State, Market and Organizational Form

Edited by
Ayşe Buğra and Behlül Üsdiken

Walter de Gruyter · Berlin · New York 1997

Ayşe Buğra, Professor of Economics, Department of Economics,
Boğaziçi University, Istanbul, Turkey
Behlül Üsdiken, Professor of Management and Organization,
Department of Management, Boğaziçi University, Istanbul, Turkey

With 5 figures and 22 tables

♾ Printed on acid-free paper which falls within the guidelines of the ANSI to ensure permanence and durability.

Library of Congress Cataloging-in-Publication Data

State, market, and organizational form / edited by Ayşe Buğra and Behlül Üsdiken.
(De Gruyter studies in organization ; 80)
Includes bibliographical references.
ISBN 3-11-015468-4
1. Industrial organization (Economic theory) – Congresses. 2. Economic stabilization – Government policy – Congresses. I. Buğra, Ayşe, 1951– . II. Üsdiken, Behlül. III. Series.
HD2326.S747 1997
338.7 – dc21 97-20076
CIP

Die Deutsche Bibliothek – Cataloging-in-Publication Data

State, market and organizatonial form / ed. by Ayşe Buğra and Behlül Üsdiken. – Berlin ; New York : de Gruyter, 1997
(De Gruyter studies in organization ; 80)
ISBN 3-11-015468-4

Printing: WB-Druck GmbH, Rieden am Forggensee – Binding: Mikolai GmbH, Berlin. – Cover Design: Johannes Rother, Berlin.

Preface

This book brings together some of the papers presented at the sub-theme "State, Market, and Organizational Forms" of the 12th EGOS (European Group for Organizational Studies) Colloquium held in Istanbul in July 1995. All but one (Katila's contribution which was presented in another group) of the papers included in the volume were presented and discussed in the working group convened around this sub-theme of the Colloquium. They are all original contributions and have not been published elsewhere.

The conceptualization of the sub-theme in question took place in a setting where the empirical reality of the transformation of the Second World War international order had begun to challenge some of the established theoretical views in economics and in organizational analysis. Hence, both the text of the call for papers and the papers themselves reflected a concern with the adequacy of our theoretical tools for studies dealing with the emergence, sustenance, and the transformation of contemporary forms of economic organization. This concern is central to the present collection of contributions which, on the basis of observations made in different societal contexts, question the relevance of "universal" theories of organizational behaviour in general, and the increasingly important impact of economic reasoning on organization studies in particular. Although they reflect a strong concern for societal specificity of organizational activity, the contributions to the volume also point at the existence of common problems that societies attempt to solve in different institutional arrangements. They provide, therefore, useful insights for all social scientists who try to avoid the problems of unrealistically universalistic and formalistic approaches in their attempts to develop rigorous tools of analysis to be used in the study of economic, political, and social phenomena.

Indeed for us, a major feature of this collection is not only the international nature of its authorship, but also the breadth of the country experiences that it brings together. The authors contributing to the volume are presently affiliated with institutions in seven different countries and the research that they report in this collection is based on work that has been carried out in even a broader range of societal settings. So apart from authors reporting their research on organizations in their native settings, we have Whitley, Henderson, Czaban and Lengyel, an international team in itself, writing on Hungary; Stryjan on the Czech Republic, Hassard and Sheehan on China, Biggart and Orrù on East Asia, Scher on Japan and Katila on Ghana.

This is another opportunity for us to thank to all of the contributors to this volume. We wish to thank them not only for agreeing to have their work to be included in the volume, but also persevering with us in what turned out to be a long process of preparation with countless postal and e-mail exchanges.

We should like to thank a number of other people who have also helped us in various ways in the preparation of this volume. Margaret Kirk, the copy editor of the Institute of Social Sciences at Boğaziçi University, helped us with textual problems and copy editing. Our research assistants, Nisan Selekler and Demet Çetin spent many hours in front of the computer trying to ensure consistency in the preparation of the final manuscript. Erhan Altunel and Turuncan Kazezoğlu were always available to help us when we had problems with PC software or e-mail transmissions.

Special thanks go to Dr. Bianka Ralle of Walter de Gruyter. From the moment we mentioned her this project during a coffee break at the EGOS Colloquium in Istanbul through to its completion she has always been a source of encouragement and support. We also appreciate the help we received from Christoph Schirmer in getting the book through to publication and from Wilhelm Schlemermeyer in copy-editing.

We are obviously very pleased that this project has come to an end and that the book has appeared in published form. What makes us bitter is the death of Marco Orrù, one of the contributors to the volume, during the course of its preparation. The book serves, we hope, to honour his memory and the contributions that he has made to the line of thinking that in many ways is reflected in the following chapters.

Istanbul, March 1997

Ayşe Buğra and Behlül Üsdiken
Boğaziçi University

Table of Contents

Introduction: State, Market and Organizational Form

Ayşe Buğra and *Behlül Üsdiken*

Granovetter (1985: 505) wrote, in his widely quoted article, that "(E)ven in organization theory, where considerable literature implements the limits placed on economic decisions by social structural complexity, little attempt has been made to demonstrate the implications of this for the neo-classical theory of the firm or for a general understanding of production or such macroeconomic outcomes as growth, inflation, and unemployment." This was a statement made in an environment increasingly characterized, on the one hand, by greater internationalization and interconnectedness of economic activity, and on the other, within what can be identified as the transformation of the post-Second World War international order, a process accentuated, since the time of Granovetter's writing, by the series of events that have unfolded notably in Eastern Europe.

The recent attempts to analyze these developments have involved an increasing degree of interdisciplinary exchange between economics and organization studies. Much of this exchange, however, has been hardly compatible with Granovetter's concerns. As such, it has led, instead, to an increasing penetration of economistic approaches into the field of organizational analysis. Yet, interdisciplinary dialogue has also manifested itself in the emergence of a different body of literature largely drawing upon neo-institutionalist ideas from sociology and political science. Altogether these theoretical developments have culminated in the sharpening of the divide between universalist positions in explaining forms of and transitions in economic organization and those who accord a central role to the national and regional settings in which such activity is located. It is in this context that the chapters in this volume make a contribution not only by addressing the problems associated with the former, universalistic position, but also by confronting the challenges that have to be faced in elaborating new tools of analysis that would be appropriate for the study of societal difference.

The value of this contribution is enhanced by the diversity of the contexts within which the authors examine organizational arrangements and organizational change. The majority of the inquiries presented in the book deal with organizational phenomena located within one of the three sets of recent developments characterizing the world economy and influencing the recent theoretical trends in the social sciences over the last two decades or so. One of these developments pertains to the spectacular economic success of some East Asian countries, starting with Japan and followed by South Korea, Taiwan, Hong Kong and Singapore. Also characterizing the current international scene are the more recent, mainly post-1980 changes in Western market societies, that have taken place in a new technological and ideological environment and have led to a widespread questioning of welfare state practices and Fordist industrial organization. "Privatization", "de-regulation" and "flexible work arrangements" are among the key terms describing the parallel efforts at political and organizational restructuring in Western industrialized countries. Finally, the post-communist transformation process in former centrally-planned economies has constituted a major element of radical change in the post-Second World War international order.

Economistic Interpretations of Global Change

There has been a strong tendency to interpret these developments with reference to the premises of standard economic analysis, as part of a general trend towards convergence of economic systems which reasserted the universal validity of "economic rationality." Neo-classical development economists, for example, have tried to explain East Asian success with reference to the undeniable superiority of "right" policy choices, namely, outward-looking, market-oriented strategies (Lal 1983; Balassa 1988). In European market economies, similar strategic choices adopted by different countries in favour of more market coordination and less state intervention again seemed to constitute a rational policy orientation directed at the dismantling of obstacles to the efficient functioning of these economies. Post-communist transformation, on the other hand, was analyzed as a smooth process whereby markets would naturally emerge as central planners leave the scene. In this context, it was claimed that markets, as coordinating mechanisms, had "a natural affinity" with private ownership and, consequently, rapid privatization of public enterprises would generate the necessary conditions for an efficiently functioning market economy (Sachs 1993; Kornai 1990).

While standard economic interpretations were characterized by an almost total neglect of the social context of economic activity, a somewhat more sophisticated line of analysis was provided by new institutionalist economics, which has emerged not only as a new orthodoxy in economic analysis but has also enjoyed increasing popularity in organization studies. In many ways, the advent of new institutionalism, especially via transaction cost and agency theory but also through the new approaches to the analysis of political processes and of economic history (Bates 1988; North 1990), has constituted an important development challenging some of the central premises of standard neo-classical economics. The basic premises of the latter can be formulated as, first, that economic activity can be conceptualized and studied as market activity, and, second, that individuals are rational. This famous rationality postulate has two implications. It means, first, that all individuals maximize their self-interest and, second, that they maximize their self-interest with full knowledge of the values of all relevant parameters. We are told, in other words, that people are not only selfish but they are also omniscient.

New institutionalism challenges the first premise of standard economics by simply stating that organizations exist, something that was not acknowledged by economists for a long time. This suggests, of course, that economic activity can not be studied merely as market activity. In spite of some notable exceptions which have nevertheless remained outside the formal body of analysis (Marshall 1890/1916), economists have, for a long time, studied business firms as if there were no difference between the firm and the market. Somewhat paradoxically, the firm, as a distinct entity, did not form part of the economic "theory of the firm." It was, of course, Coase's seminal article (1937), written as an undergraduate paper, which first called this strange state of affairs to the attention of the discipline. "Why do firms exist?" was the question that Coase asked, and neither the question nor his answer to it did not make much impact on the profession until Williamson's formalization in the 1970s (1975; 1985), following which economics has acknowledged the existence of economic organizations other than markets.

The second premise is also challenged by the new institutionalists who, following Simon (1976), have highlighted the fact that individuals are not omniscient; that rationality is bounded. Nevertheless, new institutional economics keeps the first part of the rationality postulate and builds the analysis on individual maximizing behaviour. Homo oeconomicus thus remains central to the economic analysis of institutions based on methodological individualism, which forms the basis of the well-established "formal" definition of economics.

Whether people are really rational in this sense and whether it is legitimate to base the analysis of economic activity on the behaviour of atomistic individuals has always been a subject of heated debates between economists as well as between the latter and critical social scientists from other disciplines. Yet, the rationality postulate constituted a very convenient first principle with reference to which one could explain all economic phenomena as links in the same chain of causality. To the discovery of general laws it was very useful. It also appeared to be a useful approximation of exchange activity on self regulating markets. As such, it depicts the relationship between "anonymous", "free" and "equal" individuals. These individuals who have no social ties with each other come together, by their own free will, to exchange goods of equal value only to maximize their own well being. In other words, the market relationship is a totally impersonal one. It is, in essence, a relationship between "men and things" and not between people (Dumont 1977). This suggests, however, that outside "free" markets where personal relations of mutual commitment and trust, habit and custom, social hierarchy, or political mechanisms of regulation are excluded, it does not only become difficult to base the analysis of economic activity on the behaviour of atomistic individuals, but it also becomes impossible to hold on the generalizations concerning individual behaviour inherent in the formal meaning of economics.

In spite of their explicit objective of extending economic analysis beyond the realm of market exchange, new institutionalist economists do not attempt to incorporate the variety of human motivations in their investigations of non-market phenomena. They reduce, instead the organizational and the political to the economic in a manner which perhaps can be regarded as yet another example of the "imperialistic expansion of economics" (Hirshleifer 1986). Hence, their promise of expanding the domain of economics beyond the market culminates in the extension of the market paradigm to all institutions including the state and the business firm. This methodological orientation has certain advantages which explains the popularity it enjoys both in economics and in studies of political and organizational issues. First, the formal economic approach based on the market paradigm confers significant advantages in terms of analytical formalization with the possibility of making predictions. The recent popularity of new institutional economics can also be attributed, however, to its conformity with the neo-liberal trends dominating the ideological atmosphere on an international scale. Based on the market paradigm, with individual interest maximizing activity as the centrepiece of analysis, new institutional economics gives support to those arguments where economic efficiency appears almost as a moral imperative that justifies the disregard for conflicts of interest and inequalities of power as well as for the societally specific ways of dealing with them. It would not be exaggerated to suggest, in fact, that formal economic analysis in its new institutionalist form constitutes an integral component of neo-liberal ideology.

In spite of its scientific advantages and its conformity to prevailing ideological trends, the problems that the new institutionalism in economics entailed in terms of the explanatory power and the relevance of the analysis have been a source of dissatisfaction for some students of real world phenomena. Hence, notwithstanding those writers who cherish the revolutionary potential that new institutional economics offers to the study of organizations (Hesterly et al. 1990), its impact on the field of organizational analysis was also seen to be dangerous in various ways for research and practice (Donaldson 1995; Ghoshal and Moran 1996). According to Perrow (1990: 149), the new institutional economics presents a challenge to organizational analysts, "a challenge that resembles the theme of the novel and the film *The Invasion of Body Snatchers*, where human forms are retained but all that we value about human behaviour — its spontaneity, unpredictability, selflessness, plurality of values, reciprocal influence, and resentment of domination — has disappeared." In a parallel fashion, Granovetter (1985: 486), who, incidentally, also mentions *The Invasion of Body Snatchers,* writes that "the main thrust of the 'new institutional economics' is to deflect the analysis of institutions from sociological, historical, and legal argumentation and show instead that they arise as the efficient solution to economic problems."

Beyond Homo Oeconomicus

Challenges to the analytical trends highlighted by writers such as Granovetter and Perrow were presented by the work of scholars applying neo-institutionalist ideas from sociology and political science to the study of organizations. Initially, a major impetus for this kind of work has come from the challenge and success of East Asian businesses in international markets. More practical concerns have been accompanied by theoretical analyses which have, in various ways, questioned the adequacy of market-based economic approaches and exchange-based organizational perspectives in explaining forms of business organization in East Asia. Various strands of this work (e.g. Hamilton and Biggart 1988; Whitley 1990) have been based on the common theme that there is a need to consider the social and the institutional context in which organizational activity is embedded. This line of reasoning has, more recently, been extended to the analysis of business structures and changes in industrial organization in "Western" settings (e.g. Whitley 1992; Lane 1995; Whitley and Kristensen 1996). Not less influential has been Piore and Sabel's (1984) flexible specialization thesis and the ensuing scholarly interest that it has generated. Pioneering attempts have also emerged within more recent but now highly influential currents of analysis in organization studies questioning the neglect of political contexts of organizations (e.g. Carroll et al. 1990; Jepperson and Meyer 1991).

More and more research attention is now being devoted to assessing the adequacy of existing analytical tools for understanding organizational responses to radical changes in institutional environments (Clark and Soulsby 1995; Peng and Heath 1996; Allmendinger and Hackmann 1996).

Such contributions jointly reassert the role of the institutional environment in which economic and organizational activity is embedded. As such they can largely be situated in a "substantivist" approach which, especially in Karl Polanyi's (1944; 1957) work, is contrasted with the formalist approach characterizing economic analysis in its neo-classical and new institutionalist variants. The substantivist view posits the economy as being embedded and enmeshed in institutions, both economic and non-economic. This view rejects the methodological individualism which is central to formal economic reasoning. This does not lead, however, to a holistic approach where agency becomes subservient to structure and where the significance of individual choice in socio-economic activity is disregarded. On the contrary, mechanistically interest maximizing agents are replaced by real individuals who define and pursue their interests in the historically shaped dynamics of social interaction. We are thus enabled to consider the patterns of competition and cooperation between individuals in particular institutional settings, which takes place against the background of history and, consequently, reflects much more than the functionalist requirements of the day. In the substantive approach, the inclusion of the non-economic is vital because, as Polanyi (1957: 250) writes, "religion and government may be as important for the structure and functioning of the economy as monetary institutions or the availability of tools and machines that lighten the toil of labor."

"Government", in particular, is a vital element in the analysis of economic activity because of the society shaping role of the state which, in turn, is shaped by historical factors that are society-specific in nature and which cannot be attributed solely to the choice of standard policy sets. This is not only important for the analysis of social formations which are different from Western market societies, but also for the empirical studies on the latter. In fact, what we unambiguously call market economies today appear as the totality of social institutions and political mechanisms of regulation which have distinct, society specific histories. The market system, in other words, is not a universal phenomenon that emerges spontaneously and functions independently of social regulation. As Polanyi, puts it, "(T)here was nothing natural about laissez faire; free markets could never come into being merely by allowing things take their course. Just as cotton manufacturers — the leading free trade industry — were created by the help of protective tariffs, export bounties, and indirect wage subsidies, laissez-faire itself was enforced by the state" (1944: 139). According to Polanyi, the role of the state in the advent of the market society was not limited to the "institution" of the market economy through extensive legislation. Equally important was the parallel legislation to control and to "contain" the free functioning of markets in order to save the social fabric from their disruptive influence. It seems, therefore, inadequate to leave the state outside the analysis of economic activity by establishing an artificial dichotomy between the state and the market as it has been done in standard neoclassical analysis. As Desai (1986) writes,

> ...it is not only that the state establishes, again and again, the conditions under which the nature of the civil society is determined. It is a fallacy to separate the two so sharply and antagonistically. In the day-to-day working of the civil society, certain public goods are necessary. These are meta-goods, such as the very process of exchange on which we rely or the system of property rights; money itself is a public good, which, like language, only gains currency from the fact that other people use it... We live in a world where public goods and externalities are pervasive, where our actions and perceptions are made in the context of households, factories, clubs. We fail to understand phenomena such as poverty, famines and the provision for social security if we view them from the point of view of the isolated individual.

What we fail to understand could perhaps be stated in more general terms as the interaction between the state, market and organizational forms as it affects the functioning of the economy. This is, precisely, what one has to understand to explain the current developments in the world economy and the organizational challenges that they have generated. In this regard, some of the studies on East Asian development were important to point at the differences between the East and the West concerning the forms of institutionalization of the economy. As Biggart and Hamilton succinctly put,

> Just as Western economies have institutionalized ways of maintaining autonomy between actors, Asian economies are rooted in institutions that encourage and maintain ties... What the American economy works so studiously to prevent — connections between individuals, links between firms — Asian economies accept as appropriate and inevitable. Moreover, Asian nations have institutionalized networks and built economic policies around the presence and presumption of social relations among market actors (1992: 474-475).

Social relations among market actors are not, of course, absent in Western economies. It is neither true that these relations manifest a continuity and similarity throughout Western history. In fact, both the differences in welfare state practices and forms of industrial organization and the divergent policy outcomes that have resulted from the attempts at political reorganization and industrial structuring suggest that the current developments in Western market economies can only be understood with reference to patterns of social interaction and interest representation in their socio-cultural specificity (Esping-Andersen 1990). We see, for example, in Kristensen's (1996: 12) analysis, the firm as a "...part of the set of institutions by which the social construction of reality takes place." As Kristensen writes with reference to Sorge's reinterpretation of the "societal effect approach", "(N)ational types of firms and their institutional context change, but because the process of change happens through and by nationally patterned relations and interactions, nothing ensures convergence." Kristensen (1996) also argues that societies go through conflictual situations where the conflicts over social space between different actors are socially reconciled in a nationally distinct manner. According to him, for most European countries the industrial revolution constituted such a conflictual period where social interaction was guided into society specific patterns of cooperation and competition. This approach is of a nature to provide useful clues for the analysis of the often overlooked differences between the post-Second World War European forms of industrial organization and social regulation on the one hand, and the current attempts at industrial restructuring and public sector reform on the other.

The social developments currently taking place in post-socialist countries constitute a very typical example of the conflictual situations to which Kristensen refers. Spender (1993), for example, describes the situation in Eastern Europe as one of "institutional collapse" and argues that the peculiarity of the social fabric in the region calls for society specific patterns of institution building, something which cannot be realized through the transfer of Western management and organizational knowledge. Child and Czegledy (1996) make the same point by arguing that managerial learning processes have to take into account people's evaluations of their social environment and their place in it. Hence, people face the challenges of adopting to a new environment through their acquired habits and expectations which are incorporated into the "tacit" managerial knowledge that they have. Totally ignoring the tacit nature of managerial knowledge and regarding it as codified knowledge which has the same validity across social boundaries creates certain illusions about the nature of organizational change in Eastern Europe. More significantly, it leads to a highly misleading interpretation of what is now happening in post-communist countries as a process of transition, which implies a lineal passage from one well-defined system to another. As Child and Czegledy (1996) argue, the term transition should be replaced by transformation, a term that denotes an open-ended process whose results would depend on the balance of international and national forces acting upon each other in different social contexts. Transition, in fact, appears as a term which reflects a certain understanding of what a market economy is: an economy consisting of self regulating markets where atomistic individuals exchange marketable rights to maximize their individual self interest. The most important lesson that one can derive from the developments in post-socialist societies is, precisely, that market economy is much more than that. These developments have revealed, very clearly, what the requirements of a market economy are and have shown, in Nuti's (1995: 87-88) words, that markets "are a time stratification of memories, expectations, traditions, legislation, trust, reputations — without which a market is a pale imitation, indeed a grotesque caricature of the real thing."

Market appears, in Nuti's statement, as a socially and politically instituted process. Thus, the statement clearly shows, as the other debates summarized above, the problems of starting with a pre-given market paradigm to be applied to organizational analysis. As the experiences of East Asian societies, western market economies and the radical transformation in former centrally planned economies all indicate, a more meaningful analysis of organizational activity requires a framework where the dynamic interaction between state, market, and organizations is taken into account.

Embeddedness of Economic and Organizational Activity: Towards a Dynamic Conceptualization

The development of such analytical frameworks is faced, however, with important challenges and requires more than the recognition of the reality of the embeddedness of economic and organizational activity. It needs to take into account, for example, the role of voluntary state intervention which significantly affects both market processes and organizational forms. Organizations can not, therefore, be seen as passively conforming to their institutional environment. The "organization-shaping" role of the state is itself also conditioned by conflicting interests that are pursued within the context of unequal power relations. The interplay between state policy and strategic action by social actors should, therefore, form an integral component of analysis if the latter is expected to provide a balanced account of structure and agency.

It is also important not to overlook the fact that the efforts to shape organizational activity in conformity with public or private interests are often, if not always, situated within the context of international relations which give rise to common challenges and common ideological orientations. Especially in today's world of growing interconnectedness, analyses of societal specificity are clearly in a position to consider the role of the international context in affecting the ways in which inter-country differences manifest themselves.

While they share a common concern with societal determinants of economic activity, the contributors to this volume also document, in varying degrees, the significance of interest, the reality of power, the crucial role of ideology, and the interplay between local and international factors by presenting a wealth of empirical evidence pertaining to a wide variety of country experiences. By drawing on different theoretical approaches and currents of analysis and dealing with different societal contexts they make a joint contribution by forcefully demonstrating that the most promising path to the elaboration of solid frameworks of analysis is to adopt a comparative perspective sensitive to both what is different and what is similar in human institutions in different parts of the world.

The contributions in the volume are presented in two parts. The chapters in the first part deal with organizational change within the context of post-communist transformation on the one hand and in European market economies on the other. In most of these approaches, state appears as the dominant agent leading the process of organizational change along particular ideological lines conforming to current ideological trends. In their discussion of the Hungarian case, Whitley et al. highlight "the paucity of economic agents able and willing to carry out radical changes." The absence of a domestic capitalist class coupled with the limited role that foreign investors could and are likely to play in the establishment of the market economy leaves the state as the sole guiding force in this direction. In his analysis of the transformation of Czech agriculture, Strjyan, too, describes a government-led attempt to establish markets which has a clear ideological blueprint reflected in the emphasis on the restitution of historical property rights. Both Whitley et al. and Stryjan document the failure of legislative processes which, faced with interests and behavioural regularities reflecting the historical legacy of the societies under investigation, have culminated in organizational practices and forms that hardly support expectations concerning the performance of privatized enterprises. State action in these contexts seem to have led either to hybrid forms of limited economic success as in the case of Czech "owners' cooperatives" or to a situation where private ownership has not appeared to be conducive to managerial policies that are significantly different from those of state economic enterprises as in the Hungarian context.

In their discussion of the role of the state in enterprise reform in China, Hassard and Sheehan deal with a society where socioeconomic transformation has followed a more gradual and more authentic path than it has in Eastern and Central Europe. They document, therefore, the development of organizational arrangements that are highly unique in their social specificity, but also subject to considerable modification by voluntary state action. Their discussion highlights the significance of ideological divisions within the state concerning the direction and pace of economic reforms that form the context in which the positive and negative aspects of emerging organizational forms are considered. They show, therefore, that ideological and political factors can at times play a more significant role than efficiency related criteria in determining the ownership structures and managerial practices that prevail in a given society.

A similar point is made, albeit in a totally different social context, in Hulsink's fascinating account of the transformations through which the Dutch Postbank has gone in the period 1945-1994 not only in its form of ownership and management, but also in its socially defined role in Dutch economy and society. The state plays, once again, a crucial role in these transformations. In the context of Dutch society this role reflects, however, the strategic interaction between conflicting interests with the outcome significantly affected by the dominant ideological trends that closely reflect the changes taking place at the international level. While in Hulsink's discussion the upsurge of neo-liberal ideas plays a crucial role in determining the balance of conflicting interests negotiated in the political arena and, along with it, the fate of the Postbank, Garsten documents how these ideas invade and transform the realm of the state by affecting the organizational dynamics in the public sector. Garsten analyses the more recent universalistic discourses on organizations as the legitimating rhetoric of current attempts at restructuring enterprises and the public sector and shows how the seemingly neutral concept of efficiency acquires a moral value of its own which disguises the inequalities of power between the parties that stand to gain and lose from market-driven social change. It is through this study of the discursive framework of social action that the chapter discusses the divergences of interest and relations of power that accompany the changing forms of interaction between the state and the market in Swedish society.

With the chapters in the second part of the book, the emphasis shifts to a broader range of institutional factors, although the analysis of the policy process and its outcomes occupy a central role in some of the contributions. In the first chapter in this part, Sorge tests the new institutionalist transaction costs theory on a sample of German and British firms whose products incorporate micro-electronic components. The comparative part of his analysis shows that transaction cost assessments are loaded with social and societal constructions which, in turn, shape choices that may be contrary to the predictions of the theory. Like Sorge, Biggart and Orrù, Scher, and Katila all present an explicit questioning of economistic approaches to the study of organizations which they attempt to "re-embed" in their societal context. This emphasis of societal specificity goes hand in hand, however, with the exploration of the role of particular socio-cultural arrangements in fulfilling certain objectives that are universally shared. Hence, Biggart and Orrù attempt to explain the success of economic policies pursued by the developmentalist states in Japan, South Korea, and Taiwan by introducing the concept of "societal strategic advantage" as a resource effectively mobilized by these states. They argue that while the East Asian societies that they study are different in their policy orientation and institutional characteristics, all three cases manifest a strategic fit between institutionalized social arrangements and the needs of the global market. The idea of societal comparative advantage implicitly enters in Scher's discussion of Japanese industrial groups and cross-shareholding where the economic success of Japan is largely attributed to traditional culture and institutions which support asymmetries of power and enable their exploitation in sustaining the concentration of wealth. While he highlights the functional role assumed by the traditionally given social arrangements in Japanese society and economy, Scher strongly argues against the possibility of emulating Japanese managerial practices in a different socio-cultural context. In Katila's ethnographic analysis of the market practices that are deeply rooted in the traditional fabric of the Ghanian society, these culturally determined practices, in their seemingly esoteric character, appear to be fulfilling the functions of certain formal mechanisms of state intervention that regulate and contain market activity. Hence, the "market queen institution" that Katila discusses serves to maintain law and order in market transactions, as well as incorporating mechanisms of information dissemination, credit provision, and social security.

The last chapter of the second part by Loveridge, introduces a different perspective from which the empirical cases discussed by some of the other contributors to the volume can be considered. Although Loveridge draws on a large variety of theoretical currents and lines of analysis, the paradigm of late industrialization is central to his interpretation of East Asian organizational forms which constitute the basis of many approaches that emphasize the social determinants of business structure and strategy. Against the emphasis of historically given institutional diversity, the author suggests an alternative explanation where British and American industrialization patterns are contrasted with the German one which, as the archetypal late-industrializing country, has served as a model first for Japan, and then, indirectly on other East Asian countries. It is thus argued that the German pattern of late industrialization constitutes a significant point of reference to understand East Asian business practices which in their sharp difference from British and American ones, significantly rely on nationalist ideologies in which conflicting interests are balanced and legitimated. Loveridge's discussion thus leads us to a reconsideration of societal diversity by drawing attention to the significance of common sources of ideology on which different countries draw in eradicating and legitimating their institutional structures.

In sum, the contributions in this volume introduce some new conceptual extensions to and serve to enrich the empirical basis of the growing body of literature on the role of the "non-economic", in particular the state, in understanding the emergence, sustenance, and transformation of organizational forms. They offer clues for future lines of inquiry and debate, demonstrating, yet again, the usefulness of inter-disciplinary and inter-perspective dialogue.

References

Allmendinger, J. and J.R. Hackman (1996): "Organizations in changing environments: The case of East German symphony orchestras." *Administrative Science Quarterly* 41: 337-369.

Balassa, B. (1988): "The lessons of East Asian development." *Economic Development and Cultural Change* 16(4): 273-290.

Bates, R.H. (ed.) (1988): *Towards a political economy of development: The rational choice perspective*. Berkeley, CA: University of California Press.

Biggart, N.W. and G. Hamilton (1992): "On the limits of a firm-based theory to explain business networks: The western bias of neoclassical economics" in N. Nohria and R.G. Eccles (eds.), *Networks and organizations: Structure, form, action*, 471-490. Boston, MA: Harvard Business School Press.

Carroll, G.R., J. Delacroix and J. Goodstein (1990): "The political environments of organizations: An ecological view" in B.M. Staw and L.L. Cummings (eds.), *The evolution and adaptation of organizations*, 67-100. Greenwich, CT: JAI Press.

Child, J. and A.P. Czegledy (1996): "Managerial learning in the transformation of Eastern Europe: Some key issues." *Organization Studies* 17: 167-179

Clark, E. and A. Soulsby (1995): "Transforming former state enterprises in the Czech Republic." *Organization Studies* 16: 215-242.

Coase, R.H. (1937): "The Nature of the firm." *Economica* 4: 386-405.

Desai, M. (1986): "Man and things." *Economica* 53: 1-10

Donaldson, L. (1995): *American anti-management theories of organization*. Cambridge: Cambridge University Press.

Dumont, L. (1977): *From Mandeville to Marx: The genesis and triumph of economic ideology*. Cambridge: Cambridge University Press.

Esping-Andersen, G. (1990): *Three worlds of welfare capitalism*. Cambridge: Polity Press.

Ghoshal S. and P. Moran (1996): "Bad for practice: A critique of the transaction cost theory." *Academy of Management Review* 21: 13-47.

Granovetter, M. (1985): "Economic action and social structure: The problem of embeddedness." *American Journal of Sociology* 91: 481-510.

Hamilton, G.G. and N.W. Biggart (1988): "Market, culture and authority: A comparative analysis of management and organization in the Far East." *American Journal of Sociology* 94: S52-S94.

Hesterly, W.S., J. Libeskind and T.R. Zenger (1990): "Organizational economics: An impending revolution in organization theory." *Academy of Management Review* 15: 402-420.

Hirshleifer, J. (1986): "Economics from a biological point of view" in J. Barney and W.G. Ouchi (eds.), *Organizational Economics*, 319-371. San Fransisco: Jossey Bass.
Jepperson, R.L. and J.W. Meyer (1991): "The public order and the construction of formal organizations" in W.W. Powell and P.J. DiMaggio (eds.), *The new institutionalism in organizational analysis*, 204-231. Chicago: The University of Chicago Press.
Kornai, J. (1990): "The Affinity between ownership forms and coordination mechanisms." *Journal of Economic Perspectives* 4(3): 131-147
Kristensen, P.H. (1996): "Variations in the nature of the firm in Europe" in R. Whitley and P.H. Kristensen (eds.), *The changing European firm: Limits to convergence*. London: Routledge.
Lal, O. (1983): *The poverty of "development economics."* London: Hobart.
Lane, C. (1995): *Industry and society in Europe*. Aldershot, UK: Edward Elgar.
Marshall, A. (1890/1916): *Principles of economics*. London: MacMillan.
North, D. (1990): *Institutions, institutional change and economic performance*. Cambridge: Cambridge University Press.
Nuti, M.D. (1995): "The restoration of markets in East-Central Europe" in M. Mendell and K. Nielsen (eds.), *Europe: Central and East*, 74-89. Montreal: Black Rose Books.
Peng, M.W. and P.S. Heath (1996): "The growth of the firm in planned economies in transition: Institutions, organizations and strategic choice." *Academy of Management Review* 21: 492-528.
Perrow, C. (1990): "Economic theories of organization" in S. Zukin and P. DiMaggio (eds.), *Structures of capital: The social organizations of the economy*, 121-152. Cambridge: Cambridge University Press.
Piore, M. and C. Sabel (1984): *The second industrial divide: Possibilities for prosperity*. New York: Basic Books.
Polanyi, K. (1944): *The great transformation*. Boston: Beacon Press.
Polanyi, K. (1957): "The economy as an instituted process" in K. Polanyi, C.M. Arensberg and H.W. Pearson (eds.), *Trade and market in the early empires*, 243-270. Chicago: Gateway.
Sachs, J. (1993): *Poland's jump to the market economy*. Cambridge, MA: Harvard University Press.
Simon, H. (1976): "From procedural to substantive rationality" in S. Latsis (ed.), *Method and Appraisal in Economics*, 129-148. Cambridge: Cambridge University Press.
Spender, J.C. (1993): "Transferring management techniques to Eastern Europe: An Institutional critique." *The International Journal of Organizational Analysis* 1(3): 237-254.
Whitley, R. (1990): "East Asian enterprise structures and the comparative analysis of forms of business organization." *Organization Studies* 11: 47-74.
Whitley, R. (ed.) (1992): *European Business Systems*. London: Sage.
Whitley, R. and P.H. Kristensen (eds.)(1996): *The changing European firm*. London: Routledge.
Williamson, O.E. (1975): *Markets and hierarchies: Analysis and antitrust implications*. New York: Free Press.
Williamson, O.E. (1985): *Economic institutions of capitalism: Firms, markets, relational contracting*. London: MacMillan.

Part One
Political Processes, Economic Interests and Organizational Re-structuring in Societal Transformation

Enterprise Change and the Management of Labour in a Transforming Society: The Case of Hungary*

Richard Whitley, Laszlo Czaban, Jeffrey Henderson, and *Gyorgy Lengyel*

Introduction

The radical transformation of state socialist societies in Eastern Europe has combined the development of democratic political systems with the establishment of market economies and varying kinds of liberal capitalism. As has been noted by many observers (e.g. Hausner and Nielsen 1992; Tatur 1995), this combination of changes is difficult to achieve successfully, especially in a short time, and political pressures can often inhibit radical economic transformation. This is particularly the case when large scale enterprise restructuring is involved, not least because it implies major changes to the workforce and radical changes in labour management strategies. Where trade unions are powerful collective agents because of their role in overthrowing the previous authoritarian regime, as in Bulgaria and Poland, such political forces are particularly likely to limit the scale and speed of this restructuring (Dittrich and Haferkemper 1995; Tatur 1995).

An additional factor limiting the extent of enterprise restructuring in many East European countries has been the paucity of economic agents able and willing to carry out radical changes. By definition, state socialist regimes did not permit the growth of private capital or a capitalist class which could take over the ownership of state owned enterprises (SOEs) and transform them into recognizable capitalist firms. Furthermore, the widely expected invasion of private foreign investors eager to buy state assets in these countries has turned out to be much more limited than anticipated. Even in Hungary which has attracted the most foreign direct investment since 1989 (Bönker 1994; Radice 1995), foreign ownership of the largest Hungarian enterprises only became important in 1993 and 1994. Additionally, where western firms do completely assume ownership of former SOEs, they do not always, indeed rather rarely, engage in radical transformation, as we shall illustrate. Although this may change as more foreign firms invest in SOEs and political stability seems more assured in many countries, the likelihood that outside investors will play the dominant role in establishing the market economy and, in effect, act as the functional equivalent of a native capitalist class seems rather limited at the moment.

Thus, the dominant agent in transforming the command economy into a decentralized market economy has been, and remains in most Eastern European countries, the state (Amsden et al. 1994; Whitley 1996). However, the state is not the strong, quasi-authoritarian state behind many of the successfully newly industrialized countries in Asia (e.g. Henderson 1993; Wade 1990; Woo 1991), but is rather weak, with greatly reduced legitimacy as a result of the state socialist period, and often fragmented into rival fractions and interest groups (Holmes 1995; Tatur 1995). As a result, its economic policies, and especially its attempts to reconstruct and restructure the large SOEs, are frequently characterized by inconsistency, incoherence and susceptibility to interest group pressures (Henderson et al. 1995). In turn, this has meant that most SOEs, and many of the recently privatized firms that rely on loans from the state owned banks to survive, remain subject to considerable political risk and often continue to rely on political alliances and interests in their battles to survive.

A further factor inhibiting large scale reorganizations and layoffs in many enterprises has been the recent growth of support for many of the transformed former "transmission belt" unions in East European countries. In Hungary, for example, the National Confederation of Hungarian Trade Unions (MSZOSZ), which inherited 42.9% of the assets of the previous regime's National Council of Trade Unions and many of its personnel, gained 50.1% of the votes in the social security board elections for pensions funds and 45.2% of those for health insurance funds in 1993. Even more impressively, it won 71.67% of the votes for works councils later that year (Lado 1994). This was despite the new government's antagonism to the "reconstituted" traditional unions on the grounds that they were dominated by ex-communists, and may reflect the quasi-autonomous role they developed under the previous regime (Hughes 1994). While these unions in general in Hungary have proved to be quite cooperative in enterprise restructuring — and often join with management in lobbying Parliament and Ministers — their significance and ability to retain support clearly has limited the ability of top managers to pursue radical changes in employment policies and work control (Mako and Novaszath 1995), albeit not perhaps to the same extent as in some Polish enterprises (Konecki and Kulpinska 1995).

In general, then, the extent of radical transformation of most SOEs in most East European countries has been less than expected by devotees of shock therapy, especially in matters of labour management, and transfers of ownership to private investors have not always resulted in the rapid adoption of distinctly "capitalist" employment practices. Furthermore, ownership change, *per se*, has proved to be a much more complex matter than the straightforward sale of publicly owned assets to private investors. As Amsden et al. (1994) among others have suggested, much of the claimed privatization of state firms that has taken place in Eastern Europe is really pseudo-privatization, with few effective owners investing their own resources in these enterprises. In most countries, a variety of ownership forms have emerged, particularly in Hungary, and these often involve some degree of state involvement through the state owned and/or controlled banks.

In this chapter we explore the contrasting effects of institutional transformation and loss of traditional markets, on the one hand, and these substantial continuities in the early transformation period, on the other hand, on the labour management policies of 14 enterprises in one former state socialist society — Hungary. Because Hungary began a long period of incremental reforms to the central planning system with the New Economic Mechanism (NEM) in 1968 — and some changes had already started before then (Berend 1990) — dominant enterprises had already moved some way from being mere branch manufacturing plants of industry Ministries before 1989 and had acquired a limited degree of autonomy from state agencies, particularly in the 1980s (Szalai 1991). According to Swaan (1993), a few of these had started to become more innovative and flexible in product lines and processes as they moved away from total dependence on CMEA markets. Insofar as any large enterprises in Eastern Europe were capable of managing the transition from state socialism to a market economy effectively, then, they are more likely to be found in Hungary than elsewhere.

In analysing how Hungarian enterprises have managed work organization and labour relation during the initial transformation period, it is obviously important to distinguish between those remaining in state ownership and those which have been privatized or have always been privately controlled, not least in view of the great emphasis placed by many international agencies and both domestic and foreign policy makers upon private ownership as the key to enterprise transformation (Gowan 1995). However, the post 1968 reforms in Hungary allowed a variety of organizational forms to develop before 1989 which provided the basis for a considerable plurality of ownership types to appear once private property rights had been established (Grabher 1995; Stark 1993). As well as state ownership continuing in various forms through the newly created agencies of the State Property Agency (SPA) and the State Holding Company (SHC) or State Asset Management Corporation, in addition to the Industrial Development Bank, and various Ministries, the number of joint ventures with foreign companies grew, often as a prelude to full foreign ownership. Privatization of all or part of SOEs generated a variety of privately owned firms, often with considerable bank influence through the provision of loans for purchasing liquidated and/or privatized assets. Finally, there are a variety of firms which have developed from different sorts of work units and enterprises established in the 1980s. These have been classified by Webster (1993) in her survey of private manufacturing firms in Hungary as: ex craftsman firms, ex Enterprise Work partnerships (VGMK), ex Business Partnerships (GMK), ex small co-operatives, and ex industrial divisions of agricultural co-operatives. Thus, the Hungarian economy contains a considerable variety of different kinds of enterprise in terms of ownership and control and there is little indication that these will converge to a standard type in the near future.

Ownership need not, of course, always lead to effective control of a company's assets and key decisions, and this is particularly the case in a society undergoing radical transformation. During a period of considerable uncertainty about formal property relations and the efficacy of the legal system, day-to-day control over an enterprise's operations and assets is often more important than formal shareownership. In analysing the relative power of owners, managers, employees, banks and other groups, we here focus on their ability to influence enterprise policies and practices directly, as well as their inclination to do so. For example, the state bank control of the investment funds in the Czech Republic has not so far led to their direct intervention in the affairs of the enterprises these funds currently own, and so the power of these banks is presently rather limited. Indeed, most of the larger enterprises "privatized" through vouchers here seem to be more "insider" manager controlled at the moment (late 1995) than investor controlled (cf. Stark and Bruszt 1995; Vickerstaff et al. 1995). Where the banks do not directly own shares on a substantial scale, their influence is primarily exercised through the conditions attached to the large enterprise debts that they have inherited, as well as through the loans made to private entrepreneurs to acquire the assets of liquidated SOEs and/or parts of SOEs being sold off by the state. Obviously as financial and political systems change in different East European countries, the significance of these types of control will vary, and other combinations of dominant groups will emerge.

An important distinction to be drawn in analysing the connections between control type and labour management policies is that between "insider" and "outsider" control (cf. Amsden et al. 1994). Given the considerable continuity in senior management personnel in most large enterprises in Hungary and elsewhere since 1989, changes in formal ownership without the owners exercising direct control over company strategies and their implementation are unlikely to lead to radical discontinuities in labour management policies. "Insider" controlled firms, then, are less likely to implement major changes than those whose owners alter substantially and take control. It is also clearly important to distinguish between "outside" controllers, especially between state agencies and foreign firms. Because the latter operate different labour policies and practices to Hungarian ones and have greater access to foreign markets and capital, they are more likely to implement novel policies than other outside controllers. It should be pointed out here that most foreign firm owners in Hungary, and elsewhere in Eastern Europe, have been able to exercise considerable management control without owning all of the shares, or even a majority in some cases.

The 14 enterprises we studied here included many of the largest firms in Hungary, as can be seen from the employment figures in Table 1, but also a few smaller ones to incorporate privately owned ones which have been celebrated as representing new and entrepreneurial kinds of firms. For confidentiality reasons we cannot be too specific about their sectors, except to say that five are in the chemical, oil and allied products industry, including pharmaceuticals, three in non-electrical machinery, including transportation equipment and components, three in electrical and electronic machinery, two in metals and metal products and one in food processing. While not claiming a high level of representativity of leading enterprises in terms of ownership or sector, these 14 firms do include most of the major kinds of ownership and control currently important in the Hungarian economy, and certainly enable us to compare SOEs with different kinds of non-SOEs.

As can be seen from Table 1, ownership patterns of Hungarian enterprises can be quite complex, including those owned by the state. In these cases, ownership was dominated by the two state agencies, the SPA and the SHC, which were established in 1990 and 1992 respectively. While there were some differences in the operations and policies of these two agencies (Henderson et al. 1995; Voszka 1995), these were not significant for enterprise labour policies and we will combine the enterprises controlled by them into a single category of state owned and controlled.

The remaining seven firms in this study were owned by a wide range of investors, firms, banks and employees. In order to clarify the roles of these various owners in their management and to identify their key controllers, we asked the top managers of these firms about the formal and informal influence of their major shareholders. The formal aspects focused on the membership and powers of the Board of Directors and owners' veto powers over capital investment, new product introduction, top management appointments and creating or closing major departments or business units. The informal ones covered the extent of owners' involvement in operational and strategic issues, such as investment decisions, the approval of a business plan, top management appointments below the CEO, prioritising customers and suppliers, pricing policies, wage policies and banking relationships, as well as their requests for information from managers.

Table 1. Ownership type, employment and sector of 14 Hungarian enterprises

Type	Ownership		Employees		Sector
		%	1990	1993	
State Owned					
A	SPA	100.0	9,360	3,932	Chemicals
B	SHC	99.8	6,892	5,253	Chemicals
	Municipalities	0.2			
C	SPA	94.0	4,522	2,250	Machinery
	Municipalities	6.0			
D	SHC	100.0	23,462	20,932	Chemicals
E	SHC	83.0	10,320	11,400	Metals
	State Development Institute	12.0			
	Municipalities	5.0			
F	SHC	40.8	12,523	7,138	Machinery
	State Development Bank	51.0			
	Municipalities	8.2			
G	SHC	61.0	12,130	8,590	Machinery
	Largest Customer	30.5			
	Commercial Bank	4.5			
	Trading Firm	3.0			
	Foreign Investors	1.0			
Foreign firm owned					
H	SHC	43.4	3,806	2,911	Chemicals
	Foreign Firm	51.0			
	Employees	5.6			
I	Foreign Firm	99.8	14,173	9,432	Electrical Products
	Commercial Bank	0.2			
Joint bank/Manager owned					
J	Commercial Bank	66.0	18,956	5,236	Electronic Products
	Top Managers	29.0			
	Foreign Investors	5.0			
Owner Managed					
K	Top Managers	40.4	278	300	Electrical and Electronic Products
	Banks	19.96			
	Foreign Investors	14.23			
	Employees, other small investors	25.41			
L	Top Managers	100.0	267	370	Metals
Employee Owned					
M	ESOP	56.6	1,832	1,411	Chemicals
	Limited	27.2			

Table 1. Ownership type, employment and sector of 14 Hungarian enterprises (cont.)

Type	Ownership		Employees		Sector
		%	1990	1993	
	Retained Shares	10.0			
	Municipalities	6.2			
Investor Owned					
N	Foreign Investor A	31.0	1,715	1,988	Food
	Foreign Investor B	19.0			
	Small Investors	32.3			
	Municipalities	3.5			
	Employees	9.2			
	SHC	5.0			

Considering the composition of Boards of Directors, owners' veto powers, information requests and managerial involvement together, owner managers were clearly the most directly involved in decision making and implementation, while the employees of the ESOP owned firm and investors in the investor owned firm were relatively remote from these activities and non-owning managers had substantial *de facto* control. The SOEs and foreign owned firms were in between these two groups in terms of owner control, with most of the SOEs being subject to frequent information requests and strong state influence on top management appointments and organizational restructuring. This owner control was especially marked in the major loss making SOEs. Foreign owned firms seemed to have more autonomy on operational matters, as might be expected from their greater managerial representation on Boards of Directors, but usually the parent firm controlled senior management appointments and also had some influence over the choice of suppliers. The joint bank/manager owned firm seemed to be very much under the control of the Chief Executive, although he was in frequent communication with the CEO of the bank.

Broadly, then, the two owner managed, the jointly bank/manager owned, the ESOP owned and the foreign investor owned firms all appeared to be substantially controlled by their top managers, although subject to varying external constraints and targets. They may, then, be termed manager-controlled, but privately owned, enterprises. The managers of the two foreign firm owned enterprises also had somewhat greater operational independence than those in the SOEs, but were becoming more integrated into their parent organization and were clearly more restricted in their policies than the manager controlled firms. Accordingly we classify them separately as foreign firm controlled. Overall, then, there were seven SOEs, two foreign firm controlled enterprises and five manager controlled ones.

As can be seen from Table 1, ownership and control type is associated with the number of employees. Five of the seven SOEs had over 5.000 staff in 1993, while only two of the privately controlled ones did. Additionally, the financial situation of the SOEs was, in general, worse than that of the rest. All five of the loss making enterprises with substantial debts in 1993 were state owned and controlled. Only one of those not making losses and without significant debts remained in state hands. In general, then, the privately owned firms here tended to be medium to large in size rather than very large, and were financially more secure — if not exactly highly profitable — than most of the SOEs.

Information about the policies being pursued by these 14 enterprises in the early transformation period in Hungary was obtained through detailed interviews about strategic issues, contractual relationships and organizational practices with their top managers in late 1993 and early 1994. In all, 56 were interviewed, and we also undertook shorter interviews about supervisor-subordinate relations with 65 middle managers and supervisors from these enterprises, as well as using the secondary literature to check on major events in their recent histories. Interview questions were translated into Hungarian and then independently back translated into English to check for consistency and accuracy of meanings. The interviews themselves were conducted in Hungarian.

Employment and Labour Management Policies in 14 Hungarian Enterprises

If ownership and control changes are as critical to firms' decisions and polices as many advocates of early and swift privatization in the former state socialist countries have suggested, we would expect the most significant differences in labour management strategies to occur between SOEs, on the one hand, and those now controlled by foreign firms, owner managers and private investors. As well as the rationalization of production capacity following the disappearance of CMEA protected markets, and so major reductions in employee numbers, the latter group of enterprises are likely to have restructured administrative systems and authority hierarchies in favour of more decentralized, divisionalized forms as central state control was removed. They can also be expected to have reduced the number of support staff and functions not directly involved in production and sales, as well as the number of specialized functional departments, and to have moved to a more market based reward system with greater differentials for people with skills in short supply (Bangert and Poor 1993). Additionally, the increasing availability of high quality supplies, together with pressures to raise the productivity and flexibility of employees, might encourage greater supervisor direction of work processes and more task variety and mobility. These changes may also lead to a move away from what Pearce et al. (1994) call the "person-based" reward system prevalent in some SOEs in the 1980s towards a more formalized, transparent system linking pay directly to personal performance.

These aspects of employment systems and labour management strategies will be considered under three headings. First, overall changes in both the total number of employees and in different groups of them will be summarized. Second, personnel and employment policies dealing with reward systems, internal and external labour markets and the development of employer-employee commitment will be discussed. Finally, policies concerning the division and control of tasks and patterns of supervision will be analyzed.

Changes in Employment

Considering first the extent of employment change in general since the beginning of 1990, it can be seen from Table 1 that all but four enterprises employed fewer people in 1993/94 than they had done in 1990, in some cases very many fewer. The only enterprises to have increased employment levels were three of the manager controlled, privately owned ones, and one SOE. This last had grown as a direct result of the acquisition of a bankrupt machinery firm to safeguard the market for some of its products.

Of those that had reduced employment levels since 1990, the most severely affected was the enterprise that had been liquidated in 1991. Current employment in its largest successor organization was only 27% of the total group's in 1990. While some other components of this group had also been resurrected, the total number of employees for all of these was still under a half of the previous one. The two other enterprises that had reduced their work force by a half or more were both making large losses and had an uncertain future. In contrast, three of the SOEs that had better prospects, had retained at least two thirds of their 1990 workforce. The foreign firm owned enterprises, it should be noted, had not radically reduced the number of employees by comparison with the state owned ones. Overall, then, it would be difficult to conclude that it was those enterprises which had undergone the most radical changes in ownership and control that had "rationalized" their workforce the most. Rather it seemed that a combination of large losses, centrality to the Hungarian economy and political influence played the major role in different rates of employment reductions.

In terms of the categories of employees that had been most reduced, the largest fall over all 14 enterprises was in technical support services, which included maintenance workers, R&D staff and all non-workflow personnel who were not clerical workers. At the beginning of 1990, this group constituted 27.9% of all employees in these enterprises, but only 21.75% in late 1993 and early 1994. However, this overall decline, masked considerable variations. In enterprises E, K and N, for instance, the number of staff in this category had grown quite considerably, whereas in A, C and J they had dropped by 73.7%, 89.1% and 93% respectively. The largest falls in this category of staff were in the SOEs, especially the severely loss making ones. Similarly, two of the three enterprises that had reduced the number of clerical workers by over 40% in this period were state owned, both making major losses, so that it seems clear the most radical reductions in non workflow personnel were made by SOEs in severe financial distress, as well as by the liquidated firm. State ownership *per se*, then, has not inhibited major restructuring of the labour force in large Hungarian enterprises.

Employment and Personnel Policies

The decentralization of economic decision making to independent firms and the intensification of competitive pressures since 1989, might be expected to change many enterprises' employment policies to more market oriented ones. However, many sectors are still dominated by a single or very small number of large vertically integrated enterprises in Hungary, so that external labour markets remain relatively weakly developed in some industries, and, in any case, employment policies very considerably between market economies so that no single pattern of effective labour management practices dominates and could be taken as the appropriate one to adopt. Given the considerably degree of continuity in many aspects of enterprise behaviour in large Hungarian organizations since 1990, especially of products, technologies and business partners (Whitley et al. 1996), it would, perhaps, be unwise to predict large scale adoption of, say, Anglo-American employment policies. Initially, we discuss the extent to which these firms have moved away from long term employment and reliance on internal promotions towards more external market based recruitment. Next, the role of market rates in determining wages and related benefits is discussed, together with the extent of differential rewards for different groups of employees and the establishment of varied employment conditions for particularly valued staff. Third, we consider their attitudes to trade unions.

As Table 2 shows, most (five) SOEs still had a workforce which had predominantly been with them since leaving school. Over 60% of the employees of these five enterprises had not worked elsewhere, but in contrast only two of the seven privately controlled firms had such a high degree of continuity in the bulk of their labour forces. Additionally, the only three enterprises where 80% of employees had only worked for this one firm were state owned. This continuity in the substantial bulk of the labour force in many of these enterprises is maintained by the widespread tendency to rely on internal recruitment when filling vacancies. For those firms that had any job vacancies in 1993, most (seven out of eleven) had filled these internally, although it should be noted that three of the four that had recruited externally were privately controlled. Given the general tendency for SOEs to discharge employees rather than recruit them in 1993, it is perhaps not surprising that when vacancies did arise, they preferred to use internal candidates.

Table 2. Employment continuity and control type in 14 Hungarian enterprises

	% Employees with organization since leaving school			
Control type	21-40	41-60	61-80	80+
State	2		2	3
Foreign firm		2		
Manager controlled	2	1	2	

This continued general preference for internal promotions in Hungary was manifested by the 12 firms here that recruited their foremen from production workers. Additionally the 12 of the 13 that made managerial appointments in 1993 did so from amongst their current employees for over 80% of these jobs. Furthermore, 11 out of these 14 enterprises claimed that they generally gave priority to internal promotions when making supervisory, technical and managerial staffing decisions. On the whole, then, the internal labour market still seems to be preferred by most of these Hungarian enterprises, although more mobility between employers does occur in privately owned and controlled firms. In some of these latter cases, this is because of the growth of the business and the need to recruit specialist staff following privatization.

Turning now to consider pay and reward systems in these 14 enterprises, there are three main issues to discuss. First, the extent to which market rates of pay have become major influences in setting wage rates for large groups of employees. Second, the development of substantial differentials in rewards between groups, especially for those whose skills are in short supply and, third, the extent to which non-financial rewards remain significant components of the reward system in privatized and privately-owned enterprises.

Most (twelve) of these fourteen enterprises' top managers said that external pay rates did affect wage rates, and ten claimed they were the key determinant in the company's pay policy. The two that did not think market rates were significant were both SOEs and relatively remote from consumer markets, as were all four that, by and large, regarded them as limited in their impact. Thus, ownership and competitive pressures here do seem to have played some role in affecting susceptibility to market influences, though it should be pointed out that three SOEs also claimed that market wage rates were very important. In terms of the individual characteristics that affected pay and other rewards, a major influence was possession of public certificates of competence, which is not surprising given the importance of the vocational secondary schools in Hungary. Only two enterprises said that such credentials were not very important in setting pay scales, the same two SOEs that did not consider market rates when deciding wage rates. Overall, five firms said that individual pay was most affected by a combination of qualifications and experience for the bulk of the workforce, with a further four adding job difficulties — typically reflected in the job grading — to that combination. Individual performance did not seem to be a critical determinant of pay for the bulk of the workforce in any of these enterprises, except for one that had a piecework based reward system.

Focusing on particular groups of employees who were thought crucial to the future of the enterprise, all 14 claimed that there were such groups, mostly amongst the managers. The only one that did not mention managers in this connection was one of the smaller owner controlled firms who referred instead to the skilled workers and technicians as being crucial. Commercial and financial managers were regarded as particularly important by five firms, all SOEs. The most common way of retaining these key staff and ensuring their continued commitment was through paying a high salary and bonuses.

In examining the growth of differentials between different groups of staff, two issues arise. First, the extent to which firms allocate rewards and general conditions of employment in different ways to different groups of employees, and so pursue segmented reward policies, and second, the amount and type of differentials in rewards between groups. Both ownership and size were related to the segmentation of reward policies. All the privately owned firms employing over 1,500 people varied their employment contracts between different groups of employees, but only the SOEs with over 8,000 employees did so. The principal group affected by these separate contracts were technical and other qualified white collar workers. Five of the six enterprises that had distinctive employment contracts with this group were privately owned and controlled.

Additionally, in five enterprises, managers received non wage benefits which were not available to other staff, such as the provision of company cars. Four of these were privately owned. Overall, then, it seems that the enterprises which had been longest in private ownership and were most distant from their SOE past were most willing to implement different reward and employment conditions for different groups and to link rewards to external market rates, but size also played a role, often interdependently with ownership and control. The actual size of pay differentials did not, though, seem to vary greatly with either size or ownership. The ratio of the Chief Executive's total remuneration package to the average operative's pay varied from 9 to 28, and although one of the two enterprises at the top end of this dimension was the largest by far in this group, the other one was one of the smallest. Among the non-SOEs, this ratio varied considerably, with size not being a major factor and, within particular size classes control type similarly did not seem to be significant.

Other pay differentials we investigated dealt with supervisors, technical staff and returns to university education. Table 3 summarizes these by control type. As can be seen, there is no indication that privately owned firms had established greater pay differentials between these groups of employees. Indeed, the reverse seems to be the case for technical staff, where five of the seven enterprises paying them less than 250% of operators pay were privately owned and controlled. It is interesting to note here that the ESOP owned form had substantially greater pay differentials for all three categories of employees than many of the other enterprises. Whether this was a legacy of its previous, state owned, existence is unclear at the moment. Overall, then, differences in ownership and control had remarkably little connection to differences in pay between the top and the bottom of the authority hierarchies in these 14 enterprises or between key groups in them. Sectoral differences as indicated by capital intensity also had little impact on these pay differentials.

Changes in control type might, though, be expected to have had a more direct impact on procedures for performance evaluation and the establishment of a more formal transparent link between such assessments and pay (cf. Pearce et al. 1994). However, the number of enterprises that claimed they undertook regular formal evaluations of manual worker performance was quite limited, only four, and these were equally divided between SOEs and non SOEs. Six firms regularly evaluated technical and managerial staff in fairly formal ways, four of these were privately owned. Over half (eight) of the fourteen claimed that such evaluations, when carried out, directly affected pay and other rewards. Overall, then, it seems that systematic, regular assessment of manual workers which impinges upon pay directly is still quite rare in leading Hungarian firms, and that SOEs as well as privately owned firms have established formal procedures to evaluate technical and managerial staff.

Table 3. Control type and pay differentials in 14 Hungarian enterprises

a) Ratio of first line supervisor's pay to operator's pay

Control type	1.50	1.50-1.99	2.00-2.49	2.50+
State	1	3	3	
Foreign firm		1	1	
Manager controlled		3		2

b) Ratio of technical staff pay to operator's pay

Control type	1.50-1.99	2.00-2.49	2.50-2.99	3.00+
State	1	1	4	1
Foreign firm	1	1		
Manager controlled	1	2	1	1

c) Ratio of university graduates' pay to non-university graduates' pay

Control type	2.00-2.49	2.50-2.99	3.00-3.49	3.50-3.99	4.00+
State		3	1		2
Foreign frm	1		1		
Manager controlled	1	1		1	2

Turning now to consider the relation between control type and provision of non-wage rewards, we might expect privately owned enterprises to be less willing to provide the extensive ancillary benefits traditionally offered by SOEs, especially since Webster (1993) found that private manufacturing firms in Hungary preferred, on the whole, to offer higher wages and fewer such benefits than their state owned counterparts. These benefits included subsidized meals, contribution towards travel expenses, housing loans, health services, child care facilities, contributions to holiday costs, life insurance policies and heating bills and so on up to 15 distinct kinds. Two enterprises, one SOE and one private, provided only three of these benefits, while two provided over eleven of them. As can be seen from Table 4, the non-SOEs were no more likely to have stopped providing a wide range of these benefits than had SOEs, partly perhaps because such non pay rewards were not taxed at this time. Equally, size seemed to have relatively little connection to the variety of benefits provided. The most obvious factor, in fact, was the financial situation of the enterprise. None of the three SOEs making heavy losses provided more than five of these kinds of benefits and the owner managed firm that offered only three of them was also in some difficulty. Enterprises providing over eight, in contrast, were in much better situations and/or had foreign owners who were investing considerably in them.

Table 4. Size of enterprise in relation to the number of ancillary benefits and rewards provided by 14 Hungarian enterprises

	Number of ancillary benefits			
	0-3	4-7	8-11	11+
Control type				
State	1	3	2	1
Foreign firm			1	1
Manager	1	3	1	
Size by employees				
<1,000	1	1		
1,000-1,999		1	1	
2,000-2,999		1		1
3,000-3,999		1		
5,000-5,999	1	1		
7,000-7,999		1		
8,000-8,999			1	
9,000-9,999				1
10,000+		1	1	

In view of the common antipathy to trade unions expressed by the manufacturing firms in Webster's (1993) study, it is worthwhile reporting on their significance in these 14 enterprises. All had unions representing at least some of the workforce, except for the owner managed firm which had grown from a business partnership in the 1980s. The other small owner managed firm only partially recognized a trade union, but all the other twelve gave full recognition to trade unions and allowed their representatives time off for union activities and provided some space for them. The dominant union in most cases was the reconstructed successor to the previous regime's transmission belt union. All but two — the ESOP and one of the small owner controlled firms — also had enterprise specific forms of worker representation but these were typically dominated by union representatives. Despite, then, the low legitimacy of the previous unions, their successor organizations were still the dominant means of representing workers' interests in most of these enterprises, including the two foreign controlled ones, and none of the top managers we spoke to in these 12 enterprises envisaged a radical change in this situation. Indeed they mostly accepted the unions' bargaining rights on a wide range of issues. While, then, the smaller owner controlled Hungarian firms may well seek to bypass or reject unions, their larger counterparts seem likely to continue to accept them and work with them. The example of Suzuki being pressured into accepting union representation on a greenfield site emphasizes the strength of the union tradition in Hungary, and their so far generally cooperative behaviour has not led foreign investors to develop antagonistic attitudes to unions (Mako and Novoszath 1995).

Work Organization and Control

The move to a market economy with "hard" budget constraints and intensified competition for customers could be expected to generate much greater concern with labour productivity and the quality of outputs than was the case under state socialism. Enterprises might, then, attempt to move from 'quasi-Taylorism' in Nagy's (1989) phrase to Taylorism and exert more direct, centrally planned control over the work process. Alternatively, they might seek to encourage greater flexibility between tasks and skills, and generate higher commitment to the firm in order to respond quickly and effectively to changing customer demands, particularly in the light of considerable skilled worker autonomy in the SOEs studied by Burawoy and Lukacs (1985; 1989; 1992). Similarly, they may encourage supervisors to develop closer relationships with subordinates while at the same time exhorting them to exert more control over task performance.

Two aspects of task organization and control are discussed here: the variety and flexibility of tasks and people on the one hand, and top managers' expectations about supervisor behaviour and control, on the other hand. Considering first of all whether different enterprises recruited staff more for a specific job, or rather preferred to select employees for broader, more varied, responsibilities, six enterprises said they almost always hired for a specific role. Four of these were quite large SOEs. On the other hand, three, relatively small, firms preferred to recruit for broader roles, only one of these was an SOE. There was, then, some tendency for the larger and state owned enterprises to focus on specific jobs when recruiting but it is not possible to say whether this is a consequence of control variations or size.

The range of tasks carried out in a single job by operators varied from one to six. Six firms said that most jobs were concerned with only one or two tasks, while seven claimed their jobs had three or four different tasks and one, a loss making SOE, allocated five or six tasks per job. These variations were not apparently connected to control type, size or sector. Considering next the flexibility of organizations in terms of moving employees between tasks and roles, this seemed rather limited in these enterprises. Mobility between jobs within small work groups of three or five people was rather rare, but did occur in the smaller owner managed firms and the ESOP owned one every few weeks, and every three days or so in one of the severely loss making SOEs. Similarly, the majority of these enterprises did not encourage mobility between jobs in larger work groups of ten or thirty, although six did have some movement every few weeks. Four of these six were non-SOEs, including one of the foreign owned firms, but size seemed equally relevant since four of the six with under 2,000 employees also encouraged some operator mobility between jobs.

If we combine all these indicators of job mobility by operators in different sized work groups from three to thirty people, seven enterprises claimed operators did move between jobs on a fairly regular basis. These included five of the six employing under 3,000 people and five of the seven privately owned firms. Dominant technology and work flow rigidity, as measured in a similar way to the "Aston" studies, do not seem to be important factors influencing these variations. In general, then, operator mobility in these enterprises is clearly linked to size and to control but we cannot distinguish which factor is more significant at the moment.

Mobility among technical and managerial staff is also related to small size and non-state ownership. In six enterprises, these employees were said to change jobs every one or two years. All six had under 4,000 employees, four were non-SOEs. The only relatively small enterprise that did not move this group around fairly regularly was the ESOP owned one. For these employees, then, it seems then that size was the critical factor, presumably because there were simply fewer managers and technicians to do the increased variety of jobs that had become required in the transformation.

On the whole, then, task flexibility and job mobility were somewhat greater for the smaller, privately controlled firms in this group of 14 Hungarian enterprises, but by no means all of the smaller non-SOEs had established highly flexible and mobile patterns of work organization and nor had all the larger SOEs developed narrow, specialized jobs which were allocated to workers for many years. Furthermore, it is not possible to separate conclusively the effects of size from those of control type, although in a number of instances, size seems rather more significant.

Turning now to consider expectations about supervisor behaviour related to task control, performance and decision making, we asked a number of questions dealing with the role of supervisors which were similar to those used by Lincoln and Kalleberg (1990) to investigate differences between American and Japanese organizations. These were intended to find out if enterprises now expected supervisors to exert more direct control over task performance, control the allocation of rewards to subordinates and perform a broadly paternalist role, as well as ascertaining if expectations differed significantly between those remaining in state ownership and privately controlled firms.

As can be seen from Table 5, nearly all these enterprises' top managers expected supervisors to be closely involved with subordinates' work activities, to allocate tasks, and to maintain a high level of work group morale and commitment. The somewhat greater expectation of supervisor control over task allocation by top managers of non-SOEs was echoed by the middle managers we interviewed. However, supervisor control over how tasks were to be performed was rather less widely expected, similarly several organizations did not expect supervisors to play the major role in evaluating subordinate performance and allocating rewards. While both of the foreign controlled enterprises, the investor shared control one and two of the owner managed ones had quite strong expectations about supervisor control of how work was to be carried out, the two that did not were both loss making SOEs. Private control does, then, seem to be associated here with high levels of desired managerial control over task performance. However, this view was not shared by the middle managers in the non-SOEs when contrasted with those in the SOEs.

Subordinate involvement in decision making was not strongly expected by most of these enterprises, although one foreign controlled and one owner managed firm claimed they did encourage supervisors to develop such involvement. Supervisor concern for subordinates' welfare and the development of personal links with them were somewhat more expected, with the owner managed firms slightly more likely to regard the former as desirable, and two SOEs not so inclined. However, it was the SOEs which were marginally more concerned that supervisors should develop strong personal ties to subordinates. Most of these Hungarian enterprises did not, though, expect supervisors to socialize with their staff out of working hours.

In terms of their technical superiority to subordinates, the bulk of these firms expected supervisors to be more knowledgeable on most issues, and they also preferred middle managers to be specialists in the area they were responsible for. However, all but three considered that top managers should be experienced over a wide range of activities. Overall, the prevalent expectations of managerial expertise and careers in these organizations seem to be focused on developing and maintaining technical competence in particular functional areas and retaining considerable continuity in expertise up the authority hierarchy. The Anglo-Saxon "generalist" middle manager did not seem to be a desirable role model here, which is not too surprising given the strength of the vocational education system in Hungary and its close links to labour market stratification.

The only substantial differences between middle managers and supervisors in the non-SOEs compared to those in SOEs on these issues concerned task allocation, the superior intelligence of supervisors and the extent to which they felt that they shared the company's values. On these dimensions, those in non-SOEs reported higher values than those in SOEs. However, these differences were not very large, and in all other respects there did not seem to be much variation in the perceptions of these employees according to ownership. Indeed, the overall homogeneity of this group in respect of authority relations and values was quite marked.

Table 5. Managerial expectations of supervisors in 14 leading Hungarian enterprises

	Very high	Considerable	Some	Not much	Not at all
a) Involvement of supervisors in group work activities					
SOEs	2	4	1	0	0
Non-SOEs	4	3	0	0	0
b) Role of supervisors in task allocation to subordinates					
SOEs	3	3	0	1	0
Non-SOEs	6	0	1	0	0
c) Role of supervisors in determining how tasks are to be performed					
SOEs	0	3	2	2	0
Non-SOEs	3	3	1	0	0
d) Role of supervisors in evaluating performance and allocating rewards					
SOEs	0	4	1	2	0
Non-SOEs	1	4	2	0	0
e) Expected involvement of subordinates in decision making					
SOEs	0	1	3	3	0
Non-SOEs	0	2	4	1	0
f) Expected involvement in non-task concerns of subordinates					
SOEs	0	2	3	2	0
Non-SOEs	0	4	3	0	0
g) Expected development of personal ties to subordinates					
SOEs	1	3	3	0	0
Non-SOEs	0	3	3	0	1
h) Expected socialisation with subordinates outside work					
SOEs	0	1	1	3	2
Non-SOEs	0	1	2	4	0
i) Extent to which supervisors are expected to be more knowledgeable than subordinates					
SOEs	2	3	2	0	0
Non-SOEs	1	4	2	0	0
j) Importance of high work group morale and commitment for evaluating managerial performance					
SOEs	3	3	0	1	0
Non-SOEs	6	1	0	0	0

Conclusions

We can conclude, then, that the ability of some SOEs, especially those in severe financial distress, to reorganize themselves without being privatized yet, the inevitably dominant role of the state in managing the transformation to a market economy and its policy oscillations in the early 1990s, the significance and largely cooperative behaviour of the trade unions in Hungary and the costs involved in making radical changes in labour management practices, have together limited the impact of private ownership and control on employment policies and work management. While privately owned and controlled enterprises have relied on market processes and norms in setting wage rates and recruiting staff, they still preferred to rely on internal promotion in making appointments and also used seniority, qualifications and job grade in deciding pay. Similarly although they also evaluated some staff more regularly than some SOEs, these differences were not so strong as to suggest a close connection between private ownership and more formal, direct linkages between performance and pay. Equally, the tendency of the smaller, privately controlled firms to move workers about between jobs and to recruit for more general organizational roles than for specific posts is just as likely to be due to size as to ownership.

These points do not, of course, imply that some privately owned firms will not undertake significant reorganization and radical changes in labour management strategies over the next five or so years, especially those owned by large foreign firms (cf. Child and Markoczy 1994). However, we suggest that such changes will be limited by: (1) the continued close connection between the large firm section of the economy and the political system, (2) the slow institutionalization of external labour markets, (3) the influence of trade unions in the larger firms and, (4) the legacies of intra-enterprise cooperation between key groups, informal agreements and negotiations and work group solidarity, particularly among skilled workers (cf. Hethy and Mako 1989). While these factors could, of course, undoubtedly be overcome by sufficiently determined employers, it is not at all obvious that the prospective benefits would outweigh the costs, or what improvements in productivity could not be easier achieved by modifying and developing existing policies and practices incrementally rather than by creative, radical destruction.

In any case, changes in ownership and control are but one factor in achieving such improvements and need by no means be determinant. Thus, relying just on privatization and ownership changes to transform state enterprises into high productivity, "efficient" capitalist firms is unlikely to be successful. As numerous examples have demonstrated elsewhere, in Europe and in East Asia (Amsden 1989; Wade 1990) state ownership *per se* need not be inimical to organizational effectiveness, what is more significant is the competitive environment, incentive structures and the nature of commercial and financial risks (Grancelli 1995), as well as the broader institutional environment.

Note

* The research reported in this chapter was funded by the British Economic and Social Research Council under grant number R234422.

References

Amsden, A. (1989): *Asia's next giant: South Korea and late industrialization.* Oxford: Oxford University Press.

Amsden, A., J. Kochanowicz and L. Taylor (1994): *The market meets its match: Restructuring the economies of Eastern Europe.* Cambridge, MA: Harvard University Press.

Bangert, D. and J. Poor (1993): "Foreign involvement in the Hungarian economy: Its impact on human resource management." *International Journal of Human Resource Management 4*: 817-840.

Berend, I.T. (1990) *The Hungarian economic reforms, 1953-1988.* Cambridge: Cambridge University Press.

Bönker, F. (1994): "External determinants of the patterns and outcomes of East-European transitions." *Emergo* 1: 34-54.

Burawoy, M. and J. Lukacs (1985): "Mythologies of work: A comparison of firms in state socialism and advanced capitalism." *American Sociological Review* 50: 723-737.

Burawoy, M. and J. Lukacs (1989): "What is socialist about socialist production? Autonomy and control in a Hungarian steel mill" in S. Wood (ed.), *The transformation of work*, 295-316. London: Unwin-Hyman.

Burawoy, M. and J. Lukacs (1992): *The radiant past: Ideology and reality in Hungary's road to capitalism.* Chicago: Chicago University Press.

Child, J. and L. Markoczy (1994): "Host country managerial behaviour in Chinese and Hungarian joint ventures: Assessment of competing explanations" in M. Boisot (ed.), *East-West business collaboration,* 127-148. London: Routledge.

Dittrich, E. and M. Haferkemper (1995): "Labour relations in the making — Bulgaria, Hungary, Poland and the Czech Republic" in E. Dittrich, G. Schmidt and R. Whitley (eds.), *Industrial transformation in Europe,* 137-162. London: Sage.

Gowan, P. (1995): "Neo-liberal theory and practice for Eastern Europe." *New Left Review*, no 213: 3-60.

Grabher, G. (1995): "The elegance of incoherence: Economic transformation in East Germany and Hungary" in E. Dittrich, G. Schmidt and R. Whitley (eds.), *Industrial transformation in Europe,* 33-53. London: Sage.

Grancelli, B. (1995): "Organizational change: Towards a new east west comparison." *Organization Studies* 16: 1-26

Hausner, J. and K. Nielsen (1992): "The post-socialist transformation process: Systematic vacuum, search processes, implementation problems and social struggle" in W. Blaas and J. Foster (eds.), *Mixed economies in Europe.* Aldershot: E. Elgar.

Henderson, J. (1993): "The role of the state in the economic transformation of East Asia" in C. Dixon and D. Drakakis-Smith (eds.), *Economic and social development in Pacific Asia*, 85-114. London: Routledge.

Henderson, J., R. Whitley, L. Czaban, and G. Lengyel (1995): "Contention and confusion in industrial transformation: Dilemmas of state economic management" in E. Dittrich, G. Schmidt and R. Whitley (eds.), *Industrial transformation in Europe*, 79-108, London: Sage.

Hethy, L. and C. Mako (1989): *Patterns of workers' behaviour and the business enterprise*. Budapest: Hungarian Academy of Sciences.

Holmes, S. (1995): "Cultural legacies or state collapse? Probing the postcommunist dilemma." Public lecture delivered at the Collegium Budapest on the 17th October, published as Public Lecture no. 13, Collegium Budapest, November.

Hughes, S. (1994) "Of monoliths and magicians: Economic transition and industrial relations in Hungary." *Work, Employment and Society* 8: 69-86.

Konecki, K. and J. Kulpinska (1995): "Enterprise transformation and the redefinition of organisational realities in Poland" in E. Dittrich, G. Schmidt and R. Whitley (eds.), *Industrial transformation in Europe*, 234-254. London: Sage.

Lado, M. (1994): Workers' and employers' interests — As they are represented in the changing industrial relations in Hungary. Working Paper no. 3, University Council for Economic and Management Education Transfer, Cracow, Poland.

Lincoln, J. and A. Kalleberg (1990): *Culture, control and commitment*. Cambridge: Cambridge University Press.

Mako, C. and P. Novoszath (1995): "Employment relations in multinational companies: The Hungarian Case" in E. Dittrich, G. Schmidt and R. Whitley (eds.), *Industrial transformation in Europe*, 255-276. London: Sage.

Nagy, K. (1989): "New technology and work in Hungary: Technological innovation without organizational adaptation" in A. Francis and P. Grootings (eds.), *New technologies and work*, 88-119. London: Routledge.

Pearce, J.L., I. Branyiczki and G. Bakacsi (1994): "Person-based reward systems: A theory of organisational reward practices in reform-communist organisations." *Journal of Organisational Behaviour* 15: 261-282.

Radice, H. (1995): "Organizing markets in Central and Eastern Europe: Competition, governance and the role of foreign capital" in E. Dittrich, G. Schmidt and R. Whitley (eds.), *Industrial transformation in Europe*, 109-133. London: Sage.

Stark, D. (1993) "Recombinant property in East European capitalism: Organisational innovation in Hungary." Paper presented to a conference on Economic Transformation in Central and Eastern Europe, WZB, Berlin, September.

Stark, D. and L. Bruszt (1995): "Network properties of assets and liabilities: Patterns of inter-enterprise ownership in the post-socialist transformation." Paper presented to an EMOT Programme Workshop on Dynamics of Industrial Transformation: East Central European and East Asian Comparisons, Budapest University of Economic Sciences, May.

Swaan, W. (1993): *Behaviour and institutions under economic reform*. Amsterdam: Thesis Publishers, Tinbergen Research Series, no. 46.

Szalai, E. (1991) "Integration of special interests in the Hungarian economy: The struggle between large companies and the party and state bureaucracy." *Journal of Comparative Economics* 15: 284-303.

Tatur, M. (1995): "Towards corporatism? The transformation of interest policy and interest regulation in Eastern Europe" in E. Dittrich, G. Schmidt and R. Whitley (eds.), *Industrial transformation in Europe*, 163-184. London: Sage.

Vickerstaff, S., J. Thirkell and R. Scase (1995): "Enterprise strategies and labour relations in Central Europe." Paper presented to an EMOT Programme Workshop on Dynamics of Industrial Transformation: East Central European and East Asian Comparisons, Budapest University of Economic Sciences, May.

Voszka, E. (1995): *Agyaglabakon allo orias. Az AyRt letrehozasaes mukodese* (The giant with feet of clay), Budapest: Penzugykutato.

Wade, R. (1990): *Governing the market.* Princeton, NJ: Princeton University Press.

Webster, L. (1993): "The emergence of private sector manufacturing in Hungary", World Bank Technical Paper no. 229, Washington, DC World Bank.

Whitley, R., J. Henderson, L. Czaban and G. Lengyel (1996): "Continuity and change in an emergent market economy: The limited transformation of large Hungarian Enterprises" in R. Whitley and P. Kristensen (eds.), *The Changing European Firm*, 210-237. London: Routledge.

Whitley, R. (1996): "There is no alternative: The necessity of state coordination of East European reindustrialisation." *Competition and Change* 1: 321-332.

Woo, J. (1991): *Race to the swift: State and finance in Korean industrialization.* New York: Columbia University Press.

The Machineries of Institutional Transformation: The Case of Czech Agriculture*

Yohanan Stryjan

Introduction: Studying Transformation

In the study of institutional transformation, a great deal of attention has been paid to dramatic changes of signal features. These, however, only mark turning points in a process of change, but do not wholly define it. A new institutional order is not built from a political centre (though whatever is happening there may be very important indeed). In fact, most of the actual change is being enacted at less heroic levels, in enterprises, in local government, in households, and in the life of individuals. Most evidently, an institutional transformation involves and entails a massive modification of populations of organizations. Understanding processes that unfold at this meso-level is vital to the understanding of transformation (Bager 1996).

The role of organizations in the shaping, maintenance and reproduction of a social order has been quite extensively researched (e.g. Meyer and Scott 1983; Perrow 1979; Sjöstrand 1985; Ahrne 1990; 1994). Due to their inherent stability, organizations may be considered the basic building blocks of a social order (Hannan and Freeman 1989). Indeed, to a major extent, organizations and their interplay are the social order. Accordingly, the transformation of organizations and of organizational populations can be seen as the nexus of the transformation process, at which micro and macro inputs converge. Inputs from the macro level consist for our purpose here, of legislative changes of the rule systems that regulate incorporation, liquidation and organizational conduct. Individuals engage in and impact on the organizational scene mostly through their faculty for organizational affiliation and the formation of new organizations. Legislative redistributions of individual entitlements may influence, trigger, and modify individual inputs.

The focus in this chapter is primarily on the transformation of a single sector of the Czech economy, namely, the agricultural sector. A chain of historical coincidences made this sector into somewhat of a convergence point for most of the problems transformation entails; normative considerations, private ownership, organizational strategies, and policy implementation — all enacted in a well-delimited sector, dominated by a single population of resourceful organizations, the collective farms of communist times. All these factors have turned the case of Czech agriculture, economically inconsequential in itself, into somewhat of a laboratory of transformation. It is believed that the findings could improve the understanding of the dynamics at work in other sectors and in other economies as well.

Background: The Privatization of the Czech Economy

Relative to other cases of post-communist transformation, the transformation of the Czech economy has largely proceeded in a legally explicit and highly formalized fashion. The Czech economy was probably the most robust of the CEE economies. It neither collapsed into chaos, nor imploded prior to the fall of communism, as was the case with many of its CEE counterparts. Cases of spontaneous disintegration and "wild" privatization were extremely rare. The Republic (particularly its Czech part, eventually reconstituted as a sovereign Czech Republic) could rely on a bureaucratic tradition and on well preserved ownership and property records stretching back, almost unbroken, to the times of Austrian Imperial rule.[1] Legislation invariably produced effects (though not necessarily the ones desired), and questions of ownership and entitlement were handled in a technically sophisticated fashion. These features (that were amply illustrated in the unprecedented orderly dissolution of the Czechoslovak Republic) greatly facilitate institutional analysis, and make it possible to relate legislation to actual development, and to trace failures back to the specific policies that precipitated them.

The re-privatization of the Czech economy was carried out as an integrated, top-steered, comprehensive project. The ambition was to transfer 70-80% of the economy into private hands in a short time (Stryjan and Maskova 1992; Frydman et al. 1993; Earle et al. 1994; Zammit and Ghai 1992). The process was started in late 1990, within the framework of the then Czecho-Slovak Federal Republic, and formally completed in the Czech Republic[2] in the first months of 1996, with the closing of the last round of voucher privatization. The project suffered some delay, but was otherwise unaffected by the demise of the Czecho-Slovak federation.

A top-managed privatization process, is essentially a procedure of structured re-matching of entitlements with *existing* productive assets. The procedures applied distinguished between different classes of privatizable assets (small and large privatization), but also between different categories of entitlements:

- *Historical entitlements*, i.e. restitution rights to property confiscated by the communist regime. In practice, these entitlements applied only to real estate and former family businesses. An expanded concept of historical entitlements was custom-tailored for the case of property held in collective farms (discussed later on in this chapter).
- *Civic entitlements*, conveyed by the state, as a citizen dividend of sorts. These entitlements could be exercised through the voucher scheme (for details and limitations of this complex and technically ingenuous scheme, see Stryjan and Maskova, 1992). In the case of agriculture, such entitlements were activated only in the privatization of the processing industry.
- *Financial entitlements*, exercised through tenders and auction bids. Due to the lack of legitimate privately-held capital in the first post-revolutionary years, this lane was, to start with, mainly open to foreign investors, eventually joined by local would be entrepreneurs with good bank contacts to back their bids. Within agriculture, direct privatization auctions/tenders were resorted to in the privatization of state-farms, and in the processing industry.

Different combinations of procedures were applied to different groups of enterprises. Thus, small enterprises and subunits separated from the unwieldy "conglomerates" of the communist times were subject to restitution where appropriate, or auctioned in the framework of "small privatization." Larger enterprises were reincorporated as joint-stock companies and blocks of stock were then either auctioned off through the voucher privatization scheme, or sold through local, national, or international tenders, as the case may be. Numerous exceptions notwithstanding, the proceedings were largely carried out in an orderly and formally proper manner.

The chief problem of the privatization programme lies in its underlying perception of the enterprises to be privatized as (passive) objects, to be designated to deserving owners. Initiatives originating in the organizations being subjected to privatization and in pre-existing inter-industry networks were discouraged. In the absence of potential competent owners (that could only have arisen within the industries in question), this policy resulted in a concentration of industrial ownership rights in the hands of emergent investment funds that arose to fill the void. The dominance of institutional ownership probably accounts for the relatively sluggish post-transformation performance of the Czech economy.

The transformation of the agricultural sector occupied a special place in the transformation process, and largely followed a path and a timetable of its own. This is due to a combination of factors of an institutional, legal, and political nature. *Institutionally*, the entire agro-industrial complex lies, formally, in the domain of a separate ministry. *Legally* speaking, large portions of the sector were not formally owned by the state and could therefore not be privatized in the ordinary manner. A disproportionate share of unresolved ownership claims in the Republic concerned farming property (to be sure, this was partly due to the way property entitlements were defined by the new regime). Viewed as a *political* issue, the "farming question" had a high symbolic value. The issue combines two key societal symbols, namely that of "free-holding peasants", enshrined in the Central European pantheon as the semi-mythical mainstay of the nation, and of private ownership, a key symbol of the new order. To manipulate agriculture is, thus, first and foremost, to manipulate symbols. The sector (in particular its key component the collective farms) was, thus, awarded disproportionately high attention by the communist regime and came to be considered as its main bastion. The disproportionately high priority awarded, for precisely the same reasons, to the question of farming by the post-communist government ought to be understood in this context. In a profound sense, the post-communist transformation of the 1990s, discussed below, is thus both a sequel and a mirror image of the communist transformation of the 1950s. Understanding the legal genesis of the organizations in the sector, and the historical sediments deposed by 40 years of the communist regime is thus necessary for understanding both the present regime's attitude to cooperation, the particular legislative approaches chosen, and the concrete organizational outcomes (Stryjan and Linhart 1996).

The Reshaping of the Agro-Industrial Complex

Czech agriculture in 1989, the communist regime's last year, stood out as both the most extensively collectivized and, probably, the best performing agricultural sector of the then East Bloc (Stryjan and Maskova 1992; Stryjan 1994b). Three distinct clusters of organizations can be said to have constituted the agricultural sector in 1989, the communist regime's final year:

- *collective farms* (CFs), which were clearly the most dominant group and the centrepiece of the entire system;
- *state farms* (SFs), a cluster of secondary importance, filling the slots not taken up by CFs;
- *enterprises in the processing industry and their distribution linkages*. Formally external to the sector, these enterprises nonetheless define the economic environment of both groups of primary producers.

Government policies in the post-communist period left their clearest mark on the reshaping of (sub)populations of organizations within the sector. The evolution of the sector is largely the story of continuity and change in these clusters.[3] As will be shown later, the development of each of the clusters was guided by a different set of rules and by its own population dynamics. The actions of enterprises in all three categories are also linked and aggregated through market mechanisms, Thus, each of the clusters affects the others' conditions of development although cases of direct interference were rare.

The government's position at the outset of the process was somewhat of an institutional designer's dream. It enjoyed a strong mandate, and the delegitimization of (pre)existing interests *within* the sector meant that normative notions at the political centre were not countervailed, to start with, by any vested interests. The vision that guided the transformation policies of successive post-communist governments since late 1990 was of an agriculture dominated by resurgent family farms, yet virtually free of any form of cooperative organization whatsoever. With this aim in sight, the government embarked on a project of restructuring existing organizations. This line, as will be shown later, has proven self defeating for the government and detrimental to agriculture in general. At first, the effort to hinder the development of producer organizations crippled the development of family farming as well. In the longer run, agriculture's mounting problems, caused, in part, by these policies, came to provide an important stimulus for the development of new cooperative solutions (Stryjan and Linhart 1994).

State interference has played an important role on three levels: (1) the redistribution of individual entitlements; (2) the setting of parameters through legislation; and (3) direct, hands-on interference of the Treuhand type in specific organizations, or groups of organizations. Owing to the government's penchant for customized legislation, designed to apply only to specific target groups[4], the three often shade into each other. The explicit, and nearly exclusive, priority of policy-makers from 1991 onwards was on the restructuring of property relations. A sequence of laws concerning agricultural property was passed to this end from the year 1991 onwards. On the whole, the sector attracted disproportionately more legislation than any other sector of the economy.[5] While closely involved in the restructuring of specific organizations (see below), the government failed to seriously involve itself in shaping the economic environment these organizations would act in. Agricultural policy proper was managed mainly by default.[6]

The prime focus of the discussion below will be on the transformation of CFs, the old systems' centrepiece, and the erstwhile proprietor of most prime production assets. Given the (sub)population's sheer weight and the strategic importance of the niche they originally occupied, the end-products of their transformation are bound to play a key role in any future alignment of the sector. The (sub)population in question was reasonably uniform, consisting of a large number of sovereign organizations, which also gives the case interesting theoretical implications.

The discussion of the evolution of the remaining two sub-populations will be relegated to the background, as it were, and will mainly concentrate on its implications for the entire sector.

Cooperative/Collective Farms (CFs)

Primary agricultural production in the Czech Republic was dominated in 1989 by about 1000 large, formally cooperative farms of an average size of slightly under 2600 ha each, that answered for the cultivation of about 65% of all agricultural land, including the largest part of prime agricultural land in the republic. Cooperative organizations have traditionally occupied a dominant place in Czech agriculture. Farmer cooperatives, organizing upstream and downstream industries, credit, and, at times, community aspects of rural life as well (Galla 1937), had already emerged under the Austro-Hungarian Empire and achieved increasing prominence under the First Republic. Cooperatives maintained a central role of sorts under the Communist regime as well, though strictly on the regime's terms. The extensive organizational network, originally created to manage farmers' transactions with their environment, was taken over, and turned inside out, as it were (Stryjan 1994a). The outward-oriented cooperative processing industry and production services were nationalized, and the focus of cooperative activity was turned *inwards*, on the integration of primary production within the framework of "integrated farming cooperatives" (JZDs in Communist terminology). It is possible to see the evolution of the population of CFs as a product of a long and patient "selective breeding program" (Stryjan 1994a). Starting initially as single-village co-ops, the population of collective farms reached its peak at 12,560 units in 1959 (Spirk 1974).[7] From this point on, collective farms were successively merged into ever bigger units. The last wave of amalgamations was completed in the 1970s. The resulting "integrated cooperatives" were modeled, in broad lines, after Soviet collective farms, though with incomparably higher standards of performance, better social cohesion, and broader autonomy, especially from the 1980s onwards, than their Soviet counterparts.

Could those formally cooperative farms be considered autonomous organizations in their own right, or should they be seen as merely an outgrowth of the state bureaucracy? I believe that the former is clearly the case. Though acting in a tightly controlled environment, the management of collective farms normally exercised a considerable range of managerial discretion. This was aided by the fact that advancement paths normally were internal to the sector.[8] The competence mix encouraged by the regime for managers within the sector was that of political docility and managerial zeal, and not the other way round.

The last wave of amalgamation was completed in 1975. The period that followed, until the collapse of the regime in 1989, was the longest period of stability that the CFs ever came to enjoy. As political developments in neighbouring Poland sharpened the regime's awareness of the importance of keeping the population well fed, the sector was flooded with cheap credits and granted an increased internal autonomy. From 1982 onwards, the scope of central planning was progressively reduced, and innovation and independent economic activity were encouraged.[9] The maverick Slusovice CF, diversifying into an array of fields, from assembly of computers to horse-racing was held up as an example. In a sense, this period constituted the best preparation for a future transformation that the regime could have ever provided (Stryjan and Linhart 1996).

The system regulating CFs' activities disintegrated with the collapse of the communist regime. Formally speaking, the CFs were the property of their members and, thus, no longer subject to state directives. For the first — and, as it eventually turned out — the only time in their history, decisions as to the future of these enterprises were fully lodged in the CFs themselves, i.e. the respective cooperative's corpus of members and its management team. Though the reactivation of historical property rights seemed imminent, the CFs were well buffered by assets accumulated in 30-40 years of operation. A legal framework for the operation and spontaneous restructuring of the existing CFs was provided by a new Law on Agricultural Cooperatives approved in May 1990.[10] The law created legal tools for the division of CFs by groups of members and for the withdrawal of property by titular owners (members and non-members alike[11]). CFs were recognized as sovereign economic subjects, free to decide on their own evolution and to negotiate with owners of collectivized land its return or continued use on a lease basis. The brief period in which this autonomy could be fully exercised provides some indication of the course of development CFs might have taken, if left alone. Generally, action was directed towards improving the structure and functioning of the CFs. The chairmen in many, probably most CFs, were replaced by new people less tainted by contact with the former regime. Some of the CFs decided to split into smaller units that better fitted existing village divisions. The number of CFs in Czechoslovakia thus increased, by division, from 1,655 in 1989, to 1,898 (Liptak and Vavra 1993). The year's harvest was the best ever to be achieved in the republic's history. Investment continued, drawing on still good credit lines. To the extent it is possible to judge by this brief period, the interest among members in disbanding the CF was virtually nonexistent. This conclusion is also supported by a number of surveys (Majerova 1992; Hudeckova and Lostak 1991; Brabenec and Sarecova 1991). A sober assessment of the future prospects of independent small to middle size farming, and of agriculture in general in the new economic reality, probably played an important role in forming these preferences.

The legislation that acknowledged the sovereignty of CFs was soon overturned by new bills that enhanced the rights of historical owners vs. those of CF members, blocked further restructuring, and placed CFs in an economically disastrous legal limbo (Mertlik 1992). In parallel, a vigorous campaign to encourage private farming was initiated, further increasing the entitlements of owners that set out to start farming on their own[12] and allocating generous subventions to family farms. The response to the latter was rather limited, as neither present farmers nor historical owners were eager to start farming on their own. The CFs would neither disintegrate as a result of a run on their assets, nor through a voluntary decision of their corpus of members.

The process was completed with the passing of the Transformation Law (Law 42/1992, Law of the 21st December 1991 on the Adjustment of Property Relations and the Settlement of Property Rights in Cooperative Societies) regulating the mandatory restructuring of CFs. The law was heavily weighted in favour of absentee (historical) owners, allotting them a right to determine the enterprises' future, and an ownership title to a major portion of the assets. Contrary to the government's initial ambitions and despite the impossible odds, the law failed to precipitate a voluntary breakup of CFs into private farms. The absolute majority of CFs underwent, instead, a metamorphosis into so-called *owner cooperatives* (OCs). The details and dynamics of this process will be discussed in more detail in a later section.

State Farms (SFs)

State farms (SFs) were initially established on state land, generally confiscated in the first post-war years from expelled Germans and Austrians, or great nobility and church estates. Contrary to Leninist orthodoxy, SFs were never hailed as "the highest form of organization" that cooperatives should be expected to emulate or eventually evolve into. On the contrary, they remained somewhat of a junior partner and a problem child throughout the communist period. A communist information brochure on Czech agriculture from the regime's last years (Zaloudek 1988) provides a fine illustration of the official priorities in the matter. It devotes five pages to organizational development within the sector of which four lines are devoted to state farms. The SFs were often used as a depository for failed collectivization attempts that were often converted into or incorporated into existing state farms.[13] In a sense, the CF population was held in trim partly through this siphoning off of bottom sediments which substituted for normal selection mechanisms. Needless to say, this policy hardly advanced the development of the SFs themselves.

As of January 1990, there were 257 SFs in the Czech Republic. Some of the most unwieldy units were divided shortly after the collapse of the regime, thus increasing the figure to 362 farms in 1991.[14]

The transformation of SFs, though of little direct impact on the developments in the remainder of the sector, provides an excellent illustration of the disparate strands of logic inherent in the Czech governments' approach to agriculture. It unfolded roughly parallel to that of CFs, though it took a considerably longer time to complete. In contrast to the highly structured, but strictly decentralized implementation in transforming the CFs, the transformation of SFs was centrally steered, yet highly unstructured.

Initially, the government decided to privatize the farms within the framework of the so-called "big privatization" programme (Stryjan and Maskova 1992). After turning down, in the first post-revolution months an informal bid for worker-takeover advanced by the farm workers' trade-union[15], it opened 302 farms for privatization bids in the first and second privatization waves. 826 privatization projects were submitted. However, as the process gathered momentum, the government started moving in an entirely different direction, namely that of extended restitution, seemingly unaware of its implications. Their shaky legal grounds notwithstanding[16], settler allotments from the agrarian reform of 1947 were recognized as full ownership rights, thus assigning titular owners to a great bulk of state-farm land that was generally believed to be under state ownership. In addition, an amendment to the Land Act (93/1992, in power from 28th February 1992) opened the way for the restitution of the great nobility estates and made further inroads into the SF's assets. The two incompatible rationales of privatization and of restitution clashed in a frontal manner in this case. While privatization rests on the individuation of economically viable units and their allocation to resourceful enterpreneurs/owners whatever their identity may be, restitution rests on restoring the historical rights of distinct owners, quite independently of current economic realities. As property was subject to restitution, debts outstanding were retained by the shrinking rump state farm, and mortgages were transferred to its remaining assets (Lux 1993). Thus, while the privatization projects were being submitted and considered, the state-farms were turned into a patchwork of odd assets and old debts, quite an unlikely privatization object. Only one state farm was fully privatized by the autumn of

1993[17] and the entire privatization scheme was quietly shelved. Planned privatization gave way to piecemeal privatization of a storm-sale character, handled by the ministry and the Land Fund on a highly particularistic, case-by-case basis. The process is likely to give rise, in the long run, to a group of powerful actors. With the eventual exception of reinstated great nobility estates, this has not occurred as yet.[18] The disintegration of state-farms indirectly affects the entire sector by further depressing the price of production assets on one hand, and by eliminating agricultural production surpluses on the other. The fall in production was offset by falling demand and by state price intervention in the form of state-subsidized imports. It did not trigger a rise in producer prices or the formation of new enterprises. The glut in production assets did, on the other hand, further diminish the value of equity and the credit-worthiness of enterprises still in business.

Processing Industry

The processing industry was never considered, in communist thinking, to be a part of the agricultural sector proper. It was formally state-owned and firmly managed by the bureaucracies of relevant ministries (industry and agriculture). Historically, the cluster was constituted by the nationalization of private industries (already partly in the pre-communist times) and the "voluntary" surrender of farmer cooperation's processing facilities that were entrusted to state monopolies. The sector underwent substantial restructuring and modernization under the communist government and numerous new plants were added to or replaced the old ones. The water-tight partition between primary production and processing was, however, maintained thereafter. This was, indeed, one of the few fields into which CFs were not encouraged to diversify in the diversification drive of the 1980s mentioned above. In a nearly full inversion of the pattern accepted in Western agriculture, the Czechoslovak "agri-food complex" came to be marked by the domination of formally cooperative organizations in primary production, their limited presence in upstream industries and virtual exclusion from downstream industries (Stryjan 1994b).

Communist times' strict separation between primary production and processing was zealously maintained by the post-communist Czech government. The restructuring of this population was intentionally decoupled from that of primary production units. This decoupling was one sided. While primary producers could not in any way affect the transformation of the industry, developments in the processing industry played a major role in shaping the economic environment of primary producer enterprises by setting the economic parameters for these populations' development, thus motivating the inclusion of this group in our discussion.

The transformation of this (sub)sector proceeded within the framework of large privatization, i.e. *previous to*, and quite independently from that of primary production. In privatizing the industry, the government decided to ignore the historical property rights of farmers, the industry's historical founders and owners. Instead, the field was opened to competitive privatization bids and, later on, to voucher privatization. Farmers ("old" as well as "new" ones) were prevented from attaining any stake in the industry, by the sequencing of the process and by procedural means[19] (Stryjan 1994b); or even through direct and indirect government intervention.[20] A considerable portion of sales to domestic enterpreneurs were de-facto leveraged sellouts to well connected individuals and groups. Bids were financed in their entirety by bank credits. The (often unrealistically assessed) assets of the company not yet bought were often used as collateral. Given that banks, at the time, were still largely controlled by the state the procedure was often swayed by political deals and influence-peddling.

Privatization seems to have strengthened, rather than weakened, oligopolistic tendencies in the industry and to have led to a network of mutual support between enterprises, reminiscent of those formed within Russian industry (Kharkhordin 1994). Thus, while milk production in the Czech Republic fell between 1989 and 1993 by nearly 30%, the number of dairies only decreased from 113 to 103 (Stryjan and Linhart 1996). In a manner of speaking, this constellation could be regarded as a specimen of a *permanently failing population* (cf. Meyer and Zucker 1990), kept afloat by the continued efforts of the population's members and creditors (including suppliers) eager to avoid bankruptcy. Thus, while the gap between farming output prices and consumer prices is approaching western standards (Brabenec and Sarecova 1993), Czech farmers, unlike their western counterparts, had no share in the revenues this gap generates, nor do they go to enhancing the industry's international competitiveness. Instead, these revenues were largely swallowed by the costs of maintaining an increasingly outdated and insufficiently utilized (due to falls in both production and demand) processing capacity. Most immediately, the situation constitutes an additional drain on the sector's financial resources, aggravating the financial distress of existing producers and discouraging potential new entrants from establishing themselves or investing in the sector. Despite government opposition, initiatives for a cooperative organization of producers challenging the existing agro-industrial complex did reemerge in 1994 (Stryjan and Linhart 1994). Since the challengers are still largely alienated from the present political establishment, while the present proprietors of the processing industry are normally well connected to banks and the state apparatus[21], the outcome of such challenges is uncertain. The repeated attempts of primary producers to gain a foothold within the processing industry are likely to remain a central feature of the Czech scene for years to come.

The Transformation of CFs

Given their specific form of incorporation, the CFs were immune to privatization legislation. The impact of restitution legislation was also rather limited to begin with, since CFs had managed, under their long career, to accumulate considerable capital and assets of their own that buffered them against restitution claims and provided their members/mandators with a firm resource base. Nonetheless, the CFs had to go, as their continued existence was not compatible with the regime's vision.

To this end, the government chose to re-class CFs, demoting them from being functioning organizations with a legitimate group of owners/mandators into being an agglomeration of assets. It then proceeded to redistribute the entitlements to these resources, as if the legal entity holding them never existed. The Transformation Law (Law 42/1992), regulating the mandatory restructuring of CFs, was posted in the Official Gazette (Exhibit 1). The law's two principal elements are (1) a drastic redistribution of entitlements that is heavily weighted in favour of historical owners (often residing now in town) at the expense of the CFs' members; and (2) a meticulously designed procedure and timetable for legal transformation.

Besides the (already legislated) right to get their historical assets back, historical owners (or their heirs, whether resident or not) were awarded an equal vote as members in determining the future of successor enterprises and a disproportionate share (up to 82%) of the considerable assets accumulated under the CFs' 30-40 years of operation. Put roughly, since the CFs declined to disintegrate of own volition, legislation created new bodies, populated by "owners" created for the purpose and who seemed more likely to reach such a decision.

As noted, each CF's future was to be decided by a body whose composition was strictly prescribed by the law, namely, the (respective) transformation assembly. While the law did not prescribe any specific outcomes, the composition of the decision-making bodies that legislation called forth was heavily weighted from the outset against the possibility of smooth succession:

- Member-owners and working members were outnumbered by about three to one by potential claimants, now residing in town (this proportion, be-

Exhibit 1. The law of transformation

Timetable: Start 28.01.92, completion within a year, on penalty of compulsory liquidation.

Transformation assembly: The decision-making body governing the transformation proceedings. May decide on formation of (eventual) successor enterprise(s). Consists of entitled persons (see below).

Entitled persons: With one vote each, are:
- members without property in the CF
- members with historical property
- non-members with property (or their heirs).

Property redistribution: Among entitled persons
a) *Historical property:* All committed property returns to original owners (equivalent replacements for livestock and movable inventories, machines, etc).*
b) *Residual property:*
- 3% set aside for unknown restitution claims;
- the remainder is distributed as capital shares/debt instruments, after the following key: 25% reserve fund for successor enterprise;
- the remaining 75% are to be allocated as retroactive dividends, as follows:
  37.5% returns to land; per ha land committed
  22.5% returns to livestock and inventories; per CZK book value
  15% returns to labour; per year employment

The transformation shares are to be redeemed by the successor enterprise within 7 years from transformation (1999-2000).

---

* This step, termed restitution, has actually been granted by earlier legislation.

Source: Stryjan and Linhart 1994 (modified).

tween farmers and ex-farmers would, in itself, be rather natural for *any* European country that underwent urbanization in the post-war period). The majority in most assemblies was thus virtually guaranteed to external owners, i.e. persons/groupings that had no commitment to the CFs continued existence — to put it mildly.

- The massive transfer of ownership of residual assets to historical owners further strengthened the hand of external claimants and commonly amounted to a de facto veto-right over any thinkable reconstruction project.
- The *de facto* disenfranchisement of non-owner members (that had no property in the CF, and whose "dividend" for years of employment barely amounted to a mediocre severance pay), neutralized the one group which had both a genuine stake in the enterprise's survival and was not involved in the divisive process of collectivization. The field was left to

(external) owners and member-owners, i.e. to those who were evicted from the village during collectivization and those who helped the then authorities to evict them. A composition that can hardly be considered a fertile ground for social coherence or for fruitful communication. Non-members (absent owners), the group least committed to the CFs survival, were often the larger group of the two.

Despite the seemingly impossible odds, the law failed to precipitate a voluntary breakup of CFs into private farms. The absolute majority of CFs underwent, instead, a metamorphosis of sorts, into the so-called *owner cooperatives* (OCs) constituted by reinstated, often absentee, owners of the assets previously held by the CF (see Table 1). This "cooperatively owned" corporate estate is operated by a workforce that may, but need not, include members. A capital share (commonly based on restitution and transformation claims) is the main and normally the only criterion for membership. Land is leased, primarily from members and patronage is to capital only.

Table 1. The transformation of CFs in the Czech Republic

	Type	Enterprises
0)	CFs before transformation	1,076
	After transformation	
1)	Owner Cooperatives (OCs)	1,221
2)	Joint stock companies	37
3)	Limited partnerships	163
4)	Others	22
5)	Liquidated	24

Sources: Lux (1993), and internal survey material of the Czech-Moravian association of agricultural cooperatives (CM SZD).

The circumstances that produced this outcome deserve some explanation. As mentioned above, decision-making that was to determine the future of CFs took place in what may be regarded as a social vacuum. Due to limited interest in return to family farming and the decreasing attraction of farming for prospective enterpreneurs, the transformation of CFs also took place in a virtual economic vacuum largely caused by the absence of a coherent government farming policy. While entitled persons were enticed to join the process by the prospect of gaining a share in the CFs' property (and, more than once, by the temptation of settling old accounts), there was no market for the assets thus gained. Both economic and social factors thus gave a pivotal role to the management teams of CFs.

The OC model and the sophisticated software required to handle the extensive amount of paperwork concerned (property claims, lists of entitled persons, mailing lists and standard summons to entitled persons etc.) made their appearance in this confused scene in about May 1992[22] and were rapidly disseminated through licensing agreements (and countless pirate applications) by private consultants throughout the Republic.

The sequence of events merits a closer look:

- A progressive deterioration of the terms of the farming sector introduced an increasing environmental strain (autumn 1990 onwards).
- Legislation set a tight timetable for conversion increasing this strain further, and disrupted internal communication (February 1992).
- An easily communicable scheme for transformation proceedings (backed by a comprehensive software package and consulting services) was introduced (ca. May 1992).
- The scheme was adopted and implemented by virtually the entire population (deadline 28 January 1993).

The scenario outlined above, of mounting stress resulting in mass adoption by a group of individuals once a model behaviour emerges, is best understood in terms of *social contagion* (Midlarsky 1978, Miller et al. 1978; Klapp 1972), a process known from studies of panics and riots. The label most suitable to the transition mechanism at work in this case would, in the same vein, be *contagious* mimesis. The behaviour adopted is not non-rational. Its envisaged outcome is preferable to that of inaction which would have meant forced liquidation. Lack of trust between the parties involved imposes a prohibitively high transaction cost threshold on any search for a truly optimal solution. The solution adopted preserves the position of management and provides a caretaker solution for external owners and member-owners' property. In this sense, it is a clear response to the government policies that shaped the preconditions for action. As it will be argued below, this outcome is clearly sub-optimal for all parties and definitely different from the one policy-makers strove to produce, namely, the emergence of family farming.

The Future of OCs

The pre-transformation agriculture was dominated, for better or worse, by the cluster of collective farms. The post-transformation scene came to be dominated by the same organizations, now reborn as OCs. The mass emergence of OCs raises a number of important theoretical questions concerning their genesis, internal structure and affiliation model (ownership vs. membership), and their future developmental path.

New organizations are problem-prone (Stinchcombe 1965). Amburgey et al. (1993) show that the same applies to "old" organizations that go through radical change. The problems that can be expected in this particular case go, however, well beyond mere "liability of newness." The OC organization form was, first and foremost, a defensive response to momentary constrains created by legislation and to severe imperfections in the markets for land and production assets. It is not oriented to the future tasks to be faced by the organizations formed. The problems evaded in the formation stage are, thus, bound to reemerge later on as management and governance problems. Being an "interim caretaker-owner" on behalf of a deeply split and an often incompetent owner group, the OC model cannot provide a satisfying answer to essential questions of governance. I observed, in the course of the project, cases of OCs debilitated by struggles between various owner-groups[23] or destroyed by a general run on the OCs assets by members and restitution claimants. Some of the major questions revolve around the cohesion and competence of the owner/member group. Resolving these so as to forge OCs into capable business actors is a prime challenge to cooperative governance and it is unlikely that it will be met by all CFs in the population:

- Cooperative organizations are normally based on affiliation through *membership* that cannot be entirely reduced to property rights (Stryjan 1989). Czech OCs stand out in this respect as a uniquely consequent attempt at deriving patronage from property rights alone (Stryjan 1994a). A cooperative is, in principle, a system of open contracts primarily safeguarded by trust relations. A joint-stock company, by comparison, is a system of closed contracts, safeguarded by institutionalized control mechanisms. While the joint stock enterprise is immune, by virtue of its legal construction, to opportunistic behaviour on the part of its owners (indeed, it nearly presupposes it) the cooperative form is not. The application of the cooperative form on a deeply split group of titular "members" is, therefore, a doubtful proposition.
- Governance presupposes a coherent mandator and, thus, in the case of cooperatives, a degree of continuity in the evolution of the corpus of members. The reproduction of membership has a central role in cooperative organizing (Stryjan 1989; 1994c). A situation in which a cooperative enterprise has a major portion of its members replaced by others (who, besides, may have old accounts to settle with the remaining members), virtually by decree, has no precedent in cooperative practice.
- Primary agricultural production normally calls for close monitoring and hands-on management (Swinnen et al. 1993). Absentee control in coop-

erative form exists primarily in extensive, long-range mono-cultures such as forestry. Absentee control of intensive multi-cultures, as attempted in the OC model, is a questionable proposition.

These problems are shared, to a varying degree, by the entire population of OCs. This opens extremely interesting population perspectives on issues of organizational adaptation and learning (Hannan and Freeman 1989; cf. also Havemen 1992). Amburgey et al. (1993) predict that the disruptive effect of change diminishes over time. This holds true at the population level as organizations that fail to resolve their teething problems are eliminated but offers no solace to any single organization. On the contrary, it can be argued that the organization form created is inherently defective and, often, essentially ungovernable (Stryjan 1994b). The weaknesses inherent in the OC construction are likely to be overcome by (and only by) OCs with a tolerably coherent corpus of members (whose membership is dominated either by worker-owners or by members of the local community) and/or under a highly competent management. The middle-range prediction for the OC population is that only this fraction would stand a chance to survive in its present form. The remainder will either disintegrate due to internal conflicts, economic failure, or a combination of both; or gravitate towards more viable forms either by changing the form of incorporation towards those that are less vulnerable to owner discord (e.g. joint-stock) and/or by modifying their corpus of members towards a more homogenous composition. There is, in fact, evidence of both processes at work in the population at present. A pivotal role in accomplishing such changes would be played by the OCs' respective management, existing or emergent.

Some homogenization of the workforce, namely, raising the proportion of members has occurred in the past years largely through the massive disenfranchisement of non owners accomplished by the transformation law and the steep fall in employment in OCs (from 403,000 in 1989[24], to 180,000 in April 1994), and the falling attraction of agricultural employment. A parallel realignment in the ranks of *members* raising the proportion of members that are committed to OCs continued existence is less likely. The exit of non committed members is complicated by the fact that members are tied to "their" cooperative by "captive property" created through transformation which is somewhat of a ticking bomb under the legal construction. A process of self-selection could only become feasible if debt instruments for the transfer and sale of transformation debts were created.

The main force shaping populations of organizations and respective populations of their members, has, until recently, been *exit*/attrition. Though some new OCs were created from the debris of the state-farms during their privatization the prospects for further diffusion of the form through the entry of new organizations are slight. Nor is recruitment of new members to existing OCs likely. Such recruitment is complicated by the unrealistically high nominal values assigned to founders' capital shares.[25] These indirectly discriminate against new capital and raise major hindrances for the reproduction of capital. Dividends are paid to capital only which serves as a powerful de-motivator for employed smaller owners to exert themselves. or for non-member employees to purchase a share.

The continued evolution (or, rather, gradual attrition) of the OC population is illustrated by Table 2.[26] The figures in the table provide an estimate of overt formal change only. A considerable amount of restructuring seems, however, to be taking place lately, *without* leaving, for the time being, its mark on official liquidation statistics. The procedure adopted is typically as follows: A new enterprise or enterprises are incorporated (normally as joint-stock companies). Stock is being offered in exchange for OC capital shares and assets that formally cover the shares' value are siphoned off from the OC to the new company. The "mother" OC is kept as a goal keeper enterprise carrying residual debts (not redeemed by stock) and an odd assortment of leftover assets that serves as formal collateral for these. This latest wave of restructuring is not motivated by organizational, nor by business or social motives any more than its predecessor was. Instead, its driving force is the mass of basically fictive, and essentially unpayable transformation liabilities that the OCs were burdened with by legislators and that now approach fruition. For obvious reasons, it is impossible to obtain any statistical data about this process.

Table 2. Enterprises created in the evolution of OCs, 1994-97 (as of 1st of January)

Type	1995	1996	1997 (prognose)
Owner cooperatives	1012	981	924-935
- in liquidation	15	19	20
Joint-stock	85	128	180-183
Limited partnerships (SRO)	300	337	346
Others	80	82	84

Source: Internal survey, CM SZD.

Just as in the first (mandatory) case, the present transformation provides fertile ground for the operation of consultants and the contagious spread of turnkey solutions. There is no ground to expect that the immediate results will be considerably more functional, in business or governance sense, than the results of the previous transformation. At best, it will increase the mobility of owners and assets and, in the long run, open a way for the spontaneous restructuring that would have taken place under more favourable circumstances five years earlier, had it not been arrested by state interference.

Discussion

Institutional Change and Natural Selection

Organizations are the building blocks of the institutional order — but also major agents in the realignment towards the formation of any new order. Plotting the futures of organizational populations can help us to understand and foresee the nature of the order now in the process of establishing itself. In understanding and evaluating transformation processes the concern here is not with the fate of any specific organization but with the future composition of the entire field or sector. This prescribes the range of available theoretical tools. Until the late 1970s, organizational theory dealt mainly with the structures and fates of specific organizations (Aldrich 1992), naturally stressing continuity, action and adaptation. The introduction of the ecological paradigm (Hannan and Freeman 1977) and the revival of institutional research (Meyer and Rowan 1977) mark a shift of attention towards higher aggregation levels, respectively, populations of organizations or organizational fields. The patterns that influence the behaviours and fates of organizations are seen as aggregate products of (all other relevant) organizations' actions. The two approaches develop two basically incommensurable paradigms (Aldrich 1992; Scott 1987). Some of their central tenets, that are relevant to this discussion are summarized in Table 3.

Table 3. Institutional and ecological approaches

Perspective	Institutional	Ecological
focus on	field	population
main mechanisms	adaptation	1) formation (births); 2) attrition (deaths)
change motive	ritual	functional
generates	isomorphy	variation
society seen as	continuity	equilibrium

Each of the two views can be highly useful in explaining the features of and dynamics of incremental change in a new system *once established*. Both, however, have serious limitations when it comes to accounting for fundamental change — even more so to predicting its future course. The crystallization of the "iron cage" envisaged by institutionalists (DiMaggio and Powell 1983) presupposes stability. The idea of changing one cage for another does not quite fit into the conceptual framework. Similarly, the population ecology approach notes that evolution proceeds through a succession of punctuated equilibria (Hannan and Freeman 1989). The hiatus *between* equilibria lies, nearly by definition, beyond the scope of a theory of equilibria.

These limitations notwithstanding, *both* approaches contribute elements vital to our understanding of the process. When dealing with clusters of organizations, we find that transformation can be seen as the product of the following component flows:

- change and transformation of communist times' organizations;
- attrition of those who fail to adapt;
- the formation of new enterprises, and the forging of new inter-organizational linkages.

Neither of the two approaches takes all three flows fully into account. Most evidently, ecologists tend to dismiss the impact of *intra*-organizational on the shaping of populations, while institutionalists seriously neglect the impact of new births in the population and tend to undervalue that of attrition (considered a basically avoidable occurrence, mainly useful as a negative example for those organizations that contrive to live forever). To capture the picture in its entirety, there is a need to balance concepts scavenged in both theoretical domains.

Policy and Reality

The institutional transformation of Czech agriculture evolved in an exceptionally formalized and politically steered framework. Initially, at least, the Czech government's policy closely approached a textbook application of (programatically defined) property rights implemented virtually in a frictionless manner. The transformation of primary production was carried through a legislative redistribution of entitlements marked by a strong programmatic emphasis on (historical) property rights and on family farming. The blueprint of future agriculture underlying this comprehensive programme projected a massive emergence of new family enterprises but did not include any cooperative organizations whatsoever. Ironically however, the number of cooperative enterprises actually increased in the course of transformation (see Table 1 above and Stryjan and Linhart 1994). Though professing to re-establish markets, policies have rather shaped market failures (1) in the market for land and production assets through wholesale *in natura* restitution, and (2) in the farming staples market, through privatization policies that facilitated emergence of processing monopolies. These market failures, in turn, did stimulate the (re)emergence of cooperatives. The attempt to attain tight control over the process of transformation created a "collective behaviour response" in the incumbent population, arrested the emergence of new organizational contenders, and, in fact, acted to inhibit the desired outcome.

It may be useful to distinguish, at this point, between *evolution* and *transformation* (the later may be called, at times, "revolution"). Evolution is gradual, and mostly borne by changes in the populations of organizations and of individuals. Major institutional changes emerge in the course of the process through aggregation of outcomes (Stryjan and Wijkström 1996). Legislators tend to pursue or profess Pareto-optimality (especially in the context of economic growth). *Transformation* is sparked off by signal changes. It needs not (and, in the case of revolutionary change, intentionally *does* not) pursue Pareto-optimality. Indeed, taking from some may be as politically important a goal as giving to others.

The Czech government's strong emphasis on property relations and, in particular, on an old-testamental restitution of historical property rights was a clearly revolutionary strategy, inasmuch as it:

- introduced a strong strain of Pareto-disoptimality, positively discriminating repossession of property from private hands in relation to return of property held by the state;
- firmly set the focus on *existing* organizations and assets and, thus, distracted attention from the potential inherent in the creation of new ones;
- introduced a non-economic mechanism for (re)allocating owners to assets.

Owing to its strong emphasis on the preexisting, a revolutionary policy is, paradoxically, rather conservative in its implications. This probably accounts for the relatively low rate of formation of new enterprises and the minimal rate of bankruptcies in the course of Czech transformation in general.[27] The creation, of long-range obligations (transformation debts) by legislation served to cement the existing organizational population. Change became an easier path to take than organizational demise.

These specific circumstances of formation, together with the strong programmatic bias on property relations as the sole legitimate organizing principle that permeates the Czech society of today, have strongly influenced the organizations being formed and stimulated the creation of hybrid organization forms that often are highly defective, and prone to future problems. The "transformation" of 1992-93 was merely the starting point for the actual process of change.

Theory and Policy

Policy-makers rarely spend time on studying organization theory. Nonetheless, policy normally incorporates implicit paradigms of sorts as to the relation between policy and effect.

The underlying paradigm of market reform is clearly institutional. It aims at the (re)construction of a set of desirable or historical institutions. A basic normative tenet of market economy is the autonomy of market actors. Consequently, policy implementation presupposes that the government implementing it relinquishes *some* of its control over outcomes. Due both to considerations of legitimacy and of expediency, policies are normally destined to handle, or manipulate, whole classes of organizations. A government cannot assume the role of a Maxwell's demon that only lets through "right" organizations. Policy impacts should thus primarily be evaluated in population terms. Schematically, the sequence of top-steered market reform would start with an *institutional phase* of partial re-modeling of institutions that sets would-be actors loose. It is followed by an essentially "ecological" phase in which the population of market-actors is stabilized. Finally, institutional interactions within this population would act to (re)produce and/or modify the institutional framework. Once we know what organizations we have, we may speculate on the nature of the iron cage they will build (Stryjan 1996).

The transformation of Czech CFs provides an interesting combination of paradigms. In this case, the government had a clear institutional vision. Relative to other post-communist regimes, it was also exceptionally well endowed to implement it. The conception of the policy implemented was nonetheless clearly ecological. Environmental (economic and legal) pressure was brought to bear on the CFs. It was believed that this should lead to the population's demise. A new population of family farms would arise instead of its own accord.

Results failed to conform with this vision. Of nearly 1,200 collective farms that were forced into the transformation mould only 24 were liquidated. This policy failure can be interpreted in two, partly complementary ways, depending on the paradigm one adopts:

- The case shows that organizations *can* and do learn. Under extreme duress, the rate and net effect of adaptation can actually exceed the combined effect of births and deaths in the population. Failure was, at least partly the result of applying an ecological prescription to an essentially institutional problem. The main problem with this interpretation is that it is difficult to envisage an institutional prescription that would have achieved the desired end. Indeed, it is plausible to assume that the end was unrealistic to start with.

- Since the organizations of the old regime were *formally* terminated and the successor enterprises *formally* registered, the result conforms, *formally* speaking, to the ecological paradigm. That the outcome deviates from expectations (i.e. other types of successor organizations were formed than those envisaged by policy-makers) may be due to inept implementation of the government's own paradigm. The excessive regulation of the process inhibited the emergence of any other organizational form than owner's cooperatives. An interpretation of this kind stretches the ecological paradigm to its utmost and points to its major weakness, the insufficiency of formal criteria as a ground for determining an enterprise's demise.

As indicated, none of the intra-paradigmatic interpretations provides a fully satisfactory account of the actual development. Both dynamics are intermittently at work and reality clearly oscillates between two different scenarios. A plausible framework for understanding the process calls for the ability to assess population effects of institutional change on one hand and the institution-building inputs of organizational populations on the other.

Conclusion: Theory and Reality

The central event of the case discussed in this chapter is a mass conversion of an entire class of organizations into a different organizational model. The phenomenon is not easily accommodated into the population-ecology framework. Transformation junctures of the type described challenge the concepts of organizational continuity and identity and, thus, the basic tenets of the ecological model. This makes the application of rigorous population-ecological approaches to the study of extreme institutional transformation processes highly problematic. One may say that the transformation scene is populated by a host of subspecies of the Phoenix Bird, a species definitely not covered by the Lotka-Volterra equations. Additional factors, unaccounted for by ecologists, are definitely at play.

Though the case is much more readily analyzable in institutional-theoretical terms, the prognostic value of such analyses is limited. While outlining general directions of institutional change, the historical explanations that institutional analysis provides are not readily extrapolated. The difficulty in assessing long term viability of emerging trends can be attributed to the theory's unwillingness to deal with the relation between performance and survival and thus, with the selective impact of attrition. Within the boundaries set by institutional requirements of propriety, organizations still have to perform and compete for resources. In the long run, the iron cage they constitute cannot be stronger than the aggregated strength of those upholding it. Thus, general failures to perform may bring about the collapse of an entire environment (as indeed was the case with the communist system) quite regardless of how institutionally proper the organizations constituting the system were. Within an institutional order, institutional prescriptions that are non-functional may wipe out precisely those classes of organizations that were most adept in following them. Thus, reform drives may falter under their own weight or spawn unexpected consequences. These issues are best approached from a population perspective. Qualitative application of ecological modes of reasoning can clearly enhance our understanding of transformation processes, and enrich the somewhat tautological projections that institutional analysis provides. The points of synergy between the two approaches can be summarized as follows:

- Sectors of the economy and of society and their transformation may be studied in terms of the organizational (sub)populations that comprise and constitute them, and their shifting balance[28].
- Institutional change may be dealt with as environmental change, inasmuch as institutional changes and government policies, as well as the economic changes they precipitate, act to modify key parameters of the environment (see Hannan and Freeman, 1977).
- Environmental change may affect various sub-populations in a *differential* fashion in terms of their relative survival prospects, competitiveness vs. other sub-populations, and attrition rates. The resultant demographic outcomes need not conform to institutional prescriptions. Plotting the ensuing population development paths can greatly improve the predictive value of the analysis and provide a valuable tool for policy evaluation and design.

Plotting population futures presupposes, however, that the mechanisms of change that are at work are identified. As noted, this is the main point of contention of the two theoretical approaches applied here. Institutional theorizing gives a clear primacy to intra-organizational change while ecologists correspondingly emphasize the import of birth and attrition rates.

The fact that organizations *do* change has, nonetheless, been acknowledged by population ecology research. Thus, Hannan and Freeman (1984) suggest that those organizations that do have a propensity to change tend to be selected against in the evolutionary process. Singh et al. (1986) distinguish between core and peripheral change and argue that observable change in organizations is generally restricted to the latter order. This explanation is hardly applicable to our case. Haveman (1992) acknowledges the possibility of populationwide change within organizations but sees this rather as an exception that confirms the rule. Amburgey et al. (1993) find that organizational change may jeopardize the viability of organizations undergoing it, further diminishing the demographic impact of intra-organizational change. Generally, the objective of research seems to be to reconcile the phenomenon with the existing body of ecological theory, somewhat in the manner that the existence of firms is of theoretical interest to transaction economists.

The original claim of ecological theorists is, after all, one of expedience, not of essence. Both phenomena undeniably exist but the impact of demographic change normally overshadows that of intra-organizational change and renders the latter negligible. In this respect, the explanations offered above seem to unnecessarily overstate the theory's positions. The case in this study suggests that the ratio between the impacts of the two mechanisms of change is, in fact, *variable* and may be influenced by a variety of factors. The ones observed in this case are reviewed below. Due to low birth and attrition levels in the population studied, the empirical material does not cover the entire range of potential inputs that may affect this balance.

- *Non-emergence*: Births or entry of new (species of) organizations into the niche are a potentially powerful agent of change at the population level. However, organizational births may be inhibited by institutional and economic factors, indirectly tipping the balance between the relative impacts of organizational and demographic change towards the former:

  a) *Contender birth rates* are influenced by the economic attraction a given field of activity has for prospective entrants and for scavengers of existing organizations. Worsening terms of trade (deterioration of the specific niche) can slow down demographic change by way of inhibiting the entry (births) of new organizations. Thus, the forced capital outflow from country to town that was accomplished by restitution and transformation legislation was reinvested in more promising sectors and did not facilitate the formation of new enterprises in farming (or, indeed, the countryside). Indirectly, this raised the life expectancy of incumbents and the likelihood that they may accomplish change before (and instead of) being competed out.

  b) *Transaction cost thresholds*: The forming of a new organization invariably entails transaction costs. Such costs are largely determined by institutional factors and by the nature of the organization to be formed. High transaction-cost thresholds may inhibit the emergence of new quite irrespective of what the potential newcomers' survival prospects would have been if ever formed. In this sense, competition between yet unborn organizations (or, indeed, between the incumbent and the unborn) may function in a different fashion than competition between incumbents. The adoption of the OC solution may be attributed to the high costs of designing better alternatives within the time and situational constraints imposed by legislation.

- *Non-attrition*: As any other organizational action, the winding down of an organization is done at a price for those involved (Meyer and Zucker 1990). In our case, the barriers to, and costs of exit were artificially raised through ineffectual bankruptcy legislation and the creation of long-term "transformation debts."

The factors listed above may be grouped under the heading of *friction* (Etzioni 1991). In slowing down the otherwise more rapid course of demographic change, friction may allow otherwise slower intra-organizational change processes to catch up and leave a clearer imprint on the population. In parallel with forces that delay attrition, other processes may be at work facilitating change and further tilting the balance between the flows that reshape the population. Organizational change requires the re-negotiation of a multiplicity of (implicit and explicit) contracts, both within and outside, that hold an organization together. That organizations commonly go under rather than change may be due to the prohibitive transaction costs change entails. The evidence of the case described above suggests that this need no longer be the case. The Czech transformation has unfolded in a technologically and organizationally sophisticated society. Organizational structures, ownership constructions, and procedures for their transformation could be codified onto PC software that was transferable across organizations in the population. Technology, and the increasing standardization of organizational structures may, in effect, be making change more communicable. Available technologies may, thus, substantially alter the balance between the relative impacts of learning and births/attritions on population change and introduce new ways of reshaping organizational populations.

Notes

* The research on which this study is based was financed by FRN grant # A13-5/66, and ACE/PHARE grant # P95-2743-F, and was made possible by the kind help and hospitality of The Czech Agricultural University (CZU) in Prague.

1 The Czech Lands have not experienced any profound boundary alterations or demographical upheavals since the Napoleonic Wars. This accounts for the remarkable stability of ownership structures.

2 This holds true for the Czech Republic only. With the division of the Czechoslovak Federal Republic, the Slovak part opted for a different path, while the economic course (and the leadership) of the Czech programme remained virtually unchanged.

3 The reemergence of family farming, though of some relevance to our topic, will not be discussed here. Economic activity in this subsector is relatively limited and only had an indirect impact (mostly, by its absence) on the transformation of the remainder of the farming sector.

4 Thus, for instance, restituents' entitlements varied in practice, depending on who they were, and what organization happened to hold their property in 1989 etc.; a point best illustrated by the law of transformation (see Exhibit 1). See also Mertl¡k (1992).

5 The laws most directly affecting the transformation of agriculture or specifically legislated to deal with this sector are: Law 403/1990 on Mitigating the Consequences of Some Property Wrongs (known as the law on restitution); Law 229/1991 on the Arrangement of Property Rights to Land and Other Agricultural Property (the Land Law); with amendments 93/1992, 183/1993, and 243/1992, 195/1993; and Law 42/1992, on the Adjustment of Property Relations and the Settlement of Property Rights in Co-operative Societies (Transformation) completed by Law 39/1993.

6 A comprehensive agricultural programme of sorts (still setting property relations, rather than farming, as the most important problem to be dealt with) was first approved by the government in 1994.

7 Data for the entire Czechoslovak Republic. The figure for the Czech Republic was probably somewhat over 8,000, as the balance between the republics was generally maintained at the 1:2 level. For figures of population development 1958-1989, see Stryjan (1994c).

8 The patterns of personal mobility contained one more interesting quirk: children of dissenting farmers who opted to leave for town, often found that their way to higher studies was blocked by "wrong class background." The Agricultural Universities, because of their strict technocratic profile, were the most permissive on this count, the consequence being that many second-generation collectivization dissidents were recycled back into administrative and (second tier) management positions within the sector.

9 Typically, Ladislav Adamec, the last communist prime-minister was a pragmatic technocrat who made his career largely within the agricultural sector and was the author of a management handbook on innovation.

10 Law 162/1990 on Agricultural Cooperation, of May 3rd. It should be noted that a large portion of ownership titles were maintained throughout the communist period by their historical owners.

11 Collectivization generally implied that the CF obtained a "right of cooperative use" for the assets in question. Somewhat paradoxically, the system conserved historical property rights. Formal ownership titles to land were maintained by original owners. Generally, such ownership records were meticulously preserved for most cooperatives throughout the communist period.

12 At this stage, owners of land were only entitled to get their land back. Claimants that declared their intention to resume farming were granted the right to claim of the CFs full and immediate in natura restitution of the inventories and livestock that they committed in 1948 or thereabouts (cow for cow, tractor for tractor, etc.). No provisions of this type were made for claimants whose land was administered by state farms, nor in any other sector of the Czech economy.

13 Massive failures arose primarily in the course of attempts to "collectivize" new settlers on expropriated (mainly German) land. Consequently, state-farms were mainly concentrated in border regions. They largely remained somewhat of an economic basket case throughout the communist period.

14 The Statistical Yearbook of the CSFR, 1991 and 1992.

15 Information obtained from (then) union officers.

16 Land distribution in 1947-48 employed the procedural and legal framework developed in the agrarian reforms of the First Republic. Expropriated land was parcelled, and offered to settlers who were to pay for it through a liberal installment plan. By the time of the communist coup, only part of these have taken physical possession and most did not complete their payments.

17 The farm of Hodonin, a former imperial estate, was turned into a state farm during the First Republic. Consequently it had no restitution claimants, and could be privatized as a going concern.

18 The Ministry's official statistics over private and corporate farms provide no breakdown for the "150 ha and above" range. My repeated efforts to obtain data on large estates were met with blank refusal.

19 Technical provisions in the voucher privatization procedures effectively blocked the possibility of plants being taken over by farmers. See Stryjan and Maskova (1992).

20 Indirect measures included the blocking of bank backing for takeover bids (the bank system was, and still remains, largely state-dominated) and preferential treatment for competing bids. Direct intervention included the vetoing of debt-for equity swaps in plants where the state had majority ownership , and, most recently, court action against associations of producers, legitimated by a broad interpretation of anti-trust legislation.

21 In perhaps the most bizarre example of government embroilment that came to my attention, in a privately managed debt-ridden dairy in Northern Bohemia, the National Property Fund, acting as a majority shareholder, rejected an offer of debt-for equity swap, declared bankruptcy, and sold the entire dairy once again to the selfsame minority shareholder cum manager who had led it to bankruptcy.

22 The kit was developed (to the best of my knowledge, as a semi-private initiative) by researchers at the (then) Federal Institute of Agricultural Research.

23 See e.g. Stryjan (1994b: 37).

24 Ministry of Agriculture of the CR: Agricultural Programme, 1993.

25 Calculated from historical book values and standard livestock prices specified in the law-text; both unrealistically high. Though these sums are being slowly reduced by inflation, the stability of the Czech Crown prevents an automatic writeoff.

26 The survey covers member and ex-member organizations of CM SZD only. The figures are, thus, not fully comparable to those given for 1993 in Table 1.

27 It is interesting to compare Czech developments to the case of Poland, that did not regulate its property relations (Earle et al. 1994).

28 For examples, see Bager (1996); Evers (1993); Stryjan and Wijkström (1996).

References

Ahrne, G. (1990): *Agency and organization*. London: Sage.

Ahrne, G. (1994): *Social organizations. Interaction inside, outside and between organizations*. London: Sage.

Aldrich, H. (1992): "Incommensurable paradigms: Vital signs from three perspectives" in M.I. Reed and M.D. Hughes (eds.), *Rethinking organization: New directions in organization theory and analysis*, 17-45. London: Sage.

Amburgey, T.L., D. Kelly and W.P. Barnett (1993): "Resetting the clock: the dynamics of organizational change and failure." *Administrative Science Quarterly* 38: 51-73.

Bager, T. (1996): *Organizations in sectors*. Esbjerg: South Jutland University Press.

Brabenec, V. and P. Sarecova (1991): "Nazor obyvatel venkova na budoucnost venkova a zemedelstvi" (The opinions of countryside dwellers concerning the prospects of the countryside and of agriculture). *Zemedelska Ekonomika* 37: 433-440.

Brabenec, V. and P. Sarecova (1993): "Vztah mezi cenovem vyvojem zemedelskych vyrobku a trhem v CR" (The relation between the price development for farming produce, and the Czech market). *Proceedings of the Conference Agrarian Perspectives II. The Transformation Phase*. The University of Agriculture, Prague: 368-372.

DiMaggio, P.J. and W.W. Powell (1983): "The iron cage revisited: Institutional isomorphism and collective rationality in organizational fields." *American Sociological Review* 48: 147-160.

Earle, J.S., R. Frydman, A. Rapaczynski and J. Turkewitz (1994): *Small privatization*. Budapest: CEU Press.

Evers, A. (1993): "The Welfare-mix approach. Understanding the pluralism of welfare systems" in A. Evers and I. Svetlik (eds.), *Balancing pluralism*, 3-32. Aldershot: Avebury Press.

Frydman, R., A. Rapaczynski and J.S. Earle (1993): *The Privatization process in Central Europe*. Budapest: CEU Press.

Galla, K. (1937): *Sany. Prispevek k sociologii druzstevnictvi v ceskoslovenske vsi* (Sany. A contribution towards a sociology of cooperation in the Czech village). Prague: Sp Pece o Blaho Venkova

Hannan, M.T. and J. Freeman (1977): "The population ecology of organizations." *American Journal of Sociology* 82: 929-964.

Hannan, M.T. and J. Freeman (1984): "Structural inertia and organizational change." *American Sociological Review* 49: 149-162.

Hannan, M.T. and J. Freeman (1989): *Organizational ecology*. Cambridge, MA: Harvard University Press.

Haveman, H.A. (1992): "Between a rock and a hard place: organizational change and performance under conditions of fundamental environmental transformation." *Administrative Science Quarterly* 37: 48-75.

Hudeckova, H. and M. Lostak (1991): "Privatization in agriculture." *Privatization in agriculture in the Results of Sociological Empirical Research Survey*. Prague: Agricultural University of Prague.

Kharkhordin, O. (1994): "The Corporate ethic, the ethic of Samostoyatelnost and the spirit of capitalism. Reflections on market building in post-Soviet Russia." *International Sociology* 9(4): 405-430.

Klapp, O.E. (1972): *Currents of unrest: An introduction to collective behavior*. New York: Holt, Rhinehart and Winston.

Liptak, M. and V. Vavra (1993): "Nektera vychodiska a prisupy k profilaci podnikatelskych struktur v privatizacnim a transformacnim procesu APK" (Some starting points and approaches to the profiling of business structures in privatization and transformation processes of the agro-food production complex). *Zemedelska ekonomika* 39(5): 369-381.

Lux, J. (1993): "The policy of privatization and restitution." Lecture delivered at the ministerial meeting Development and Harmonization of Agricultural Policies in Central and Eastern Europe. Gödölö, Hungary, August.
Majerova, V. (1992): "Sociologicky pohled na zmeny v ceskoslovensk,m zemedelstv po roce 1989 (A sociological perspective on changes in Czechoslovak agriculture after 1989)." *Sociologie Venkova a Zemedelstvi* 28(1): 31-34.
Mertlik, P. (1992): "Institutional reform of co-operatives in Czecho-Slovakia." Paper presented to ISS conference, Arciccia, October
Meyer, J.W. and B. Rowan (1977): "Institutionalized organizations: formal structure as myth and ceremony." *American Journal of Sociology* 83: 340-363.
Meyer, J.W. and W.R. Scott (1983): *Organizational environments*. Beverly Hills, CA: Sage.
Meyer J.W. and L. Zucker (1990): *Permanently failing organizations*. London: Sage.
Midlarsky, A. (1978): "Analyzing diffusion and contagion effects: the urban disorders of the 60's." *American Political Science Review* 72(3): 996-1008.
Miller, D.L., K.J. Mietus and R.A. Mathers (1978): "Examination of social contagion image of collective behavior — case of Enfield Monster." *Sociological Quarterly* 19(1): 129-140.
Perrow, C. (1979): *Complex organizations: a critical essay* (2nd edition). Glenview, IL: Scott, Foresman and Company.
Scott, W.R. (1987): *Organizations: Rational, natural, and open systems* (2nd edition). London: Prentice Hall International.
Singh, J.V. , R.J. House and D.J. Tucker (1986): "Organizational change and organizational mortality." *Administrative Science Quarterly* 31: 587-611.
Sjöstrand, S.E. (1985): *Samhallsorganisation*. Lund, Sweden: Doxa.
Spirk, L. (1974): "Agricultural policy in Czechoslovakia at the time of the socialist transformation of agriculture." *Czechoslovakia's Socialist Cooperative Movement*: 47-56. Prague: URD.
Stinchcombe, A. (1965): "Social structure and organizations" in J.D. March (ed.), *Handbook of Organizations,* 142-193. Chicago: Rand McNaly.
Stryjan, Y. (1989): *Impossible organizations: Self-management and organizational reproduction*. London: Greenwood Press.
Stryjan, Y. (1994a): "From collective farms to owners' cooperatives: ownership and membership in the transformation of Czech agriculture." Paper presented to the XIII ISA World Congress, Bielefeld, July.
Stryjan, Y. (1994b): "Czech agriculture: the vagaries of institutional transformation." Berliner Hefte zum internationalen Genossenschaftswesen, Institut für Genossenschaftswesen an der Humboldt-Universität zu Berlin.
Stryjan, Y. (1994c): "Understanding cooperatives. The reproduction perspective." *Annals of Public and Cooperative Economics* 65(1): 59-80.
Stryjan, Y. (1996): "Systemskiftets irrgangar" (The meanders of Swedish system transformation). Stockholm School of Business research report 1.
Stryjan, Y. and Z. Linhart (1994): "Co-operatives in the transformation of Czech agriculture. Problems and prospects" in *The World of Co-operative Enterprise*, 81-90. Oxford: Plunkett Foundation.
Stryjan, Y. and Z. Linhart (1996): "The transformation of Czech cooperation." Paper presented to XII Internationale Genossenschaftliche Tagung, Berlin, September.
Stryjan, Y. and E. Maskova (1992): "The reshaping of the Czechoslovak economy." *Economic and Industrial Democracy* 13. 561-581.

Stryjan, Y. and F. Wijkström (1996): "Cooperatives and nonprofit organizations in Swedish social welfare." *Annals of Public and Cooperative Economics* 67: 5-27.
Swinnen, J., L. Christiaensen and L. Felton-Taylor (1993): "Agricultural production structures." Paper presented to the OECD/Hungarian Government Seminar on Agricultural Cooperatives and Emerging Farm Structures in Hungary. Budapest, October.
Zammit, J.A. and D. Ghai (1992): *Czechoslovakia: Which way to the market?*. Geneva: UNRISD.
Zaloudek, J. (1988): *Czechoslovak agriculture*. Prague: Orbis.

Enterprise Reform and the Role of the State: The Case of the Capital Iron and Steel Works, Beijing*

John Hassard and *Jackie Sheehan*

Introduction

This chapter explores issues of economic restructuring and the role of the state in the context of enterprise reform in the Chinese steel industry. Theoretical debates on economic restructuring in China have revolved primarily around the adoption of market mechanisms in a gradual transition away from the centrally-planned economy which existed in China up until 1978. Contributions to these theoretical debates as they pertain to the reform of state-owned enterprises include recent studies by Hay et al. (1994) and Chen (1995) which have documented in particular the property rights and ownership and the enterprise autonomy and incentives debates. In this chapter we examine one particular aspect of these debates, that relating to the discontinuation of the Contract Responsibility System (CRS) which governed relations between the enterprise and the state in China from the early 1980s until 1994/5. It concentrates mainly on Beijing's Capital Iron and Steel Corporation (Shougang), since this was the flagship of the CRS experiment and exemplifies some of the system's problems which are now perceived by the state to outweigh its benefits. Shougang is an untypical enterprise in some important respects, but despite its special status in China, its experience with the CRS and its problematic transition from this system make it an important case study in the debate on reform of the state-enterprise relationship in China.

The chapter then goes on to look at alternative models of enterprise reform now being piloted in a limited number of SOEs, specifically the Modern Enterprise System (MES) and the Group Company System (GCS). In addition to the Contract Responsibility System (CRS) flagship Shougang, four other large state-owned steel corporations in China involved in these pilot projects are taken as case studies. The chapter focuses in particular on the question of whether any of the new reform models can solve the problems of property rights, separation of government and management functions, over-manning, welfare burdens and debt which still affect many large SOEs in China, problems which the CRS either did not address or failed to solve.

The Shougang Corporation

We begin with an overview of the Shougang Corporation's operations during the 1980s and early 1990s. Steel has long been the main business of the Corporation, and the Shougang Iron and Steel Works in west Beijing employs 120,000 of the Corporation's total workforce of 280,000. Many more are employed at the Corporation's iron ore mine north of Beijing. But the Shougang Corporation has also emerged in recent years as a major industrial enterprise on the world stage. The company literature notes that since the late 1980s, Shougang has been empowered to "engage directly in import and export business, set up plants and run joint ventures abroad, and conduct labour services. Shougang has also been empowered to do business in the fields of finance and foreign trade." The Corporation's ambition has been to become a "transnational enterprise", following a decision to accelerate the expansion of its activities abroad made in late 1992.

Shougang, however, which is China's fourth-largest industrial enterprise and third-largest steel producer, had already signalled its ambitions in the international market-place. For example, through its wholly-owned subsidiary Shougang Holdings (Hong Kong Ltd) it acquired a series of listed Hong Kong companies, and in the process forged some powerful alliances, including a partnership with billionaire Li Ka-shing in a steel company (Shougang Concord International Enterprises). The company's Hong Kong investments also facilitated additional capital-raising in the local market. Other notable overseas investments include taking control of the Mesta Engineering Company of the U.S. in 1988, and purchasing the Hierro iron-ore mine in Peru for U.S. $ 180m in 1992. Within China, the company has diversified into shipping, construction, computers and tourism.

Shougang was only able to reform its business practices and develop its business interests in this way because from the early 1980s, state controls over the company's activities were considerably relaxed. In 1979 the decision was taken to develop the CRS experiment as part of China's economic reform programme, and Shougang, as one of China's largest and best-known state enterprises, was selected as the flagship of the CRS programme. Before the CRS was introduced, Shougang was state-owned and state-managed; net incomes had to be handed over to the state, and funds for investment had to be examined, approved and distributed by the state. In

1978, the President of Shougang could only approve expenditure of up to 800 yuan (about £65 at present exchange rates). The task was one of reforming a large state-owned corporation through integrating government administration with enterprise management, and creating a sense of "enterprise" on the part of workers in the process.

It should be noted that Shougang was not chosen to pioneer the CRS in large SOEs solely because of its size and significance in the regional and national economy. The unusual scope granted to it to diversify into businesses other than steel, such as its licence to run its own bank, is attributed by many of its competitors in China as well as by outside observers to the superior political connections of the recently-retired head of the Corporation, Zhou Guanwu, who was in charge from 1954 until the spring of 1995. In particular, Zhou's close relationship with Deng Xiaoping, under whom he served during the civil war of the late 1940s, is seen as the key to his almost unparalleled freedom to pursue business opportunities at home and abroad. It has been noted that Shougang's most recent round of international acquisitions, several of which were mentioned above, followed hard upon Deng Xiaoping's highly publicized visit to Shougang in May 1992 (*Far Eastern Economic Review* [subsequently *FEER*] 23.3.95: 46-47). The changing fortunes of the Shougang Corporation and the rise and fall of the CRS more generally are bound up with issues of elite factional rivalry within the Chinese Communist Party (CCP) and the post-Deng succession struggle which has been going on more or less openly for a number of years, and without digressing too far into obscure kremlinological speculation, the political context has to be borne in mind when considering even apparently neutral aspects of the SOE reform programme in recent times. Where an enterprise has been as closely associated with a top Party leader for as long as Shougang has with Deng Xiaoping, the influence of intra-elite rivalries is highly relevant.

We now go on to a brief examination of the CRS in general and as it operated at Shougang until 1994/5. This will be followed by an account of the problems with the CRS that became apparent during the years in which it was in operation, problems which eventually led to the discontinuation of the programme in 1994/5. We will then look at the specific experience of Shougang under the CRS and at the roots of the Corporation's recent troubles, concluding with a look at the new reform models now being piloted by large SOEs in China and a consideration of how Shougang is likely to fare as it attempts to make the transition from the CRS.

The Contract Responsibility System

The CRS operated at two main levels: enterprise-level contracting with the state (the state contract system), and internal contracting within the enterprise's businesses (the internal contract system). Although the phasing-out of the CRS has been going on since 1994/5, many enterprises, including Shougang, have opted to retain the internal contract system, which is usually termed the economic responsibility system. The CRS was introduced in the steel industry during the course of the Sixth Five-Year Plan, 1980-85, and was eventually adopted by 85% of enterprises within the industry (Interview 3 1995: see Appendix 1). It was modified several times during its existence in the light of enterprises' experiences in applying it. The main variations were a mid-1980s shift from profit remittance to taxation of profits, which proved unpopular with enterprises since it generally required them to turn over more money to the state and retain less for investment and development, and the subsequent return to the system of contracted profit remittance (Interview 1 1995).

The State Contract System

Under the CRS, two types of state-enterprise contract existed. An enterprise would contract either to turn over a fixed percentage of its profits each year to the state during the course of the contract, or to turn over a certain amount out of profits which would be increased annually at a fixed rate. Shougang's CRS contract was of the latter type; in 1980 when the term of its contract began, it agreed to pay the state a certain sum based on 1978 profit figures, and this sum was to rise at an annual rate of 7.2% for the term of the contract, 14 years. Most state-enterprise contracts, it should be noted, ran for a much shorter period than Shougang's 14-year term, typically for three years or at most five. This is another respect in which the Corporation was treated as a special case. Where a fixed percentage of profit was turned over to the state by an enterprise, this could vary between 5-20%. In both types of state-enterprise contract, surplus profits were then at the disposal of the corporation for purposes of investment, acquisitions, restructuring etc.. The concept was akin to the Western notion of the corporation as "legal person." The CRS replaced the policy whereby only government agencies could represent state enterprises.

The Internal Contract System

While the state contract system operated at the government-institutional level, at the organizational level was the internal contract system, which operated as a form of target-setting cascade. To quote Shougang Iron and Steel Works President, Luo Bingsheng, "First we broke down the profits Shougang contracted to the government and our operating goals into various targets of profit, quantity, cost, quality, consumption etc., which were contracted by second-level companies to Shougang, then those targets were decomposed level by level through factories and mines, workshops, teams and groups to each post and individual" (Luo 1993: 14). This cascade of targets thus encompasses operational requirements, levels of material consumption, the maintenance of facilities, and conformance to regulations. As Luo outlines, "By so doing, a contracting network of 'from top to bottom, from centre to margin' was formed in the whole company, which had every staff member and worker know his/her definite contract task ... The internal contract system has created an initiative of all staff members and workers" (Luo 1993: 15). Internal contracting at Shougang, as in other large corporations, is both vertical, as described above by Luo, and horizontal, between Shougang's component sub-companies (Interview 3 1995).

A more nebulous aspect of the internal contract system at Shougang has been the attempt to develop an "enterprise culture" under the "Essence of the People" philosophy. This policy is based on six main principles — "value of innovation"; "enterprise spirit"; "excellent work style"; "business morals"; "responsibility of ownership"; and "consideration to national interests, enterprise interests, and individual interests." The latter principle repeats the familiar mantra of the whole industrial reform programme in China, that the state, the enterprise and the individual will all benefit from increased enterprise autonomy. In fact, as we shall see below, Shougang now stands accused of seeking to benefit only itself and its workers under the CRS, flouting central reform policies and guidelines.

Effects of the Contract Responsibility System

The CRS was apparently a great success at Shougang, with transnational and transbusiness diversification contributing to very high annual growth in profits of about 20% during the period of the reforms. Like other enterprises, it is seen to have benefited from increased autonomy in investment and management; improved staff commitment to CRS enterprises in the steel industry generally has also been noted by analysts (Interview 3 1995). However, a number of problems were also identified while the CRS was in force which were regarded as sufficiently serious to warrant the gradual phasing-out of the system and the development of new reform models to tackle the "deep" problems of enterprise reform. The following discussion of these problems refers to the generality of Chinese steel-makers which operated the CRS during the 1980s and early 1990s, as well as to the specific case of the Shougang Corporation.

Disparities between Enterprises

One of the main problems with the CRS has been the disparities between enterprises which it has created, a result of the process of bilateral negotiation of contracts for individual enterprises with state authorities. There were no definite regulations regarding the level at which profit quotas were set; as mentioned above, a range of 5-20% existed. The precise terms of the state-enterprise contract varied according to such factors as the nature of the enterprise, the industrial sector and geographical area to which it belonged, to what extent it was burdened with obsolete equipment, pre-CRS levels of investment, and so on. In the case of the Shougang Corporation, it was allowed very generous contract terms because of its need to invest in improved technology. As well as retaining the lion's share of its profits during the 14-year course of its CRS contract, it also benefited from artificially low depreciation rates enshrined in the terms of the contract (Interview 3 1995). This flexibility was built into the CRS from the start, because it was intended as a transitional stage in enterprises' development and because across-the-board regulations on state-enterprise contracts would have resulted in many enterprises failing to reach their targets. SOEs, particularly the largest of them in important industries such as steel, were not to be set up to fail under the CRS; bankruptcy was not an option at this stage. This meant of course that the CRS ultimately would not promote more efficient allocation of scarce resources, despite this being an important aim of the reform programme as a whole.

It is generally accepted that the CRS did have definite benefits for many enterprises in terms of increased autonomy and improved management; retained profits in CRS enterprises increased four-fold between 1986 and 1993 (Interview 1 1995). But the lack of a standard contract or of transparent, definite regulations governing profit remittance eventually resulted in management and state dissatisfaction with the system. Re-negotiation of contracts and disputes over profit quotas became common, especially where one enterprise found out that a comparable one had negotiated a better deal. Since the process of quota-setting relied so much on bilateral negotiation, politically well-connected enterprises were able to use these connections to their advantage. This seems to have been the case at Shougang, since the terms of its contract were unusually favourable to the enterprise rather than the state: the profit turned over to the state was based on 1978 figures, before the Chinese economic reforms had really begun in industry, and although Shougang's actual profits increased at an annual rate of 20% during the 1980s and early 1990s, its remittance to the state only increased at 7.2% per year. Thus the Corporation was one of the few which "got rich first", as Deng Xiaoping had urged. The state authorities did of course receive more money from Shougang than they had done before the CRS was introduced, but they did not benefit to the same extent as the Corporation itself, thus violating the fundamental principle of reform benefiting state, enterprise and individual alike.

Short-termism

This has been widely noted as a direct effect of the CRS, particularly in the many enterprises where a three-year contract was the norm. Although in some respects the CRS is viewed as having improved management performance in the enterprises involved (Interview 3 1995), there was also a clear tendency for managers to concentrate solely on the quantitative targets laid down in the contract and to neglect fixed-asset maintenance and investment and technological improvement. As the pursuit of short-term profits came to the fore, some enterprises did seem to be achieving greatly increased profits under the CRS, but reported profit rates were often misleading since there was no longer-term development strategy behind them. This short-termism seems to have been a direct result of the system of above-quota profit retention and thus integral to the structure of the CRS itself. Additionally, depreciation costs were not always included in contracts, or if they were, as with Shougang, the rate might be set artificially low. Despite its efforts in the direction of vertical integration (such as its overseas purchases in Peru and the United States), and despite the unusually long term of its contract with the state, Shougang was not immune from the problem of short-termism either. Although rapid technological development did take place during the 14-year term of its contract with the state in Shougang's core steel-making business (Interview 3 1995), the Corporation is also reported to have relied upon importing second-hand sets of equipment to introduce new lines of production which would bring quick returns to boost short-term profitability. The problems of short-termism were widely discussed within Shougang while the CRS was still in operation (Shougang Reforms Editorial Committee 1992), but evidently were not resolved.

The neglect of technological innovation (except where this would result in a quick increase in production volume and increased profit) and prioritizing of quantity over quality were particularly disappointing outcomes of the CRS, since the industrial reforms had been specifically aimed at improving enterprises' performance in these two areas which had long been a weak point of the state sector in China.

Impact on the Tax System and Government Revenue-raising

As was noted above in our description of the CRS system, there was a change in the system from the mid-1980s as profit remittance by enterprises was replaced by taxation of profits, followed by a reversion to the original scheme of fixed-rate profit remittance as a result of enterprise objections to having to hand over more to the state under the taxation scheme (Liu 1987). This caused confusion in the tax system as a whole, and the situation was complicated further by the fact that some CRS enterprises negotiated special fixed rates of VAT and other taxes as part of their contracts with the state, thus placing limits on state revenue. Recent fiscal and enterprise reforms were intended to disentangle profit and tax and to ensure that not only all SOEs, but enterprises of all types, including collectives and joint ventures, were subject to the same rates of tax, with no special deals for favoured institutions (Interview 1 1995). The 1992 CCP decision to implement the "socialist market economy" (as distinct from the previous "planned commodity economy") is reflected in the new emphasis on competition between enterprises of all ownership types on an equal basis, including the establishment of a level playing-field as far as taxation is concerned. This not only removes discrepancies in the tax treatment of state and other enterprises in China, but also ends the special arrangements from which certain SOEs had particularly benefited under the CRS.

Limits to Enterprise Autonomy

Although enterprises were to a large extent responsible for their own profits under the CRS, the state remained responsible for losses (Liu 1987). Since more than half of all SOEs in China are loss-making (and many of these have made losses for years), this represented a considerable drain on limited resources. This lack of responsibility for losses within CRS enterprises casts doubt over the claimed success of the system; and in any case, given the continued losses in many of the SOEs involved, it clearly did not succeed in all of them (Interview 5 1996). The other side of this equation is that the

CRS was unable to prevent continued government interference in the running of state-owned steel-makers. This remains a major problem in the industry in China, and a removal or reduction of government interference is one of the primary aims of the new MES reform programme (Interview 5 1996).

Excessive Enterprise Autonomy

To some extent the CRS seems to have brought the state the worst of both worlds, since at the same time as it remained responsible for SOE losses, and while many managers operating the CRS reportedly failed to come to terms with the increased decision-making powers they gained under the system, in a few cases autonomy was perceived to have gone too far, with certain top managers seemingly able to do whatever they wanted, including engaging in forms of business from which competitors were excluded. Again, Shougang is often mentioned as a prime example of this, and no doubt the Corporation's top political connections were a factor in its favourable treatment. But in other, less exceptional cases, the problem of autonomy without responsibility is frequently mentioned as a feature of past reform experiments, and as part of the new reform models now being introduced, managers are being explicitly reminded of their responsibilities to the state as well as to their staff.

Limited Improvement in Management Quality

While, as noted above, some improvement in state-enterprise management has been observed in enterprises practising the CRS during the 15 years of its existence, in general serious problems at the level of operational management in enterprises still exist (Interview 1 1995; Interviews 3 and 4 1996). Financial and cost management have been singled out as areas of particular weakness, and it has even been claimed that managers focused solely on the terms of their contract with the state under the CRS, effectively abandoning normal management in all other respects (Interview 1 1995), hence the widespread incidence of short-termism and other related problems in CRS enterprises. It has long been a criticism of some managers in Chinese SOEs that they are only concerned with telling the higher levels of the industrial bureaucracy what these officials want to hear regardless of what is actually happening within their enterprise, and comments along these lines are still commonly made by academic analysts of management in the steel industry and by managers themselves, as well as by workers. Doubts were expressed to us regarding how far management behaviour has changed or will change in Chinese SOEs while the "iron arm-chair" of job security regardless of performance is still in existence (Interview 5 1996).

Failure to Resolve the Problem of Property Rights

As noted by Keun Lee in a recent paper, under the CRS, "ambiguous property rights between the state and the enterprises resulted in ambiguous distributional and control relations" (Lee 1996: 109), the problem being one of both insufficiently clear regulations on income and control rights over retained profits, and also the considerable amount of bargaining, rule-bending, and collusion between state and enterprise authorities which went on in practice (Lee 1996). Once China embarked on the course of economic reform, and specifically reform of SOEs, it was necessary to consider how to separate management from ownership, and the CRS was originally intended as a new institutional arrangement which would facilitate this separation (Chen 1995). But making the terms of the state-enterprise contract legally enforceable failed to alter significantly the behaviour of either state organs or enterprises in respect of questions of property rights (Lee 1996), and so the need for a real separation of management and ownership is now commonly cited as a reason for abandoning the CRS and adopting new models of enterprise reform (Interview 2 1995; Interviews 3, 4 and 5 1996). The negotiation which was an integral part of setting state-enterprise contract profit quotas under the CRS also tended to institutionalize in the reform era older state habits of direct interference in or control over the running of SOEs (Lee 1996: 109).

One important manifestation of this problem has been the question of management disposal of state assets. This was permitted under the CRS provided that the funds so acquired were applied to technological improvement (Chen 1995), but in practice, as discussed above in the section on short-termism, technological improvement was extremely limited, with technical and maintenance departments among the biggest losers in terms of influence within the enterprise (Interview 3 1995). It is now believed that the decentralization of authority which took place during the CRS allowed considerable abuse of state assets for quick profit (Interview 2 1995; Interview 4 1996), and under new systems of enterprise reform, managers' responsibilities now include an obligation at least to maintain the value of state assets, if not to increase it. This will be discussed further when we come to look at the MES in greater detail.

The Continued Social Welfare Burden on Large Enterprises

Clearly this is a problem of the external institutional environment rather than a flaw of the CRS itself, but it is still something which was not provided for under that system, and which has to be dealt with if the autonomy of large SOEs is to mean anything in practice. Enterprises implementing the CRS continued to be responsible for providing a wide variety of social and other services to employees and their dependants, and this necessarily had a significant impact on their profitability and autonomy over personnel matters. Under new models of reform, responsibility for employees' social welfare is in many cases, though not all, beginning to be transferred from enterprises to local government. As was stressed by several of our informants in the Chinese steel industry recently, enterprises could not, and still cannot, create a socialist market economy on their own; the government has to play its part as well with the creation of a social-security system over the next fifteen years (Interviews 1 and 5 1996).

Given this list of defects, failures and undesirable side-effects, it might seem surprising that the CRS lasted as long as it did, so it should perhaps be stressed that despite the above criticisms now forming the conventional wisdom on the subject, both within China and overseas, the CRS was regarded as a fairly successful stage of the economic reforms at the time (Hay et al. 1994). But it is now perceived to have outlived its usefulness and to have failed to tackle the "deep" problems of reform, in particular the vexed questions of property rights and the separation of government and management functions. Having made a number of breakthroughs thus far in the course of the reforms, those who would transform China's SOEs are now faced with only the most difficult and intractable problems remaining to be solved, and it is therefore not surprising that a programme such as the CRS, at least as this relates to the state-enterprise relationship, is no longer considered likely to provide workable solutions.

Fate of a CRS Flagship

Arguments against the CRS were seriously raised by Chinese analysts as early as the mid-1980s (Lee 1996), and because of the problems listed above, by the early 1990s the argument over the future of SOE reform in China had basically been won by those who were critical of the limitations and side-effects of the CRS in practice. But there still remained two powerful arguments in favour of the CRS: Shougang's much-vaunted success, and the personal backing of China's paramount leader which this CRS flagship still enjoyed. Both of these arguments have now all but evaporated. Shougang's success had always been attributed by its rivals to the special terms of its particular deal with state authorities under the CRS rather than to the superiority of its reform blueprint; these special terms included the unusually long term of its contract (14 years), its low depreciation rates, its permission to exclude bonuses from normal wage costs, and its freedom to make overseas acquisitions and gain some of its companies a Hong Kong listing. Given that even with all these advantages, Shougang still fell prey to many of the common defects of the CRS, this argument seems a persuasive one. In addition, Deng Xiaoping's advanced age and failing health have sharply reduced his influence over the direction of future enterprise reform, and seem also to have weakened significantly his ability to protect what was known throughout China as his favourite SOE from its critics and rivals. For since the decision was taken to bring to an end the CRS experiment, the problems with this particular reform system have come to be seen as the very least of Shougang's difficulties. In brief, the Corporation has, since early 1995, experienced accusations of high-level corruption and of seriously polluting the capital, and has had its freedom to run non-steel businesses curtailed, having been compelled recently to sell 80% of its 100% stake in its own Huaxia Bank because of unspecified "organizational difficulties" (*FEER* 7.12.95: 83).

Zhou Beifang, the chairman of the Corporation's Hong Kong subsidiary, Shougang Concord International Enterprises, and the son of Zhou Guanwu, was arrested on corruption charges in mid-February 1995, and his father retired from his post at the head of the Corporation immediately afterwards. This corruption investigation is continuing at the time of writing, and the specific allegations involved are still not known (*FEER* 2.3.95: 16; 23.3.95: 46-47). What is now clear, though, is that the Shougang case is not directly connected to the bigger Beijing corruption scandal which has already resulted in the resignation of Chen Xitong, head of the Beijing Party apparatus, and the suicide of Beijing Vice-Mayor Wang Baosen. This major investigation is expected to continue for some time yet, whereas the Zhou Beifang case is scheduled to be concluded by the end of calendar 1996 (*FEER* 13.6.96: 29). But both of these corruption investigations, and no doubt many others besides, are clearly being used as political weapons in the struggle to succeed the ailing Deng Xiaoping and to define his legacy.

The pollution accusations are another sign that, rather than simply returning to the normal status of a large SOE in need of reform now that the CRS is no more, Shougang is actually being victimized by critics who are looking for ammunition against the Corporation beyond the deficiencies of its CRS programme. These accusations were made in mid-1996 when the company was visited by an inspection team from the National People's Congress

(China's parliament) and accused of being responsible for half of Beijing's sulphur-dioxide emissions and two-thirds of its carbon-monoxide emissions (*FEER* 27.6.96: 30). This serious pollution of the capital was said to date back to the late 1970s. Even if these figures are accurate (they seem to be suspiciously round numbers, but on the other hand Shougang's main plant, located not far out in the city's western suburbs, is an enormous one which lacks modern, environmentally-friendly technology to deal with its emissions), it seems somewhat surprising that no-one noticed this huge pollution problem at any point during the preceding 20 years. A plausible conclusion is that, without its powerful protectors in high places, Shougang is now considered fair game by critics who would have had to hold their peace in the past.

To appreciate the extent of the difficulties in which Shougang has recently found itself, it is necessary to be aware of how far this particular enterprise had to fall from its position of almost unparalleled privilege. Shougang is not just another state-owned steel-maker; it is not even just another very large state-owned steel-maker employing a quarter of a million people who would be likely to cause the state serious problems were they ever to find themselves out of pocket or out of a job in significant numbers. The unusual political significance which accrues to things which happen at Shougang can be illustrated with reference to two recent incidents involving the Corporation's workers. Firstly, there is the matter of the participation of Shougang workers in the independent unions formed during the 1989 democracy movement in Beijing (and in more than a dozen other cities as well). The participation of workers from Shougang is well documented; these workers were seen and spoken to, and their banners photographed, by reliable eyewitnesses to the demonstrations (Han 1990; Lu Ping 1990; *South China Morning Post* 9.3.90). Yet even before the crackdown on the movement had really begun, the official trade unions, the Shougang Corporation itself, and the local and national Party authorities went to enormous lengths to try to prove that no genuine employees of the Corporation were involved and that work attendance and production were at normal levels (*China Daily* 19.5.89; *Foreign Broadcast Information Service Daily Report - China* 13.6.89).

In part this display of concern is simply a reflection of Chinese authorities' general anxiety about any serious unrest involving workers, and in particular about any attempts by workers to organize themselves. The large-scale involvement in 1989 of workers from large and relatively successful SOEs such as Shougang was also a new phenomenon. In the past, workers' protests had tended to involve the relatively disadvantaged in China's industrial hierarchy, such as temporary and contract workers, apprentices etc. (Sheehan 1995). But the focus on Shougang and the lengths to which the authorities went, protesting perhaps too much that everything was normal in the western suburbs, demonstrates the particular importance attached to Deng's "pet state enterprise" (*FEER* 11.3.93: 25). Despite the relatively high wages and bonuses received by most Shougang employees in the hey-day of the CRS, occasionally mutterings of workforce discontent were still heard (*FEER* 18.11.93: 64).

Similarly, in a second incident, when retired women workers from the Corporation demonstrated outside the central leadership compound in Beijing over disputed pension entitlements, it made headline news (*South China Morning Post* 17.2.93: 10) not just because a public demonstration at such a sensitive political site was still a rarity in China, but also because of Shougang's status as a model of enterprise reform enjoying Deng's close personal support.

As the flagship of the CRS programme and the recipient of great publicity in this role, Shougang might well have expected to experience some sort of backlash once the system had become discredited, becoming as much of a focal point for criticism of the CRS as it had once been for its praise. While he was still in charge of the corporation, Zhou Guanwu had attempted to mount a last-ditch campaign to defend the CRS and Shougang immediately before the Party plenum which took the decision to abandon the (external) CRS in late 1993 (*FEER* 23.12.93: 9), demonstrating his concern about possible repercussions for Shougang if the programme it had pioneered were to be completely discredited. There was reportedly some support even within Shougang itself for ending the CRS, however. Managers' (and workers') attitudes here tended to be determined by whether or not they could easily meet the targets which were set for them under the CRS, and by the early 1990s those managers who were feeling under pressure from tough targets did favour abandoning the CRS (Interview 3 1995).

Yet if it was true that Shougang's success owed more to the political connections of its top leadership than to the CRS, it could also be argued that the Corporation ought to be able to ride out the criticism of a particular phase of the reforms and go on to take its place among the enterprises piloting the next reform programme, bolstered by its well-known links to Deng Xiaoping and others. Indeed, even after the official abandonment of the CRS, the Corporation's President, Luo Bingsheng, announced that Shougang still had ambitions to be the world's largest steel producer by the turn of the century, and was still hoping to list in New York at some point (*FEER* 9.6.94: 73). But this optimism evaporated the following year. Shougang was not in fact originally included among the enterprises piloting either of the two main SOE reform programmes launched in recent years, the MES and the GCS (it has now been included in the latter group of 56, and as such will be implementing the MES as well in future).

Given that the decision to abandon the CRS was well-founded in the light of the experiences of so many enterprises implementing it, and that this decision had already been taken in the late autumn of 1993, more than a year before Shougang ran into serious difficulties, it seems to be the case that the Corporation's woes are more bound up with the Deng succession struggle in itself than they are with any continuing need to attack proponents of improving and refining, rather than abandoning, the CRS. The Shougang Corporation's sudden fall from grace in reality seems not to have been brought about by its high-profile association with a discredited reform programme. The converse line of reasoning, that the Corporation's other difficulties, detailed above, have been used to further discredit the CRS programme, is not really convincing either since the argument about the defects of this system had basically been won before 1995. Rather it seems to be the case that those who live by their political connections, die by them also. Times have changed since the publication of the three-volume celebration of the Corporation's reforms, including contributions from both Chinese and foreign observers, in 1992 (Shougang Reforms Editorial Committee 1992). Shougang's most powerful patron, Deng himself, is now apparently unable to defend either his own reform strategy or his best-known protege from their detractors. If Shougang is viewed more broadly as a representative of Deng's whole enterprise reform strategy, then recent attacks on the Corporation make more sense than if the already-defunct CRS programme were the target of the criticism.

That Shougang's difficulties are closely linked to the political transition currently taking place in China was confirmed in February 1996, when the *China Reform Daily* newspaper, the organ of the State Commission for Economic Restructuring, launched an open attack on the Corporation's management and direction under Zhou Guanwu. The new leadership of the Corporation was praised for having "shifted their emphasis from being unique and defiant towards the state's macro-level control and adjustment (policy) to toeing the line of the party's central committee... This has enabled Shougang to intensify its reform drive." In a direct swipe at Zhou Guanwu himself, the article also noted that "[m]anagement at Shougang has changed from a patriarchal dictatorship to a democratic and scientific decision-making system which respects opinions of experts and the workers." More generally, the report blames not only Shougang itself, but Deng Xiaoping's rapid reform strategy, for the problems of economic overheating which have only recently been brought under control by a three-year austerity programme overseen by Vice-Premier Zhu Rongji (*Hong Kong Standard* 17.2.96). Cautious growth targets set by the party centre in 1992 were disregarded after Deng Xiaoping's famous remark that "slow economic growth is not socialism" gave the green light to the more developed coastal provinces to push ahead regardless. His visit to Shougang the same year, which sparked off a new round of international acquisitions for the Corporation, is seen in the same light. So now both Shougang's recent conduct and Deng's broader reform strategy are being discredited and disavowed by the so-called "third generation" of top Chinese leaders.

With the external (state-enterprise) CRS abandoned by its flagship and throughout the industrial hierarchy, there was clearly a need for some sort of new reform blueprint, preferably one which could tackle some of the outstanding problems in enterprise structure and management which the CRS had either failed to resolve or had not addressed at all. These new reform models will be discussed in the next section.

New Models of Enterprise Reform

We will examine two interlinked reform programmes for large and medium-sized SOEs, the MES and the GCS, which have been developed recently as possible successors to the CRS in state-owned industry, including the steel industry. These two pilot programmes were launched in 1994 and 1992 respectively, and are to run until 2010 (although preliminary results are expected by 2000). Both are intended to promote the "corporatization" of large and medium-sized SOEs, bringing in some features of Western company structure such as Boards of Directors and shareholders, reducing government interference in the running of enterprises, and making them more entrepreneurial and less reliant on the state.

We have argued above that the timing of the decision to end the CRS programme (as it related to state-enterprise contracting) in late 1993 refutes the argument that the problems of the erstwhile CRS flagship, Shougang, were being exploited as an opportunity to discredit the CRS reform model once its powerful patrons were no longer in a position to defend it. But the underlying reasoning about the likely direction of future enterprise reforms in China which underpinned this assumption has to a certain extent been borne out by subsequent developments. For the argument was that Shougang had been intended as a showcase for the CRS reform which would prove that state enterprises could succeed if managers were freed from the confines of state planning and given more autonomy over matters of finance, marketing and product mix, personnel, and foreign acquisitions and listings. In other words, Shougang's success would prove that more autonomy under the CRS was all that was needed to revitalize the stagnating state sector, and that there was no real case for privatization in China. Thus some difficult ideological problems of enterprise reform could be avoided. Conversely, once both Shougang and the CRS had been shown to be inadequate as models for the future of Chinese SOEs, alternative views within the top leadership could be expected to have more impact on the future of enterprise reform. Most often mentioned in this context was Vice-Premier Zhu Rongji and his supporters, who were believed to be more favourably disposed towards eventual partial privatization of at least some SOEs as a resolution of the property-rights dilemma (*FEER* 2.3.95: 16).

It is certainly true that the recent emphasis on "corporatization" of SOEs, including the formation of shareholding and limited-liability companies, has moved China's enterprise reform programme an important step further down the path towards eventual privatization of at least some state enterprises. As Keun Lee has argued, the logic of recent developments is that share ownership by individuals, rather than by "public-oriented legal persons" (banks, the state insurance company, other non-private enterprises, trade unions etc.), is likely to increase, and with it the likelihood of real privatization in the longer term (Lee 1996). At the time of writing, our information on the steel industry was that privatization is still not an option for the really large state-owned steel-makers; likewise, where their component sub-companies have been transformed into shareholding companies, the holding company intends to retain at least a 51% share, and in some cases shares are not to be sold to individuals at all (Interview 4 1996). However, further moves towards actual privatization within the next few years can certainly not be ruled out in the light of the rapid developments in recent years.

The MES and Group-Company Experiments in the Chinese Steel Industry

The main focus of reform efforts at the moment is a group of 156 medium and large state enterprises in China, including a number of large steel corporations. 56 of these enterprises are piloting the GCS (developing a parent holding company and a large group of subsidiary companies which will have a high degree of management autonomy from the parent), and 100 are involved in the MES programme. In fact, though, the 56 group-company pilots are also undertaking MES reforms internally, so what we have in effect is 156 MES pilot enterprises. In addition to these enterprises which are part of the national reform experiment, provincial governments have also selected pilot enterprises, including some steel-makers, locally for "corporatization" reforms. Nationally, there are also 22 state enterprises involved in a shareholding-company experiment under the auspices of the State Economic and Trade Commission. These 22 are expected to list on the stock-market in the near future, whereas it is anticipated that it will be some time before the 156 national MES pilots are allowed by the government to list. As noted above, Shougang was initially omitted from the original group of 155 national pilot enterprises, but has now been included as a group-company pilot.

The working definition of the MES reform programme in China is *gaige, gaizao, gaizu* (reform, reconstruction, restructuring). This includes the following main elements:

- clarification of property rights;
- clear definition of rights and responsibilities;
- distinguishing between government and management functions;
- scientific enterprise management.

This list gives an indication of the main areas in which the CRS is perceived to have failed in large and medium-sized SOEs.

To realize these aims in practice:

- reform (*gaige*) means the adoption of new enterprise management mechanisms;
- reconstruction (*gaizao*) will consist of technical transformation and improvement;
- restructuring (*gaizu*) will involve a reorganization of property rights and assets (Interview 4 1996).

As described to us by informants in the steel industry, the GCS is intended to create large companies which can be internationally competitive in world markets, reorganizing their resources, assets and structure. The MES is intended to bring in to Chinese SOEs modern management mechanisms and more elements of the Western company system. The Chinese see this as something which has enabled Western companies to fend off government interference more successfully than their Chinese counterparts. Reducing government interference in enterprise management is a primary aim of the MES (Interview 5 1996). Another important aspect of the programme is the removal, or at least the reduction, of the social-service burden on enterprises. Traditionally large SOEs in China have been responsible for the cradle-to-grave welfare (including education and health-care) of not only their employees, but also employees' dependants. In many cases, though not all, this burden on enterprises is now beginning to be shifted onto local government. Many Chinese provinces and municipalities are now in the process of setting up schemes to provide unemployment and health insurance and pensions to their citizens.

Restructuring within Enterprises

Over the past two to four years a new corporate structure has begun to emerge in the steel corporations involved in the new reform experiments. These corporations are in the process of separating off all component parts which are involved in their core line of production (i.e. iron and steel) from others which may be engaged in completely unrelated lines of business. What will result is a parent holding company and a range of subsidiary companies. The core iron and steel subsidiaries will maintain a fairly close relationship with the parent company, although still enjoying some degree of management autonomy, while the other sub-companies, including social-service companies, will have a higher degree of autonomy.

All sub-companies will eventually be formed into shareholding or limited-liability companies which will be responsible for their own profit and loss, and which will be able to attract outside investment, borrow from banks, and enter into joint ventures with foreign companies in their own right. A distinction is made here between shareholding companies, which are destined for an early stock-market listing and whose shares can be bought by anyone, including individuals, and limited-liability companies, whose shares can only be bought by institutional investors. These "public-oriented legal persons" (Lee 1996) might be state-owned banks or insurance companies, other SOEs, or state trade unions. At the moment the parent company always retains a controlling stake of at least 51% in all of these sub-companies, and in practice the smallest stake we have come across is one of 66% of shares in a sub-company held by the parent company. In other cases more than 80% of total sub-company shares are held by the parent group company.

The formation of sub-companies serves a number of related purposes. The sub-companies are intended to spread responsibility for results throughout the group, to provide more opportunities for gaining access to capital, especially overseas, and to absorb surplus labour from the core iron and steel businesses. Dividend income from sub-companies (or profit quotas) can be used by the parent company to help cover social welfare costs where these have not been transferred to local government; in addition, since the relationships within the group are now to be governed by market principles, sub-companies will be expected to pay for the provision of social services by the parent company.

Below we comment briefly on several key aspects of the MES and group-company programmes as these are now taking shape in the Chinese steel industry, before turning to Shougang's prospects under the new SOE reform blueprint. Since these reform experiments have only been going on for at most four years, and in many cases for only two, these comments should be taken as preliminary observations only. Since little has been published in English on the latest reform experiments to date, however, we do consider it worthwhile to include here some details of how the new schemes are intended to work and what the results have been so far, despite the reforms still being at a very early stage.

Downsizing and Absorption of Surplus Labour

Several of the steel corporations involved in the MES and group-company experiments consider themselves to be overmanned and are planning reductions in employees of between 16% and 50% in their core iron and steel businesses. In all cases both production workers and management will see their numbers reduced (Interviews 2, 3, and 4 1996). The creation of service sub-companies is a key method of absorbing surplus labour. These large corporations now typically contain within them sub-companies running shops, hotels, restaurants and travel agencies, as well as social-service companies and companies engaged in any kind of manufacturing or service provision where profits can be made (not necessarily steel-related). In one case the number of employees hived off into such sub-companies now exceeds the number employed in iron and steel production by 40% (Interview 4 1996).

Corporations are also employing a number of other methods in their efforts to achieve often drastic workforce reductions. Early retirement is encouraged, and in some cases employees taking advantage of this can receive a lump-sum investment from the group company in order to help them start up their own business. To make voluntary severance for workers of any age more attractive to those wishing to change jobs or go into business on their own, the requirement on these employees to pay back the costs of their training if they leave the corporation has been removed (Interview 3 1996). Inevitably, companies have found that it is not necessarily the employees of whom they would most like to be rid who volunteer for this sort of scheme, and have had to take steps to retain key technical personnel in particular (Interview 3 1996).

One steel corporation has set up its own group labour pool where surplus employees can receive re-training for other work within the group, and is also replacing part-time and contract workers with otherwise redundant permanent employees (Interview 2 1996). All steel-industry managers and analysts are acutely aware of the political sensitivity of unemployment in the Chinese context; social stability remains the party's first priority, and so making large numbers of employees redundant and shifting the burden onto society is simply not an option for them. However, where a surplus employee has been unable to find suitable work within the group for two years, it is acknowledged that there would be a case for compulsory termination of employment, and some steel corporations are setting quotas for employment reduction at various levels within the organization, which also suggests that the process will be coercive in some cases. Although China cannot really be said to have a labour market at present, the recently-passed Labour Law does shift some of the responsibility for helping people to find work onto local government institutions rather than leaving enterprises to bear the whole burden (Interview 3 1996). Employees can also now look for alternative employment on their own initiative in the local "talent market."

The steel corporations undertaking large workforce reductions all admit that there had been considerable resistance to these changes, but say they are seeking to explain to reluctant employees that it is futile for everyone to try to remain in their present position, since if the workforce is not reduced, the company will face serious difficulties in the next few years and no-one will prosper. It has been reported that reducing management numbers is still the most difficult task; the "iron arm-chair" of lifetime employment (the management equivalent of the production workers' "iron rice-bowl") persists, as does the tendency to move under-performing managers sideways rather than down. Under the MES, however, managers are now being put on three-year contracts which can be terminated at any time if they do not meet certain set performance criteria (Interviews 3 and 5 1996). Given the unintended consequences of the CRS in some enterprises, managers' targets are not now limited to levels of profit. They also include an obligation to increase, or at least maintain, the value of state assets. Systems of audit and appraisal, both internal and external, are being developed to check that assets are not being run down or disposed of improperly (Interviews 4 and 5 1996).

There is some scope for reducing managerial numbers in the streamlining and merging of administrative departments which have duplicated or overlapping functions. For example, one steel corporation of which we have knowledge has merged four separate departments responsible for different aspects of construction projects into one entity. Separate HRM departments and training centres for production workers and managers have also been successfully combined (Interviews 2 and 3 1996). In some cases, finance and other departments have been abolished at the sub-company level and their responsibilities taken over by delegated personnel from the parent company's administrative departments. This can only be done in core iron and steel sub-companies, however; for other sub-companies, it would cause an unacceptable reduction in managerial autonomy (Interview 4 1996). But perhaps the biggest difficulty enterprises face when dealing with surplus managers is that most at the top levels are party members and derive their appointments and authority from that status. Therefore questions of efficient staff allocation come into conflict with wider political imperatives. We return to this question below in the section on separating government and management functions.

Managerial Autonomy in Sub-companies

Sub-companies are responsible for their own profit and loss, since the parent company is only responsible for the money which it has invested in the sub-company (however, some sub-companies at this very early stage of the reform are still 100% funded by the group). In principle they can decide on their own staffing levels and appoint their own managers, but in practice they would be expected to consult with the parent company over any large reduction in their workforce. Transferring employees between sub-companies or from sub-companies into the group labour pool has started to happen, but as yet no surplus employees have in fact been forced out of the group altogether in any of the corporations for which we have information. Sub-companies are allowed to recruit new staff from outside the group, but clearly there is also pressure on them to take up the slack where redundant workers in other parts of the group are in need of new work (Interview 2 1996).

The degree of control which sub-companies have over their production targets varies depending on whether the group company is their main customer or whether they sell most of their production outside the group (Interviews 1 and 2 1996). In general they are free to look for markets anywhere, but where they provide a key input to group steel production (such as an iron-ore mining sub-company), the group's orders must be met before production can be sold outside to the highest bidder. Inputs can in theory be bought in from any competitive supplier, but in practice many of our informants observed that it was common for sub-companies to choose to work mainly within existing group relationships whether seeking markets or materials. The parent company was still admitted to have considerable influence over most sub-companies whatever the regulations on corporate structure and governance might say on paper (Interviews 1 and 3 1996). The parent company must be informed of all sub-company investment decisions, and must give permission for any investment above a certain amount; at one steel corporation for which we have figures, the investment ceiling for sub-companies above which the parent company's permission has to be sought is 30 million *yuan* (about £2.5 million).

Enterprise Debt

One large state-owned steel corporation on which we have information has a particularly serious debt problem which is to be tackled as part of the present phase of MES reforms. This enterprise has debts of about 80% of its total asset value, which is on the high side, though certainly not unheard-of, among Chinese SOEs of all sizes. In the West it would probably go bankrupt, but in China this is still not allowed to happen to such a big company (although some small SOEs have already gone bankrupt or will be allowed to do so in the near future. Many others have been sold off to their workers, or "given" to other, profitable state enterprises to turn around (*FEER* 12.9.96: 62-68)). The debt is owed mainly to state banks and industrial ministries and to materials suppliers. The corporation is enmeshed in the typical web of "triangular debt" between SOEs in China.

As well as freeing sub-companies to seek additional funding in overseas capital markets, this corporation is also resorting to a form of debt write-off, which seems to be the only way in which it will be able to continue to operate and possibly show a profit in future. Funds from government ministries and state-owned banks are to be converted from loans to investment; thus these institutions will become part-owners of the corporation. Enterprise debts will be converted to investment in the same way. The corporation will also issue shares, and part of the proceeds of this issue will be used to pay off debts. This plan has been accepted because none of the corporation's creditors, whether ministries, banks or other enterprises, stand any chance of recovering their money in any other way, and the possibility of future dividends if the corporation can turn a profit is better than nothing at all. It should be noted, however, that although this sort of debt write-off may be an option for a few large SOEs, not every indebted state enterprise can do the same, since their net losses amount to more than the total equity of all China's banks (*FEER* 12.9.96: 62).

In other cases, however, what is happening in the re-organization of enterprises seems to achieve little beyond moving the problem around between institutions. For example, one of the steel corporations which is part of the group-company reform experiment has been compelled by its local government to take smaller loss-making SOEs (whose losses were previously the responsibility of local government) into the group as sub-companies. The finances of these autonomous sub-companies are kept separate from those of the parent company, so only limited financial help will be forthcoming from the parent if the sub-companies continue to make losses. Therefore little benefit is gained from this shifting around of unprofitable enterprises by anyone except the local government, which divests itself of the responsibility for enterprises' losses. The large steel corporation in question is one which did not volunteer for the group-company experiment in the first place, but was pressed into it by the government; it is also one which has no immediate plans to shift its social welfare burden onto local government. Clearly there are questions of specific political contexts and relationships at work here which still have a big impact on the direction and progress of enterprise reform. This brings us on to the question of government interference in enterprise management.

Separation of Government and Management Functions

It is certainly true that, superficially at least, MES enterprises in China now more closely resemble typical Western corporate structures. Each of the steel corporations taking part in the latest reform experiments now has a Board of Directors which is supposed to be chosen by its shareholders and which selects the general manager. But for large, state-owned steel-makers, in most cases the sole shareholder is still the state, which means that in practice most candidates for the Board are recommended and appointed by the government (which is indistinguishable from the ruling CCP), just as enterprise managers always were before the reforms. It is admitted by many within these steel corporations that changes in corporate structure are more form than substance at the present time, with the ideal of shareholder control falling prey to continued direct government interference. The reportedly high level of government interference in the appointment of Boards of Directors has thus negated one of the main purposes of the MES programme, the separation of government and management functions. There are no indications that this problem will be resolved in the near future. Indeed, it is questionable whether the large SOEs involved in the national reform experiments really want to be free of state control, since a large majority of them have opted to remain "exclusively state-funded" rather than aiming for the intended "corporatization", i.e. shareholder or limited-liability company status (*FEER* 12.9.96: 68).

A similar picture emerges when we examine the distribution of power within the enterprise. Before the reforms, power mainly rested with the so-called "old three committees", the party, management, and the official trade union. Under the MES, these are to be replaced by the "new three committees": the Board of Directors, the Board of Supervisors, and the Shareholders' Congress. So if it were carried out as intended, this reform would directly attack the vested interests of many in the old structure, notably the party and the trade union, generating resistance. Under the MES, the Board of Directors ought to be the highest level of decision-making, but this was always the role of the party in the past, and the party is proving reluctant to give up its power. Many enterprises, including some in the steel industry, have fudged the issue by appointing the branch party chairperson as chair of the Board of Directors as well, so that the same person can give orders wearing either "hat." Similarly, existing managers have been transformed into a new "Board of Directors" by a stroke of the pen, and party and union organizations have also found a place on the Board of Supervisors, allowing power to remain in essentially the same hands but under different titles. The question of how to break up the old vested interests in state-owned industry has been described to us as a "forbidden area" of reform, since it touches on the question of the party's role now and what the limits of its power should be. The contradictions in the situation are obvious to many Chinese enterprise managers and academic analysts, but there is little open discussion of how to resolve them because of the issue's great political sensitivity.

Discussion

Shougang's Transition from CRS to MES

Shougang's original exclusion from the national group of pilot enterprises may have been as much for political reasons as economic ones: The State Economic Restructuring Commission, the institution behind the *China Reform Daily* which recently attacked Shougang's record under Zhou Guanwu, had a hand in selecting the national pilot enterprises (Interview 4 1996). But clearly the transition is likely to be a difficult one, as Shougang loses much of the special treatment which contributed to its success under the CRS and has to find ways of maintaining its profitability in a changed economic environment. Now that the CRS is no more, the Corporation will have to pay tax at the same rate as every other enterprise, its depreciation rates will be revised upwards, and its bonuses will be part of its regular wage costs, rather than coming straight out of retained profit. All these changes necessitate a marked improvement in the Corporation's finances to cope with the downward pressure on its profitability.

Staff and workers at Shougang benefited from its high level of retained profits during the term of its CRS contract in the form of bonus increases some 40-60% higher than increases in basic salary during the same period. Since bonuses generally form such a significant proportion of state workers' monthly pay (typically around 15%), any marked reduction in levels of bonus is likely to have an appreciable impact on workers' budgets and morale. Workers' bonuses were suspended for a while during the spring of 1995 when accusations of high-level corruption at the Corporation first became public and Zhou Guanwu retired (*FEER* 23.3.95: 46). Given the changed circumstances in which Shougang is now operating, bonuses are unlikely to return to their previous high levels, and this may engender workforce dissatisfaction with management. Attempts to downsize the core steel workforce in these circumstances would only exacerbate the situation, and Shougang is likely to meet with the same sort of resistance and foot-dragging that similar large steel corporations in China have experienced.

Despite its much-vaunted levels of profit under the CRS, the Shougang Corporation also had a serious debt problem by 1993, the penultimate year of its CRS contract. The many competitive advantages enshrined in its contract with the state, the focus of much resentment elsewhere in the industry, could not protect it entirely from the general problems of Chinese industry, and like others, it was trapped in a web of triangular debt between SOEs, as well as being affected by falling demand for steel from the domestic construction industry, still one of the main markets for all large steel-makers in China. In late 1993 the Corporation was granted an emergency state loan of 400 million *yuan* (about £33 million) to deal with this situation (*FEER* 18.11.93: 63). Given the size of the Corporation, like other comparable Chinese steel-makers it will continue to receive state subsidies in one form or another and will not be allowed to go bankrupt, in keeping with the official policy slogan of "grasping the large and releasing the small" (i.e. keeping hold of a core of large, heavy-industrial SOEs but letting go of smaller ones which may then be sold off or merged). So although its era of enjoying special treatment is at an end, it still belongs to a class of enterprises which the state is not yet prepared to abandon completely to the mercies of the market. To sum up, it is likely to face the same difficulties (debt, downsizing, finding new markets) as other large steel-makers, added to which will be the contrast for workers and management alike between their previous privileged position and the harsher realities of the late 1990s. Where questions of pay and job security arise, this may lead to a deterioration in labour-management relations which can only make the Corporation's transition more difficult.

MES and GCS Prospects in the Chinese Steel Industry

Western observers of the Chinese economic reforms, particularly those familiar with the whole process dating back to the late 1970s, can perhaps be forgiven for displaying some scepticism about the extent to which things have really changed inside China's SOEs. When a new reform programme is launched, inevitably very ambitious claims are made for its efficacy and the problems it will be able to solve. While it is underway, reports of its success in model enterprises receive great publicity and everything seems to be going well. But when a programme is brought to an end and its successor launched, a litany of very serious defects in the old reform programme then comes to light which seems to cast doubt on previous reports of its success in enterprises. Shougang's abrupt fall from the status of a successful reform flagship held up for universal emulation to that of a problem case and negative example for others is an illustration of how quickly and how completely the party line on these matters can change. It is true, however, that the environment in which enterprise reform has been taking place has itself been changing so rapidly that apparently successful phases of reform are bound to outlive their usefulness fairly quickly; this does not necessarily mean that reports of their success were greatly exaggerated, or that nothing of value can be taken from the experience.

Since our informants in the steel industry so often commented themselves that whatever changes had recently taken place on paper, power within and over enterprises was still essentially in the same hands, the question obviously arises as to what, if anything, is really new about the latest phase of reform. Several of our informants insisted that managers' attitudes really had undergone a sea-change, so that they no longer resorted to asking for instructions from the higher level (higher management or government) as soon as a problem arose. The new MES contracts for managers, which lay down clear responsibilities which must be fulfilled if they are to remain employed, are often cited as an example of real enforcement of paper rights and responsibilities, and a real cultural change within enterprises. However, it should be remembered that contract employment, introduced in 1986, was supposed to have brought an end to the "iron rice-bowl" of job security by now, yet managers still complain of the difficulty in practice of firing workers (and managers), whatever the regulations say about their right to do this. It is true that some large steel corporations are dealing with their overmanning by dismissing contract employees and replacing them with permanent staff, but targets for the proportion of employees on fixed-term contracts have themselves not been met, and many have their contracts automatically renewed every time they expire regardless of their performance or the enterprise's continuing need for their services. So the existence of these three-year MES contracts for managers does not of itself mean that real accountability for results is now going to be enforced. It is not yet clear what is happening in practice since the MES has been running for less than three years at the time of writing, but it seems entirely possible that although regulations have changed, actual behaviour will not.

If there are doubts about the extent to which managerial accountability is going to become a reality under the MES, there are even greater question-marks over the reform programme's chances of doing away with, or at least reducing, government interference in enterprises. Solving this problem brings into question the party's own role and professed ideology in the 1990s, hence the difficulty for Chinese analysts in even discussing it openly. Keun Lee has argued (1996) that the logic of so-called "legal-person socialism" (where state banks, insurers, unions and SOEs hold shares in reformed state enterprises) is that it will develop more and more in the direction of "capitalism with Chinese characteristics", i.e. with individual shareholders playing a much bigger role than is presently envisaged, since in China today it is individuals, not public institutions, which are accumulating the money that enterprises need (Lee 1996: 118). This is something which is already creeping in by the back door, but the party still is not prepared for large corporations of the sort we have been studying to be anything other than state-owned and state-controlled. While it seems possible that the MES and group-company reforms will give SOEs greater access to much-needed capital, the encouragement of share issues inevitably raises difficult ideological problems for what is still an avowedly socialist government.

The problem of surplus labour is also likely to cause difficulties over the next five years. The service sector of the Chinese economy, which outside three or four major cities was still in its infancy even ten years ago, does still have considerable capacity to absorb surplus labour from big, heavy-industrial SOEs, but it is not yet clear whether the numbers affected by this next round of downsizing can be accommodated in the same way. Nothing on this scale has really been tried in China before. The Chinese government's own figures on urban unemployment put it at a level of three per cent, but it was recently admitted that state-sector unemployment is in fact at least eight per cent, and overall, the urban unemployment figure may be as high as fifteen per cent. So there must be some doubt as to whether the scale of workforce reductions which most reforming steel corporations believe to be necessary for production efficiency can be accomplished without threatening the social stability which is still the first priority of the government.

Added to these major difficulties — continued party interference in enterprises and the problem of surplus labour — is the question of divesting enterprises of their social-welfare burden. Although the general policy is to transfer the running of social services to local government, with enterprises contributing to costs through the tax system rather than directly operating services themselves, this is not happening in all cases, and it is evident that a certain amount of negotiation and horse-trading is still going on in the relationship between enterprises and state authorities. A lot still depends on this relationship, and thus large SOEs in the steel industry still cannot be said to be operating on a level playing-field in all respects. Thus this is one defect of the CRS which more recent reform blueprints do not in themselves seem to be able to remedy. All in all, it seems that the successful completion of this round of enterprise reform may depend not only on successful fiscal and welfare reform nationally, but also on the outcome of political reform in China. That in turn is unlikely to begin until the succession to Deng Xiaoping has been settled.

Note

* This chapter is one of the products of a research project funded by the Economic and Social Research Council's Pacific Asia initiative. It is based in part on interviews conducted during 1995 and 1996 with senior managers from five large state-owned steel corporations in China, including Shougang, and with state officials and analysts of the Chinese steel industry. The authors would like to thank Professor Chen Zhicheng of the Institute of Management Science, University of Science and Technology, Beijing, and Mr Xiao Yuxin of the School of Management, University of Keele, for their invaluable assistance in the arrangement and conduct of these interviews, further details of which can be found in Appendix 1.

Appendix 1

Interview 1 1995 was with a senior academic expert on management and fiscal science based in Beijing.

Interview 2 1995 was with a senior specialist in economic management at a leading Chinese Communist Party academic institution.

Interview 3 1995 was with an economic specialist working in the Metallurgical Industry Ministry in Beijing.

Interview 4 1995 was with a senior member of staff specializing in research and development at a large steel corporation in Beijing.

Interview 1 1996 was with two group-level directors at a large steel corporation in eastern China.

Interview 2 1996 was with two group-level managers responsible for Human Resource Management and the plant CCP Party branch respectively at the same east China steel corporation.

Interview 3 1996 was with an engineering specialist and former group director of a long-established steel corporation in west-central China.

Interview 4 1996 was with a group-level manager previously responsible for enterprise restructuring and now working in economic research and development, and another senior member of the economic research and development institute of a large steel corporation in central China.

Interview 5 1996 was with a senior academic management specialist from a University of Metallurgical Science and Technology in central China.

Interview 6 1996 was with senior group-level managers from a large steel corporation on China's eastern seaboard.

These were all semi-structured interviews conducted in Chinese and English via an interpreter, and typically lasted for two or four hours. All except Interview 4 1996 were tape-recorded with the permission of the interviewees. The corporations visited were chosen to provide a range of experiences under the CRS and MES reforms. Although all would be classed as large enterprises from a Western perspective, a variety of different enterprise sizes in terms of output, profit and workforce numbers is represented within the sample, and the sample includes both enterprises chosen for the national MES and GCS pilot projects and those selected to pioneer these reforms by provincial authorities. The enterprises all have diverse histories, with the oldest having been established at the end of the nineteenth century and the newest during the early 1980s, and there is also a contrast in the health of the balance-sheets of the various corporations, with some heavily indebted while others are making a good profit. Thus they were chosen to provide the researchers with some idea of how the MES and GCS reforms are likely to perform in the different conditions obtaining across the state-owned steel sector throughout China.

References

Chen, D. (1995): *Chinese Firms Between Hierarchy and Market*. London: St. Martin's Press.

China Daily (19.5.89): "Workers rally for students." *FBIS-CHI*-89-097: 81-82.

Far Eastern Economic Review (11.3.93): "Congressional record." 23-25.

Far Eastern Economic Review (18.11.93): "Model on the rocks." 63-64.

Far Eastern Economic Review (23.12.93): "Smelted down." 9.

Far Eastern Economic Review (9.6.94): "Shougang sets goals." 73.

Far Eastern Economic Review (2.3.95): "The reckoning begins." 16.

Far Eastern Economic Review (23.3.95): "Goodbye to all that." 46-47.

Far Eastern Economic Review (7.12.95): "Shougang sheds shares." 83.

Far Eastern Economic Review (13.6.96): "Teams investigating corruption cases are proliferating in Beijing." 29.

Far Eastern Economic Review (27.6.96): "Former model enterprise in Beijing is now the target of an anti-pollution campaign." 30.

Far Eastern Economic Review (12.9.96): "Trials by fire." 62-68.

Foreign Broadcast Information Service Daily Report — China (13.6.89): "Beijing workers urged to make losses." *FBIS-CHI*-89-112: 30.

Han, M. (1990): *Cries for democracy: Writings and speeches from the 1989 Chinese democracy movement*. Princeton, NJ: Princeton University Press.

Hay, D.A., D.J. Morris, G. Liu and Y. Shujie (1994): *Economic reform and state-owned enterprises in China 1979-1987*. Oxford: Clarendon Press.

Hong Kong Standard (17.2.96): "'Veiled attack' on model state firm reported." *FBIS-CHI*-96-035: 16-17.

Lee, K. (1996): "An assessment of the state sector reform in China: Viability of legal person socialism." *Journal of the Asia Pacific Economy* 1(1): 105-121.

Liu, G. (1987): "Problems in the reform of ownership relations in China" in M. Warner (ed.), *Management Reforms in China,* 165-175. London: Frances Pinter.

Lu, P. (1990): *A moment of truth: Workers' participation in China's 1989 democracy movement and the emergence of independent unions.* Hong Kong: Hong Kong Trade Union Education Centre/Asia Monitor Resource Centre.

Luo, B. (1993): "The Shougang Contract Management Responsibility System: Effects, Practices and Thoughts." Keynote address to International Seminar on the Shougang Contract Management Responsibility System, Beijing, October.

Sheehan, J. (1995): *Conflict between workers and the party-state in China and the development of autonomous workers' organizations, 1949-1984.* Unpublished doctoral dissertation, University of London.

Shougang Reforms Editorial Committee (1992): *The Reforms at Shougang.* Beijing: Beijing Municipal CCP Propaganda Department, Beijing Municipal Research Group on Ideological and political work, and the Shougang Iron and Steel Works (3 volumes).

South China Morning Post (9.3.90): "Cases of industrial unrest in 1989 viewed." *FBIS-CHI*-90-047: 26-27.

South China Morning Post (17.2.93): "Retired workers in daring Beijing pensions protest." 10.

Monopolized, Privatized, Diversified, and Incorporated: An Institutional Analysis of the Evolution of the Dutch Postbank (1945-1994)*

Willem Hulsink

Introduction

From the 1960s onwards Postal Savings Bank (RPS) and Postal Giro (PCGD), both government-owned and politically controlled, had increasingly started to work together in *retail banking* as PTT Moneyservices, providing financial services to the general public. The need to integrate the administratively separated RPS and PCGD became urgent when they were confronted with strong competition from the private banking community. As a consequence of the aggressive diversification strategies of individual banks, the boundaries between the traditionally separate domains of merchant banking, savings, giro, credits, and mortgages became eroded. Starting with the early 1970s, PTT Moneyservices was losing ground to the commercial banks, even threatening the long-term provision of savings and payments services to the public. The ability of PTT Moneyservices to react to this competitive challenge was limited. The company's overall strategies were constrained by political interference: marketing of new products and services required political approval and the carrying out of its operational functions was subjected to parliamentary supervision. These institutional restrictions to entering new markets, together with the time-consuming character of political decision-making, prevented PTT Moneyservices from effectively responding to the threat posed by the commercial banks, which had started to enter its domain of retail banking. The RPS and the PCGD responded by increasingly working together on retail banking, eventually becoming fully integrated into the Moneyservices Directorate within the PTT administration.

In the mid-1970s, the centre-left government hoped to counteract this negative trend through the establishment of a strong and fully integrated Postbank, thereby consolidating the Giro service and the Savings bank. In addition to safeguarding the continuation of the public PTT Moneyservices through the creation of Postbank, a second, more controversial policy objective was involved, making the situation more complicated. The prediction was that a strong and diversified Postbank would act as a countervailing state bank to promote competition in the concentrated and cartelized Dutch banking sector. Government, in the original plans, therefore, allowed Postbank to enter the *wholesale banking* market, i.e. to offer customized financial services to the business community.

The Parliament received these proposals with mixed feelings. Although supported by the political parties represented in the Cabinet, it was strongly opposed by the liberal-conservatives and the banking community, who argued that competition in the banking sector was sufficient and that there was no necessity for the government to intervene in the wholesale banking market. Furthermore, it was believed that a non-profit Postbank could not operate under the same market conditions as would the other banks. Therefore, the existing banks argued that the portfolio of a future Postbank needed to be restricted to its core business of providing public giro services and that PTT Moneyservices should be excluded from providing "wholesale" financial services.

The situation became even more complicated through the coincidence of the reorganization of PTT Moneyservices, the harmonization of the PCGD network and the payments system of the banking community in the policy process, and the cabinet shifts between 1975 and 1985; from centre-left to centre-right, then centre-left and to centre-right again.

Finally in 1984, a minimal compromise was reached within Parliament and the larger community of organized banking over a less ambitious plan for PTT Moneyservices. The RPS and PCGD would be integrated within Postbank, allowing it economies of scale and scope to safeguard the provision of public giro services in the immediate future. This Postbank would become an ordinary retail bank with only limited access to wholesale banking. The lobby of the banking community proved effective. The proposal to grant Postbank the privileged status of a state bank was replaced by the alternative of becoming corporatized and privatized that would meet the rules and conditions of fair competition. On 1 January 1986, the RPS and the PCGD merged into the limited liability Postbank, thereby changing status from government-owned and politically controlled institutions to that of a semi-commercial bank. After almost ten years of laborious negotiations between government, PTT Moneyservices and organized banking over the structure of the Dutch market for giro and financial services, privatization of PTT Moneyservices, together with a controlled expansion of Postbank in wholesale banking, was seen as the only solution to the political stalemate. Neither Government, Moneyservices and the larger PTT administration, nor organized banking could agree about the degree of government intervention in the financial sector.

The research questions addressed in this study are the following: How did PTT Moneyservices/Postbank manage the major techno-economic and (de)regulatory challenges in its business environment, and how did it cope with the interests of the various stakeholders in the Dutch financial community? The focus will be on the various configurations of certain public and private actors in the political decision-making process and the problems, policies, and political events that emerge within that policy-making process. More specifically, attention will be paid to unravelling the complex web of strategic interactions between PTT and other parties over the policy issues of reconsidering PTT's responsibilities and re-defining the governance structures of the Dutch giro system. The emphasis will be on how the (near) monopolies on giro/postal savings of Moneyservices/Postbank were broken down and opened up to (more) competition. This chapter analyses at first the consolidation of Postal Giro and Postal Savings Bank into the integrated Moneyservices directorate, followed by the divestiture of Moneyservices from the PTT administration and its corporate transformation into a (semi-) commercial bank. These drastic changes in the status and organization of the public Moneyservices were shaped of course by the focal organizations, Postal Giro, Postal Savings Bank and PTT, and also by other actors and groups in the larger policy community (e.g. Cabinet and Parliament, the labour unions and the larger banking community), either stimulating or blocking institutional change.

Theoretical Background

In this study I will follow an actor-oriented and institutional perspective. Such an approach acknowledges both the strategic and tactical moves of actors driven by calculated self-interest and the collective dynamics of competition and collaboration, as well as the institutional conditions and rules constraining strategic interactions on the definition of problems and the formulation of appropriate solutions. I will focus on the search for and negotiation over more appropriate governing arrangements by public and private stakeholders, producers and consumers in both the market place and the policy arena. This action logic does not automatically involve an imperative for continuous change, it could also imply institutional inheritance and persistence. The degree of governance transformation seems to depend upon the distribution of power and interests among the stakeholders, shifts in the technological and economic characteristics of industries and the larger political-institutional setting promoting and foreclosing particular courses of action. In today's policy process one can see, along with De Swaan (1990), a change from policy-making by command towards policy-making through negotiation. This means that the policy process increasingly depends upon the specific structural dependencies between public and private stakeholders and their ongoing negotiation over the maintenance or reconstitution of rules. In order to analyse the politics of policy-making I will consider the policy process as a complex action system, in which actors or *stakeholders* are involved in forming temporary alliances for particular limited purposes, collectively promoting certain issues or hiding others from political attention. The stakeholder concept refers to any group whose collective behaviour can directly affect the focal organization's future, but which is not under the organization's direct control (Evan 1976; Freeman 1984). Stakeholder analysis attempts to identify the major and minor parties and their interests that are critical to the firm's functioning, and how they affect and are affected by the focal organization. The stakeholders in the policy process do act and pursue their objectives within the rules defined by the established institutional framework. At the same time, these rules also provide a (potential) arena for conflict, in which some actors strive to change any institutional constraints in their favour. I will, therefore, focus on the importance of firms, strategic alliances or industrial groups as economic actors, and their increasing ability to shape the rules of the competitive process.

The policy process itself could be typified as a game of antagonistic co-operation embedded within specific government-industry networks, which encompasses multi-level and mixed sub-games, nested games and multiple ties among numerous interdependent stakeholders (Wassenberg 1985). The participation of the stakeholders, their mutual dependencies and the strategic interactions between them to (re)shape the negotiated order, are the central elements in such an approach. Wassenberg (1991: 183) has defined negotiation as "a process of potentially opportunistic transactions by which two or more parties (organizations, groups and individuals) with partly conflicting interests try to reach a more satisfactory result, by co-ordinating their behaviour, than they might have done otherwise." The negotiation behaviour of actors is aimed at the scope of their mutual dependence, by recognizing the ambitions, plans and interests of their allies and adversaries, and also by getting support from the various stakeholders, for or against, a change in public policy. The negotiation perspective attempts to make it clear that the availability of blueprints is no guarantee of effective development of policies, but basically, policy and strategy are the products of bargaining within and between mutually dependent organizations. The disposal of discretionary power for the players involved in that respect is crucial, i.e. whether the possessor of power is able to change the range of options open to others without apparently putting pressure on them directly to take one decision or make one choice rather than another.

In a democratic society, politics means discussion, bargaining and searching for compromises. The policy struggle basically takes the form of competing efforts to influence those in a position to make the formal allocation of values and resources. Also the laying down of industrial regulation by government involves values, interests, conflicts between politicians, administrators and other stakeholders. The strategic choice between different governance modes of industry can be considered as a strategic game in which interests and values of the involved parties matter and where the political-economic organization of society is at stake. Regulated firms and industries, public agencies and other actors operate within the political and administrative process just as they operate in the market (Vietor 1989). For public or private companies that want to operate effectively in a regulatory environment, they must be active in both the market place and the political arena and link their business plans with complementary political action. For instance, a strategy often followed by organizations operating in (semi-)public spheres to control their (potentially) hostile environment is co-optation, defined by Selznick (1949/1980: 13) as: "the process of absorbing new elements into the leadership or policy determining structure of an organization as a means of averting threats to its stability or existence." The larger business environment provides opportunities for strategic and tactical behaviour: the realization of economic objectives and innovation could be used as offensive means and information gathering, co-optation of experts, lobbying, cross-subsidization and litigation are illustrations of more defensive means of strengthening one's position. Both established parties and prospective entrants try to make extensive strategic use of information in the administrative process; these actors take virtually every opportunity to make detailed economic and technical information available and understandable in ways which emphasize the strengths of their cases and diminish, or at least obscure, the weaker points. The affected parties in regulatory policy-making can also respond by pursuing delaying tactics: for instance, by flooding the agency with more information than it can absorb. The responsibility of regulators is to sift through the information received and differentiate between arguments that reflect only special interests and those that support the public interest (as perceived by the policy-makers).

The negotiation perspective provides a lucid process-oriented perspective on policy-making and strategic interactions among public and private actors. The theory disregards, however, the persistent influence of institutional arrangements that constrain bargaining processes. In this study I acknowledge the relatively independent roles of both economic and socio-political institutions. The term "institutions" is used in the study in a general sense, referring to a relatively persistent set of rules, norms and values that constrain and shape exchange patterns between stakeholders. From the 1970s onwards, academic interest in the study of economic, political and legal institutions has increased in the social sciences. New Institutional Economics, "institutionalism" in economic sociology, and "institutionalism" in political science, have started to conceptualize and investigate institutions respectively as organizational forms, socially constructed and routinely reproduced rule systems, and particular state-society arrangements structuring politics. According to the New Institutional Economics (NIE), institutions are interpreted as being incentive and governance structures designed by rational actors to respond to economic needs by reducing transaction costs and information uncertainty (Williamson 1991; North 1990). The emergence, functioning and transformation of institutions is explained with the help of micro-economics, focusing on the rational choices for the most efficient outcome as well as the incentives and the benefits, associated with particular institutional structures. For instance, it is argued that the transaction costs associated with hierarchical forms tend to be lower than the costs of market co-ordination under conditions of high frequency, high asset specificity and high uncertainty. According to the New Economic Sociology, institutions are more than merely efficient instruments in the structuring of economic activities. Moreover, the underlying assumptions of NIE of the primacy of economic goals, rational actors pursuing self-interest and the emergence of institutions as efficient outcomes to external requirements are strongly criticized. According to the New Economic Sociology, institutions are shared cognitions and socially constructed rule systems by agents whose actions are embedded in concrete ongoing networks of social relations (Powell and DiMaggio 1991; Granovetter 1985). Besides pursuing the goal of economic efficiency, actors strive also for non-economic objectives, such as power, dominance, status and public recognition. The development and the transformation of both political and economic institutions are contingent upon lasting interaction patterns, shared norms and the constraints imposed by the historical background of institutional settings and the overall structure of society. In the domain of political science, institutions refer to "formal rules, compliance procedures, and standard operating practices that structure the relationships in various units of the polity and economy" (Hall 1986: 19). The central element in this respect is the notion of institution as a set of rules affecting the structure of particular situations at various levels and in particular ways by requiring certain actions, prohibiting certain outcomes and/or allowing others (Ostrom 1986). In the political version of institutionalism, it is assumed that the socio-economic organization of a country both conditions and reflects the distribution of power among the key stakeholders affected by particular state-society arrangements and policy outcomes (March and Olsen 1989). Specific institutional arrangements structure particular kinds of politics by affecting an actor's definition of his or her own interests as well as the degree of power that any set of agents has over policy outcomes. These institutions are the result of previous situations and rule-settings in which human actors have found themselves and that led policy makers into particular courses of action. Given the fact that each alternative course of action tends to favour the interests of particular stakeholders over others, the parties involved will bargain over certain institutions and policy outcomes to enhance their well being. Thus agents actively attempt to further their interests and particular policy outcomes while at the same time being subject to larger institutional structures that impose limitations on their operations and interactions.

In this study institutional change will be interpreted as being initiated by shifts in the dependencies of the major stakeholders in the policy network and changes in prevailing economic ideas and governing structures, that together make up the governance regime of a sector. Governance transformations are the result of dynamic interplay between the strategic interactions of stakeholders in favour of change and reactions of actors preserving the *status quo* and the larger technological, economic, cultural and institutional context, constraining the actions and interactions of private and public actors. In an explanation of why governance regimes emerge, persist or are transformed, Campbell and Lindberg (1991) suggest five possible factors: the search for economic efficiency, innovation and technological developments, the quest for power and control, shaping cultural beliefs, and the role of the state.

The first factor pressing for governance transformation, i.e. economic efficiency, relies upon rational actors trying to find more efficient and/or effective ways of doing business. Consequently, economic actors will probably select those governance structures which they believe will reduce transaction costs and improve economies of scale and scope. Technology provides new opportunities for governance transformation by expanding the range of choices to make innovations in production, to restructure product markets and to facilitate new entry for outsiders. Besides the search for economic efficiency, the importance of power struggles and the pursuit of control over technology, critical dependencies and market competition in maintaining or challenging established governance structures must be considered. In other words, actors are also concerned with safeguarding their private interests, balancing the power relations with their stakeholders and controlling the terms of exchange under which these transactions and economic activities occur. Culture also plays a role in the occurrence and transformation of economic governance, although its explanatory power is limited. Cultural and ideological factors constrain the range of available governance mechanisms from which actors might choose by inhibiting or facilitating particular coordination mechanism to fit within the encompassing system of beliefs, norms and values of a particular sector. The role of the state in the structuring and transformation of governance regimes is more complex. State actors shape the selection of governance regimes by defining and enforcing the property rights within the economy and determine the conditions under which each of the governance arrangements may exist. The national government and its associated administrative bodies devise policies that might create pressures for change. They initiate adjustments of the existing socio-economic regime and legitimize and stabilize the newly established governance regime.

In explaining policy change, shifts in power dependencies between stakeholders in the policy network and the larger governance regime play a dominant role, but one should not overlook the role of new persuasive ideas, intellectual debates and prior experiences in related policies in the political process. Social scientists seem to be more interested in the "political" aspects of the policy process, referring to elements like power struggles, bargaining and conflict resolution, and overlooking cognitive and argumentative aspects, like problem-solving, advocacy, communication, deliberation, persuasion and learning. Ideas, acting as a propelling force to seek and devise new solutions to collective societal problems, are also thought to be relevant in explaining the formation and development of public policy (Hall 1989; Majone 1989). Whether these policy alternatives become widely accepted and implemented depends on their techno-economic, political and administrative viability and the support for these proposals from communities of experts, leading socio-economic groups, politicians, and administrators (Hall 1986; 1989). From a dialectic view on the relationships between institutions, problems, policies and political events, March and Olsen (1989) and Kingdon (1984) have referred to the linkage of four largely independent streams, namely the flows of the energy from participants, problem recognition, available alternatives and choice opportunities, that together make policy breakthroughs possible. Derthick and Quirk (1985) give an account of how drastic changes in regulatory policies in the United States were achieved as the outcome of shifting constellations of dominant interests, joined with conceptual innovation through the generation of new arguments, evidence and proposals, that supported the deregulation of transport, airlines and telecommunications. Originally, the policy alternative of regulatory reform was developed by economic experts, who advocated deregulation as a way to cut back often unnecessary forms of regulation and hence to reduce social costs. These intellectual suggestions for pro-competition policies were picked up and supported by leading politicians, responsive to public concerns about high levels of inflation and government intervention and/or inclined to free market ideologies. Although hindered by a relatively late and ineffective reaction from the affected industries to protect their vested interests and slow down far-reaching reform measures, entrepreneurial office-holders, commissions and advisory working groups further advanced the ideas for deregulation and eventually implemented them.

The Political-administrative Framework of Dutch Banking

In the early 1980s the Dutch banking system consisted of a number of clearly defined groups of financial institutions: the central bank, the commercial banks, the co-operative or agricultural credit banks, the savings banks and PTT Moneyservices (Bosman 1986). The pivot in the Dutch financial industry is the Netherlands Central Bank (DNB), acting as Government's bank, the Bankers' Bank and the Bankers' watchdog. Although wholly-owned by the state, the Central Bank has private law status to safeguard its autonomy vis-à-vis the government (e.g. the Treasury) and the Parliament. The 1948 Banking Act granted advisory, executive and regulatory functions to the DNB. The DNB could be regarded as one of the main advisory bodies of government on macro-economic and fiscal policy. As an executive agency, the DNB was responsible for implementation of certain aspects of monetary policy, like the issuing of bank notes, control of official reserves and inflation levels, management of national debt and regulation of the exchange value of the national currency. In order to compensate for the main imperfections of financial markets, like asymmetric information and systemic risks, and to secure overall market stability, DNB was responsible for the regulation and supervision of the financial sector in the Netherlands. The DNB adopted a prudential system of regulating the banking institutions involved by monitoring closely their market behaviour and their performance. On the basis of the 1978 Credit Control Act, the Central Bank was endowed with considerable power over the individual banks to set levels for their capital reserves, liquidity, solvency and rate-of-return ratios.

Besides scrutinising the individual banks at the micro-level, the DNB was also in charge of structural supervision at the industry level in controlling entry and exit conditions of the banking sector vis-à-vis non-banking firms and industries. Until 1990 there was a clear administrative division between Dutch banking and insurance markets. The two independent agencies responsible for regulating these two financial sectors, the DNB and the Insurance Chamber, had established a clear-cut division of jurisdiction. For instance, banks were allowed to sell insurance services, but only as independent intermediaries, for more than one insurance company. Furthermore, the participation of banks in insurance and other companies (and vice versa) was limited. The reason for the regulatory separation of banking and insurance was to protect consumers from the consequences of an undesirable concentration of market power by financial conglomerates and to restrict the risk-taking activities of financial institutions in corporate ventures, project planning and real estate. The internationalization of capital markets and the emergence of the European Common Market by 1992, both challenging the existing boundaries in financial markets, made it clear that the restrictions on market entry for foreign participants and the separation between banking and insurance could no longer be maintained. In 1986 the Dutch Government decided to liberalize entry to the domestic capital market. Three years after this modest deregulation programme was implemented, Government decided to abolish the regulatory division between banking and insurance. From 1990 onwards, as a consequence of the adoption of an amendment to the Credit Control Act, banks were allowed to provide insurance services and insurance companies were allowed to enter the banking sector. The two regulatory agencies in charge of supervising the financial services sector, DNB and the Insurance Chamber, reconfirmed their established division of labour in the newly deregulated situation. The restriction on ownership and participation in non-related businesses imposed on Dutch banks was left untouched.

As stipulated in the Banking Act, DNB was also responsible for the co-ordination and promotion of payments systems. DNB was concerned about the cashflows between financial institutions and the "public" functions of funds transfer, such as ensuring equal access for providers, standardization, efficiency, security and privacy, and promoting the development of new financial services. Originally, DNB had been involved in the transfer of funds between financial institutions, but gradually its clearing facilities were replaced by the giro systems of the PCGD (Post Office) and the BGC (the banking community). Two departments were responsible for the giro services in the Netherlands: the Ministries of Finance and Transport and Public Works — the former was responsible for reasons of monetary policy, the national interest of giro services and the stimulation of public saving, while the latter was responsible for the infrastructural aspect of the giro services and the relations with the other PTT directorates (notably Post and Telecommunications). Former RPS/PCGD president, Schotsman (1990), characterized the relationship between the Ministry of Finance and the Ministry of Transport and Public Works as an "unstable relationship", demonstrated by an unclear division of tasks and battles over turf.

In the shaping of monetary policy and the performance of its administrative functions, DNB relied upon the participation of stakeholders, such as the individual banks as well as PTT Moneyservices and branch associations, to represent the collective interests of a group of financial institutions. The DNB recognized the following collective organizations, as speaking on behalf of a clearly-defined group of actors within one (sub)sector: the Dutch Bankers' Association (representing the commercial banks), the Raiffeisenbank and the Boerenleenbank (representing the co-operative banks), and the Netherlands Association of Savings Banks, representing the interests of the various savings institutions. In the domain of securities trade, DNB recognized the Association for the Stock Market as its interlocutor in the policy process. The commercial, co-operative and savings banks (including the Dutch subsidiaries of foreign banks) co-ordinated and promoted their common interests through the Consultative Board of Organized Banking. This collective banking association had a representational monopoly on the intermediation of interests between individual banks and government agencies like DNB, the Treasury and the Parliament. The Consultative Board functioned as an informal platform, through which the various banks could structure internal discussions to set political priorities and develop joint projects, such as the establishment of a joint clearing house, and the introduction of salary accounts and guaranteed cheques. In 1989 the Netherlands Association for Banking (NVB) was established, and included both the commercial and the co-operative banks as well as the privatized Postbank.

The co-operative banks formed a group of financial institutions clearly distinguished from the commercial banks and the savings banks. At the turn of the century two central co-operative banks had been established: the *Raiffeisenbank* for the protestant community and the *Boerenleenbank* for the catholic groups in the country. The co-operative banks granted short and medium-term credit to farmers, shopkeepers and co-operative societies in the local community. In rural areas the co-operative banks fulfilled the roles of both a commercial bank and a savings bank. In the 1960s, however, the co-operative banks extended their domain to urban areas by establishing a large number of branch offices in the cities. They have a nation-wide network of outlets and have built up a solid customer base among small and medium-sized businesses and the bigger customers. In 1972 the two co-operative banks merged into one central co-operative bank, Rabobank, and effectively became a serious competitor of the other banks. The main objective of the Dutch savings banks, organized within the Netherlands Association of Savings Banks, was to promote savings services to the public, the legal form of these institutions being essentially that of a foundation. For a long time this was their only objective, but in the 1960s they followed the same path as the co-operative banks by extending their services to a whole range of financial services (e.g. mortgages, credits, and travel insurance). In 1971 the majority of the savings banks merged in the Associated Savings Bank, and became officially registered as a commercial bank, called VSB.

Postal Savings Bank (RPS) and Postal Cheque and Giro Service (PCGD) were part of the Moneyservices Directorate of the PTT administration. Obviously the RPS and PCGD had close links with the other PTT services. The post offices were available for the cash payments of both the RPS and the PCGD, and the Telecommunications branch provided the communication links for carrying out funds transfer. The PCGD and RPS were conceived as public utilities to provide basic financial services. The RPS was originally established as a savings institution for the "general public" by government in 1881, because the commercial and savings banks at that time did not fully meet the needs of low income groups for savings opportunities. The PCGD was established in 1918 and had a near-monopoly on giro services (postal cheques and giro traffic) in the Netherlands. Postal Giro was originally called into being by government to meet the banking needs of the general public through a close network of local post office outlets with convenient opening hours. Furthermore, the large majority of government authorities and businesses had giro accounts to facilitate the transfer of money to households (giro was the "poor man's bank").

Gradually RPS and PCGD started to work together in PTT Moneyservices directorate in providing financial services to the public. The portfolio of Moneyservices gradually expanded through the 1960s and 1970s from giro salary accounts, automated debits and credits, payments and funds transfer, to savings, mortgages, consumer credits, travel insurance, etc. Entry to the wholesale market (e.g. credits to business, stockbroking, securities etc.) was prohibited. A real asset to Moneyservices/Postbank business strategy was its large customer base of more than five million account holders and its dense network of post offices, functioning as distribution channels for direct marketing and providing ideal outlets for a variety of financial services.

Techno-economic Developments in Dutch Banking

Originally the commercial banks were active in the wholesale market by granting credit to business, and mostly, short-term loans to industry and well-to-do securities customers. They acted as full service banks, providing a wide range of financial services to businesses: credit provision, investment banking, corporate financing, mergers and acquisitions, equity broking, the underwriting of shares and bonds etc. These commercial banks also looked after the national and international transfer of large payments, mainly on behalf of enterprises, to one another and from and to government. Savings accounts as a rule were not offered. Later, the commercial banks diversified into the retail banking market by successfully enlarging their customer base and extending their range of financial services. The rising economic prosperity in the post-war period and the associated wage boom of the late 1960s strongly increased the demand for retail banking services. An increasing number of people opened bank accounts and employers started to pay wages through the bank or giro, rather than in cash. As a consequence, the volume of transactions through each account increased substantially and the retail banking market finally came into being.

The banking sector is a highly information-intensive industry in which dependence on information and communication technology and automation expertize is great. By introducing information systems and with the development of new ICT-based services, banks sought to increase internal efficiency, handle the traffic flows among banks and between banks and their customers more effectively and, increase the quality of their service. The automation process in Dutch banking began with the automation of back office operations in the late 1960s. The introduction of mainframe computers and centralized data-processing departments allowed for the automation of manual and clerical tasks connected with customer accounts, book-keeping and information handling. Facilitated by the advancement in the early 1980s of digital switching and other rapid transmission methods, the automation of financial transactions spread from banking headquarters to the lower level of the branches with the establishment of integrated network systems, and to wholesale operations between banks via electronic transfer of funds. During the 1980s front office terminals, like cash dispensers and point-of-sale terminals, were installed which allowed for another stage in automation of money transfers in Dutch retail banking. While the workforce in the Dutch banking sector increased at the end of the 1970s, it stabilized in the 1980s and has decreased gradually in the 1990s. The recent shedding of labour is caused by front office automation, cutbacks in the number of branch offices and the further integration and rationalization of overlapping businesses activities (especially within the newly-created ING and ABN AMRO conglomerates).

A distinction can be made between two different payments systems, which have different patterns of automation and diffusion of innovation: a cheque system and a giro payment system (De Wit 1990). The first system gave clear priority to strengthening the relationships of the banks with their clients by promoting the use and the handling of cheques. The implementation of front office automation and electronic banking systems actively stimulated various modes of self-banking like credit cards, cash dispensers and point-of-sale terminals. The second system followed a different path by automating the account records of clients and giro transfers, relying upon mainframe computer systems at the central back office of banks, automated clearing houses and harmonized interbanking data networks. Such an extensive giro system among the larger banking community also facilitated the development and introduction of new services, based on the automation of regular transactions, like giro salary accounts, automated debits and credits and regular payments (such as salaries, mortgage payments and monthly rents).

The banking system in the Netherlands is an illustration of the giro model. Because of their excellent transfer payment system and high density of branches, the Dutch banks were reluctant to invest time, money and energy into encouraging innovation in the provision of financial services (Aders 1984; Tijdens 1993). Although densely populated in the provision of nationwide giro services, bank accounts, branch offices and outlets, the Netherlands was lagging in the penetration of new banking devices, like electronic funds transfer, cash dispensers, home banking and smartcards. Later, the Dutch banks have also started to introduce front office automation and promoted new electronic banking services to cut back the ever-increasing expense of handling payments and funds transfers. The downward pressure on the interest margins of banks has led to a policy of improving efficiency levels, large-scale automation programmes, and increasing income through commission fees in the wholesale services market. Besides the continuous efficiency drive and the search for new services, another incentive to speed up the automation of funds transfer was the potential entry of relative outsiders into the domestic financial domain. This threat came from foreign banks, insurance companies, petrol stations, department stores, mail order companies, credit card companies, and institutional investors, who all had the potential to develop near-banking activities on the basis of new technologies (e.g. smartcards) or alternative distribution channels (direct marketing and direct writing). In order to maintain effective control over output levels, prices and markets, the banking institutions had to monitor the moves of these non-banking institutions closely.

The commercial and the co-operative banks started to diversify their service provision by entering the classical market segment of bulk payments and savings of PTT Moneyservices. To attack the fairly strong position of PTT Moneyservices in the mass market of private savings and payments and its lead in automating financial transactions, the commercial banks (and to a degree also the co-operative and the savings banks) took three initiatives: the introduction of cash or salary accounts with high interest rates, the guaranteed cheque, and the standardization and interconnection of interbanking transfers by way of an alternative automated clearing house, the private Bank Giro Centre (as an alternative to the "public" Giro).

Before World War II the market for financial services was strongly compartmentalized and de-concentrated. There was a clear division of labour between commercial banks, co-operative banks, savings banks and PTT Moneyservices, each respecting the others' domains. But after World War II this peaceful picture changed, mainly as a result of the erosion of the established boundaries between market segments and the increase in competition through diversification strategies of the individual banks. The wider banking community changed from a stable and well-organized sector, divided up between the various banking institutions into a dynamic and concentrated system. The individual banks, that previously had had nothing to do with one other, gradually entered into competitive relationships with each other or joined forces by consolidating their business activities. From the 1960s onwards, the level of market concentration increased dramatically: the C-5 ratio went up from 55% in 1960 to more than 90% in 1991 (De Jong 1991). Concentration started in the 1960s when *Nederlandsche Handelsmaatschappij* and *Twentsche Bank* consolidated into ABN Bank, and *Amsterdamsche Bank* and *Rotterdamsche Bank* became integrated in AMRO Bank. In 1972 the two co-operative banks, *Raiffeissenbank* and *Boerenleenbank,* merged into the central co-operative *Rabobank*. In 1975 the commercial banks, AMRO and ABN, acquired the medium-sized trade banks, Pierson, Heldring and Pierson Bank and Mees and Hope Bank, respectively. Three years later, Amsterdam Municipal Giro Office, then the last remaining local giro institution, was incorporated in Postal Giro Service (PCGD). In 1986 a merger took place between RPS and PCGD into a privatized Postbank NV.

This was not the end of the concentration trend in Dutch banking, however. The structure of the Dutch financial system has changed radically over the last ten years under the combined pressures of increasing domestic and international competition, the impact of new technologies and drastic automation of financial transactions and accelerated pace of financial innovation. As a result of international deregulation pressures, the completion of the European Internal market by 1992, and the diversification strategies pursued by the banks in their home market, an international and domestic restructuring of the banking industry has taken place. The deregulatory process at the global, European and national levels and the concomitant increase in competition has resulted in a new wave of concentration in the European financial sector and in a rapid erosion of the traditional boundaries, separating the various market segments of commercial banking, insurance, underwriting and investment banking. This process of sectoral convergence in the financial industry is illustrated by the launching of concepts like *all-finanz* or *bancassurances,* and *banques des affaires* or *industrie bank*. The former includes the joint provision of banking and insurance services by large financial conglomerates and the latter refers to the integration of the roles of trade bank and institutional investor within one financial institution (e.g. Deutsche Bank). The rationale behind the mergers, acquisitions and strategic alliances that occurred between 1990 and 1992 was to achieve economies of scale, to rationalize automation, marketing, advertising, and management operations and to cut back on branch offices. This concentration process, however, cannot be explained solely by the search for economies of scale and scope but includes other factors (De Jong 1991; Metze 1993). One explanation of the decreasing number of banks in the domestic market is the cartel-like closure strategies adopted by individual banks to control the stagnating market of traditional banking products by establishing strategic alliances, acquisitions and mergers and diversifying jointly into new financial services. Another imperative stimulating economic concentration was the threat of competition from foreign banks or from insurance companies and credit card businesses becoming active in the Dutch market. The merging of domestic banks would of course strengthen the position of Dutch banks in the European Market, but would also protect their solid position in the home market against (potentially) hostile take-overs by bigger foreign banks.

In the Dutch case, the international and deregulatory constraints of the last decade has led to another concentration trend among banks and to the emergence of various cross-sectoral alliances and mergers between banks, insurance and investment companies. The merger of Postbank with NMB Bank (ranked as the fifth and fourth banks respectively), into the private holding *NMB Postbank Groep NV* in October 1989, was the first stage in a new period of concentration in Dutch banking. With this move, NMB Postbank Group anticipated the deregulation of the domestic financial market by 1990 and became the second ranked bank in the Netherlands, behind ABN/AMRO and just ahead of the Rabobank. The merger of Postbank and NMB was said to be profitable for both parties and major synergies were expected to occur (Barkema et al. 1992). Postbank, with its stronghold in providing bulk retail services to households, and NMB, with its stronghold in providing wholesale banking services to small and medium-sized businesses, could now jointly achieve economies of scale in the provision of a complete range of retail and wholesale financial services to households and business. The, until then, inextricable connection between the capital stock of the State and the legislative restrictions on corporate autonomy became significantly loosened by the transfer of government shares into the joint venture NMB Postbank Groep, and Postbank had the chance to develop into a general commercial bank. Another important merger took place in 1990 between the two big commercial banks, ABN and AMRO, resulting in by far the biggest financial conglomerate in the Netherlands, ranking the eighth largest bank in Europe in terms of market capitalization (*Financial Times* 1996).

As a result of the erosion of the sectoral boundaries between payments, savings, mortgages and insurance, the insurance companies had become involved in the mortgage banking segment. At the end of the 1980s the two major mortgage banks, *Westland Utrecht Hypotheekbank* and the *Friesch-Groningsche Hypotheekbank,* were acquired respectively by *Nationale Nederlanden* and *AEGON*, two large insurers. The business activities of insurance companies and banks became more and more interdependent on the marketing of "full service" provision in the financial domain. The insurers needed the collaboration of banks to enlarge their customer base and banks in turn could widen their product range by collaborating with insurance companies. The next big step in the restructuring of the Dutch financial sector was the merger of NMB Postbank Group and the biggest insurance company in the Netherlands, Nationale Nederlanden. This new organization, the Internationale Nederlanden Group ING, is a financial giant in the Netherlands, and ranks as Europe's fifth largest bank (in terms of market capitalization and net income) (*Financial Times* 1996). After having acquired the British merchant bank Barings, ING strengthened its position in underwriting and started to act as a *banque d'affaires* by financing large-scale infrastructural projects. This first merger between a bank and insurance company was quickly followed by Rabobank, acquiring the medium-sized insurance company Interpolis in 1990, in which it already had a minority share (see Table 1). One year later Rabobank established a strong strategic tie with the Robeco group, the biggest institutional investor in the country. Instead of linking up with an insurance company, the newly created ABN AMRO holding decided to enter the insurance business by establishing a fully-controlled subsidiary, called ABN AMRO Risico BV.

The Change from Postal Giro and Postal Savings Bank to PTT Moneyservices

PTT Moneyservices consisted of a giro service and a savings bank. In 1983 Postal Giro had a market share in retail banking of 40% and 2,700 branch offices in the Netherlands, against Rabobank's market share of 30% and 3,000 branch offices, ABN and AMRO both with market shares of 7% and 800 branch offices and NMB with a market share of 2% and 500 branch offices (Slaa 1983). The dominant position and technological superiority of Postal Giro in retail banking irritated the private banking community. To streamline the bulk of their giro transactions, Postal Giro and Postal Savings had started early automating their transactions. In the 1950s and 1960s PTT Moneyservices became very successful, owing to the speed and the quality of their services. Also the high density of the Dutch giro system was widely acknowledged: almost a third of the population had a giro account. The quality and intensity of giro transactions in the Netherlands has reached a high level over the years, compared to other European countries (see Table 2). The number of accounts and payments per capita is one of the highest in the world. The services offered to the Dutch account holders are unmatched in other countries, and both for the financial institutions and for their customers the efficiency of the system is without equal in the world. It could be said that PTT Moneyservices has succeeded in creating a national giro system which is all-encompassing and accessible to everyone; they have created one of the most advanced networks for giro transactions in the world (Peekel and Veluwenkamp 1984).

Table 1. Overview of Dutch financial conglomerates

	Turnover 1993 (in bDFL)	Workforce	Branch office (domestic)	Major Subsidiaries
ABN AMRO	14.1	37,300 (EA: 21,000)	1,330	ABN, AMRO, Mees Pierson, ABN AMRO Verzekeringen, Hollandse Bankunie
ING	49.6	49,000 (Banking: D: 21,000; EA: 3,000)	±4,000 (incl. post offices, agents, branches)	Postbank, ING-bank, Westland/Utrecht Hypotheekbank, RVS, Nationale Nederlanden, Crediet & Effectenbank
RABO	8.4	38,500 (EA: 1,200)	744	RABOBANK, Robeco, Interpolis, Lage Landen
Fortis NL/B (AMEV-VSB & AG)	20.8	32,900	not available	VSB Bank, GWK Bank, KBW Effectenbank, ASLK-CGER Bank, AMEV, AG, Caifor

D: Domestic; EA: Employees abroad

Source: ABN AMRO (1993); ING (1993); RABO (1993); Fortis (1993).

Table 2. Giro density (per 1,000 inhabitants)

	1970	1972	1974	1976	1978
Netherlands	157.2	198.1	231.3	254.5	277.1
France	137.9	140.6	136.0	136.1	134.2
Belgium	105.3	108.6	111.6	111.3	111.0
Federal Republic of Germany	44.3	56.5	62.4	58.3	59.0
Italy	9.2	9.8	10.7	10.3	10.0

Source: PTT (1950-1989).

The successful computerization of bulk transactions offered the opportunity to attach new giro services for specialized markets to a highly advanced giro infrastructure. Combined with the fact that the market for giro services became saturated in the 1970s (the growth in giro transactions stagnated) it was decided that the services provided should be expanded. Postal Giro and Postal Savings Bank began to co-ordinate their activities in retail banking. They shifted their attention from a single product towards a diversified range of financial services (such as personal loans, deposits, consumer credits, and mortgages), comparable to the ones offered by the commercial banks. Together Postal Giro and Postal Savings Bank promoted innovative approaches to the provision of financial services through marketing concepts like home banking and telebanking. A further step was their organizational integration by combining the management of the two institutions. Gradually, Postal Giro and Postal Savings Bank were incorporated within PTT Moneyservices in 1978, the emphasis being on the concentration of management and powerful functional staffs. Continuously diminishing funds and insufficient harmonization between the two separate giro systems of the private banks and Moneyservices made co-operation with other financial institutions inevitable. The acquisition of the Municipal Giro of Amsterdam in 1979 proved successful, but the efforts to link up with medium-sized commercial banks were not (Schotsman 1990). The attempt to collaborate with Nederlandse Credietbank (NCB), Nederlandse Middenstandsbank (NMB), and the private savings banks (i.e. Bondsspaarbanken) came to nothing.

The strategy of PTT Moneyservices in entering the business market, however, entailed legal impracticalities: offering financial services to business account holders, for example, was prohibited. PTT Moneyservices argued for an increase of corporate flexibility by the lessening of legislative restrictions to entering the market for business services (Schotsman 1990). It had become clear that PTT Moneyservices was subject to a legislation that had become more and more obsolete. The idea of installing two government-owned institutions to carry out giro transactions and public savings was developed in a period when the financial markets were still divided into the clear-cut market segments of the commercial banks, the co-operative banks, the savings banks and PTT Moneyservices. The previously discussed process of diversification and concentration changed this stable picture. The move of the commercial and co-operative banks into the retail banking market of Moneyservices made a revision of legislation necessary. The activities of PTT Moneyservices were too strictly regulated and de-regulation of legislation was needed. Legal hindrances, however, could not really obstruct a bottom-up product diversification of the giro and savings bank services; the range of financial services was gradually extended to include loans, consumer credits and travel insurance.

The expansionist strategy of PTT Moneyservices of slowly entering the business market was opposed by the banking community. From the 1960s onwards, the commercial and co-operative banks, impressed by the large market share of Moneyservices and the speed, quality and capacity of its giro system, increasingly diversified their services, aiming at the general public. A dense network of branch offices and a separate clearing system for the private banking community was established with the explicit purpose of competing with the existing public giro system. After negotiations with the "public" PCGD about jointly developing a clearing centre for handling payments came to nought, the commercial banks, the co-operative banks and the savings banks established in 1967 the Bank Giro Centre (BGC) as an alternative clearing house for giro transfers. Technically speaking, there was no need to create a new giro system. According to Schotsman (1990), the automated giro system of the PCGD could have accommodated all the giro transactions in the Netherlands (those conducted at the commercial and co-operative banks included). The banks, however, wanted to organize their clients' payments and funds, without involvement from or dependence on PTT Moneyservices and its public giro system. PTT Moneyservices of course was opposed to the idea of a competing Bank Giro Centre, which implied a duplication of giro infrastructures. Consequently, Moneyservices were against the idea of establishing interfaces between these two systems. Until the present day, attempts to harmonize the two systems into one National Payments System (NBC) did not prove successful.

The Proposal for a State Bank

In the mid-1970s, PTT Moneyservices was thrown into disorder by the inroads of the commercials banks on their retail territory. Among other things, the formation of the alternative Bank Giro Centre proved very successful. Balances drained away from the Post Office's Giro System to the BGC of the banking community and the broad range of financial services provided by the commercial and co-operative banks. The business portfolio of PTT Moneyservices, restricted to transfer payments and savings was insufficient to compete with that of the commercial and co-operative banks. So the growth of both Postal Giro and Postal Savings Bank stagnated (see Appendix 1 and 2). Survival in the long run required a change of objectives and immediate action by PTT Moneyservices, but they were hampered by strict government regulations.

The social-democratic Minister of Finance Duisenberg in the centre-left Den Uyl Government had to make two important political choices about the restructuring of Dutch banking during his term of office (1973-1977):

- to restructure and integrate Postal Giro and Postal Savings Bank into Postbank, which would be more independent of government and PTT and would compete with the private banking sector;
- to harmonize the two separate giro systems, in order to make the transfer of domestic payments between Post Office and the banking community more efficient and to develop new innovative services like cash dispensers and EFT-POS.

In 1974 the Cabinet established an Interdepartmental Committee, made up of representatives of the Ministry of Finance, Postal Giro, Postal Savings Bank and PTT (the Ministry of Transport and Public Works, also politically responsible for PTT Moneyservices, was not represented). The Committee for "Restructuring RPS/PCGD" had to make recommendations to government about the future corporate development of Moneyservices and to prepare a new "Postbank Bill", about which two preconditions were laid down:

- to ensure a continuation of the public services of the giro and the savings bank by integrating them into a retailbank;
- to encourage open competition in the banking sector through a State bank (Commissie 1976).

The Committee finished its preliminary outline of the bill in January 1976 and in July 1977 the Postbank Bill was submitted to Parliament. In keeping with its assignment the Committee proposed that the continuity of PTT Moneyservices had to be safeguarded by a further expansion of Postal Savings Bank as a fully-equipped state-controlled bank, which would stimulate fair competition in the domestic banking sector. Due to a cabinet crisis within government coalition and heavy criticism from both the Central Bank and organized banking, parliamentary discussion of the Bill was postponed. On the whole, the proposals were controversial and lacked general support, with the exception of the continuity of PTT Moneyservices, which was accepted by nearly everyone. The notion of a strong state-owned wholesale bank to encourage open competition uncovered fierce political tensions and proved to be unacceptable to the liberal-conservative Members of Parliament and the private banking and business communities. The Cabinet stated that the market structure in banking at that time was highly concentrated, the oligopoly of ABN, AMRO and Rabobank representing 60% of the total balance sheet in Dutch banking (TK 1977-1983 14632, no.1-4). This concentration suggested that the Cabinet was afraid of anti-competitive practices occurring in Dutch banking. The fear of cartel-like behaviour was further exacerbated by the successful effort of private banking to break the (near) monopoly of Postal Giro for giro traffic by establishing the Bank Giro Centre. The Cabinet had to conclude that its set of legal instruments to control the financial services market, as provided by the Credit Control Act and the Fair Competition Act, were respectively ineffective and repressive. Government decided to restore healthy competition in the banking sector by installing "a competitive state enterprise as a countervailing power aimed at breaking the banking cartel" (Kulsdom and Van De Westeringh 1983: 95). The Cabinet hoped that integrating Postal Giro and Postal Savings Bank into a state-owned Postbank, empowered to expand its portfolio of activities would be an effective countermeasure to stop the losses and decreasing profits of Postal Giro and Postal Savings Bank and would also encourage competition. This reasoning was represented in the official objective of Postbank, as formulated in the Postbank Bill:

> It is Postbank's objective to provide banking services in the interest of continuity of the desired services of Postal Savings Bank and Postal Giro to society, and in the interest of a healthy competition within the banking community, all the while aiming for an acceptable profit on capital active within the bank and a balanced promotion of the interests of all those involved. ... Postbank is part of the state's public services (TK 1977-1983 14632, no.1-4).

The legal status chosen for Postbank was a *sui generis* form, to guarantee a definite influence of government and without affecting the civil servant statute (Reinders 1981). Furthermore a substantial degree of government control of the corporate strategy of Postbank and the giro services had to remain. Vis-à-vis the future Postbank the Minister of Finance would have the following responsibilities: to give broad indications concerning its corporate strategy, to appoint high ranking officials, and to approve its business plan and the financial objectives to be achieved.

During the discussions of the Postbank Bill in Parliament, the private banking sector showed at first a tight coalition between the commercial banks, the co-operative and the savings banks. The banking front was not against a further integration of Postal Giro and Post Savings Bank as such, as long as the scope of the new Postbank was to remain restricted to retail banking (i.e. the traditional areas of PTT Moneyservices). The community of commercial, co-operative and savings banks was against the idea of a powerful state bank in the banking sector, which, along with providing payments and savings services to households, would be allowed to enter wholesale banking by providing financial services to businesses. According to the banking community, this would cause a serious distortion of competition in the domestic market. The private banking community of commercial, co-operative and savings banks was not against the merger of Postal Giro and Postal Savings Bank into one banking institution as such. An integrated Postbank could be accepted if its field of activities and its services were similar to the ones Postal Giro and Postal Savings Bank offered separately. Government's proposals to extend the scope of Postbank's activities to include credit services to business in order to secure the continuity of PTT Moneyservices and stimulate further competition in banking, as laid down in the Bill, were unacceptable to the banking community. Another element which aroused fierce criticism from the commercial banks was that a state-owned Postbank would have a number of privileges, such as tax advantages, the civil servant status of its employees and financial backing by government (i.e. state guarantees). Furthermore, Postbank could rely upon an extensive and free distribution network through the post office outlets.

The Consultative Board of Organized Banking, representing the commercial, co-operative and savings banks, suggested that the financial situation of Moneyservices was not as bad as had been stated in the explanatory memorandum to the Postbank Bill. The Consultative Board argued that the reasons for a state bank to develop banking activities were either non-existent or inappropriate. Private monopoly positions or anti-competitive activities in the markets for financial services were absent and the Dutch banking industry was performing relatively well, offering a wide range of services at competitive prices (CvO 1977). The Consultative Board criticized the Cabinet for arguing for open and fair competition by creating a state bank without having proved the need for it. The causal link between the existing oligopoly structure of Dutch banking and the emergence of cartel-like behaviour was *not* based on or demonstrated by any research, but simply *assumed*. Evidence of cartel-like behaviour in this case was quite hard to find; a decrease in the number of competitors would not necessarily mean a decrease in competition (De Jong 1977). The Consultative Board argued that competition in banking had not decreased and, as a result of diversification and the settlement of international banks in the Netherlands, had even increased. The individual banks were performing reasonably well and did not neglect their societal functions. Interfering with Dutch banking by way of creating a state bank in these circumstances, in which competition between the banks was sufficient, would create an undesirable precedent with respect to government regulation of industry.

The Consultative Board argued further that the proposal to establish a strong state bank contained several elements that could distort fair competition in banking. Unlike the private banks, Postbank would remain subject to civil law, implying that the future Postbank, just like Postal Savings Bank, would have the status of a legal body *sui generis* and its employees would retain the status of civil servants. Government involvement in stipulating the corporate targets and financial conditions of the future Postbank could seriously hamper fair competition, for instance by setting the rate-of-return ratios for Postbank at a significantly low level, by allowing cross-subsidization between Postbank's public and private services and by the overall sponsorship of government, of any of its (potential) lame-duck activities. Furthermore, Postbank would be exempted from paying turnover tax and would be subject to a soft regime as far as the payment of corporate income tax was concerned. The proposal to create a state bank, according to the Consultative Board, showed a conflict of interests between Postbank as a commercial banking company on the one hand and a policy instrument utilized by government to stir up competition in the banking sector and to serve public interest by securing an efficient and differentiated supply of financial services on the other. The Minister of Finance was responsible for both supporting the corporate strategy and monitoring the performance of Postbank (on the basis of the Postbank Bill) and supervising, together with the Central Bank, all the individual financial institutions and the banking sector as such (on the basis of its overall responsibility for monetary policy and banking regulation).

The commercial banks, organized in the Dutch Bankers' Association (NBV 1980), blamed government for wishing to transform PTT Moneyservices into a general state-bank, which was allowed to offer business services and thereby to enter the sphere of wholesale banking. The Bankers' Association argued that the state should not enter the field of business services and wholesale banking, unless private enterprise was unable or unwilling to meet the needs of certain financial services. According to the Bankers' Association, this was definitely not the case. The employers' association VNO (Federation of Netherlands' Industries) was also deeply concerned about government entering a traditional private sector activity. VNO argued that the creation of Postbank, instigated by the state to counteract the "unproved" collusive behaviour of business, could establish a precedent for other industries:

> A Postbank, however, would be an entirely new precedent: government presents itself as a competitor to private banking, neither because certain financial services are not being offered, nor to save a needy industry from mass unemployment, but for purely political reasons. And if one sheep (i.e. Postbank) has leaped over the ditch, who is to say no more will follow soon? In practice this is bound to lead to political interference: the state will take on tasks belonging to the business community that are adequately performed by that business community *(Onderneming* 1976: 4).

Another point of criticism was that VNO considered the conditions for regulation of competition in the domestic banking market, as stipulated in the Bill, were insufficient. The Cabinet suggested that the Minister of Finance should be responsible for general supervision and monetary affairs while the Dutch Central Bank should be in charge of supervising the individual banks. Postbank would be controlled by the Ministry of Finance and be exempted from structural supervision by the DNB. Like the banking community, VNO expected a conflict of interests between government operating as a guardian of the public interest and government acting as a banker through the "public" Postbank amidst the private banking sector. In order to achieve fair competition, the employers' association argued for scrutiny of Postbank by the DNB as part of its overall regulatory responsibility to supervise the credit system and the provision of financial services in the country. The requirement of functionally separating the administrative and the business-like activities of government and establishing a systems of checks and balances was not met in the Postbank Bill. In short, VNO argued that any special links between Postbank and central government would seriously distort competition in the market place and should therefore be abolished. The public sector union (ABVA/KABO 1981) was positive about the plans to reorganize Moneyservices and extend its range of services to wholesale banking, as proposed by government. For them, the future Postbank would be able to safeguard its existing position on the retail market and could expand into the new markets of providing financial services to the business community. For the labour unions, representing about 40% of the workforce, the consequences of government proposals were minor. Postbank was able to respond to the competitive challenge of the private banks and to a large extent to keep up employment levels, and its employees would retain their civil servant status.

The Political Discussion Widened: Struggling to Harmonize Public and Private Giro

Although the internal efficiency and effectiveness of the two intrabanking systems was acknowledged, traffic and transfer payments between the "public" Postal Giro and the "private" Bank Giro Centre were problematic and cumbersome, taking more time and effort than transferring balances just within either the Post Office Giro or the Bank Giro System. Although the private banks and Moneyservices had reached agreement about a standard pre-printed giro credit slip in 1975, the centralized PCGD and the decentralized BGC giro systems were basically incompatible and transferring funds from one system to another was only possible after conversion from computer tape to paper to computer tape again. The banking community became increasingly irritated by the fact that the exchange of payments took place on the terms set by Postal Giro; the closed and exclusive topology of the Post Giro network required that the commercial, co-operative and the savings banks kept a PCGD-account to make transactions between PCGD and the banking community possible. Unlike its domestic household consumers, the PCGD did not pay any interest on current accounts to its business customers, including the banks. The transfer of funds from the interbanking system to the giro system of the PCGD was possible, while traffic from the Postal Giro to the BGC system of the banking community could only be structured through the channelling of money through the giro accounts of the individual banks.

Thus traffic between these two incompatible giro systems was highly inefficient with the banking community losing high amounts of interest on their Postal Giro accounts. A possible termination of the accounts of the individual banks at Postal Giro, as a consequence of the harmonization of the two giro systems, would imply that the banking community could keep interest revenues for themselves and attract the vast money pool offered by the large number of PCGD account holders. With competition between Postal Giro and the Bank Giro Centre increasing even further and with the potential entry of foreign banks, and with department stores and petrol stations developing "near banking" activities, the banking community decided to take countermeasures by openly contesting the centralized public giro system and enlarging their market share at the expense of Postal Giro. The commercial banks developed a masterplan to break up the (near) monopoly of Postal Giro network by attempting to harmonize and interconnect the public giro system with their private automated clearing house BGC (Kulsdom and Van De Westeringh 1983). According to the banking community such a harmonized national payments system had to be an open network, to which all the participants should have equal access, in spite of differences in software and hardware standards. Such an integrated network for funds transfer would offer substantial cost savings and facilitate the future development of automated banking services.

The idea to rationalize and harmonize the national payments system was supported also by the Central Bank. As a regulatory body the Central Bank was responsible for promoting giro payments and it also had a private interest in integrating its internal giro system into a future National Payments System. The banks needed the Minister's co-operation in forcing the PCGD to participate, because Postal Giro refused to participate in negotiations over the harmonization of the two incompatible giro systems. The PCGD foresaw an erosion of its financial and economic strengths, because such harmonized system would make the giro accounts of the banks at the PCGD (estimated about 500 mDFL) redundant and furthermore would provoke a draining away of funds and accounts of its customers to the commercial banks (estimated about 2.5 bDFL). As a compensation for these (potential) losses caused by its involvement in the formation of the future National Payments System, Postal Giro demanded support for its plans to integrate Postal Savings Bank into a strong and fully-equipped Postbank that would be allowed to enter the "wholesale" market of business services.

Notwithstanding the criticism and opposition of Moneyservices, the Ministry of Finance responded positively to the banking communities' complaints about a duplication of the giro infrastructure and to the suggestion that the efficiency of Dutch banking should be stimulated through creating technical interfaces between the two systems. Also the Central Bank and the Municipal Giro Amsterdam had separate giro networks, which could be harmonized with a future fully integrated giro system. In 1975 the Minister installed an official Steering Committee, which had to study the technical, economic, political-administrative and social feasibility of harmonising the two separate giro system of the PCGD and the banking community into one National Payments System. The following organizations were represented in the Committee: the Consultative Board of Banking Organizations (representing the four commercial banks: ABN, AMRO, NMB and Rabobank), Postal Giro/PTT, Municipal Giro Amsterdam, the Central Bank, and the Ministry of Finance. The Committee was chaired by the Central Bank. Surprisingly, the small and medium-sized banks, business account holders, consumers and labour unions were not represented. The Steering Committee was asked to study whether the efficiency of Dutch payment traffic could be increased by integrating the two main giro networks of Post Office and the private banking community into an integrated national giro network (Stuurgroep 1975). Such a National Payments System would not only contribute to the efficiency of the Dutch banking system by reducing the speed and costs of money transactions between the two giro systems, but it could also function as an infrastructural system facilitating the provision of various financial services in the future. The establishment of such an integrated nation-wide giro system would, however, be a complicated technical and organizational process, implying long-term investment and commitment by the stakeholders. The final implementation of the National Payments System was not foreseen before the end of the 1980s.

In the beginning the main problem confronting the Committee was how to choose between the Postal Giro system and the Bank Giro network of the private banks. The former was centralized, tailor-made for the postal giro applications and closed to other systems; the latter was decentralized, connecting all the associated banks through its automated clearing house. The disagreement between the banking community and Postal Giro was not merely technical: the two parties also had major political and strategic differences. As part of their strategy of penetrating the retail market and building up a large customer base, the commercial and co-operative banks asked for an opening up of the PCGD giro system and an integration of the two networks into one National Payments System. Postal Giro wanted to be compensated for their potential losses by gaining permission to enter the wholesale market to provide financial services to businesses. Postal Giro made an explicit connection between the issues of establishing a National Payments System and becoming a wholesale Postbank with their slogan: *No National Payments System without a Postbank.* In its claim Moneyservices, in compensation for its participation in the harmonization of national payments networks, demanded permission to widen the range of financial services to be provided to the general public and the business community. It was believed that this would strengthen the financial and economic position of Moneyservices.

The stalemate between Postal Giro, supported by Municipal Giro Amsterdam, and the other parties was broken in 1979, when agreement was reached between the representatives of public giro and private (banking) giro over the interface and common standards between the two giro systems. The public data network DN-1 of PTT Telecommunications made it possible to harmonize the two giro systems (Van der Vlist 1988). The choice of PTT's DN-1 as the technological infrastructure for the National Payments System caused Postal Giro to abandon its irreconcilable attitude and to increase its readiness to be somehow more involved in the project. The interests of the two PTT directorates, Moneyservices and Telecommunications, were played off against each other by the banking community. Against the tightly-knit lobby of private banking stood the internally divided PTT: the interests of the directorate of Telecommunication and Moneyservices in harmonising the two giro networks conflicted. PTT Moneyservices refused to open up its giro network and to join the project for the National Payments System and PTT Telecommunications promoted the use of its newly developed public DN-1 as the technical interface between the public and the private giro networks. PTT's Management Board feared that the private banks would develop their own private data-network, and by allowing Moneyservices to join the harmonization project, hoped to increase the chances of supplying the necessary interface by way of DN-1. The participation of the Telecommunications Directorate in the National Payments System would offer the opportunity for PTT Management to promote DN-1 as the future infrastructure for such a system.

In January 1979 the Steering Committee was expanded with the addition of representatives of PTT Telecommunications, and the public data network DN-1 was accepted as the official standard for integrating the two giro systems. Through an agreement among the participants involved, the Committee was obligated to present a preliminary sketch for the National Payments System, allowing for direct giro transactions between the account holders of all the participating institutions. To make the negotiations over the implementation of the plan for a National Payments System more binding and effective, the Steering Committee was reshuffled. In addition to the consolidation of Postal Giro and Municipal Giro Amsterdam, the composition changed because of replacement of the Consultative Board of Banking Organizations by its four constituent members: ABN, AMRO, Rabobank and NMB bank. From 1979 onwards, the Committee consisted of eight parties: the four banks (the three commercial banks, ABN, AMRO, and NMB, and the co-operative Rabobank), the Netherlands' Association of Savings Banks, the Central Bank, PTT and the Ministry of Finance. In May 1980 the Steering Committee produced an interim report and in 1982 the final report was published (Stuurgroep 1980; 1982). These feasibility studies provided a long-term perspective on the technical, legal, commercial and social aspects of the Dutch giro infrastructure, electronic banking activities and future financial services. Reaction to these reports was mixed, with responses correlating with whether the organization had participated in the formulation of the reports.

Not surprisingly, the feasibility study received strong support from the Central Bank and the Ministry of Finance. However, it was heavily criticized by the labour unions, consumer organizations and small and medium-sized businesses which complained that the interests of end-users and employees have been overlooked in the whole process. The labour unions had strong doubts about the figures on the effects of the introduction of a National Payments System upon employment, as provided by the Steering Committee (Dienstenbond FNV et al. 1983). The Committee had estimated that the net number of lay-offs would be 700 (the generation of 900 new jobs and the redundancy of 1600 employees), including the workforce of the Bank Giro Centre of around 750. The labour unions argued that the figures on the consequences of the harmonization of the two giro systems upon employment levels, as suggested by the Committee, were far from realistic. The unions expected that the shedding of labour would be more drastic, made up of 3,293 lay-offs (1,219 generated, 4,512 job cuts) as a direct consequence of the introduction of the National Payments System (NBC) and another 3,493 redundancies related to the introduction of new terminal applications facilitated by a harmonized national payments system. A request from the side of the labour unions, consumer organizations, representatives of small business account holders in 1981 for expanding the Steering Committee, supported by the social-democratic party in Parliament, was refused by the banking community. The preparation for this National Payments System turned out to be the technical and exclusive affair of the financial community, made up of the commercial banks, the PCGD, the Central Bank and the Ministry of Finance, and some minor involvement from PTT Telecom. There was hardly any public debate or parliamentary discussion of privacy issues, the legal-institutional framework of the system, (un)-

employment consequences and the like. Societal actors were kept out of the Steering Committee's decision-making and parliament was only officially informed about the progress of the project after the main feasibility study of 1982 had been published.

Although the parties within the Committee, as early as 1983, had agreed upon the system specifications, functional design, and the implementation of the national payments system in the medium-term, the attempts to merge the two systems into one National Payments System continued to have complications and difficulties. Job redundancies, but also market developments and changes in government policy, as a result of which a kind of privatized Postbank was preferred to a State Bank, hampered the bargaining process even further. The emergence of relative outsiders in the (electronic) banking arena, such as influential department stores and oil companies and petrol stations which engaged in near-banking activities, had already resulted in leaving the point-of-sale terminals in shops and petrol stations out of the National Payments System. The mixed reactions to plans for an integrated national payment system from its external environment, together with internal frictions within the Steering Committee between the commercial and co-operative banks and the RPS/PCGD, caused the actual introduction of the National Payment System to be delayed until October 1985, when a compromise was reached with a less-ambitious system and for a Postbank which was to function at arm's length from government. The impasse between Moneyservices and the banking community was broken when the final proposals for Postbank were discussed in Parliament. In the near future Moneyservices was to become integrated and privatized into Postbank but would still be somewhat restricted in the provision of business services (wholesale banking). As a consequence of these measures the opposition to connecting the public PCGD system and the private Bank Giro system was weakened and the plans for the National Payments System were further elaborated. In 1987, after twelve years of laborious preparation and negotiation, agreement was reached between the major parties about the actual implementation, in phases, of the National Payment System before 1995.

The decision-making process in the Steering Committee had a rather closed character, dominated as it was by the banking community and excluding consumers, labour unions, business account holders and the Parliament (Slaa 1983). In the 1960s the banking community was challenged by the near-monopoly of the PCGD/RPS on public giro services to develop a counter-strategy through the establishment of the Bank Giro Centre to control this market even more and increase efficiencies through interfaces between the two systems. The development towards harmonization in a technical and administrative sense was characterized by laborious negotiations and sometimes even blocked by sabotage. PTT Moneyservices made an explicit connection between the harmonization of the public and private giro systems networks and the creation of Postbank. Moneyservices felt threatened by the National Payments System, because such an integrated system would put an end to the necessity for business account holders to keep, next to their bank account, a second giro account for making payments to their personnel and customers. In order to guarantee its continuity, Moneyservices had to ask to be treated like the private banks as far as the provision of a broad range of financial services was concerned (e.g. wholesale banking):

> The arrival of Postbank and the possible creation of the NBC are to be expected. There is a connection between the two, in that such a national payments system may seriously affect the market position of PTT Moneyservices while it is not in a position to compete with the existing banks (PTT 1981: 5).

The Final Policy Proposal: No State Bank but a Privatized Postbank

The period between the first Postbank Bill of 1977 and its revision in 1985 can at first sight be characterized as a period of non-decision (Kulsdom and Van De Westeringh 1983; Reinders 1981). As a result of opposing interests between the public enterprise of PTT Moneyservices and the private banking community and between the political left and right, and the centre Christian-Democratic party not knowing what to do, decision-making over the creation of Postbank was slowed down. On the surface nothing spectacular happened. At a deeper level it was a period of endless deliberation, discussion and negotiation between government, parliament, PTT and organized banking which prepared the way for a stripped-down Postbank. Eventually it became clear that something had to happen; the position of PTT Moneyservices would become seriously endangered as long as a political decision concerning the first Postbank Bill was not made. In the meantime, nothing was done to stop small and medium-sized business customers from transferring their accounts from PTT Moneyservices to the private banks. Moneyservices was not allowed to introduce new financial services to keep its current customers and to attract business account holders. The deficiency of activity on the business market, due to legal impediments, seriously threatened the position of PTT Moneyservices.

The social-democratic party had two main objectives with the installation of a strong and fully-fledged Postbank under far-reaching government influence. For the social-democrats the continuity and reasonable rate-of-return ratios for Moneyservices were important, but at the same time public service provision and the interests of account holders and employers of PTT Moneyservices should be guaranteed. Furthermore there was the idea of the state-controlled Postbank as a countervailing power which would promote and stir up competition in the cartel-like banking sector. For the Christian-Democratic party the main object in reorganizing PTT Moneyservices was to guarantee continuity in the provision of giro services by integrating Postal Giro and Postal Savings Bank. Their attitude with regard to the notion of a state bank was moderate. They were not in principle against the idea of a fully-fledged Postbank. The liberal-conservative party opposed the idea of a state bank, which for them was just an ideological pet subject on the part of the social-democrats. A widening of the scope of activities of Moneyservices was not desirable because, according to the liberal-conservatives, Postal Giro and Postal Savings Bank were financially strong enough to continue competition with the other banks. The idea of state intervention was not valid because market failure was absent; commercial banking was performing very well by offering all the services the public wanted at reasonable prices.

A change in government coalition of the social-democrats and Christian-democrats to a Cabinet of Christian-democrats and liberal-conservatives in 1977 prevented quick materialization of the first Postbank Bill. The liberal-conservatives in the centre-right Van Agt I Cabinet were not convinced of the urgent need to reorganize PTT Moneyservices; they were sensitive to the complaints of organized banking about the idea of a state bank. The consequence of their opposition was a deliberate postponement of the Bill. The Cabinet found itself in a dilemma: the Christian-democratic faction was convinced of the necessity to take action by integrating and widening the scope of activities of Moneyservices into Postbank, while the liberal-conservatives kept postponing and slowing down the discussions about the original Postbank Bill. In November 1980 the possibility of privatization was put forward by the centre-right Van Agt I Cabinet (1977-1981). The Social-Democratic party indicated that the notion of privatization was just another ploy to slow down the discussions on the creation of a strong and integrated Postbank. If Moneyservices was privatized, the public sector union (ABVA/KABO 1984) feared a relatively large number of lay-offs and loss of the privileges of the civil servant statute.

Under the influence of the threat of another centre-left-wing cabinet, the liberal-conservatives took the initiative and dropped the Postbank Bill of 1977. They opted for a political revision of the Postbank Bill. The revised Bill of 1984 was a political compromise between the two governing parties in cabinet. The Christian-democrats got their societal guarantee of the continuity of PTT Moneyservices and the notion of state intervention in banking was abandoned. In their turn the liberal-conservatives had their demand for fair competition and the retreat of state intervention complied with, namely, the creation of a level playing field in Dutch banking that would not be distorted by government interference ("market conformity").

A factor which hastened acceptance of the revised Postbank Bill was that the broad coalition of commercial, co-operative and savings banks fell apart as a result of diverging interests between the commercial banks and the co-operative banks. The opposition of organized banking lost its impetus when the co-operative Rabobank put forward that Postbank should be subject to the same rules as the other commercial banks. Rabobank argued for the option of market conformity: Postbank should not be equipped with competitive advantages with respect to the other banking institutions. Therefore Postbank should function as independently from the State as possible (Rabobank 1984; Bosman 1984). After the postponement of the first Postbank Bill (1977), the revised Postbank Bill was introduced and passed in 1984 and came into force in January 1986. In the revision of the Postbank Bill the interests of organized banking were taken into account. The result was that the second objective, encouragement of competition in the cartel-like banking sector, was converted into market conformity. In the new Bill the aim of Postbank became:

> The goal of the company is the carrying out of banking services in view of the continuation of provision of services as offered by Postal Giro and Postal Savings Bank, it being the company's task to aim for continuity of the institution as well as, economically speaking, a reasonable return on the company-controlled capital (TK 1983-1984 18346, no.23).

The change in the political and economic climate caused the notion of encouraging fair competition through a state bank to be abolished. An alternative was found in some kind of privatization of Postbank into a limited liability company, to be called Postbank NV, subject to private law with only indirect government supervision and control. As a consequence its employees lost their civil servant status and became subject to the collective labour agreements of the banking sector. This half-way privatization process, however, would generate conflicting interests between Postbank as a commercial bank, at arm's length from government on the one hand and as a fully state-owned enterprise with continuing government interference (for example, through the appointment of members of the management board and political concerns about issues like capitalization of corporate value and dividends) on the other.

Postbank was given permission to act as a "normal" general bank in the retail banking market with only restricted access to the wholesale business market. The only goal of Postbank was that of any private enterprise — to strive for continuation of the company and for a reasonable return on its business capital. Compared with the original proposals, Postbank no longer had any special privileges or special goals and was now subject to the general rules prevailing in the banking market with no direct state involvement and its banking activities were subjected to supervision by the Central Bank. This meant that Postbank was subject to the same tax regimes, had to follow the same salary structure, and pay a market-related price for the lease of the post offices. Postbank had to devote itself basically to retail banking and was allowed to take up a limited position with respect to wholesale banking, but was nevertheless given permission to offer some financial services to business. In this respect government had followed the aforementioned recommendations made by the banking community and the Central Bank. In its comment on the revised Postbank Bill the DNB suggested a cautious entrance of Postbank into wholesale banking (DNB 1983). Postbank developed into a limited liability company although 100% of its shares would be in the hands of the Dutch government (there was however, no legal impediment to private shareholding). Government and parliamentary influence on the affairs of the former PTT Moneyservices was restricted. The Minister of Finance no longer had any special authority over Postbank's policy. Direct state interference was absent, although two indirect links remained: the state still owned all the shares and the post offices continued to serve as branches of Postbank. And thanks to the privatization of Postbank, the turf war between the Ministries of Finance and Transport and Public Works was finally solved (Schotsman 1990).

The privatization of Postbank became a fact in 1986. Its objective was to conduct banking business in order to guarantee the continuity of the services rendered by the merger of Postal Giro and Postal Savings Bank. The continuity of the two institutions and a reasonable return on their own resources were regarded as prerequisites. Postbank's starting assets were made up of claims on public authorities or of a guarantee by these authorities, a substantial amount of mortgage loans, personal loans and current accounts. For PTT Moneyservices the decision to merge the giro and savings banks removed a great deal of uncertainty, as it provided them with the opportunity to introduce new services and thus to strengthen their management by changing from a functional into a divisional organization. Privatization also meant that it was easier to attract more highly qualified personnel. The price that had to be paid for all this was a severance of the close ties with the "mother" PTT company and with the public sector unions. PTT lost its Moneyservices directorate and 11,000 employees lost their civil servant status. Some years after implementation of the (semi-) privatization of Postbank the members of the public sector union ABVA/KABO were transferred to the FNV Services Union which has, among others, banking and insurance as its major domains. In 1988 government evaluated the market position of Postbank. The results were far from optimistic. Postbank was still without a solid base in the business market and its market share of the payments market had decreased from 50% in 1980 to 43% in 1989 (Scholtens 1992).

Government responded by granting Postbank permission to enter the insurance and the brokerage markets (under certain conditions) and to consider the alternative of privatising and selling off a substantial proportion of shares. The continuation of Postbank and the prolonging of providing money services to the general public could only be secured by incorporation into a bigger financial conglomerate. As early as in 1987, NMB bank (in which the state then had a minority share) started negotiations with Postbank to merge their banking activities. The merger of Postbank NV with NMB bank, culminating in the private holding called NMB Postbank Group NV was confirmed in October 1989. The inextricable connection between the capital stock fully owned by the State and the legal impediments on the business scope of Postbank was succeeded by a combined equity swap and sale of shares, thus gradually phasing out the participation of the state from 100% to less than 50%. In 1989 the Management Boards of Postbank and NMB reached agreement with the unions about keeping up employment levels for the first five years (NMB: 12,000; Postbank: 11,000 employees). The merger with a commercial bank considerably accelerated the development of Postbank towards a fully-fledged commercial bank, which became even more pronounced with the merger of NMB Postbank Group with the insurance company Nationale Nederlanden into the financial conglomerate Internationale Nederlanden Groep. This strategic move reduced the share of the state even further to less than seven per cent in the newly created financial conglomerate ING Groep. The last phase of the privatization process was completed in October 1993, when the remainder of government's shares was sold at the Amsterdam Stock Exchange.

The merger of Postbank with NMB changed power relations even more. With this move Postbank finally became a general wholesale bank subject to the regulations of the banking sector. Thanks to the process of privatization and incorporation in the development of Postbank, the far-reaching harmonization of Postal Giro and the Bank Giro system finally seemed feasible. From 1987 onwards the incompatibility between the giro systems had been reduced to an exchange of computer tapes, reducing paperwork but still presupposing physical transport between the two institutions. Since 1991 the creation of an on-line communications systems has allowed for the settlement of standing order and remittance services. Before the end of 1995 the National Payments Systems was to be completed with the inclusion of direct debits, guaranteed cheques, EFT-POS, normal transfers and rushing orders in the automation of transactions between several financial institutions. Until the end, the creation of the National Payments Systems was a strategic game in which both Postbank and the private banking community, notwithstanding their commitments to collaborate, pursued their individual interests and attempted to preserve their financial and customer base.

In 1987 the commercial banks and Postbank decided to work together in the creation of a joint network for electronic funds transfer at points-of-sale. This sector-wide EFT-POS network, called Beanet and installed in 1989, was temporarily exempted from anti-trust rulings by the Dutch government because of its experimental character. This collaborative effort to create a joint network was instigated by the banking community and Postbank between 1985-87 to co-ordinate the various competitive experiments with on-line payment systems more closely. Originally in 1985 the BGC and Postbank had together initiated a pilot with EFT-POS at petrol stations, together with PTT (supplying the X-25 data links), Philips (supplying terminals) and the oil companies. According to the retailers participating in the experiment, the on-line payment system was considered to be too expensive and had no practical applicability. They suggested the utilization of alternative off-line technologies like smartcards (Kolijn 1995). After its initial teething problems, the EFT-POS network, Beanet, became a big commercial success to a large extent facilitated by enabling data communications via telephone lines with associated cost cuts and low tariffs for consumers (Kolijn 1995). In the early 1990s the banking community, together with the representative bodies of shopkeepers and consumers, launched a campaign to cut back the expenses of payments and money transfers. The banks also proposed the step-by-step introduction of cost-based charges in the provision of some financial services (like fees for standard packages and charges for additional services). In 1994, the Dutch banks decided to merge their electronic banking activities, namely Beanet, the Bank Giro Centre, and Eurocard (handling of credit cards) into the newly created Interpay company. Postbank, however, has not given up its corporate autonomy completely. Recently, it established *Postkantoren BV*, a joint venture with its former sister PTT Post. Together with 13 other European girobanks, Postbank participated in the formation of EuroGironetworks, which competes with the international interbanking SWIFT network.

Before 1986, Postbank and the private banking community differed in the tariffing of services: the then non-profit-oriented Moneyservices argued that the transfer of payments and the provision of standardized financial services was a free and accessible "public" service. The banking community argued for a more business oriented position, so that charges, either transaction or subscription-based, had to be included in the provision of services. According to the banking community, money transfer was loss-making and had to be cross-subsidized from the interest margins of current accounts and savings, commission fees and value day management. Given the then significant rivalry and competition between the public Postbank and the banking community, the individual banks did not have the courage to introduce tariffs for the provision of services. After 1986-1990, when Postbank became gradually incorporated in the bigger financial conglomerates of NMB Postbank Groep and the ING Groep, the banking community more or less successfully attempted to co-opt Postbank into their cartel-like arrangements concerning the introduction of new services and to make deals about the harmonization of the tariffication of services, extra-service charges and payments systems. Today the Dutch banking market shows a clear market division, in which ABN AMRO has a solid domestic and international position in corporate finance and credits and brokerage, the ING is strong in payments and insurance, while Rabobank has its market niches in consumer credits and mortgages (see Table 3 below).

Table 3. Market shares of the big three in 1993 (in %)

	ABN AMRO	ING	RABO	Other institutions
credit (business)	55	20	15	10
consumer credit	17	33	40	20
mortgages	16	22	30	32
securities	50	5	5	40
payments	20	40	35	5

Source: ABN AMRO (1993); ING (1993); RABO (1993).

Concluding Remarks

After almost ten years of negotiations Postal Giro and Postal Savings Bank were separated from PTT and integrated within the limited liability company of Postbank on 1st January 1986. Moneyservices/Postbank adjusted itself to the newly emerging business environment and the political and market pressures of the private banking community by following a strategy of reorganization, privatization and incorporation into the financial conglomerate ING. It has become a recognized member of the private banking community; in other words, the concentrated banking sector has absorbed its former contender, the "public" Moneyservices, into its policy determining framework.

The different banking organizations, i.e. the Dutch Central Bank, the commercial banks, the co-operative and the savings banks, played key roles in breaking the (potential) powers of PTT Moneyservices. The commercial and co-operative banks successfully penetrated the retail and the savings market in which Postal Giro, Postal Savings Bank and the other smaller savings banks had substantial market shares. The larger commercial and co-operative banks created their own alternative Bank Giro network, in parallel with the large-scale giro infrastructure of PTT Moneyservices, to attract new business customers and erode the latter's solid base in large-scale financial payments granted as credits to business and industry. The commercial and co-operative banks were not only successful in commercial terms, but also effective in political terms. The banking community, dispersed and divided between the interest of the commercial, co-operative and savings banks in the early 1970s, became integrated by market concentration but also by actively pursuing joint interests going beyond their particular individual interests and establishing a representational monopoly for the entire banking sector. The commercial and co-operative banks started the discussions about harmonising the two networks and argued that in order to prevent a further duplication of infrastructure the giro system of the PCGD needed to be opened up. The legally constrained PTT Moneyservices had to accept that funds drained away from Moneyservices to the commercial and co-operative banks and that its power position in retail banking was weakening progressively. Opposite the organized banking front stood the internally divided PTT with its conflicting interests between Moneyservices and the Telecommunications Directorates.

So organized banking was in a strong bargaining position and could play off the interests of the two PTT directorates against each other. Given the fact that Moneyservices' position became weaker and weaker, it had to give in and make political concessions to their competitors. Moneyservices was forced to drop its claim of *No National Payment System without a Postbank.* The postponement of the original Postbank Bill was to the advantage of private banking and implied a continuing weakened position of Moneyservices. The history of the development of Postbank is a perfect illustration of a conflict-oriented decision-making process generating a non-decision. The politically sensitive Bill brought about serious tensions, conflicts and tactical manoeuvres which slowed down and disrupted an objective discussion of the original Bill and finally made cabinets — for more than five years — powerless to take action.

The introduction of the politically coloured idea of privatization in public policy-making proved a turning point in the long discussion about Postbank. In the second draft of the Postbank Bill of 1985 privatization was given the shape of a private limited liability company. The changed political and economic climate of the 1980s saw the end of any desire to encourage competition through a state bank, the alternative being the integration of Postal Giro and Postal Savings Bank into Postbank NV, a limited liability company eventually to be privatized. Although the decision to privatize PTT Moneyservices was taken by a centre-right cabinet with a neo-liberal economic ideology in the mid-1980s, this case study suggests that privatization was *not* a deliberate political strategy to cut back the public sector but an opportunistic solution to a long-lasting and complicated policy problem. Originally, the 1977 Postbank Bill was conceived by the centre-left government as a form of state intervention designed to restructure the oligopolistic market structure of the banking sector. Thanks to an effective representation of the private interests of organized banking and the changed politico-economic climate, its interpretation changed from the encouragement of competition through the creation of a countervailing power to the banking cartel to a future Postbank subject to fair competition rules. In the revised Postbank Bill of 1985 the interests of organized banking were taken into account and as a consequence the idea of state intervention in the banking sector was rejected. The emergence of the notion of privatization in public policy changed the ongoing discussions about the future of Postbank. The proposals of the centre-right wing government (1981-1985), which were mostly concerned with reducing the size of the public sector, could easily be combined with the already existing plans for a reorganization of PTT Moneyservices. Privatization plans offered an ideal opportunity to break the stalemate between government, organized banking and Moneyservices by dropping the option of the state bank. The combination of the political trend towards a changed politico-ideological climate and new ideas with regard to banking policy, resulted in the construction of a new, privatized, limited liability company, the Postbank.

The two-fold objective of the original Postbank Bill — the guarantee of financial services offered by PTT and the creation of a strong state bank to break the banking cartel — could no longer be wholeheartedly supported, especially in the new political climate following the replacement of the centre-left government by a centre-right one. In the political compromise reached between the groups involved (government, PTT Moneyservices and banking) every party got a share. By privatizing PTT Moneyservices government solved the vexed question of the future development of Postbank and, at the same time, achieved an easy and direct result with their just initiated privatization programme. When Postbank was converted into a fully state-owned company in 1986, its portfolio was deliberately restricted in order to prevent an increase in competition with private banks which was considered politically undesirable at that time. For Moneyservices the formal creation of Postbank offered opportunities to enter the business market (albeit with restrictions) and thus put an end to the draining of funds to the commercial banks. But, above all, organized banking got its way because the proposition of a state bank was dropped. In exchange for the political guarantee that such a newly organized Postbank should act in accordance with fair competition rules, organized banking withdrew its opposition to the creation of Postbank. By a mixed strategy of attacking the market position of PTT Moneyservices in retail banking and at the same time postponing or opposing an extension of the sphere of action of Moneyservices, organized banking succeeded in weakening the latter's position.

The conditions under which a new Postbank could function were at first unilaterally defined by government — the notion of a state bank in cartel-like banking — but in the end became a bilateral arrangement between the banks themselves. A Postbank characterized by market conformity was formed and the private banking oligopoly was re-established. Before the partial sale of the state shares in Postbank in 1989-1990, related to the merger with NMB, the remit of the bank was extended to that of a normal commercial bank in order to increase its effectiveness and market value. As a result of the merger between Postbank and NMB and a subsequent merger with the insurer Nationale Nederlanden, the state's holding became reduced to less than seven per cent and recently was phased out. So, one could see in the Postbank case, a change from government intervention by proposing a strong state bank in order to induce competition in banking, to self-regulation by the private banks themselves. Postbank has become a bank, just like the others subject to the agreed and operative rules of conduct in the banking sector. Now that the privatized Postbank has become incorporated into the large financial ING conglomerate and to some extent been co-opted by the private banking community, it is difficult to imagine its predecessor as a unique public service institution, namely the government-controlled PTT Moneyservices.

Note

* The title was inspired by Folded, Spindled and Mutilated: Economic Analysis and U.S. vs. IBM, a discussion of the anti-trust case against IBM as provided by Fisher, McGowan and Greenwood (1983). I would like to thank Cynthia Little for editorial assistance.

Appendix 1
Volume of Dutch Giro transactions

	in millions DFL		in %	
Year	Postgiro	Bankgiro	Postgiro	Bankgiro
1968	330			
1970	397			
1972	451	62	88	12
1974	508	192	73	27
1976	584	319	65	35
1978	633	409	61	39
1980	714	482	60	40
1982	746	558	57	43
1984	766	620	55	45

Source: BGC (1968-1985) and PTT (1950-1989).

Appendix 2
Results of the Postal Giro and the Postal Savings Bank

	Postal Savings Bank		Postal Giro	
Year	No. of accounts ('000)	Trading results (millions DFL)	No. of accounts ('000)	Trading results (millions DFL)
1881	24	0		
1890	282	0		
1900	829	0		
1910	1,510	1		
1920	1,908	3	33	0
1930	2,144	6	168	2
1940	2,333	7	392	5
1950	3,877	13	534	7
1955	4,607	11	640	4
1960	5,177	17	788	8
1965	5,678	26	1,079	13
1970	5,638	28	2,225	26
1975	5,866	97	3,418	46
1980	6,559	225	4,554	90
1985	7,332	5	5,114	- 39

Source: RPS (1950-1985) and PTT (1950-1989).

References

ABN AMRO (1993): *Jaarverslag* (Annual reports). Amsterdam.

ABVA/KABO (1981): *Beleids — en Actieprogramma 1981-1984* (Policy and action programme 1981-1984). Zoetermeer.

ABVA/KABO (1984): *Beleids — en Actieprogramma 1984-1988* (Policy and action programme 1984-1988). Zoetermeer.

Aders, J.H.J. (1984): *Marketing van bankdiensten. Ontwikkelingen in de particuliere sector* (Marketing of banking services: Developments in the private aector). Deventer: Kluwer/NIBE.

Barkema, H.G., S.W. Douma and B.T.M. Steins Bischop (1992): *Analyse van een fusie. Strategische, financieel-economische en juridische aspecten van de fusie tussen nationale Nederlanden en de NMB Postbank groep* (Analysis of a merger: Strategic, financial, and legal aspects of the merger between Nationale Nederlanden and the NMB Postbank group). Schoonhoven: Academic Service.

BGC (1968-1985): *Jaarverslagen* (Annual reports). Amsterdam.

Bosman, H.W.J. (1984): "Eindelijk de Postbank? (At last: the Postbank?)". *Bank — en Effectenbedrijf* August/September: 236-241.

Bosman, H.W.J. (1986): *The Netherlands banking system.* Amsterdam: NIBE.

Campbell, J.L. and L.N. Lindberg (1991): "The evolution of governance regimes" in J.L. Campbell, J.R. Hollingsworth and L.N. Lindberg (eds.), *Governance of the American industry*, 319-355. Cambridge UK: Cambridge University Press.

Commissie Herstructurering RPS/PCGD (1976): *Voorontwerp Postbankwet. Advies van de Commissie Herstructurering RPS/PCGD* (Preliminary sketch of the Postbank Bill. Recommendations from the Committee Restructuring RPS/PCGD). Den Haag.

CvO (1977): *Commentaar op het Ontwerp Postbankwet. 27.10.1977* (Comment on Postbank Bill October 27, 1977). Amsterdam: College van Overleg van de Gezamelijke Banken.

De Jong, A.D. (1977): "Het Ontwerp Postbankwet (The Postbank Bill)" *Economisch-Statistische Berichten* December 7: 1226-1228.

De Jong, H.W. (1991): "De Concentratie in het Bank — en Verzekeringswezen. (Concentation in banking and insurance)" *Economisch Statistische Berichten* May 1: 445-449.

De Swaan, A. (1990): *The management of normality. Critical essays in health and welfare.* London: Routledge.

De Wit, G.R. (1990): "The character of technological change and employment in banking: A case study of the automated clearing house (BGC)" in C. Freeman and L. Soete (eds.), *New Explorations in the Economics of Technical Change*, 95-119. London: Pinter.

Derthick, M. and P.J Quirk (1985): *The politics of deregulation.* Washington: Brookings.

Dienstenbond FNV, Dienstenbond CNV, ABVA/KABO and CFO (1983): *Werkgelegendheidsconsequenties van het Nationaal Betalingscircuit* (Employment consequences of the National Payments System). Woerden.

DNB De Nederlandsche Bank (1983): Postbank. Letter November 16. Amsterdam.

Evan, W.M. (1976): *Organization theory. Structures, systems, and environments.* New York: Wiley and Sons.

Financial Times (1996): "European results analysis: banks." June 17: 25.

Fisher, F.M., J.J. McGowan and J.E. Greenwood (1983): *Folded, spindled and mutilated: Economic analysis and U.S. vs. IBM.* Cambridge MA: MIT Press.

Fortis (1993): *Jaarverslag* (Annual reports). Brussels.

Freeman, R.E. (1984): *Strategic management: A stakeholder's approach.* Marshfield: Pitman.

Granovetter, M. (1985): "Economic action and social structure: The problem of embeddedness." *American Journal of Sociology* 91: 481-510.

Hall, P. (1986): *Governing the economy: The politics of state intervention in Britain and France.* New York: Oxford University Press.

Hall, P. (ed.) (1989): *The political power of economic ideas: Keynesianism across nations.* Princeton: Princeton University Press.

ING (1993): *Jaarverslag* (Annual reports). Amsterdam.

Johnson, C. (1982): *MITI and the Japanese miracle. The growth of industrial policy 1925-1975.* Stanford: Stanford University Press.

Kingdon, J.W. (1984): *Agendas, alternatives and public policies.* Boston: Little, Brown and Company.

Kolijn, R.J. (1995): "De ontwikkeling van het elektronisch betalen in Nederland (The development of electronic banking in the Netherlands)." *Informatie* 37 (2): 123-128.

Kulsdom, D. and M. Van De Westeringh (1983): "Postbank en particuliere banken. Kan eenstaatsbedrijf overleven? (Postbank and private banks: Can a state enterprise survive?)." *Tijdschrift voor politieke economie* 7 (1): 88-102.

Majone, G. (1989): *Evidence, argument, and persuasion in the policy process.* New Haven: Yale University Press.

March, J.G. and J.P. Olsen (1989): *Rediscovering institutions. The organizational basis of politics.* New York: Free Press.

Metze, M. (1993): *De geur van geld. Een opmerkelijk Bankafschrift* (The smell of money: A striking bank statement). Nijmegen: SUN.

NBV Nederlandse Bankiers Vereniging (1980): Letter to the Second Chamber of Parliament, June 23. Amsterdam.

North, D.C. (1990): *Institutions, institutional change and economic performance.* Cambridge: Cambridge University Press.

Onderneming (periodical of the Federation of Netherlands' Industries VNO) (1976): "Postbank: gevaarlijk precedent (Postbank: dangerous precedent)." May 7. The Hague: VNO.

Ostrom, E. (1986): "An agenda for the study of institutions." *Public Choice* 48: 3-25.

Peekel, M. and J.W. Veluwenkamp (1984): *Het girale betalingsverkeer in Nederland* (Giral payments traffic in the Netherlands). Deventer: Kluwer.

Powell, W.W. and P.J. DiMaggio (eds.) (1991): *The new institutionalism in organizational analysis.* Chicago: University of Chicago Press.

PTT (1950-1989): *Jaarverslagen* (Annual reports). The Hague.

RABO (1993): *Jaarverslag* (Annual report). Utrecht/Eindhoven.

Rabobank (1984): Brief aan de bijzondere Tweede Kamer Commissie inzake de Postbank (Letter to the Parliamentary Commission in the matter of the Postbank), August 28. Utrecht/Eindhoven.

Reinders, A. (1981): "Het wetsontwerp Postbank (The Postbank Bill)." *Beleid en maatschappij* March/April: 121-129.

RPS (1950-1985): *Jaarverslagen* (Annual reports). The Hague.

Scholtens, L.J.R. (1992): "Opkomst en ondergang van de Postbank (Rise and fall of the Postbank)." *Bedrijfskunde* 64: 180-189.

Schotsman, C.J. (1990): *De Postbank. ontstaan en ontplooiing* (The Postbank: Origin and development). Gravenhage: SDU.

Selznick, P. (1949/1980): *TVA and the grass roots. A study of politics and organization.* Berkeley: University of California Press.
Slaa, P. (1983): "Elektronische Betaalsystemen en het Nationaal Betalingscircuit. Beheersbaar of niet? (Electronic payments systems and the National Payment System. Controllable or not?)." *Tijdschrift voor Politieke Ekonomie* 7(1): 65-87.
Stuurgroep Integratie Giroverkeer (1975): *Mandaat* (Mandate). 25.11.1975. Amsterdam: DNB.
Stuurgroep Integratie Giroverkeer (1980): *Onderzoek Voorontwerp Nationaal Betalingscircuitmet Gebruikmaking van het Openbare Datanet DN-1* (Preliminary sketch of a National Payments Systems utilizing the the public datanetwork DN-1). Amsterdam.
Stuurgroep Integratie Giroverkeer (1982): *Contouren van een Nationaal Betalingscircuit* (Shaping the National Payments System). Amsterdam.
Tijdens, K. (1993): "25 Jaar produkt — en procesinnovatieprocessen van het binnenlandse girale betalingsverkeer in het bankwezen. De ontwikkeling van informatietechnologie in de dienstensector. (25 Year product — and process innovation processes of domestic giro payments in banking. The development of information technology in the services sector.)." *Tijdschrift voor Politieke Economie* 15(3): 67-89.
TK Dutch Parliament (1977-1983): "Regelingen inzake de Postbank (Postbank regulations)." No.14632. Den Haag.
TK Dutch Parliament (1983-1984): "Regelen met betrekking tot de Oprichting van de PostbankN.V. (Postbank Bill)." 18346, no.23. Den Haag.
Van der Vlist, P. (1988): *Telematica netwerken* (Telematics Networks). Amsterdam: Tutein Nolthenius.
Vietor, R.H.K. (1989): *Strategic management in the regulatory environment. Cases and industry notes.* Englewood Cliffs: Prentice Hall.
Wassenberg, A.F.P. (1985): "Organizational instinct: On the political economy of bargaining" in A.H.G. Rinnooy-Kan (ed.), *New challenges for management research,* 159-177. Amsterdam: North-Holland.
Wassenberg, A.F.P. (1991): "Onderhandelen: Arena, agenda en timing. Een politiek — en economisch-sociologisch perspectief (Negotiating: Arena, agenda and timing — a political and economic-sociological perspective)." in M.J.G.P. Kaplan (ed.), with the collaboration of A.H.G. Rinnooy Kan, *Onderhandelen. Structuren en toepassingen* (Negotiating. Structures and applications), 179-203. Schoonhoven: Academic Service.
Williamson, O. E. (1991): "Comparative economic organization: The analysis of discrete structural alternatives." *Administrative Science Quarterly* 36: 269-296.

The Double-dealing of Rhetoric — An Anthropological Perspective on the Dynamics of Organizing in the Swedish Public Sector

Christina Garsten

Introduction

In Sweden, financial and social developments in recent years have stimulated, as well as reflected, actions of change in the public sector and its areas of activity. Such changes have involved many aspects and issues, and have encouraged debate and research among social scientists and the general public. "The state", as a concept and as an institutional framework occupies a central position in the minds of Swedes, and carries strong emotional charge. In relation to major structural changes in Swedish society, involving not least privatization and changing conditions on the labour market, the domain of the state appears as an arena where institutional change can favourably be studied, both in the shape of steering mechanisms and rhetoric formulated on a central level, and as locally generated processes brought about by individuals and professional categories in specific contexts of interaction. Taking a social anthropological perspective on recent trends of change and their legitimating rhetoric, the chapter will set the ideological context of the current attempts at organizational restructuring. The following discussion highlights the significance of the place of rhetoric in this ideological context and raises some questions as to the relationships between current ideology and rhetoric of organizational change and the nature of power relations prevailing in public and private sector organizations. The chapter looks particularly at the role of legitimating rhetoric in the dynamics of interaction between the state and the market. The most vital question in this context is then; Who is holding the reins in current processes of organizational restructuring? The chapter hopes to contribute to discussions of the powerful role of rhetoric in initiating and directing processes of change in organizational structures.

Current Debates on New Forms of Organization

Organizations, as the locus of interaction between individuals and the social mechanisms that connect a large number of human wishes and hopes into common consolidated actions (Ahrne 1994), occupy a great deal of the attention of both academics and practitioners. The studying, managing and changing of organizations is a huge industry in itself, besieged by fads and fashions as well as more sophisticated conceptualizations. The abundance of rhetoric and the liveliness of the public and academic discourse on the need for new types of organizations and for new personal and interpersonal competencies, might in fact be seen as a reflection of the significant role attributed to the production and distribution of ideas in present-day society. As Meyer (1996: 247-248) puts it; "In the modern system, the carriers of ideas have more standing than the carriers of action." This means, reading Meyer, that membership in the world of ideas also bestows interactional advantages in organizational transactions. A similar argument is put forth by Reich (1992), who in his analysis of the present economic and social prospects of nations, particularly the United States, outlines three emergent broad categories of work, corresponding to the different competitive positions of individuals. He calls them *routine production services*, *in-person services*, and *symbolic-analytic services*. What is of interest to this argument is the latter category; the symbolic-analytic services category, expected to take a leading role in tomorrow's global economy. It includes problem-solving, problem-identifying, and strategic brokering activities of researchers, management consultants, management information specialists, strategic planners, marketing strategists, journalists, to mention only a few professional categories. Their trade is the manipulations of symbols — data, words, oral and visual representations, and the like:

> Symbolic analysts solve, identify, and broker problems by manipulating symbols. They simplify reality into abstract images that can be rearranged, juggled, experimented with, communicated to other specialists, and then, eventually, transformed back into reality. The manipulations are done with analytic tools, sharpened by experience. The tools may be mathematical algorithms, legal arguments, financial gimmicks, scientific principles, psychological insights about how to persuade or to amuse, systems of induction or deduction, or any other set of techniques for doing conceptual puzzles (Reich 1992: 178).

Some of the manipulations may yield new inventions, arguments, or advertising campaigns. Others serve to entertain the recipients, or cause them to reflect more deeply on the human condition. Reich (1992: 179) provides a rather amusing ethnographic glimpse of what may occupy the day of a symbolic analyst:

When not conversing with their teammates, symbolic analysts sit before computer terminals - examining words and numbers, moving them, altering them, trying out new words and numbers, formulating and testing hypotheses, designing or strategizing. They also spend long hours in meetings or on the telephone, and even longer hours in jet planes and hotels - advising, making presentations, giving briefings, doing deals. Periodically, they issue reports, plans, designs, memoranda, layouts, renderings, scripts, or projections - which in turn precipitate more meetings to clarify what has been proposed and to get agreement on how it will be implemented, by whom, and for how much money.

The conceptualization of the symbolic analyst, then, is a reflection of the significant role of information and rhetoric in times of structural change. In the same manner, the increasing interest in organizational culture is to some extent a consequence of the way in which the idea is marketed. Here, consultants, described by Czarniawska-Jœrges (1988) as "merchants of meaning" are especially important. Burrell (1992: 87) describes them as "seeking to provide the expensive but quick fix to an industrial and commercial audience who, ever hungry for novelty, are eager to consume different ideas before turning greedily to a newer fad in the relentless pursuit of busyness" (cited from Alvesson 1993: 5).

The universalistic character of the discourse on organizing creates large-scale arenas for development and communication of such ideas. Adopting ideas that derive from places and people that none of the actors has ever been in face-to-face contact with becomes rather easy. The discourse often transcends local circumstances and experiences, and may be reembedded in a variety of locales. As Meyer (1996: 248) puts it, "The idea market is much larger, and contains much more usable material, than the market of actions and transactions." A similar idea is expressed by Hannerz (1990) in the context of a discussion of local — cosmopolitan orientations to the outer world. Here, cosmopolitans are seen to base whatever influence they have on a knowledge less tied to particular others, or to the unique community setting. Their specialized knowledge makes them able to leave and take it with them without devaluating it. As Hannerz puts it; "They are 'the new class,' people with credentials, decontextualized cultural capital" (1990: 246). Furthermore, their overall orientation towards structures of meaning, to which the notion of the "culture of critical discourse" refers, carries a reflexive, problematizing tendency, concerned with metacommunication (Gouldner 1979):

I would also describe it as generally expansionist in its management of meaning. It pushes relentlessly in its analysis of the order of ideas, striving toward explicitness where common sense, as a contrasting mode of meaning management, might come to rest comfortably with the tacit, the ambiguous, and the contradictory. In the end, it strives toward mastery (Hannerz 1990: 246-247).

From the above, the current state of affairs may be described in terms of an overall drift from a preoccupation with actual change and reorganizing experiments to an emphasis on ideological construction. In this, symbolic analysts and other categories of "the new class" who enact and experiment with a rhetoric of enchanting power, in some sense contribute to creating the market they then live off. The celebration of certain aspects of market-driven change and the forms of organizing and professional competencies needed are by the same token a way of constructing an apotheosis of themselves as visionaries of a future social order.

What, then, are the dominant aspects of the forms of organizing put forth by symbolic analysts and other "actors on the market"? A quick glance at some current titles in the domain of organization studies gives a clue; *The hara-kiri of hierarchies* [*Hierarkiernas harakiri*, my translation] (Johnson 1995); *The virtual corporation* (Davidow and Malone 1993); *The network nation* (Hiltz and Turoff 1993), to mention only a few. According to these writings, hierarchies are looked upon as obsolete ways of organizing, whereas "virtual organizations" convey a more desirable form, in the absence of clear structure. The preferred form is rather more like a network of more or less loosely connected nodes of individuals, offices, or computers. These networked, cobweb-like organizations are becoming more important at rapid rate; organizations are themselves becoming notably more temporary, losing important elements of permanence. As March (1994: 63) puts it: "The key conception is summarized in the dictum: Don't repair! Replace!" Corollary to the idea of the "disposable organization" is the idea of contingent or disposable employees, in other words an increasing reliance upon temping, contracting, consulting, and outsourcing. Many organizations, both public and private, are now reducing the number of core workers and turn increasingly to "just-in-time" employment. At stake here is a trade-off between short-run concerns and long-run concerns and between gains to individual knowledge and gains to collective knowledge.[1]

Quite obviously, information technology carries the torch of futuristic visions. Interestingly, the discourse on organizing and the discourse of information technology are parallel discourses, whose content closely resembles each other. Overall, they both imply integrative and disintegrative elements. In a relatively recent article in one of the major Swedish morning papers, *Svenska Dagbladet* (1994), Dahlbom and Janlert argue that behind the enthusiasm for "networking" is the basic need for human communication. By networking we are able to confirm ourselves as individuals in a social context; networking as a way of communicating creates both individuality and community. The rhetoric of networking in its various shapes is thus at the core an expression of psycho-social needs for integration with a wider social context. A similar argument is put forth by Bauman (1992), in reflecting upon the viable character of contemporary social structures. Under such conditions, he argues, the need for reflexive thinking and conscious creation of social formations (such as networks, we may add) increases. Talking about our work organizations in terms of networks carries the promise to bring people together in organizations where hierarchies have committed *hara-kiri*, and where decision making is done closer to the individual.

Within the business of information technology and computing, Apple Computer has elaborated what is often referred to as the informal hierarchy of an organization, at the same time downplaying the importance and value of clear, formal lines of hierarchy and communication channels (Garsten 1994). The discourse of networking relates closely to the rhetoric of equality and change. It is ripe with positive connotations suggesting a "flat" model of organizing that emphasizes the role of each individual as an important node in the network, rather than one's position in a hierarchy. "The beauty of a network is that it has no center", John Sculley (1987: 96) asserts. "It is a process more than a structure..." The network model of organizing is supported by Apple's technology, it is believed. This can also be seen from advertisements. During my fieldwork at the Swedish subsidiary in Stockholm, an ad was designed in the shape of a network, where the nodes were made up of tiny Apple logos with the name of each employee of the Swedish subsidiary printed underneath. The title read: "Would you like to work in a network with us and tear down pyramids?" The lines which followed asserted that "The Macintosh ... stimulates a flatter network organization where the integrated powers of individuals give the organization its strength."

The importance of "networking" is also a theme that leavens all through the introductory classes for new employees at Apple. As reflecting the approach of lay thought to social science, which Giddens (1990) claims is a central feature of late modernity, the notion of networking as a verb and conscious activity occupies a central place in the organization. From the introductory class onwards, the individual is encouraged to develop a wide network of personal contacts. Networking is envisaged as a way to get to know your colleagues, as a way to get information, and as a mode of organizing. The emphasis placed on networking can be better understood when related to the fact that there is not a great deal of formalized knowledge at Apple, and only modest amounts of it is used on a day-to-day basis to affect decisions and influence actions. Neither is information to any significant degree routinely passed on to employees and only to some degree is it documented and archived. Tracking information therefore becomes an essential activity, and knowing people becomes a crucial means to get access to knowledge. It is explicitly stated that you as an individual are responsible for actively seeking information. Although a certain amount of bureaucratization and routinization has developed over the years, as the organization has become more complex and its employees more numerous, the overall aim is to keep such tendencies at bay. Therefore, attempts at structuring and routinizing the flow of information are relatively restricted and cursory. Frequent reorganizations on both larger and minor scales accentuate the significance of networking. In times of reorganization, it becomes more vital than ever to have a network of contacts, since generally very little advance information is given to the employees. To have a network of contacts increases possibilities of obtaining information about what is going to happen. In other words, it constitutes a powerful resource, and hence a basis for power within the organization.

The latest bait of information technology is "the virtual reality", as an imagined social world where one may spend time, act, and interact. One may "surf on the net", "walk the netwalk", "work the network", or simply "network." The social constellations that may arise in these imaginary worlds are often called "communities", as in the book *Virtual reality and the exploration of cyberspace* (Hamit 1993), where the author in the foreword acknowledges the contributions of the people in the developing "Virtual Reality Community." Indeed, we may see here new variants of Benedict Anderson's *Imagined communities* (1983) being about to form. Overall, the picture given in the media and by debaters is that of a common land of computers; transparent, flowing, and open. Perhaps the strongest version of this idea is that expressed by the "zippy" (Zen-inspired professional pagan), a kind of contemporary hippie who has appropriated information technology as a means to change the world for the better. As an article in *Wired* puts it:

> A new and contagious cultural virus is ripping through the British Isles, a meme, an 'idea with attitude'. Like all successful memes, it confers advantages on its host: Those infected suffer attacks of optimism, strong feelings of community, lowered stress levels, and outbreaks of 'pronoia' — the sneaking feeling one has that others are conspiring behind your back to help you.
>
> If these were not sufficient to ensure the meme's continued spread in this mutating, anxiety-inducing age of ours, add the effects of unselfconscious dancing till dawn, a strong dose of underground hipness, and a belief that technology can - indeed, should — be put to the furtherance of hedonistic and spiritual goals (Marshall 1994: 80).

Even in the world of youth subculture, then, the same kind of ideas of community, equality and empowerment show up, albeit in different shapes.

The democratic, communitarian idea of transparency is apparent as well in Davidow and Malone's book *The virtual corporation* (1993), as an example of how technology may be used to cut down hierarchies and bureaucratic levels. They tell how T.J. Rodgers, CEO of Cypress Semiconductor, has taken a technological approach to the challenge of removing layers of bureaucracy. In order to maintain a flexible, adaptive organization no matter how large the company grew, Rodgers refused to allow middle-management to form. Instead, he installed a computer system to track the daily objectives of every company employee. Such a system makes him able to stay abreast of each employee and his team, to check who is doing what, whether someone has got a light enough workload to be put on a new team, and who is having trouble. Rodgers can review the goals of all 1,500 employees in about four hours, which he (according to Davidow and Malone 1993) does each week. He looks only for those falling behind, and calls to ask if there is anything he can do to help. The example shows not only how a rhetoric of democratic closeness and flat organizations works in practice, but also the degree of centralization such a system may involve. We may in this context note Simmel's (1964) observation that secret societies also combine despotism or centralized authority with a brotherly equality of members.

The urge for change, reorganization, and flexibility is apparent as well in the traits of character emphasized among employees-to-be. Organizations now look for "socially competent" people, who embrace the idea of change and are flexible enough to rapidly adjust themselves to new circumstances. Such a capacity or readiness has come to be valued as a significant characteristic of individual competence in societies with a high degree of change readiness. Davidow and Malone (1993) even speak of "a new breed" of employees, whose characteristics will be contrary to those who have been encouraged during the industrial era. The availability of a variable workforce, seemingly willing to adjust itself to the demands of the client organizations, favours the notion of "*à la carte* services" (which also happens to be the name of an American temporary placement firm). Employers may pick and choose among professionals according to their demands at the moment. For employees the challenge is to learn the ropes as quickly as possible, to engage in the competitive race for knowledge, and to stage one's performance in a convincing and winning manner. All of this requires a great deal of self-monitoring and self-instruction.

Among the characteristics making up the Apple employee, the ability to cope with change stands out as one of the most significant. By recurrent comments, the new recruits are reminded of the need to be alert to changes and to welcome them as they arrive. The success of the company, it is said, rests on the ability of its employees to act creatively and innovatively, to be flexible and to resist tendencies of stagnation and routinization. Not least does the vision of the company itself — "to change the world" — reflect the idea of continuous change. Not surprisingly, the term "oldtimer" has a double edge to it; connoting both cultural competency, but also inertia and resistance to change. Slogans, advertisements and media messages project an image of the company as being part of the frontier of new technology and modes of organizing. "The Journey is the Reward" is a catchphrase that appears in all kinds of contexts as a rhetorical device, leading employees to think in terms of development, change, and learning.

In fact, Giddens (1990) argues, it is the conditions of late-modernity under which we live, characterized by a discontinuity between abstract knowledge systems and the everyday knowledge of the lay agent, that bring about the continuous need for reskilling. The need to learn and to reskill is, according to Giddens, an expression of a change of social conditions, and of the sensitive relation between abstract systems and the individual. It speaks of the interdependency of individuals and organizations; of macro and micro. The emphasis on learning speaks of changes to which the individual has to react in some way, by adjusting, questioning, or otherwise responding.

The Rhetoric of Reorganization

Hand in hand with transformations in both public and private organizations and among professions, there is hence a boom in the use of rhetoric to describe and define the ongoing process. For example, we are all "customers", "actors on the market." Parts of the public sector become "exposed to competition" and have to "package" and "customize" goods and services. Concepts such as "lean-production", "outsourcing", and "just-in-time production" echo a change of direction and logic. A choice of words with associative links to a neo-liberal political discourse characterizes the discursive flow. As Gustafsson (1994) notes, the urge to be efficient, rational, and diligent, are for senior managers not only a trivial must in order to survive in the business, it has become a dominant moralist imperative. In contemporary society efficiency and rationality constitute values in and of themselves. What has happened, according to Gustafsson, is that modern culture and society have formed new virtues, new moral duties, which are rapidly replacing the classical ones. The "morality of efficiency" is spreading to other aspects of reality than the clearly market driven, to areas which do not as easily lend themselves to be treated according to the same conceptual frame of reference. In the world of neo-liberalism, nearly all societal happenings and processes are to be seen in a particular kind of perspective; a perspective that speaks of practices that were earlier confined to corporate business in the private sector. As Gustafsson (1994: 184) rightly points out; "It becomes increasingly difficult for us, each and every one of us, to question the imperative of the efficiency moral. Even play is slowly being pulled into the sawmill [my translation]."[2]

Obviously, we learn from social discourse. Most of the time, these processes of learning are unconscious, pre-intellectual and assimilative. "Talk" is quite simply the dominant part of an individual's environment; it constitutes the environment; it describes the environment; it interprets the environment. In this way, moralistic talk contributes to continuously shape and reshape people's perceptions of what is good and evil, right and wrong (Gustafsson 1994). Hence, we should view changes in the Swedish public sector as closely intertwined with rhetoric, where a dominant discourse of more or less clearly formulated perceptions of the desirable aspects of "the new society" influences future actions.

To begin with, let me cursorily outline my conceptual bias as regards the term rhetoric. Taking as a springboard the frame of reference outlined by Schieffelin (1985), rhetoric leads us to think about the social context in a particular way. It makes us associate in certain directions, captures our interest and directs it towards a particular point. Among social anthropologists it has been common to view rhetoric as integral to the symbolic production of meaning. Following Schieffelin, I want to put forward the view of rhetoric as being to some degree enforcing, not only for the cognitive space, but also for the social space; engaging actors to participate in the creation of a social reality. Rhetorical discourse enacts and defines limits for our frame of action, which in turn creates our thought-world. In this sense, rhetoric is an act with intentions. It carries enormous potential for influencing our way of perceiving reality, and hence, for creating and legitimating it.

Rhetoric and the moral imperatives that guide our daily work are, according to this perspective, culture producing devices, carrying social intentionality. The use of value-laden words is, in other words, a process through which market actors, politicians, analysts and other stakeholders aim to gain and legitimize a particular kind of perspective and authority. In this particular case, a market-oriented perspective is imposed on the public sector.

In conditions of increasing globalization, we are also experiencing an intensification of transnational relations, which in turn further contributes to the complexity and intermingling of social and ideological patterns on the local scene. The symbolic forms transmitted by the media of mass communication are central to contemporary cultural forms, since they greatly expand ideological scope, permit new kinds of interaction, and produce images that are diverse and pluralistic (Lash and Urry 1994). This argument is further developed by Appadurai (1990) who attempts to detail five different dimensions of such global cultural flows. Of particular interest here are *ideoscapes* — concatenations of images often in part linked to the ideologies of states or of movements of opposition; *mediascapes* — the distribution of electronic capabilities to produce and disseminate images and the proliferation of images thereby generated; and *finanscapes* — the movement of vast sums of money through national turnstiles at bewildering speed via currency markets, national stock exchanges and commodity speculations (Lash and Urry 1994; Appadurai 1990). All these landscapes are characterized by deterritorialization. Furthermore, the relationship between them is deeply disjunctive and profoundly unpredictable, since each of them is subject to its own constraints and incentives, at the same time as each acts as a constraint and a parameter for movements in the other. This intermingling of images, ideological keywords, and financial speculations creates ever new terminological kaleidoscopes in discussions of the state — market relationship.

Bauman (1988) argues clearly that the shift to post-modern society is premised on the replacement of older modernist and intellectual notions of rationality with the reality of the marketplace as the privileged pathway through which all traffic increasingly must pass. Clegg (1993) interprets this development in terms of an obligation such that "consumer freedom", premised on and geared to the market, has become the cognitive and moral focus of life, the integrative bond of society, and the focus of systemic management. Such a conceptualization has major implications for our understanding of the role and appearance of power under new structural conditions. "In the post-modern world", Clegg (1993: 275) writes, "power consists less in the relational field of force in each circuit and more in the way in which the obligatory passage point of the market has become a 'black hole,' sucking in ever more agency and spewing out an ever more diffuse power as the pursuit of things becomes an all encompassing passion." Only for those for whom membership in the new order has either not been proffered or rejected where it was offered does power manifest itself in the traditional form of repression. The rhetoric of organization is, I suggest, rooted in structures of meaning that emphasize market-driven efficiency and rationality, but expands beyond the particular structural conditions of corporate business towards the public sector and its domains of responsibility. The abstract and universal character of the rhetoric does not, however, mean that it will necessarily be translated into a "working" practice in the particularities of specific local contexts.

The Swedish Debate on Public Sector Reform: Rhetoric at Work

During the latter years, discussions on the organization, efficiency, direction, and scope of the Swedish public sector have been intense and continuous. Not only have commentators been quick in pointing to weaknesses, but some have also put forth claims as to how these weaknesses could be managed. In turn, this has led to reorganizing experiments in municipalities and at state level aiming at creating more efficient spheres of action. It seems as though our perceptions of what is obvious and desirable in terms of organization and governance are changing (Jacobsson 1994). In this section, I will look into the relation of public and private sector organization with particular focus on rhetoric, hence consciously leaving out much of the empirical details of current changes. The aim here is rather to point to the expansionist flow of ideas on organizing and to suggest a perspective from which it may be understood.

A significant aspect of the ideological construction of Swedish society has been that of an opposition between the state and the market. The public sector has during the latter decades constituted the basis of what we may call institutionalized solidarity, and been associated with the good will of humans to take care of each other and to care for the weak and the poor. The private sector as its counterpart has been portrayed as profit-oriented, exploitative, and "cool." Reflecting the struggle for establishing a dominant perspective on the relation between the two, leftist politicians talk in terms of "restraining the market", while right-wing politicians prefer to call the public sector "the common sector" to avoid socialist connotations. Labour market issues and policies have almost exclusively been a matter for the public sector, where the rights of the workforce have been protected by careful laws and regulations. Recently, however, the labour market has been subject to de-regulation, with the aim of catering to the needs of employers for a more flexible workforce, both in terms of time and skills, while attempting to secure the needs of individuals for a certain amount of security and continuity.

Let me here connect back to the notion of "the network" as outlined in reference to organizational changes in private organizations. Parallel directions of change are being propagated for the public sector, aiming to increase flexibility and effectiveness. With reference to municipalities — under the subtitle "The virtual municipality" [my translation] — Johnson in the above mentioned book *The hara-kiri of hierarchies* (1995: 150), makes the following claim; "Even if concepts like privatization, corporatization, contract purchasing, and competitive exposure are still politically controversial, there is strong agreement that the public sector has to reorient itself from hierarchies to networks [my translation]." He then goes on to argue in favour of "virtual municipalities":

> An interesting alternative to the industrial municipality is the virtual municipality. Like IKEA [the Swedish international home furnishing chain (author's note)], the virtual municipality constitutes the spider in a value-creating network. The municipality could in fact borrow its motto from IKEA: 'A better everyday life for all people.' The object of this organizational form is to contribute to the solution of two problems, on the one hand the financial problem — to get more service for less money, on the other hand the demo-

cratic problem — to restore the citizens' confidence in the local democracy. As in the private economic sector, it is all about trying to combine the best of two worlds: the broad participation of the old municipality and the efficiency of the large-scale municipality [my translation] (Johnson 1995: 152).

Networks, it is assumed, have an integrating function, and imply a more democratic way of organizing in both the private and the public sector. Public sector reforms are pictured as though they would benefit in several respects by taking on the characteristics propagated for competitive business corporations.

Speaking of flexibility, Johnson (1995: 188) ends his book with a musical touch. He states emphatically that:

We must go from the march-time of the hierarchies to the collective improvisation of the jam-session. In this, the leaders are responsible for the section of rhythm in the background that provides the pace, the rhythm, and the harmony. The front-line-musicians use the accompaniment as a common frame of reference for their continuously renewed extravagances. All are free to solve their tasks in a manner that is not foreseeable, but listen at the same time to what all others are playing. In their fingers are years of stored competence, but the solutions are born just in time. The moment of truth [my translation].

The message is that the public sector should not be set apart from developments in the market. Accordingly, an article by Södersten (1995), clearly argues in favour of a dramatic change in the public sector. Those who oppose change are described as always seeking refuge in "the world of excuses." The author asks who has given the local politicians in the municipalities of Sweden the right to promise the employed a treatment that is entirely absent in the private sector, and how is it that they can guarantee that things will not change. What we need in order to diminish the rate of unemployment is, according to Södersten, among other things, increased flexibility and reasonable demands on people to re-educate themselves, and to relocate.

The opposition between state and market having been one of the organizing principles of Swedish society, the development sketched above becomes all the more drastic. According to some, however, for example Arvidsson (1992), the opposition between state and market is a thought trap. Currently, politics is swinging between a belief in the basic conditions of the market and a belief in the supreme rule of the state; "the modern dilemma's two poles." Periods of expectations on the state are followed by periods of dreams about the blessings of the market. In this context, we might pause for a while to reflect upon the content of the rhetoric and what it tells us of the character of the transformations we are undergoing.

The construction and direction of this intentionality has, according to Boréus (1994), been largely in the hands of neo-liberals, who have used language as a strategy for directing thought and action. For example, trade and industry in the Swedish private sector used in the 1970s to refer to a particular activity. In the 1980s, a new interpretation had established itself; trade and industry became instead the private alternative to the public sector. As a way to establish the new interpretation, several private organizations were given names which in Swedish echo of authorities; *Näringslivets Ekonomifakta, Näringslivets EU-fakta* (in English: Business and Industry Information Group), etc. (Boréus 1994). Overall, a new "lingo" is spreading throughout the Swedish society, in which market- and business-oriented concepts are replacing concepts relating to bureaucracy and hierarchy in privatized companies, at the same time as private corporations take on names with connotations to authority.

As regards the labour market, a drift in perspective and use of language has as well taken place. An often cited study of change in the labour market; *Workforce 2000 — Work and workers for the 21st century* — conducted by the American Hudson-institute, pointed to rising demands on the level of knowledge within new work areas. *Workforce 2000* became an igniting spark for a growing conviction that we live in a "knowledge society", where competence, creativity, and other intellectual skills constitute the future capital of both individuals and societies. However, the perception of higher demands on knowledge were seen to spread faster than the real changes in daily work for most groups of the working population. At the beginning of the 1980s, the image of Sweden having taken a significant leap towards the knowledge society was hence spread. The old educational society had lost its role as the leading perception. Still, there was a long way to go before half of the production could be said to be located within the sector of information, something which partly characterized the United States, but hardly Sweden by that point in time (Abrahamsson 1995). Nevertheless, images of Sweden as a "neo-industrial knowledge society" (as propagated by e.g. SIFO AB, Sweden's largest private marketing research and poll institute) took hold long before information-processing labour took on a significant proportion. It was a statement of direction rather than a description of the current situation as such.

A concept coined by Schwartz and Thompson (1990) may in this context elucidate the use of market-driven rhetoric for describing public sector change. From within a discussion of differing political cultures and their relation to nature and technology, Schwartz and Thompson draw on the concept of *stolen rhetoric* to make sense of rhetoric that does not match up with the way the actors are socially organized. Differing political cultures are, following Schwartz and Thompson (1990), viewed as having differing preferred ways of organizing, differing views on rationality, differing scopes of knowledge and cultural biases, to mention only a few of the outlined differences. If, for instance, an actor's definition and solution to a problem are not those appropriate to its clearly discernible way of organizing then that actor is, for some reason, using *stolen rhetoric*.

We may conceptualize the use of rhetoric to describe the changes taking place in the Swedish public sector as use of *stolen rhetoric*. The character of the concepts and images invoked derive mainly from the private sector and the particular kind of generalized conditions that apply for business-driven organizations. In broad terms, private sector organizations imply as well a particular kind of relation to the market and its actors, to customers and the supposed needs. Hence, their ways of communicating with the market are, or at least have been, substantially different. In many respects, the rhetoric is moving at a pace much faster than the changes themselves in the public sector, sketching a picture of the structural conditions, desirable type of skills, competencies, and state of mind among employees-to-be and clients. At present, the rhetoric points rather to a state of affairs more similar to that characterizing the private sector (however internally varied this may be).

However, continuous use of *stolen rhetoric* contributes to changing the culture, which is what we are witnessing in terms of the public sector. What used to be relatively discrete or finite cultures (at least according to our general understanding of them) — the market on the one hand, and the public institutions on the other hand — are now becoming more complex and intertwined, and their boundaries blurred.

Virtual Realities and Imagined Communities: Elusive Powers

The use of an empowering rhetoric with utopian signature does not, however, mean that power has become forgotten or obsolete. On the contrary, it covers a new and equally significant economy and culture of power, in which a plethora of new competencies, skills, empowerments, and states of mind play the leading roles. Our failure to grasp it may be because, using Clegg's (1993: 275) phrasing, "The canvas is not fixed; the palette not given; the style not dictated. Representations can be fixed anywhere, anyhow, anyway. This is the post-modern democratic freedom of the market."

All forms of organizational affiliation entail a relation to a specific set of resources (Ahrne 1994). Somewhat tentatively, a few reflections may be made as to the nature of power in new, emerging organizational contexts. As regards the preference for networks as opposed to organizations, much of the alluring capacity of the term network may in fact be attributed to our hopes that such a way of organizing would combine *Gemeinschaft* with *Gesellschaft*; a social formation characterized by organic unity, sense of belonging, and direct and closely intertwined relations with that of a mechanistic constellation of separate individuals with rational motives for group formation.[3] Arvidsson (1992) claims that all the expectations that were tied up to the idea of a powerful state and what it could do to integrate people into stable social structures, are in fact contributing to dissolve them. Public institutions may at best offer good professional service, but seldom a continual sense of community, he argues. Through the professionalization of all sorts of needs the state is enforcing individualism and speeding the disintegration of existing collective communities. Network-rhetoric nurtures hopes for a new civil sphere of action.

The concept of network, as an alternative to that of organization, connotes personal relations between people rather than bureaucracy and hierarchy. It is perceived as more dynamic and creative. In networks, patterns of authority are not clearcut, and their boundaries are floating (Ahrne 1994). Networks have a double side to them; they promise to make relations transparent, but they also have a capacity for opacity. While networks may enhance the human aspect of relations as well as a sense of flexibility and equality, power becomes more elusive. There is a sliding scale of meaning as to what collective resources constitute the source of power and authority, who is a friend and who is a manager. In virtual or imaginary organizations, where networks are the preferred mode of organizing, organizational positions in relation to resources are not always obvious. The question then arises as to who controls the change, the reorganizations, and the legitimating rhetoric?

Interactions between people inside and between organizations are to a large extent guided by the notions of potential resources that each actor has access to through his or her organizational affiliation. The particular character of bonds between actors are essential for understanding the pattern of interaction between them, even though they appear to be equals (Ahrne 1994). At Apple, the volatile character of the organization accounts for much of the networking and perpetuates a degree of arbitrariness in the structure of relations. Just as important, it continually creates a new demand for what Crozier (1964: 197) calls "authoritarian reformer figures", who "play an indirect but powerful role in shaping the values and counter-values or the organization." Such figures resemble the stereotyped "big men" of anthropological literature. Like the Kwaio big man of the Solomon Islands, a leader at Apple gains influence, authority and leadership from success in mobilizing wealth (read information). Like the "big man", his strategy is to make people obligated to him by contributing something not to their feasts or marriages, as the case would be, but rather to their careers, and otherwise investing his resources (cf. Keesing 1978). Gilles, a French middle-level manager in the Finance department at Apple's European headquarters tells me that "When you know a reorg is coming up, you devote much more attention to talking to the right groups." In reorganizations, awareness of the limits to individual power increases. In Kanter's words (1989: 65), "Restructuring makes clear the realities of power." The relations one may have to the level of top managers who design the new organization may prove vital. Top managers, or somebody else in the social network, may be in control of information about what the restructuring will entail; who will be laid-off, who will be promoted, who will change teams, etc. Connecting, talking, or otherwise trying to find out about who is in control of core potential resources and securing one's interests is a constant preoccupation. Here, not only actions but wordings are important. Behind reorganizations, there is thus a political system where rhetoric is a central ingredient (cf. March and Olsen 1989). The more fluid modes of organizing stress the accumulation of information as a significant resource and basis of power in relations between organizational members.

Following Ahrne (1994: 3), "organization is a link that unites some people, while separating them from others." While ideas and theories on organizations have during the past years claimed that they are loose and nebulous entities, organizational boundary-drawing and exclusive control of resources has not lost its significance. Concentration of information is likely to occur within organizational boundaries of some sort. Again, networks suggest accessible and more egalitarian organizations, while implying as well a capacity for increasingly centralized powers. With increased reliance on temporary workforces, sub-contracting and outsourcing in both the public and the private sector the number of actors working outside of organizations are becoming more numerous. True, many of them are in turn employed by temporary agencies or run their own small companies as contractors or consultants. The fact remains, however, that more people will find themselves circling in and out of organizations to a greater extent than before. While this may for some categories entail new opportunities and increased sense of control, for others it means being peripheral to key resources concentrated at the core of organizations and, hence, at a loss in terms of power. The latter category may be seen to include people with little professional training and expertise, who have had difficulties getting into the labour market in the first place, and who will hardly stand a chance of getting closer to where resources are located and decisions are made. These may very well become a modern parallel to the reserve armies of unemployed witnessed throughout the history of labour. On the other hand, when organizations are down-sizing and threaten to fall apart, those who are outside of them, employed by temp agencies, may even be better off, having the opportunity to quickly be reassigned to another client organization. Organizations are dependent on affiliates with unique qualities and skills, and a person that is difficult to substitute is also more difficult to control (Ahrne 1994). A strong sense of professionalism and adherence to professional codes of conduct and ethics as well as long experience in the field speaks in favour of the independence of temporaries in relation to client organizations and temp agencies. The networked organization entails both threats and possibilities for employees in its peripheries. In a competitive and liberalized labour market, we may also expect changes in the relative strength of professions, with some categories gaining increased weight and others withering.

Flexibility, too, carries ambiguous connotations. In the case of an increasing use of "flexible workforces", numerical adaptability is a key notion, promising benefits for both corporations and individuals. However, there seems to be a contradictory relationship between demands for flexibility on the one hand, in the shape of a smaller core troop of employees, and an outer circle of "loose horses" — and on the other hand a need for increased competence in many jobs. Production may demand levels of knowledge and qualifications that are not possible to fill at short notice. In case of a period of economic recovery, the shortage in qualified workforce may become a bottleneck, which makes companies unable to grasp the possibilities of the business upturn. Also, while the massive advertising for skilled secretaries, economists, assistants, and technicians supports the idea of specialized and highly competent temporaries by glamorous and extravagant promises of "personnel power", individuals may at times find themselves unable to do the job they were assigned for or educated and trained for, being instead "living backups" (as an advertising slogan for temporary employees has it) for whatever vacant position needs to be filled.

Hence, we may ask whether the new type of flexible corporations with temporary demands for what may be called "just-in-time workforce" means in terms of conditions for maintaining a sense of professional identity. In the case of administrative staff such as secretaries, who are in the midst of structural change and facing a rhetoric of flexibility and learning, the development has been said to offer new opportunities for secretaries in the wake of rationalizations. Computerization of routine tasks may entail that formerly sharp boundaries between professions are now being blurred. The duties of the secretary, the assistant, and the clerk are being divided among several individuals. Old tasks disappear, while new ones emerge. Herein lie the possibilities for secretaries to work on more qualified tasks, supporting the manager, working on project administration, etc. Hence, the allround secretary — the spider in the web of work relations — is said to become more professional (Ebbeskog 1995). It is an open question whether a development towards flexible working conditions actually brings about increasing professionalization, or whether it implies a "de-professionalization", where boundaries of skill and competence get blurred.

Professions, Schwartz and Thompson (1990) tell us, have to be socially viable to be successful; they have in other words to be *mediating* institutions; they have to contain within themselves a variety of approach and definition sufficient to match that which they will encounter among their diverse clients. Such a view speaks of the precarious balancing act of temporary staff, where changing conditions may entail new opportunities for mediating functions but also a loss of professional identity and a sense of wholeness and integrity in work.

Temporary personnel especially, it would seem, are caught in a squeeze-play of opposing forces. Both public and private organizations continually have to deal with forces that threaten to draw the affiliates apart and forces that keep affiliates closer together; what Ahrne calls *centrifugal* and *centripetal forces* (Ahrne 1994: 92). Currently, the centrifugal forces are seen to have the upper hand in providing points of direction for private business organizations as well as the public sector. This tension informs much of the shape and cultural character of organizations, and it is also within this zone of tension that a temporary workforce has to act. On the one hand, the increased reliance on temporaries enhances the dissolution of the organization and its boundaries. On the other hand, the central ideological and rhetorical tenets of an organization helps to keep it together, and thereby facilitates the substitutability of affiliates. As Ahrne (1994: 18) puts it: "The recognition and identification of individual affiliates is indispensable for the running of an organization. Still, for the organization to last and survive no affiliate can be indispensable (see Selznick 1948: 25). This is the paradox of organization." The rhetoric of temporary services mirrors these core organizational dilemmas and dynamics.

Obviously, an intriguing aspect of organizing processes and temporary or flexible work conditions is the construction and passing on of messages, aspirations, and normative rules of conduct — in short, of a symbolic package — surrounding new models of employment, the nature of engagement and character of tasks of temporary employees. What type of rhetoric is involved and how is it put to use? The impact of rhetoric, however subtle, may be far-reaching, in terms of setting the framework against which organizational changes and our roles as employees within or between them are to be understood. The rhetoric of organizing is basically to do with relations, as between state and market or between temp agencies, temporary personnel and client organizations. Power, too, is basically relational (Ahrne 1994) and lodges to a great extent in the accumulation and diffusion of information (Lash 1994). It is in looking into the relations of dependence and the allocation of resources between interacting parties that an understanding of power relations emerge. Rhetoric may or may not image power relations in a way that provides a fair representation of dependencies.

Increasingly, the complexity of conditions and solutions implies that different categories of individuals may have competing perceptions of the situation. The intense discourse on change in the labour market is also a reflection of the battle over whose socio-cognitive problem definition should prevail. The above discussion actualizes Brunsson's (1989) discussion of "hypocrisy" as a common aspect of organizations experiencing inconsistencies within themselves or between internal functioning and external imaging and claims. Talk among organizational members and talk directed externally may expose differential norms and values of an organization. It is an intriguing question whether we will be seeing organizational forms and competencies in accordance with the desirable rhetorical formulations, or whether we will see more of "the organization of hypocrisy" as a way of adapting to divergent contextual demands.

Concluding Discussion

The orientation towards a more market-driven and competitive public sector and labour market poses new demands on both employers and employees. We are now experiencing this in terms of rationalization of workforces, increasing use of information technology, a concentration to core activities where specialist competence is assured, demands for more flexible working hours and temporary assignments. The aim of this chapter was to set the ideological context of current attempts at restructuring, highlighting the role of rhetoric in changes in direction of the public sector in Sweden. The rhetoric in use is more than "just talk" on current and future modes of relating and organizing; it sets the framework for action and for the ways in which we understand power relations. Here, I have argued that the current rhetoric of organizing is mainly a rhetoric with elusive conceptions and locations of power. While it may claim that organizations are loose and nebulous entities, concentration of resources is still likely to occur within organizational boundaries of some sort. And even though flexible workforces may move in and out of organizations, organizational boundary-drawing has not lost its significance.

In organizing processes, rhetoric and ideology play significant roles, promoting ways of imaging problems and solutions. These ways of imaging do have powerful effects. Not least, the current rhetoric on organizational change locate the source of influence beyond the immediate volition of organizational leaders, thereby absolving both organizations and managers of responsibility. Just like the efficiency metaphor of Taylorism seized business and education in its day, so does the re-engineering and "just-in-time" rhetoric seize much of today's organizing processes. We may connect back to Kanter (1989), in saying that the restructuring of relations between the public and the private domains in Swedish society, while dimmed by a rhetoric with empowering promises for individuals as well as for organizations, also offers a clear view of the realities of power, if we care to look. The canvas may not be fixed, but we should not be induced to think that it is a free-floating and ever-changing one, either. The market-influenced rhetoric is not necessarily a reflection of people's actual understanding of themselves, their relations, and activities within organizations and in labour markets. Nevertheless, there cannot be a sharp divide between the rhetorical and the literal, because there is no sharp divide between action and discourse. The important question to ask is where these ideas and images come from and in what direction they are going, to understand the discursive framework for actions and transactions. In an increasingly informated society, the flows and accumulations of conceptual symbols, of ideology and rhetoric, are also to a large extent manifestations of the relations and assemblages of power.

Notes

1 Related to this issue are issues of institutionalization and de-institutionalization of organizations (see e.g. Scott 1995) as well as issues of organizational learning (see March 1991). These very relevant and timely subjects have not been made key to this chapter, but remain intriguing fields of research.

2 We may note here that Bellah et al (1985) in their study of American life argue that an outstanding feature of American industrial life is that the manipulative, achievement-oriented practices of the workplace and the practices and values that guide intimate relations with spouse, children, friends, community and the like, have become radically discontinuous in the kinds of traits emphasized and the moral understandings that guide individuals within them. With the coming of the managerial society, the organization of work, place of residence, and social status have come to be decided by criteria of economic effectiveness. Those same economic criteria further facilitate the growth of national mass marketing and, with it, expanded consumer choice.

3 Bengt-Erik Borgström, Department of Social Anthropology, Stockholm University, personal conversation.

References

Abrahamsson, K. (1995): "Strukturomvandlingen och de utsatta grupperna (Structural transformation and groups at risk)." in M. Utbult and B. Frejhagen (eds.), *Det nya kompetenslyftet. Idèskrift om utveckling av arbetsplatser och anställda i Sverige och Europa* (The new skills enhancement. A policy study on the development of workplaces in Sweden and Europe), 6-11. Stockholm: Arbetsmiljöfonden.

Ahrne, G. (1994): *Social organizations: interaction inside, outside and between organizations*. London: Sage.
Alvesson, M. (1993): *Cultural perspectives on organizations*. Cambridge: Cambridge University Press.
Anderson, B. (1983): *Imagined communities*. London: Verso.
Appadurai, A. (1990): "Disjuncture and difference in the global cultural economy" in M. Featherstone (ed.), *Global culture: nationalism, globalization and modernity*, 295-310. London: Sage.
Arvidsson, H. (1992): "Staten kan inte fylla tomrummet (The state can not fill the void)." *Dagens Nyheter*, 2 July.
Bauman, Z. (1988): "Viewpoint: sociology and postmodernity." *Sociological Review* 36(4): 790-813.
Bauman, Z. (1992): *Intimations of postmodernity*. London: Routledge and Kegan Paul.
Bellah, R.N., R. Madsen, W.M. Sullivan, A. Swidler and S.M. Tipton: (1985): *Habits of the heart: Individualism and commitment in American life*. New York: Harper and Row Publishers.
Boréus, K. (1994): *Högervåg – nyliberalism och kampen om språket i svensk offentlig debatt 1969-1989* (The shift to the right – The influence of neo-liberalism on the Svedish public debate 1969-1989 and the struggle of language). Stockholm: Tidens Förlag.
Brunsson, N. (1989): *The organization of hypocrisy*. Chichester: John Wiley.
Burrell, G. (1992): "The organization of pleasure" in M. Alvesson and M. Willmott (eds.), *Critical management studies*. London: Sage.
Clegg, S. (1993): *Frameworks of power*. London: Sage.
Crozier, M. (1964): *The bureaucratic phenomenon*. Chicago: The University of Chicago Press.
Czarniawska-Jœrges, B. (1988): *To coin a phrase: on organizational talk, organizational control and management consulting*. Stockholm: Stockholm School of Economics.
Dahlbom, B. and L.-E. Janlert (1994): "Se upp: nätverkssvärmare i farten! (Look out: network dreamers on the go!)." *Svenska Dagbladet*, 8 May.
Davidow, W.H. and M.S. Malone (1993): *The virtual corporation: Structuring and revitalizing the corporation for the 21st century*. New York: Harper Business.
Ebbeskog, C. (1995): "Bättre med ett halvt men överkomligt kliv (A small and realistic change is better than the great step)." in M. Utbult and B. Frejhagen (eds.), *Det nya kompetenslyftet* (The new skills enhancement. A policy study on the development of workplaces in Sweden and Europe), 50-57. Stockholm: Arbetsmiljöfonden.
Garsten, C. (1994): *Apple world: core and periphery in a transnational organizational culture*. Stockholm: Stockholm Studies in Social Anthropology 33.
Giddens, A. (1990): *The consequences of modernity*. Stanford: Stanford University Press.
Gouldner, A.W. (1979): *The future of the intellectuals and the rise of the new class*. London: Macmillan.
Gustafsson, C. (1994): *Produktion av allvar. Om det ekonomiska förnuftets metafysik* (Productions of seriousness. The metaphysics of economical reason). Stockholm: Nerenius & Santérus Förlag.
Hamit, F. (1993): *Virtual reality and the exploration of cyberspace*. Carmel, IN: Sams Publishing.
Hannerz, U. (1990): "Cosmopolitans and locals in world culture" in M. Featherstone (ed.), *Global culture: nationalism, globalization and modernity*, 237-251. London: Sage.
Hiltz, S.R. and M. Turoff (1993): *The network nation: human communication via computer*. London: MIT Press.

Jacobsson, B. (ed.) (1994): *Organisationsexperiment i kommuner och landsting* (Organizational experiments in local governments). Stockholm: Nerenius & Santérus Förlag.

Johnson, A. (1995): *Hierarkiernas harakiri - leve nätverken!* (The hara-kiri of hierachies - long live the networks). Stockholm: Ekerlids Förlag.

Kanter, R.M. (1989): *When giants learn to dance: mastering the challenges of strategy, management, and careers in the 1990s*. London: Simon and Schuster.

Keesing, R.M. (1978): *Elota's story: the life and times of a Solomon Islands big man*. New York: St. Martin's Press; St. Lucia, Queensland: University of Queensland Press.

Lash, S. (1994): "Reflexivity and its doubles: structure, aesthetics, community" in U. Beck, A. Giddens and S. Lash (eds.), *Reflexive modernization: politics, tradition and aesthetics in the modern social order*, 110-173. Stanford: Stanford University Press.

Lash, S. and J. Urry (1994): *Economies of signs and space*. London: Sage.

March, J.G. (1991): "Exploration and exploitation in organizational learning." *Organization Science* 2(1): 71-87, February.

March, J.G. (1994): "Organizations and the future" in J.G. March, *Three lectures on efficiency and adaptiveness in organizations*, 47-65. Helsingfors: Swedish School of Economics and Business Administration, Research Report 32.

March, J.G. and J.P. Olsen (1989): *Rediscovering institutions: the organizational basis of politics*. New York: The Free Press.

Marshall, J. (1994): "Zippies!" *Wired*, May: 79-84, 130-134.

Meyer, J.W. (1996): "Otherhood: the promulgation and transmission of ideas in the modern organizational environment" in B. Czarniawska-Jœrges and G. Sevón (eds.), *Translating organizational change*, 241-252. Berlin: Walter de Gruyter.

Reich, R.B. (1992): *The work of nations: preparing ourselves for 21st-century capitalism*. New York: Vintage Books.

Schieffelin, E.L. (1985): "Performance and the cultural construction of reality." *American Ethnologist* 12: 707-724.

Schwartz, M. and M. Thompson (1990): *Divided we stand: Redefining politics, technology and social choice*. New York: Harvester Wheatsheaf.

Scott, R.W. (1995): *Institutions and organizations*. Thousand Oaks: Sage.

Sculley, J. with J.A. Byrne (1987): *Odyssey. Pepsi to Apple...A journey of adventure, ideas, and the future*. New York: Harper and Row Publishers.

Selznick, P. (1948): "Foundations on the theory of organization." *American Sociological Review* 13 (1): 25-35.

Simmel, G. (1964): "The secret society" in K.H. Wolff (ed.), *The sociology of Georg Simmel*, 345-376. New York: Free Press.

Södersten, B. (1995): "Sätt klockan på vården! (Time measure health care services!)." *Dagens Nyheter*, February 11.

Part Two
Economic Challenges, Societal Resources, and Organizational Forms

Vertical Integration into Electronics: Transaction Costs and Organization Domain

Arndt Sorge

Introduction

Transaction cost theory (TCT) had been posited, by Oliver Williamson, as a theoretically rigorous way of explaining the institutions that regulate transactions in the face of bounded rationality and opportunism in capitalist economies. The approach was developed with a particular concern with theoretical stringency, developing a complex array of typologies and predictions from a parsimonious foundation of assumptions. There have been a number of attempts to test the approach (Baur 1990). Despite divergent results and interpretations, the relevance of Williamson's explanation of vertical integration has become well established. Vertical integration has been the "core business" of TCT since its inception.

On the other hand, there has also been criticism of this approach which has pointed at the neglect of social relations and factors such as power, legitimacy, domination and coalitions of interests (Scarbrough 1995). Such critiques have emphasized the need to consider the "embeddedness" of transactions, rather than starting with the characteristics of individual transactions. The single-mindedness of the opposition between "market" and "hierarchy" as alternative mechanisms of co-ordination has also been criticized (Hennart 1993). An argument was built for a continuum between markets and hierarchies with a "swollen middle", in which "relational contracting" mediates between the more extreme co-ordination mechanisms. However, choices made in the "swollen middle" between market and hierarchy might be taken into consideration in a way to refine TCT instead of contradicting it. Intermediate degrees of vertical integration, with relational contracting in alliances or networks, can be perceived as linked with intermediate degrees of asset specificity, complexity/uncertainty and frequency.

Douma and Schreuder (1992) have made the simple but important point that TCT is ignorant about the variety of internal coordination forms used in organizations, and their prevalence under specific contexts. TCT has become excessively concerned with hierarchical control. On the other hand, the theoretical core of the approach is sufficiently general to allow further refinement of co-ordination mechanisms, all of them related to specific transaction cost situations characterized by different combinations of values on acknowledged TCT contingencies. There have been difficulties of measuring transaction costs, and the explanatory contingencies of asset specificity, technological separability and information impactedness. Researchers have, nevertheless, found specific operationalizations for certain tests.

Such tests have also been carried out in the electronic components industry and they have confirmed, to a large extent, the effects of asset specificity and information impactedness on vertical integration (Anderson 1985; Anderson and Schmittlein 1984). What they addressed, however, was the vertical integration of the sales force. The present study tests TCT in the more technical (development and production) fields of electronic components and modules. It looks at the introduction into manufactured products of microelectronics components (memory chips, micro-processors and other highly miniaturized, condensed and integrated circuits of transistor functions) and modules, or of complete sets of equipment incorporating such components. Microelectronics has become increasingly applied, not only in electronics and data processing products proper, but also within other products like motor cars, aeroplanes, machine-tools, washing machines, even Christmas cards with a jingle on. This diffusion process of microelectronics into all kinds of products has evidently given rise to the question, which every manufacturer had to answer, where to have such components, modules or sets developed, designed and produced. This is a classical make-or-buy decision which can be analyzed by applying TCT.

The chapter will introduce, first, some theoretical and operational concepts in the line of TCT and summarize the hypotheses to be tested. Subsequently, the methodology of the research projects which supplied the information for these tests will be discussed. The main data source is a study of the diffusion of microelectronics into products in West Germany in which the author was involved (Beuschel et al. 1988). TCT will then be tested against cross-sectional information, gathered in firms about their vertical integration situation at the time of investigation. This will be followed by an examination of changes in vertical integration arrangements over time in the sites that were studied and the motivation and experience with which these changes were associated. Although longitudinal studies are potentially very informative for learning about the motives behind the vertical integration of enterprises, such longitudinal comparisons are hard to find in this field. The present chapter will show that the longitudinal element in the study leads to results with an accent that is different from the one that emerges from the cross-sectional part of the comparison.

Since the field investigation was duplicated in Britain, this chapter will also examine to what extent TCT helped explain Anglo-German differences that have already been reported (Campbell et al. 1989). In the final section of the chapter interpretations are summarized and some more general conclusions with regard to the position of TCT in organization theory are put forward.

Conceptual Framework and Hypotheses

Williamson (1985) has argued that the costs of a transaction will determine the choice that economic actors make between alternative institutional arrangements, with regard to the arrangement under which the transaction is to be carried out. Actors will compare transaction costs under alternative arrangements, and they will strive for that arrangement which minimizes their transaction costs. They will thus arrive at market transactions, transactions within organizations, or intermediate solutions in which socially instituted relations and market contracts of different types are blended.

The costs of a transaction under respective institutional arrangements, will depend on a number of factors, which were summarized by Douma and Schreuder (1992) as asset specificity, uncertainty/complexity and frequency. What these authors call uncertainty/complexity boils down to the Williamsonian notion of information impactedness. The authors then discuss combinations of factor constellations, in such a way that asymmetrical relationships between partners in a transaction are considered along with symmetrical relations. It is suggested, in other words, that partners may opt for different degrees of asset specificity and uncertainty/complexity in the transaction. This renders the approach more sophisticated. Yet, a simpler version will be used here since the aim is to test TCT from the perspective of focal organizations which are confronted with vertical integration choices. It was not possible to investigate both of the partners in a transaction, or both of the potential parties to a contract. TCT suggests that focal firms extend vertical integration further through the value chain (1) the greater the specificity of assets required to carry out the transaction is; (2) the greater the uncertainty and complexity of transaction outcomes are; and (3) the more frequently and regularly a transaction occurs.

Such hypotheses construe economic actors as seeking an arrangement which enables them to exercise a better control over opportunistic behaviour and the complexity/uncertainty of transactions. The question remains as to which kinds of costs are to be included. A notion of costs, which is probably more wide-ranging and explicit than TCT puts forward but well established in economics and at least implicit to the Williamsonian argument as it has evolved in discussion with critics, is opportunity costs. The opportunity cost of any kind of arrangement or decision is what it costs to implement this decision or arrangement in terms of foregoing the next best alternative. Such costs include revenue, value-added, profit margin or profit differentials. This concept of costs is not as restrictive as costs in accountancy terminology. Opportunity costs also include benefits foregone.

It is generally acknowledged, in TCT and by its critics, that economic organizations are not able to make a rigorous and substantiated calculation of transaction costs, most certainly not prior to making a decision. This is the essence of the idea of bounded rationality which is also fundamental for Williamson. Yet, TCT sees actors as following rules of thumb, intuition, conjecture and not quite articulate experience in order to put in place at least a rough-shod transaction cost assessment despite incomplete information. Actors also learn to develop or adopt an economic institution by trial-and-error, rationalizing the choice made *ex post facto*. It is therefore quite appropriate to test TCT by eliciting information from actors about the less articulate and reproducible ingredients of a transaction cost assessment, and to relate these to the central factors which impinge on vertical integration that are mentioned above. These can be described as *core relationships*.

The suggestive power of TCT lies in the elegance and plausibility with which the demarcation of an *organizational domain* is explained. An organizational domain is, in the first instance, the sum total of those transactions which are vertically and laterally integrated within the meaningful borders which organized units draw around themselves. However, since "the whole is more than the sum of its elements" this domain is more than a sum of its transactions. Possibly not quite identical with the borders that bound internalized transactions, there is an organizational domain in the sense of a body of competence, experience, habitual or formal routines and knowledge which is considered as constitutive of the identity of the unit, including that part of the identity which is shared with similar units in an organizational species. This part of the organizational domain is often described as "template" or "comps" (core competencies within the behavioural repertoire) (McKelvey 1982).

The fundamental contribution of TCT is to derive organizational domains from transaction cost assessments. This applies, in the first instance, to organizational domain as bounded by internalized transactions. The hypothesis that integration will occur in those transactions that are governed by idiosyncrasy, uncertainty/complexity and asset specificity suggests, however, that a template or comps are formed in order to optimize the domain of internalized transactions. The fundamental idea of transaction cost assessments determining the organizational domain and the more specific hypotheses about how this happens are to be examined in the following.

Whereas the critics of TCT have pointed out the role of social embeddedness, they have not seriously challenged the salience of its core contingencies and relations that have been summarized above. There can be, in other words, two types of critiques. A more moderate critique would argue that TCT contingencies are socially embedded and constructed. A more fundamental critique would doubt whether core contingencies and relations do in fact explain vertical integration, arguing that different explanatory factors directly lead to vertical integration policies, so that TCT contingencies are not required or disconfirmed as mediating concepts. These are the countervailing hypotheses to be tested here.

Note that the issue is not whether factors such as power or other embeddedness characteristics are important or not. TCT would argue that such factors, where they exist and are important, will translate themselves into transaction costs and influence vertical integration and co-ordination via this route. This is a methodologically individualist argument, which focusses on the individual transaction and actor, as an explanatory juncture that is both inevitable and fundamental, and it is in parallel with the argument put forward by rational choice approaches in sociology. In such frameworks social or societal arrangements are not denied but they are seen to operate through a utility or efficiency oriented individual assessment.

It is striking how much both proponents and critics of TCT refer to common-sense stylized examples (see for example, Douma and Schreuder 1992; Perrow 1986). To a considerable extent, the controversy around TCT is one about dogma rather than substance. The dogmatism is due to the difficulty of distinguishing between two shades of meaning associated with efficiency, just like other economic generalities such as utility, of deciding to interpret it either as a tautological but useful heuristic tool or a substantively meaningful testable proposition. This dogmatism thrives on the difficulty of operationalizing transaction costs, on the relative absence of empirical findings about factual integration processes and motives in a longitudinal perspective, and on the specialization of TCT literature on large North American or international conglomerates.

Research Method

The data base originates from a study of industrial firms that applied microelectronics in their products. The investigation was commissioned by the *VDI/VDE-Technologiezentrum Informationstechnik GmbH*, a "quasi non-governmental organization" which is run by the professional associations in engineering but mainly acts as a consultancy and funding body for the Federal Ministry of Research and Technology in Germany. This body had commissioned a study about strategy, and organizational and human resource aspects of the introduction of microelectronics into products of manufacturing firms, including their sales and service components. The investigation was carried out by a research unit in the *Wissenschaftszentrum Berlin* for Social Research, in which the author worked at the time, and by researchers in the Fraunhofer Institute for Human Resources and Organization (*FhG-IAO*) and the German Institute for Economic Research (*DIW*). Data collection was carried out in 1985-1987, a period in which problems related to the introduction of microelectronics into products were intensively discussed. These problems not only included the acute shortage of up-to-date engineering skills and experience in electronics and software but they also appeared in firm strategies in areas such as handling of microelectronics in vertical integration, designing of contracts and cooperative arrangements, as well as work organization, training and recruitment. Whilst the study had, in the first instance, a policy-advisory role, it clearly had relevant information for analysis in a more academic context.

The research methodology emphasized case studies in companies, carried out according to a semi-structured interview guideline, by interviewing key respondents such as engineering and production managers, hardware and software engineers, and workforce representatives. A case study lasted on average two days, depending on the size of the establishment. Responses were noted down verbatim in the interview guideline. The information for the present analysis was obtained from responses to questions about vertical and horizontal integration and disintegration policies in both, electronic components' design and production, the way this related to the design, development and production of non-electronic components, and the reasons for particular integration or disintegration policies, as well as the evolution of such strategies and practice over time, within an open-ended process of experimentation, learning and re-orientation.

Firms or, in the cases of multi-site firms, local sites with research, development and production facilities, were selected according to the results of a representative survey among German industrial firms (Behringer and Brasche 1986). This had yielded a quota selection roster, specifying selection criteria and numbers of cases (Beuschel et al. 1988). The criteria included establishment size, industrial sector and more specific characteristics related to the history, strategy and relative volume of the firm's involvement in electronics. Table 1 depicts the cases that were selected, with respect to establishment size, industry and the nature of the product.

Table 1. Sites investigated

Code	Product
ME-S1	Milking machines
ME-S2	Production fixtures and automatic machines with programmable controllers
ME-S3	Recoiling machines
ME-S4	Storage and transport systems for paper coils
ME-S5	Labelling machines
ME-S6	Measurement gauges for inside and outside spherical objects
ME-M1	Galvanizing plant
ME-M2	Glass floating and cutting machines, transfer equipment for production lines
ME-M3	Safety locks, door access systems
ME-M4	Gas control equipment
ME-M5	Compressors
ME-M6	Ticket and stamp vending machines, post-marking machines
ME-M7	Road building machines
ME-B1	Steel-rolling mill lines, shear cutters
ME-B2	Lifts
ME-B3	Printing machines
ME-B4	Gear-boxes for motor vehicles
TR-B1	Aerospace and armament
TR-B2	Cars and lorries
TR-B3	Cars
ED-S1	Programmable controllers for integrated lines
ED-S2	Controls (for hangar doors, presses, grinding machines, paper machines, etc.)
ED-S3	Overhaul and installation of electrical motors and controls
ED-S4	Local area networks and controls
ED-S5	Ultra-sound test equipment and controls
ED-S6	Hydrotherapeutical equipment
ED-S7	Coal-mining equipment controls
ED-M1	Telecommunications, office, point-of-sale computing and trading systems
ED-M2	Controls for electrical, sanitation and heating installations
ED-M3	Keyboards and sensors
ED-M4	CAD and NC programming systems
ED-M5	Clocks, high frequency measurement equipment
ED-B1	Telephone exchanges and communication systems
ED-B2	Air navigation beacons, railway safety and control installations
ED-B3	Weighing scales
ED-B4	Electronic measurement systems
ED-B5	Communication systems

The codes in the first row of Table 1 also indicate the industrial sector and the personnel size of the business unit which constituted the site, or in which the site is located. S stands for small units, with up to 100 employees, M for medium-sized units with between 100 and 1,000 employees, B for large units with over 1,000 employees. ME stands for mechanical engineering, ED for electrical, electronic and data-processing, and TR for transport equipment industries, the latter including passenger cars, lorries, trucks, civil and military aircraft, and space systems. The number in the code is just a serial number without any substantive meaning. Thus, ED-M2 denotes the second medium-sized site in the electrical engineering, electronics and data-processing equipment industries.

In total 40 cases were thus selected and studied. These included three cases which are not reflected in Table 1. They were eliminated for the purpose of the present re-analysis because they had been selected to represent specific producer-user constellations. Whilst these cases illustrated specific situations with regard to competence needs and competence formation quite well, they were not focussed on that range of the value chain which is discussed here. This would have made their comparison with the other sites, in terms of their vertical integration arrangements, rather futile. Their elimination leads to n = 37 as the total number of sites investigated and analyzed.

The selection of sites was done in a way to enable the research team to cover the total amount of qualitatively different settings with a reasonable number of cases for each setting. This is different from random or quota sampling in the strict sense. However, the reader can see from Table 1 that a very large part of the product, sector and unit size variance within the larger population of firms is covered by cases, the numbers of which in each setting somewhat reduce the risk of unrepresentativeness.

The information from the field investigation was gathered in response to open questions and further prompts, with regard to a number of areas. The information which is analyzed here, came from questions directed towards the following areas:

- Respondents were asked about the kinds of activities internalized and externalized. There were questions about the flow of activities around the development and production of microelectronics in the unit in question and beyond, as well as about the nature of the firms and personnel that carried out the externalized activities. Externalization could both mean the transaction of a service (such as making up software under a contract) and of a tangible product (such as a chip, computer board or other subassembly, or a complete control or communication product).
- Respondents were further asked to comment on why particular vertical integration or disintegration arrangements were chosen. The answers were usually phrased in such a form that they could be translated into transaction cost economic terms. It was not necessary to impose standard operational definitions of such terms, for they were directly implied by responses in unambiguous ways. It is also clear, however, that the trans-

action cost motivations offered by respondents had a strong "conjectural" element. They were not derived from calculations, based on objective accounting and economic information. But respondents were clearly manufacturing, construing and interpreting behaviour on a transaction cost basis, which formed something between a subjective and an intersubjectively validated yardstick.

- There were further questions and prompts to obtain information about how the vertical integration practice and thinking of the unit had evolved over time, what the experience with established integration practice was, what changes had resulted from learning under previous vertical integration arrangements, how perception of the merits of alternative arrangements had evolved, and which developments the unit was thinking of for the future. As far as the motivation for past, present and future changes, or stability, is concerned, the respondents again had a habit of implying transaction cost aspects in their deliberations.

Parallel with the German study, a British team conducted an investigation in the same population of firms for the British economy. Methodology and selection criteria were identical, but the number of cases investigated was smaller (n = 27). The results of this study were published by the British team separately and the cross-national comparison of the two studies was reported in Campbell et al. (1989). Cross-nationally comparative results will also be referred to later in the chapter.

Whilst the overall methodology should be described as "qualitative" in the first instance, and, by that token, as "exploratory" rather than congenial to the testing of hypotheses, it also had more cases than usual under a purely exploratory research design. Furthermore, it was possible to define and measure standardized empirical concepts in our material. In conjunction with the number of cases, this allows a tentative testing of hypotheses.

Synchronic Analysis

The first step is to analyze information about the firms in the sample within a cross-sectional perspective, i.e. the variance addressed is the one with regard to vertical integration practice at a certain point in time. This point in time is located in a chronic, rather than substantively meaningful, time dimension. Units were investigated at the same moment, but at this moment, they may be found within different phases of their experience, policy and thinking, concerning vertical integration of microelectronics. We had early and recent adoptors, all studied at the same moment. This diversity is partly explored in the subsequent section, which deals with diachronic perspectives and is therefore able to cover changes in vertical integration practices over time. In the present section, this part of the variance is deliberately left out.

On the basis of responses to questions about vertical integration, units were categorized on two dimensions: Vertical integration in electronics design and development, and vertical integration in the manufacturing of electronic components and sub-assemblies. On these dimensions, the following categories were distinguished:

- *Vertical integration in electronics design and development*
  High: Internalization of the development of electronic individual components, sub-assemblies and sets.
  Medium: Internalization of the development of electronic sub-assemblies or software.
  Low: External development of hardware and software.

- *Vertical integration in electronics production*
  High: Down to the mounting of electronic parts on boards (insertion or surface-mounting).
  Low: Fitting of sub-assemblies or sets supplied by an external manufacturer.

The implication, clearly, is that vertical integration levels in design and development, and in production, did not coincide. As Table 2 will show, they varied against each other to an extent that the relationship could not even be described by a close correlation. Before discussing empirical results, it is useful to remember the relevance of the indicators in terms of TCT. High integration in electronics design and development means that pervasive internal control is achieved over the full length of the development chain, starting from the hardware "wiring" of individual chips, over the lay-out of circuit boards and the writing of software, down to the rest of the product into which the electronic components and sub-assemblies are integrated. Conversely, low integration denotes the absence of any sort of electronic or software design and development activities, not counting minor adaptation or specification activities, although the product does have electronic control, information or communication functions. In this case, either the development of this part of the product is contracted out, or the product receives a module, programme or set that is available "on the market."

Many of the firms, even with high integration in development, still had a habit of contracting out some software activities. However, this did not detract from their categorization as highly integrated, since they contracted out jobs without abandoning either the controlling responsibility or day-to-day involvement in software and hardware design. Furthermore, in all cases of high development integration, it was reported that contracting out was a response to the problems that were not crucial or central for the functioning of the product as a whole; it simply constituted a way of coping with time peaks and deadline pressures. It can be seen that this already implies a typical TCT argument: Where the incidence of transactions is irregular, and where the transactions are not concerned with more "proprietary" aspects of the product, where the specificity of skills and knowledge required to do the job is therefore lower, firms will externalize more readily than where transactions occur regularly or where they address the more specific and proprietory core of the product.

This logic of "mixing" internal and external transactions is all the more pronounced in the intermediate category, of medium vertical integration in development. Here, individual electronic components were simply bought on the market, but either their circuit board environment, or the software with which they were loaded, or both, were developed internally. This is a "modular" solution, in which unspecific and therefore "marketed" modules are combined with elements that are more specifically developed to suit particular perceived requirements. In common sense terms, this was usually expressed as a compromise between the benefits of standardization (sharing in professional expertise and reducing the fixed costs and price of a standard module) and the benefits of customization (appropriation or maintenance of specific skills and knowledge, and quality assurance with a product which is not understood by external agents).

With respect to the production of electronic sub-sets or individual components, only two alternatives were needed, and the decision on whether to mount individual components on boards or not appeared to constitute a decisive cut-off point. In-house manufacture of complete individual electronic parts was not found in any of the firms. The aerospace site, TR B1, which featured the highest degree of production integration in the sample, still had its wafers manufactured in a foreign specialized company. This was, to be sure, a wholly-owned subsidiary. ED M5 made only some of their integrated electronic circuits in-house, in the form of thin-slice components. On the whole, it was highly unusual to manufacture wafers in-house, but the hardware structure of wafers was quite often determined by development engineers in the firm that used the wafer, rather than by the firm that manufactured it.

The distribution of sites over different degrees of vertical integration can be visualized in Table 2. The table shows that the most frequent solution to integration of development was medium integration. The reasons adduced for this degree of internalizing development included the following arguments:

- Existing standard equipment or software is insufficiently adapted to the requirements perceived in specific product environments and the context of application of the product, on the part of the end-user. Thus, manufacturers of ME products in the "medium" column in the table invariably pointed out that makers of standard controls, software or computer modules were insufficiently aware of the requirements posited by the functioning and use of the machines they made. Such specific knowledge had to be used in the design of control or information technology. This is a clear argument in favour of asset specificity, especially in the form of human resources specificity.
- Making specific knowledge related to the product environment and the context of application available to a different firm, would have implied the risk that specific knowledge "slipped" out of control of the firm which considered itself proprietory of this knowledge, thereby improving the bargaining power of a control or information technology manufacturer and running the risk that proprietory knowledge also slipped to competitors. This argument implies opportunistic behaviour on the part of suppliers and competitors, and it suggests that vertical integration may reduce dependency on suppliers. Dependency means the liability to be subjected to opportunistic behaviour, with the effect of either, eroding the focal firm's business, or making it incur price or other disadvantages.

Table 2. Vertical integration of electronics development and production

Production	Development		
	High	Medium	Low
High	ED M1 TR B1 ED M3 TR B2 ED M5 ED B1 ED B2 ED B5	ED S1 ME S1 ME B3 ED S2 ME S5 ED S3 ME M2 ED S5 ME M4 ED M2 ME M6 ED B3 ME M7 ED B4	ED S7 ME S6
Low		ED S4 ME S2 ME B4 ED M4 ME S3 ME M1 ME M5 ME B2	ME S4 ED S6 ME M3 ME B1 TR B3

Similar arguments were also made by the ED sites in the middle column of Table 2, but to such firms, identification of internal development as "natural" for an electrical and electronic products manufacturer was also easier.

It fitted in with the established identity of the firm, as one concerned with the development and manufacture of electronic and electrical products. With the change-over to microelectronics and software in state-of-the-art technology, the firms were seen to have to engage in its development, in order to develop and guard their own source of value-added. This value-added resided in the competence to develop specific electronics and software, tailored to specific industrial problems and challenges.

The specificity of assets and solutions in such "medium" development integration firms was, on the other hand, limited by the perceived advantage of standard micro-electronic components, software and computing boards, as supplied by outside manufacturers. Programmable controls, computer boards or other modules, programmable memory chips and microprocessors, are all examples of standardized equipment which yet gives the user some leeway of loading it with more specific software and programmes, and of adapting hardware to suit specific technical environments. They were seen to combine the relative advantages of standardization with those of customization. This avoided the problems of "re-inventing the wheel", those of offering products with functional or competitive deficiencies, and those of letting competence and value-added slip to a supplier. In-house design of electronic boards and software, including the precise choice of individual electronic components to be used, was particularly mentioned as necessary in order to cope with the following problems that outside suppliers were only imperfectly aware of: (1) exposure of equipment to electromagnetic field effects in the product or its environment of use; (2) exposure to heat, fumes, radiation or other physical influences; (3) compatibility with safety standards, redundancy requirements, operating standards, emergency stop facilities etc., in diversified markets with different rules, regulations and habitual professional norms.

Such arguments all attach to the salient transaction cost notions of specificity, opportunistic bargaining, complexity and uncertainty of transaction outcomes. The observed intermediate degree of vertical integration in development tallies with a perception that combines the relative advantages of "markets" (standard components, modules and software, general electronics and software development competence) with those of internalization (protection of product-specific proprietory experience and competence, value-added on the basis of intermediate product and asset specificity). This mixture of "market" and "hierarchy" is thus well predicted by TCT.

Changing over to the "high" vertical integration of development column, we found that similar themes were touched upon, but the result of the argument was evidently different. On the product engineering side, a physical concentration of electronic functions and lack of space (in the product or its immediate environment) were themes mentioned in addition to those for the "medium" integration of development column. Use of microelectronics in such products as anti-tank robots or aeroplane controls and instruments (TR B1), various bus and truck (including engine) control systems (TR B2), keyboards and sensors (ED M3), communication and office equipment (ED M1, ED B1, ED B2, ED B5) were seen to require specifically designed micro-electronic components, in view of the high density of information functions in a compressed space. In addition, there were the motives of protection of proprietory interests and assurance of safety and quality under very specific product and usage environments, which were also mentioned by firms in the "medium" column. They were stressed even more in the "high" firms. Circuits having to function reliably for ten years without maintenance, in the unfriendly environment of outer space (TR B1), or the devastating effects of hardware or software deficiencies in bus or truck control systems (TR B2) are cases in point.

This argument implied requirements for product and asset specificity to an extent which is higher than for the "medium" column firms, and this shows in that not only specific software programmes or modules but specifically designed individual components were seen to be called for. Technically, such requirements were met by the development of fully customer specific components and circuits, and by the use of gate-arrays and standard cells. The necessity to develop specific sensors and actuators, closely tuned to computing modules and partly integrated with these on a single chip or on its immediate periphery, was also emphasized. All this was said to depend on a close integration of experience and knowledge in teams or in work roles. Again, we see that a level of vertical integration is founded upon a reasoning in terms of transaction and asset specificity, the assumption of opportunistic behaviour and the desire to be protected against its negative effects.

In the "low" development integration column, we found a reasoning which was opposed to that formulated in the cases of "high" integration. Externalization of development was preferred for opposite reasons. Interestingly, the most frequent reason adduced was not the lack of specificity of the transactions concerned. There were, to be sure, cases in which programmable controls or other equipment available "on the market" were felt to be sufficiently capable of handling the control and informational functions in the product. Such cases were ME S4, ED S6, and in part TR B3 and ME B1, but the other firms in the column, and a part of the product modules in TR B3 and ME B1, were specifically developed by outside engineering consultancies and electronics suppliers. In these cases, the specificity of transactions and assets involved is not low at all. Informants in ME B1 and TR B3 indicated that externalization practice had more to do with the location of specific assets than the extent of their specificity. Reference was made to the established engineering competence and market power of outside suppliers, which supplied both specific development effort and standardized modules or sets.

In ME B1 in particular, it was said that in principle, because of the specificity involved and due to the growing share of information and control equipment as a part of value added in the selling price of steel-rolling mills, it was desirable to extend the internalization of such development effort. On the other hand, the choice of control equipment was made by individual customers anyway, and controls developed internally could not be imposed on customers. The co-operation of outside suppliers thus had to be guaranteed, and it was feared that this co-operation might deteriorate if the firm decided to go into the steel rolling mill control market more substantially. Interestingly, this firm, therefore, evaluated the transaction costs of the internal solution as being higher, despite noticeable specificity of the transaction and the assets. The high level of these transaction costs was determined by the threat of opportunistic behaviour of allies which might turn into rivals. It should be noted that this is a perfectly good transaction cost argument, but it casts the net of transaction costs more widely than usual. The consequence is that transaction costs have to be seen as opportunity costs, and such costs are here seen to include friction with co-operating suppliers in the value chain because of latent rivalry.

On a less explicit note, in the case of TR B3, it was also said that the combined competence, i.e. specialized competence, and market power in automobile electronics of the supplier group made internal development difficult to justify, so that external development and supply were advantageous. In the small and medium-sized sites in this column, there was also a tendency to consider the competence of consultancies and suppliers as more highly developed. Again, this means that use of market transactions as a co-ordination mechanism, and the location of specific assets, in response to complex, uncertain and idiosyncratic transaction characteristics, happen contrary to the predictions of TCT which would be a tendency to internalize. It might be suggested that alternative explanatory concepts, such as the frequency or the "coarse grain" of transactions, to borrow a term from population ecology, would have predicted low vertical integration. However, nearly all the firms in the "low" column are distinctive for persisting electronic development needs, although the amount of requirements may fluctuate somewhat over time.

To change the scene to vertical integration of production, Table 2 shows a striking pattern: the "high development integration — low production integration" cell was empty, and there were only two cases in the "low development integration — high production integration" cell. This creates the impression of a diagonal regression line in the table. However, this regression line runs through a great deal of scatter. In the "medium" development integration category, there are half as many sites with low production integration as there are in the "high" box. In a way, vertical integration in development influences integration in production, because firms will tend to translate development integration arrangements into production arrangements. The explanatory variables of transaction and asset specificity, which are associated with the amount of development integration, will also impinge on production, because what is an idiosyncratic design or development will also entail idiosyncratic production arrangements and experience.

This expectation is corroborated, but the association is far from strong. Let us look at the most evident deviant cases, which clearly are to be found in the "low-high" cell. In ED S7, the production of electronic modules was seen as governed by highly specific safety requirements, the product being used underground in coal mines. Similar safety considerations had not, however, worked themselves into the choice of the development integration level. The firm seemed more concerned with production, installation and service rather than development. In ME S6, mounting of chips on printed circuit boards occurred regularly and was identified as similar to the manufacture and assembly of smaller mechanical parts on a regular basis, which was identified as the mainstay of the firm in production.

In the less strikingly deviant part of the variance, the following pattern emerges from Table 2. In ED sites which, because of the nature of the product, handle more electronic and electrical modules, low production integration is infrequent (only three cases). Similarly, ED sites had also exhibited a greater tendency to internalize electronics development. For the ME cases, it is so far not possible to explain why "low" or "high" production integration was adopted in the "medium" development integration column. The ratio of "high" to "low" here is 7:5. There is no evident relationship, on the basis of the interviews, with perceived opportunistic behaviour, specificity of transactions or assets, volume or frequency of activities. Here, TCT performs less well in predicting arrangements. However, on the whole, it does not do badly, as the difference between the distributions of ME and ED sites is related to, on average, higher volume and frequency of electronics assembly operations, and by the identification of electronics production as related to the specific assets of the site in ED cases, and more tenuously related to it in the ME cases. It appeared, however, that the choice of production integration was more fortuitous or inexplicable than that with regard to development integration, which seemed to hold greater salience.

On balance, in a cross-sectional analysis, TCT seems to do rather well in explaining vertical integration. It performs better in predicting integration of development, and it is at its best in predicting high integration. Medium integration is also well explained. In the case of low integration the explanatory success is more limited. Less well explained is, in addition, production integration, but the difference between ED and ME firms is to some extent accounted for. From this part of the analysis, it appears that reference to TCT factors and reasoning is a strong characteristic of managerial behaviour and organization design, albeit with varying emphasis in different contexts.

Diachronic Analysis

In a diachronic perspective, attention will be focused on changes in vertical integration policies over time, both in the past and in the foreseeable future, mentioned in the interviews. The first step is to identify those sites which had substantially changed their integration policy or were about to do so. Table 3 lists those firms in which substantial changes had taken place or were about to take place. Again, integration in development came forward as a much more salient issue than integration in production. This is why Table 3 only lists changes in development policy. A distinction is made between those firms that increased and those that decreased their vertical integration. Another distinction concerns the difference between largely completed change, and change that was about to begin or planned. This yields a fourfold table.

Table 3. Changes in vertical integration of development policy

	Completed		About to start or planned
Increase	ME S6 ED M5	TR B1 TR B2	ME B1 ME B4
Decrease	ED S7 ME S5 ME M3 ME M5		

In total, 10 sites had changed, or were about to change, their vertical integration considerably. This amounts to over a quarter of the number of cases. The great majority of these are, as can be seen from Table 3, ME and TR firms. It is plausible that sites from outside the electrical, electronics and data processing equipment industries experience the degree of integration as more contentious. ED firms, because of their professional embeddedness in this industry context, apparently feel more certain about the degree of integration. ME and TR firms, however, manifest much more experimentation and learning experience, in order to achieve a desirable mode of integration. Interestingly, their evolution may point in both directions, towards an increase or a decrease of integration, with equal probability.

It is also significant that the firms where changes towards greater backward integration are observed are the bigger ones, whereas those that are changing towards lesser integration are smaller. Apparently, the professional and industrial scope of larger firms generates a tendency and a capacity to integrate backwards. Thus, conventional organizational context criteria such as size, industry and scope (referred to as "charter" in the Aston studies) turn out to be good predictors. This does not exclude that TCT factors do play a role. Increasing size of a firm, being associated with professional and functional differentiation of departments and work roles, can be seen to favour the incorporation of more specific assets. Possibly, asset specificity, in this case human resource assets, is an intermediate variable between organization context and vertical integration. Greater size may imply easier incorporation of broader scope or charter, since the opportunity cost of internal transactions is perceived to be lower. It is also conceivable that the greater volume and frequency of transactions of a similar kind, which will arise in larger firms, make trial-and-error learning in the direction of higher integration more probable.

However, a sharper test of TCT requires examination of the motivation and experience that underlie changes in integration policy. Let us consider, first, the cases of increasing vertical integration. In the case of ED M5 this was achieved by diversifying the product portfolio. This firm broadened out, from the manufacture of alarm clocks and larger clocks, into the development and production of thin-film circuits. Here, the change in policy was thus a consequence of the decision to go into related product fields and be active in less mature, technically more dynamic markets with the prospect of higher value-added and profit margins. This integration motive is explained by the product life cycle idea (Hatten and Hatten 1988).

ME S6 had electronicized the measurement system in its gauges, first, by contracting-out the development of the mechanism to an engineering consultancy. That gave it a "low" position in Table 2. The experience with the design was subsequently highly disappointing. There were programming faults, and chips and printed circuits were not sufficiently resistant against fumes, shock and electric magnetism in their "natural" environment of use. Workmen will not treat a gauge gently at all times, and it will be left lying next to an oil puddle or in a cloud of cooling liquid. Product malfunctioning for all these reasons led to the firm being deluged with rejects and complaints. This is a nice case to show how tacit knowledge which is self-evident to the maker or user of a technical implement, and in retrospect quite apparent even to the layman, can be disregarded by external specialists because no-one ever thought about entering it into the formal brief for a development contract. ME S6 thus took the decision to re-engineer present products and go over to developing its own electronics modules. An electronic engineer had been hired for that, but he was at the moment of investigation still very busy repairing rejects. Note that the engineer was hired, not only for his electronics knowledge and experience but specifically, for his experience in electronics for use in maritime equipment, i.e. in an environment that needed equally robust electronics as measurement gauges. This policy change provides an example of learning that internalization of transactions and assets pays because the complexity/uncertainty of transactions and the specificity of assets required, are higher than originally imagined.

The decision in ME B1 to increase integration was based on totally different reasons: Low integration was not felt to lead to deficient or unreliable outcomes. It was also thought that the highly specific experience in making controls for steel-rolling mills was available, but it had become incorporated into a division of a leading national industrial electronics group. This is, therefore, a case in which vertical disintegration coincides with high asset specificity. However, the firm wanted to increase its involvement in controls development in order to maintain its share in the value-added of the larger product. The perception was that electronic controls were steadily increasing their share in the price of rolling-mill equipment. To put a foot in this domain, the firm had started by developing a less significant control for a spindle, itself. This was a cautious step, set in order not to antagonize the industrial group which appeared to have an effective quasi-monopoly, both of this particular controls market and of the engineering specialists needed to do the job.

This case is highly ambiguous with regard to TCT, not because the steps were not set in the directions predicted by it, but because the firm was rather reluctant to pursue this course for reasons which did not confirm the explanation that would normally be given by TCT. The change was felt to be hazardous because the transaction costs of vertical integration were thought to be high, even in a situation of high asset specificity. Transaction costs evidently did matter, but they mattered in a different way than predicted on the basis of transaction specificity. On the other hand, it could also be argued that the expansion of electronic controls' share in the price of rolling mills meant an increase in frequency and volume, and therefore went in favour of integration.

An increase in the frequency and volume of electronics development is also evident in ME B4. This firm was not changing its position in Table 2, but it had recently established "system leadership" for itself, in an alliance with an automobile electronics group, for a specific part of the gears controls market. It also saw the increasing importance of electronics for gears control, and was busy increasing its importance in this specific field. As in the previous case, this did not happen for reasons of dissatisfaction with the performance of the cooperating electronics group, but in order to internalize the shifting emphasis in the value chain, from mechanical engineering to electronics and software.

Similar reasons were also adduced in TR B1 and TR B2. These firms had in the past made great efforts to establish and deepen their own electronics competence, and intertwine it more systematically with other branches of engineering, by mixing teams and forming multi-specialists. Yet in these sites, it was also said that greater integration was called for, in view of the very stringent requirements for reliability and safety of electronics in crucial functions of the car, lorry, aeroplane, satellite or battlefield robot. It is also interesting that a concern with specificity and value-added was mixed with status and prestige considerations. Where electronics crept into products in increasing numbers of places and received an ever more central function, mechanical, aeronautical and automobile manufacturers mentioned that they would not be content to turn into subservient "metal-bashers."

What unites all the cases in which an increase in integration was observed, is the proven or assumed capacity to control transactions to the advantage of the firm, better than in the past, by increasing vertical integration. This confidence was based on different motives, partly implied directly or indirectly by TCT, partly ambiguous, and partly originating from outside the TCT ambit. It would be futile to attempt a quantification, in view of the nature of the study and the number of cases in this particular bracket. Nevertheless, it is quite clear that TCT explanations are better when we enmesh them with contingency theory and straightforward business strategy arguments.

However, the picture turns out to be different when we look at the sites which had decreased their integration. In none of these cases was there an experience, or assumption, of being able to control transactions better by integrating backwards, in response to high specificity and increasing volume and frequency. Neither was there a feeling that opportunistic behaviour could be checked by integration. Instead, in all the cases was disintegration set in motion because internal electronic engineers and, worst of all, software specialists, were seen as potentially uncontrollable. They did not understand the product, rode their own hobby-horses, had different cognitive patterns, unconventional working times and habits, longer hair and more casual clothing. In return, it was reported that electronics engineers and software specialists viewed other engineers as intellectually inferior, not quite articulate about their work, unable to "think in terms of functions" but liable to the fallacy of misplaced concreteness, conservative and rigid. The clash of professional cultures thus made control over specific transactions via integration fail.

There were also disappointing experiences at the technical level. Introducing electronics into products was confronted with poor specification of requirements, malfunctioning of experimental equipment, need for re-design and over-running of scheduled deadlines. "Normal" working life in firms was upset even at the technical level. In ME M3, telephones would start ringing in the building when experiments were conducted. Relations with customers were upset, and antagonism between parts of the workforce built up for reasons which were related to a conundrum of technical, organizational and working culture clashes. In this situation, the firms went over to partial disintegration. This mainly happened by electronics and software specialists leaving the firm but continuing on the project in a new or independent firm that was provided with a development contract. ME S5 and ED S7 established cooperation with small electronics and software firms in their vicinity, and ME M3 even set up a new firm itself, to handle the project on contract, under the assumption that this firm was also to look elsewhere for orders.

This did not mean that electronics and software expertise were completely jettisoned. All the sites did keep some staff for the specification of contractual and technical requirements, project management, coordination with internal development activities, technical supervision and monitoring. Such staff continued to serve as "bridges" between the separate professional fields and firms. They were said to have a more intimate understanding of the firm's products, in addition to electronics and software experience. However, it is highly significant that externalization was increased in order to control highly specific transactions better, not by integration but via relational contracting between formally independent partners. Apparently, a separation of professional and industrial cultures and the use of formal contracts with fixed deadlines, formalized requirements and sanctions, were thought to perform better after integration had led to deadlocks, delays and defects.

This result is at odds with TCT. The theory would have predicted that the above mentioned problems of opportunistic behaviour, combined with high specificity and complexity/uncertainty, should lead to increasing integration, because that would have facilitated the use of "hierarchy" as the appropriate mechanism of coordination and control. However, this logic could only be established for larger firms, whereas smaller firms were more likely to go the opposite way. Again, we see that TCT works better at the "high" end of vertical integration, whereas it performs poorly at the "low" end.

A Cross-national Comparison

Along with the "German study" of microelectronics application in products, we had also carried out a comparison with a parallel British study that had been coordinated with the German one throughout (Campbell et al. 1989). Since the results were published in detail, they will only be referred to briefly here, insofar as they help to extend the present argument in testing TCT. With regard to vertical integration in development, we had found that the British sites were less vertically integrated. They were more inclined to buy in standard control and information technology sets or modules, or to subcontract development to other firms. On the other hand, despite the differences between ED and ME firms established in the German study, the German sites exhibited greater similarity between ED and ME firms than did the British sites.

In their reasoning, firms were different between Britain and Germany in the following way: British firms were more likely to say that "you should not re-invent the wheel" but buy in or contract out what you could get on the market. This argument was, above all, made by the British ME sites. In the German firms, there was a comparatively greater tendency to argue that controls or information technology available on the market, or developed by external suppliers and consultants, were not sufficiently adapted to the specific problems that appeared in their product range and during the use of such products with which the firm was concerned currently or potentially.

This is a case of TCT logic which is also useful in a cross-national comparison. Cross-national differences might also be linked to my previously developed argument that the respective, societally based transaction cost assessment made in firms, appears to be related to the relative separation of professional domains in engineering sectors. British engineering culture and institutions appeared as more split up, divided by both lateral (specialism, career, industry) and vertical (status, prestige, assumed intellectual calibre in a profession and an industrial sector) criteria. German engineering culture and institutions also showed similar divisions, as our case material had documented, but they were less deep and less frequent. Consequently, we could explain the "choice" of vertical integration arrangements as loaded by societal settings in the working culture and organization of enterprises, and in competence formation and labour market institutions. This argument boils down to the conclusion that transaction cost assessments, as made by actors in enterprises and elsewhere, will be a factor that mediates between societal institutions and culture on the one hand and integration policies on the other. These assessments, therefore, are much more of a socially or societally constructed phenomena than TCT concedes

That would put a new perspective on TCT, but it would not shake it seriously. However, the question is if contracts and openness to the market, in the British case, are not simply due to lower asset specificity and complexity/uncertainty, might they also be a generalized societally specific response which is invoked in order to control specific transactions and assets and which colours the perception of asset specificity and complexity/uncertainty? There is no empirical answer to this question at the present moment. But the interpretation would be in line with the situation in the German firms which reduced vertical integration. To the extent that these firms had difficulties of internally controlling clashes or rifts between differentiated working cultures and approaches to engineering, they had also intensified recourse to external suppliers via contracts. The likelihood is quite strong that the strength of the "cash nexus" and the frequency of market-type or contractual relations in British society load "choices" towards disintegration and contract, as mechanisms that will be considered more "efficient" to address problems of specificity, complexity/uncertainty and opportunistic behaviour in general.

Thus, the evidence from the cross-national comparison is also mixed. On the one hand, transaction cost considerations can have a role to play, but most likely as an intervening concept between socially and societally constructed, cultural and institutional factors. On the other hand, such social and societal constructions may load assessments and behaviour in a way which is contrary to TCT.

Interpretation and Conclusions

The results of this investigation can be summarized and interpreted under two major headings. To some extent, it confirms previous research and conclusions. It also leads, however, to a more substantial questioning of the approach. On balance, it is not possible to refute or support the approach categorically. The investigation has presented a great deal of evidence in favour, and also a great deal against. Let us examine the first set of interpretations which confirm other literature.

To start with, this study clearly shows that transaction cost assessment has an important role to play in organizational life, and actors implicitly refer to such concepts. Also, in a cross-sectional analysis, the adoption of vertical integration policies appears well explained by factors such as specificity, uncertainty/complexity, volume and frequency, as well as the threat of opportunistic behaviour. Specifically, "medium" vertical integration, and the characteristic mixture of integration, alliances and relational contracting, is well accounted for, in comparison with "high" integration; "higher" vertical integration is also associated with higher specificity and complexity/ uncertainty.

It can also be said that the cross-national comparison referred to confirms TCT to some extent. The approach seems to extend the argument the cross-national comparison has made. Instead of competing with alternative approaches, TCT may form a bridge between the social and societal construction of culture and institutions on the one hand, and "choices" made in the demarcation of organizational domains on the other. A strategy of greater vertical integration, as in Germany, appears linked with a proclivity to consider transactions in the value chain and assets as governed by specificity, complexity and uncertainty. By contrast, the tendency to use markets and contracts, as in Britain, appears to tie in with the identification of transactions and assets as less specific, complex and uncertain.

So far, TCT seems to profit from greater "embeddedness" in other approaches. This is a well-established critique of the approach, which aims at making it blend in with other kinds of organization theory (Scarbrough 1995). In the light of this critique, TCT is valuable in identifying certain core relationships. The latter are not to be seen, however, as attached to characteristics of a transaction as such. Instead, the transaction is attributed with characteristics by actors that have a personal and social experience, strategies, values, industrial recipes (Grinyer and Spender 1979) and other predispositions. Once such a socialized attribution of transaction costs is made, core relationships of the approach seem to work.

This critique is supported by the present investigation, which has shown how transaction cost assessments are rooted in strategies, and in professional and industrial postures of actors. I would add here the finding about the complementarity between contingency theory and TCT and to assert that TCT works better if it is intertwined with contingency theory explanations, which refer to company size and industry characteristics. Again, this kind of critique is not seriously unsettling for TCT. The approach probably can very well position itself as a kind of mandatory stop, en route between various explanatory factors as starting points, and organizational arrangements as the targets of our explanatory effort. TCT could argue that, wherever one starts out from, one cannot help referring to its theoretical apparatus if one wants to make the explanation more rigorous, thanks to the robust core relationships of the approach.

Nevertheless, the analysis of changes in vertical integration over time raises doubts about the pertinence of this interpretation. It gives rise to a Gestalt switch, because it shows that the same transaction cost assessment may lead to radically opposed outcomes. The outcome will be greater integration, in response to perceived specificity and complexity/uncertainty under the condition that actors can incorporate specific assets in the organizational domain without losing control. The opposite outcome, a reduction of integration, will prevail where an organizational domain is thought to be riven apart. In this situation, vertical integration is associated with lack of control, and control will be sought via disintegration, contracts and markets. This would imply that the solution to problems posed by opportunistic behaviour and the other TCT determinants is sought via the opposite of what core relations in TCT predict.

This means that transaction cost assessments are translated into organizational action on the basis of a constrained definition of the organizational domain. It is the actors' assessment of the organizational domain which influences conclusions from a transaction cost assessment. Here, it is organizational templates or comps that constrain the internalization of transactions and the level of transaction costs incurred. This is the opposite of transaction cost assessments impinging on the demarcation of an organizational domain. This critique is more serious. It suggests that TCT has to be turned on its head: Organizational domain influences the attribution of transaction costs, and it also influences whether vertical integration or disintegration will prevail.

This particular critique also views transaction cost assessments as socially, culturally and institutionally conditioned. Yet it argues, in addition to the moderate critique mentioned in the theoretical part, that the core relations of TCT do not work the way TCT suggests. This defect occurs whenever there are limits to the expansion of an organizational domain. These limits are given by the limited capacity of actors to achieve effective social integration, as opposed to vertical integration in the sense of hierarchical sub-ordination. Hierarchical subordination is overburdened as a mechanism of coordination and control. TCT tends to over-rate hierarchy as the major internal co-ordination and control mechanism and it neglects mutual adjustment and the standardization of both skills and procedures (Mintzberg 1983).

Where actors expand the organizational domain beyond the capacity of the organization to have a unit-wide integrating cultural and institutional template or comps, of a professional, industrial or enterprise specific nature, vertical integration loses its function of co-ordination and control. From a mechanism that hedges against opportunistic behaviour (the self-seeking interests of different segments), and which enables an organization to control idiosyncratic transactions by integrating forwards and backwards, it turns into a source of confusion and disorganization. If this happens or is feared to happen, then actors will turn to markets and contracts. The latter therefore are much more functionally equivalent to hierarchical integration, and less dependent on the acknowledged TCT contingencies.

The type of coordination mechanism that is adopted is indeed a matter of transaction costs, but relative transaction costs, and not asset specificity, complexity/uncertainty or frequency. The experienced or perceived costs of a transaction arrangement do not simply depend on the nature of the transaction in its institutional casing (market vs. organizational co-ordination). They are also a function of the organizational domain, either in its static form or its evolution over time. The present investigation suggests that larger units, at least within the size band studied here, offer a better dynamic potential, to expand an organizational domain. Possibly, this is so because the same absolute addition to an organizational domain will imply an incremental change for a large unit which has already integrated differentiated segments effectively, whilst it may very well signify a more revolutionary transformation for a small unit.

The importance of organizational domain, template, comps and industrial recipes, also sheds a light on the differences between firms in the electrical, electronics and data-processing industries, and those in other industries. Whilst these differences do not go against TCT, they are better understood if the relativity of transaction cost assessments to organizational domain is borne in mind. Where transactions are seen to imply specific assets which are *related* to the organizational domain and associated procedures, competence or forms of mutual adjustment, there will be vertical integration because the costs of integration will appear as low. On the other hand, where transactions imply *unrelated* but equally specific assets, firms will prefer contracts with external suppliers. This interpretation is sufficiently general to explain differences in vertical integration across a wider range, including those occasioned by industrial, firm size, other contextual and societal differences.

Is all this then to mean that we can do away with TCT? On the basis of the evidence presented here, not quite. Transaction costs are a salient motive in vertical integration policies. However, their impact is more contextually relative, and the explanation of the impact depends on theoretical cross-fertilization with other organization theories (see also Grandori 1996; Douma and Schreuder 1992). In the longitudinal analysis of vertical integration changes, the core relations put forward by TCT are largely disconfirmed. It may be that the discrepancy between cross-sectional and longitudinal tests of TCT indicates a familiar problem: Actors tend to legitimate current states of vertical integration by implicitly referring to a transaction cost framework which is normatively plausible; however, when actual policy developments are examined in comparison, it turns out that transaction costs cannot be attributed to those coordination mechanisms directly, but only to coordination mechanisms relative to organizational domain, and relative to those co-ordination mechanisms which TCT has chosen to disregard or de-emphasize.

TCT is, therefore, neither fundamentally superior nor theoretically autonomous. The same conclusion was reached by Noorderhaven (1995), from a critique of the argumentational texture of TCT. Transaction cost assessments and their organizational consequences lead in a different direction than core relations in TCT predict, when an organizational domain is constrained. They are strongly influenced by factors which TCT does not address, but which contingency theory, theories of action and the societal effect approach do incorporate. In a way, transaction costs appear like a new version of hallowed economic terms such as "utility", and they have a rationalist connotation which obscures the factual rationale of behaviour in enterprises. This suggests that TCT involves certain methodological problems which might limit its contribution to organizational studies unless a meaningful dialogue is established between this particular approach and some other currents of analysis in the field.

References

Anderson, E. (1985): "The salesperson as outside agent or employee: A transaction cost analysis." *Marketing Science* 4: 234-254.

Anderson, E. and D.C. Schmittlein (1984): "Integration of the sales force. An empirical examination." *Rand Journal of Economics* 15: 385-395.

Baur, C. (1990): *Make-or-buy-Entscheidungen in einem Unternehmen der Automobilindustrie* (Make-or-buy-decisions in an automobile industry enterprise). Munich: Verlag V. Florentz.

Behringer, F. and U. Brasche (1986): *Mikroelektronik und Mitarbeiterqualifikation. Die Bedeutung der Personalentwicklung für die Produktinnovation — Ergebnisse einer Befragung* (Microelectronics and employee conpetence. The importance of human resource development for product innovation — survey results). Berlin: VDI/VDE-Technologiezentrum Informationstechnik.

Beuschel, W., S. Gensior and A. Sorge (1988): *Mikroelektonik, Qualifikation und Produktinnovation. Ergebnisse von Fallstudien* (Microelectronics, competence and productinnovation. Case study results). Berlin: Edition Sigma.

Campbell, A., A. Sorge and M. Warner (1989): *Microelectronic product applications in Great Britain and West Germany: Strategies, competence and training*. Aldershot: Gower-Avebury.

Douma, S., and H. Schreuder (1992): *Economic approaches to organizations*. New York: Prentice Hall.

Grandori, A. (1996): "Agency, markets and hierarchies" in M. Warner (ed.), *International encyclopedia of business and management*, vol. 1:199-213. London: Routledge.

Grinyer, P.A., and J.C. Spender (1979): *Turnaround: The fall and rise of the Newton Chamber Group*. London: Associated Business Press.

Hatten, K.J. and M.L. Hatten (1988): *Effective strategic management. Analysis and action*. Englewood Cliffs, NJ: Prentice Hall.

Hennart, J.-F. (1993): "Explaining the swollen middle: Why most transactions are a mix of 'market and hierarchy'." *Organization Science* 4: 529-547.

McKelvey, B. (1982): *Organizational systematics. Taxonomy, evolution, classification*. Berkeley, CA: University of California Press.

Mintzberg, H. (1983): *Structure in fives: Designing effective organizations*. Englewood Cliffs, NJ: Prentice-Hall.

Noorderhaven, N. (1995): "The argumentational texture of transaction cost economics." *Organization Studies* 16: 605-623.

Perrow, C. (1986): *Complex organizations. A critical essay*. New York: McGraw-Hill, 3rd edition.

Scarbrough, H. (1995): "Blackboxes, hostages and prisoners: Organizing technical knowledge for innovation." *Organization Studies* 16: 991-1020.

Williamson, O.E. (1985): *The economic institutions of capitalism*. New York: Free Press.

Societal Strategic Advantage: Institutional Structure and Path Dependence in the Automotive and Electronics Industries of East Asia

Nicole Woolsey Biggart and *Marco Orrù*

What strategy should a developing nation pursue to ensure a successful position in the global economy? What industries should it promote, and what organizational arrangements and practices need it encourage? Specialists assisting the development of markets and international economic integration in Latin America, sub-Saharan Africa, and most recently, Eastern Europe, have no shortage of theories from which to draw, such as those by Hirschman, Gershenkron, Haggard, and Wallerstein. Examples of successful development are harder to find but many development theories draw their lessons from the expansion of the East Asian economies of Japan, South Korea, and Taiwan in the period after World War II and the Korean War. These Asian neighbors are often grouped together and positioned in contrast to the problematic development of Latin American nations such as Mexico and Brazil. Asian success has variously been attributed to economic factors such as their export-oriented industrial policies (Balassa 1981), to strong state control (Evans 1979), and to common cultural factors conducive to discipline and entrepreneurial drive (Berger 1984; Redding 1990). In this chapter we, too, argue that these Asian countries can serve as exemplars of development for aspiring nations. However, we believe the lesson is not in what they did the same, but rather, what they did *differently*, each from the other.

We believe the lesson to be learned from these countries is not found only or primarily in factors or practices they hold in common. Rather, we will argue, the reason each has done well is that it has organized crucial industrial sectors in ways unlike their neighbors, ways that make sense given the social relations and historically developed institutional patterns that prevail in each country (Hamilton and Biggart 1988). None has attempted to find an elusive "best way" or abstractly "most efficient" economic model to organize their entry into global markets.

Each, we will argue, has entered the global economy in ways that provide a strategic fit between their institutionalized social structural arrangements and the needs of global commodity markets. Japanese, Taiwanese, and Korean industries have pursued market strategies for which their social patterns give them advantages in comparison with other nations. We have described this development orientation as the pursuit of *societal comparative advantage,* the adaptation of well-understood social arrangements to new business opportunities and manufacturing technologies (Biggart and Hamilton 1989; see also Sorge 1991 for a related conceptualization). Comparative advantages in industry are rooted not only in economic factors, as important as they are, but also in social arrangements that prove to be advantageous in attempting a course of economic action.

In this chapter we pursue a related line of thought: we argue that strategic economic choices are path dependent, and that the "paths" economic actors are likely to follow are shaped by socially and materially constructed institutions. In other words, economic actors' strategic calculations are shaped, constrained, and potentially advantaged, by the social structural arrangements of the milieu in which they act. Further, we argue that development strategies, if they hope to be successful, must match the institutional arrangements of societies with the needs of global commodity markets. We pursue this argument by looking retrospectively at the automotive and electronics manufacturing sectors of Japan, South Korea, and Taiwan. Notwithstanding recent downturns, all three have economies that have been on a dramatic path of growth in the last 30-40 years and during this period all three established automotive and electronics industries. While these countries have important similarities, such as geographic proximity, common Confucian and other cultural heritages, poor natural resources, and until recently, an abundance of labour resources, none of these nations can be said to be following the same path as the others. Nor are they emulating earlier-developed countries, as some theorists have argued "late-industrializing nations" are wont to do. Rather, each has pursued industrial strategies in the automotive and electronics sectors that take advantage of, or are constrained by, the underlying institutional structure of their society. For the most part, but with exceptions we will note, these three countries have had societal strategic advantages — and disadvantages — that can explain their choices, successes, and occasional failures in the global marketplace.

We first discuss the concept of "societal strategic advantage" as an economic resource. This is a term that combines the insights of classical and institutional economics and the institutional school of organizational sociology. We draw, too, from the resource-based view of the firm, a recent perspective in strategic management studies. Second, we characterize very briefly the institutional structure of Japan, South Korea, and Taiwan. Third, we look in turn at the automotive and electronics industries in each nation to demonstrate how each has utilized its institutionalized social arrangements to achieve economic success. Finally, in the conclusion, we argue that social institutions confer important advantages and constraints in pursuing economic strategies. We believe that the insights of Weberian developmental sociology and evolutionary economics correctly turn our attention to the constrained paths that economies can take in pursuing prosperity. Nations have no determined path to the future, but nor are they able to pursue all economic strategies to their advantage. Development can only take place successfully within the bounds of deeply rooted social arrangements.

Societal Strategic Advantage

The concept of comparative advantage dates to Adam Smith, David Ricardo and the other classical economists. Smith (1776/1843), concerned with promoting economic prosperity, argued that some economic actors can produce goods more efficiently than others by specializing and gaining "absolute advantages" of skill and scale. Specialization leads to increased productivity and also to interdependence as actors must trade for goods they do not produce. Smith saw overall output, and hence well-being, enhanced by specialization. Ricardo (1817/1951) argued, however, that trade across national boundaries was fundamentally different than exchange between individuals: political and social institutions place barriers to the movement of labour, capital, and other resources necessary to efficient specialization. Therefore, the goods that a nation uses for trade are those that it produces with the least cost, not "absolutely" in terms of a global economic system to which it is imperfectly connected, but in comparison to other domestic goods it produces. In other words, nations will do best by exporting those goods it can produce with the greatest "comparative advantage" when contrasted to the other goods it produces. The classical thinkers focused on economic factors such as land, labour, and the transportation advantages conferred by favourable geographic location to understand why certain nations developed comparative advantages in trading different items (Irwin and Kasarda 1994).

Comparative advantage is concerned with strategizing *which* product markets a nation or other economic actor can most effectively enter for trade purposes (e.g. cotton textiles or steel). A related concept, competitive advantage, is concerned with an effective strategy *within* a product market (e.g. mass produced cotton sheeting vs. luxury designer cottons). Whereas comparative advantage is a concept used by trade economists and development specialists who are concerned with the prosperity of nations, regions, or other bounded markets, competitive advantage is a concern of management strategy theorists who study firm behaviour within industries. One school of thought, developed out of the economics of Mason (1939) and Bain (1956; 1968), and most recently associated with Michael Porter (1985), argues that firms can gain competitive advantages by exploiting weaknesses in their industry's structure. For example, in an industry that is dominated by a few large firms, a small firm might develop a specialized product niche too narrow to be of interest to large producers. This is a perspective that attributes competitive advantage to the ability to exploit a product strategy considering the industrial environment *external* to the firm.

More recently, frustrated by inattention to the internal capabilities of firms to pursue different economic strategies to their competitive advantage, strategy scholars have developed what has come to be known as the "resource-based view" of the firm. Like classical economics, which looked at the factor resources of nations, the resource-based view focuses on the factor endowments *internal* to a firm that confer an advantage when compared to competitors in the market place. Firms are conceptualized as bundles of resources — technical, economic, but especially social resources. Firms that are faster, smarter, more efficient have competitive advantages when compared to slower, less innovative, and inefficient firms. Internal endowments may enable an organization to achieve superior performance (generate greater rents, in economic terms) than other firms, with the same economic profile, in the same markets. The resource-based view, unlike earlier structural strategy theories, places importance on the capabilities of management, the culture and values of a firm, the cognitive-learning capabilities of firms, more effective organization, access to social networks, and on other *social and organizational factors* that are assets or resources that confer advantages when compared with competitors (Castanias and Helfat 1991; Connor 1991; Barney 1991).

From the perspective of resource-based view scholarship, each firm is unique in that it has historically-developed social relations, culture, and organizational routines that no other firm can claim. These social resources, however, only confer comparative advantages when they are useful in pursuit of economic profits and when they are difficult to imitate and causally complex. Techniques of management and structures of organization that everyone can copy offer no competitive advantage. It is also true that because social resources are often deeply embedded in the fabric of a firm, firms cannot easily change strategies even when it is to their advantage to do so; their social resources, unlike financial resources, are not fungible.

While the concept of comparative advantage has been applied primarily to nations selecting the markets in which they will compete in globally, and the concept of competitive advantage applied mostly to firms choosing a strategic posture within product market sectors, we believe that both comparative and competitive strategy can be understood more generally as calculated efforts to achieve economic advantage. Both levels of strategic calculation, the comparative and the competitive, are made by actors at all levels — entrepreneurs, firms, regional economies, and nations. At all of these levels strategic choices are made, not in a vacuum, but in an institutional environment that shapes both what is possible and what is economically advantageous. Material factors, such as labour costs and the cost of capital, are certainly part of any calculus, but social resources and limits are a necessary element in successful strategizing at any level. The institutional environment creates background factors that precede and logically shape both comparative and competitive strategic action. While most strategy scholarship looks from the present moment and projects to a future economic outcome, we would argue that the institutional heritage of the past offers important insights as to which strategic paths have a chance of successful implementation. In fact, we believe, knowledgeable actors — entrepreneurs, executives, industrial planners — make strategic choices in light of an intimate knowledge of institutional factors that can help or hinder economic action.

While the resource-based view of strategic competitive advantage has been applied only to firms, we believe that it functions equally well as a way to understand why economic actors at other levels of aggregation such as business networks, regions, and nations are able to sustain both comparative and competitive advantages in the global marketplace, that is, for example, why some nations are favoured exporters of some goods in some markets, but not other goods or other markets. Returning to the macro level of analysis favoured by Ricardo and Mill, but incorporating the insights of a resource-based view, we can begin to unravel the non-economic reasons that some nations are advantaged in certain industries, and why they successfully pursue the strategies they do within global industrial sectors.

While nations do not "act" in the global economy — firms do — firms within a society draw from the same institutional heritage and have many of the same organizational resources from which to draw, an observation made increasingly by scholars concerned with regional development in areas such as Italy (Orrù 1991), Germany (Piore and Sabel 1984), and the U.S. (Saxenian 1994). Firms within a nation may differ from each other, but in comparison to firms in other nations they are broadly similar: Japanese firms share many organizational attributes and social resources (are "isomorphic") when compared with Brazilian firms (see Orrù et al. 1991).

The sociological institutional school of organizational analysis, which focuses on the socially-constructed rules, routines, and other social factors that undergird industrial organization (Powell and DiMaggio 1991), can be joined usefully to the resource-based view. We believe that "societal comparative advantage", an appreciation of the leverage that different forms of social organization confer when attempting different economic strategies, helps to answer questions about which industrial strategy different nations might reasonably attempt in pursuing a national development strategy (Gereffi 1994).

Institutional Logics in Japan, South Korea, and Taiwan

In previous works we identified three distinct organizational patterns in the economies of Japan, South Korea, and Taiwan (Hamilton and Biggart 1988; Orrù et al. 1991). Japan's economy is dominated by very large clusters of firms that are social, but not legal entities. The clusters are organized for the mutual benefit of affiliated firms. Two types of clusters are important: giant inter-market *keiretsu* groups such as Mitsubishi and Sumitomo, that have affiliated firms in all major market sectors. Independent groups, such as Toyota, Nissan, and Hitachi are large manufacturers that have hierarchical relations with affiliated subcontractors that see themselves as part of the larger firm's community. In both types of groups relationships internal to the group are communitarian and they compete with outside groups. However, even groups may be networked through cross-holding of shares or other financial relations. Institutional cooperation — or what Michael Gerlach (1992) calls alliance capitalism — is typical of Japan's economic organization and has historical roots in pre-modern *zaibatsu* groups of family firms that date to the Tokugawa shogunate. The Japanese state also maintains cooperative relations with business and often works to orchestrate business interests.

Corporate patrimonialism, on the other hand, is typical of South Korea's socio-economic structure. Korea is dominated by *chaebol* or family-owned business groups. This, too, is a form of organizational structure that can be traced to a pre-industrial economic era characterized by the rule of competing aristocratic families (Biggart 1990). *Chaebol* are structured on authoritarian and hierarchical principles under the domination of a patriarchal head of household who, with the assistance of family members and personally-loyal professional managers, rules over his holdings which he treats like a fiefdom. Relations internal to *chaebol* are stratified and authoritarian at all levels and relations between *chaebol* are often deeply antagonistic and competitive. State-business relations are also hierarchical with the state attempting, with greater or lesser effectiveness at different historical periods, to control the *chaebol* through personalistic, political, and financial means.

Unlike Japan with its enormous enterprise groups, and Korea with its large groups of family-run conglomerates, networks of very small to medium-sized firms characterize the Taiwanese economy. Firms in Taiwan rarely grow large and are divided every generation or so in order to give equal inheritances to sons. This institutional pattern, which dates to Imperial China, has mitigated against the formation of large, economically powerful groups. The Taiwanese state has had selective influence in Taiwanese economic policy, but neither the important orchestrating role of the Japanese state nor the controlling role of the South Korean state.

Given these distinctive organizational structures, we want to suggest how each structure affects the relative performance and possibilities of each economy in specific industrial sectors. We believe that each nation's organizational arrangements give it relative advantages — and disadvantages — in pursuing industrial growth.

The Automobile Industry in Japan, South Korea, and Taiwan: Overview

The automobile industry is a key sector of all advanced industrial economies; symbolically and substantively, the rise of Japan as the world leader in automobile production during the 1980s sealed its position as an international industrial giant. Japanese automakers' growth has been truly astounding. In 1960, Japan accounted for 1% of the world production of passenger cars, while the U.S. accounted for 52% of that total; in a little more than a quarter century, by 1987, Japan's share had grown to 23% of the total, while the U.S. share had shrunk to 21% (see Ward's Automotive Yearbook 1988: 73). South Korea's automobile industry has also emerged rapidly: it was virtually non-existent in 1960, but in 1987 it reached almost the one million vehicle mark, and accounted for two per cent of world production of passenger cars.

The growth of the auto industry in all three East Asian economies has been phenomenal, especially when considering the general decline in the auto industry of most other non-Asian economies. From 1986 to 1987, the production of motor vehicles declined by 4% in the U.S. and Canada, but increased 1.5% in Japan; more significantly, South Korea's production increased 63%, and Taiwan's 29%. These growth figures show the strong dynamism of these three East Asian economies when compared with the industrialized West, but, as Table 1 below shows, the size of each of the three economies' auto industry needs to be put in perspective.

In 1987, Japan produced 12.25 million vehicles, South Korea produced 980,000, and Taiwan 224,000. In terms of its industry's capacity, South Korean auto production lags 25 years behind Japan, and Taiwan is 30 years behind; but one would be mistaken in taking the size of auto production in each country at face value in comparing the three economies. On the one hand, consider that in the mid-1960s Japan produced the same number of passenger cars as South Korea does today, but only ten per cent of Japanese production was exported; in 1987, 67% of passenger cars produced in South Korea were exported. On the other hand, Taiwan, who in 1972 had twice the passenger car production of South Korea, fifteen years later, in 1987, Taiwan's production is only one fourth Korea's, and Taiwan has no export component except for Ford Lio Ho Motor's small export of Mercury Tracer cars to Canada. Clearly, the three economies have historically developed, and are currently developing, along different paths which follow clearly distinct organizational strategies. The organization of the automobile sector in the three economies differs widely, as we endeavor to show in detail in the remainder of this chapter. Three levels of organizational analysis are relevant for understanding the distinctive features of the auto industry in each economy: the structure of the sector at the level of the largest automakers in each country, the kind of structural relationship between auto assemblers and ancillary firms in each auto industry, and the relationship between state and private business characterizing the auto industry development in each country.

Table 1. Production and export of passenger cars in Japan, South Korea, and Taiwan, 1952-1987

	Japan			South Korea			Taiwan
Year	Production	Export	%	Production	Export	%	Production
1952	4,837						
1957	47,121	410	1				
1962	268,784	16,011	6	1,710			
1967	1,375,755	223,491	16	4,983			
1972	4,022,289	1,407,340	35	9,525			25,000
1977	5,431,045	2,958,879	54	43,981	5,075	12	
1982	7,358,938	4,232,042	57	94,460	14,133	15	134,192
1987	9,303,606	5,897,462	63	793,125	535,231	67	195,315

Sources: MVMA, *World Motor Vehicle* Data, 1989 edition, pp. 60-99.

Organization of Major Automakers in the Three Economies

In Japan, the auto industry is characterized by eleven giant automakers who either form their own industrial groups, like the Toyota Motor and Nissan Motor groups, or who are members of Japan's largest inter-market groups: Mitsubishi Motors belongs to the Mitsubishi group, Mazda to the Sumitomo group, Isuzu to the DKB group, and Suzuki to the Tokai group (see Dodwell 1986). All together, in 1987 ten Japanese firms (more than any other country) were included among the top forty world automakers, and accounted for 28.5% of world vehicle production (MVMA 1989:16). The Japanese auto industry is fairly dispersed among producers; as Table 2 below demonstrates, the top three automakers (Toyota, Nissan, and Honda) account for less than 60% of total vehicle production, and 70% of passenger cars, with an average of 65% export rate.

Table 2. Top three producers and exporters of passenger cars in Japan, South Korea, and Taiwan, 1987

	Hourly Wages	Production	Export	% of Export
Japan	US$ 14.33			
Toyota		2,984,964	1,465,216	49
Nissan		2,023,438	1,175,257	58
Honda		1,504,842	1,169,349	78
Top Three		6,513,244	3,809,822	58
% for Japan		70	65	
Korea	US$ 2.17			
Hyundai		544,648	403,419	74
Daewoo		149,639	71,082	48
Kia		95,532	60,336	63
Top Three		789,819	534,837	68
% for Korea		100	100	
Taiwan	US$ 2.99			
Yue Loong		55,980		
Ford Lio Ho		51,202		
San Yang		35,053		
Top Three		142,235		
% for Taiwan		73		

Sources: MVMA, *World Motor Vehicle Data*, 1989 edition, pp. 60-99.

Most Japanese industrial groups are, directly or indirectly, involved in the automobile sector, and are often simultaneously tied with several carmakers. For instance, the Sumitomo group is a major shareholder of Toyota Motor, but has also its own group member in the auto industry, Mazda Motor. Collaboration with foreign carmakers is also spread around all firms, and often constitutes an overlapping web of linkages. General Motors, for instance, has tie-ups with Toyota, but also with Isuzu, Suzuki, and Fuji (makers of Subaru cars); Ford has linkages with Mazda (which in turn is linked to Isuzu), and with Nissan; Chrysler is linked with Mitsubishi Motor; and Honda has ties with the British Rover.

South Korea's auto industry, in contrast to Japan, is heavily concentrated among three carmakers: Hyundai Motor Company, Daewoo Motor, and Kia Motors Corporation (see Table 2 above). Taken together, these three companies accounted for 99% of Korea's total vehicles production in 1987, and for 100% of the country's production of passenger cars. Of the three, Hyundai Motor, a member of the Hyundai industrial group, is by far the largest, accounting alone for 63% of Korean vehicles production in 1987. Japan's Mitsubishi group owns 15% of Hyundai Motor, making Hyundai also the most independent of Korean carmakers. In comparison, Daewoo Motor, a member of the Daewoo industrial group, is 50% owned by General Motors; Kia Motors is heavily linked with both Ford Motor Co., and Mazda Motor. While Hyundai produces its own line of automobiles for the Korean and the international markets, especially North America, Daewoo Motor and Kia Motor owe a large share of their production to passenger cars they respectively assemble for General Motors (Pontiac LeMans) and Ford (the Ford Festiva). The organizational pattern of Korea's auto industry, when compared to Japan's, is characterized by industrial concentration, strong competition, and the absence of collaborative linkages among the three domestic carmakers. The organization of South Korean industrial groups, and of the carmakers within them, is autarkic: collaboration with other groups is anathema, and moreover, foreign firms which do business with one industrial group are automatically excluded from doing business with any of the other groups. Accordingly, Hyundai, Daewoo, and Kia have no linkages with each other, nor do foreign firms link up with more than one industrial group. GM is only linked with Daewoo Motor, Ford and Mazda are linked with Kia Motor, and Mitsubishi (and Chrysler through it) is only linked with Hyundai. South Korean automakers sought to enter the export market on the basis of the comparative advantage in labour costs which were one-fifth Japanese carmakers'; but after turbulent years of strikes, slowdowns, and wage bargaining, the gap in labour costs is today considerably narrower, and estimated at 75% of the Japanese automakers'. Hyundai exports, which started with a bang in 1986 and 1987, declined sharply by 50% in 1989, with a little over 200,000 units exported. In terms of overall production, however, the growth of the domestic car market in Korea has absorbed the wide swing in export activities.

Taiwan's auto industry is structured in a yet distinctive way, differing from both Japan and South Korea. Vehicle production in Taiwan is distributed among a half-dozen small automakers, and is almost exclusively devoted to filling the needs of the domestic market. Table 2 above shows that the three largest producers, Yue Loong Motor, Ford Lio Ho, and San Yang, accounted, in 1987, for about 70% of Taiwan's vehicle output. In 1990, their combined share had declined drastically because of the substantial loss of market share by Yue Loong Motor (Far Eastern Economic Review [subsequently *FEER*] 21.6.1990).

The top three carmakers are members of top Taiwanese industrial groups headed by family entrepreneurs, but are on average much smaller than Japanese or South Korean industrial groups. To sustain their domestic production, Taiwanese automakers have strong linkages with foreign firms from Japan, the U.S., and Western Europe. Yue Loong Motor, the industrial group founded by a wealthy Shangainese entrepreneur in the 1950s, is 25% owned by Japan's Nissan Motor. Ford Lio Ho, related to the Lio Ho Cotton Weaving group, is 70% owned by Ford Motor Company and is thus considered a foreign subsidiary; the San Yang Industry group has a longstanding partnership with Honda Motor which owns 13.5% of the Taiwanese carmaker; other smaller auto assemblers have linkages with such foreign firms as Renault, Citroen, Peugeot, Isuzu, Toyota, Subaru, Mitsubishi, and Suzuki, among others. In contrast to both Japan and South Korea, Taiwan's vehicle production has yet to enter the export sector, although it is poised to do so in the near future. It is unlikely, however, that Taiwan's vehicle exports will be of any significance. The Taiwanese government has seldom been interested in the growth of the domestic auto industry; when it tried to facilitate a joint venture between GM and Hua Tung for the production of trucks, buses, and diesel engines in the early 1980s, the venture failed (Noble 1987). The policies of the Taiwanese government have in some cases been counterproductive for the strengthening of a domestic auto industry. Beginning in 1985, Taiwan reduced tariffs on imported cars from 75% to 60% and down to 30% by the end of 1990, thereby stimulating an already growing market for imported cars. Between 1985 and 1989, favoured also by the revaluation of the NT dollar, the production of domestic cars more than doubled from 152,000 to 334,000 units, while the growth in foreign car imports jumped tenfold, from about 16,000 in 1985 to 166,000 in 1989. The Taiwanese import policy contrasts sharply with South Korea's policy which was to close its domestic market to car imports, especially from Japan. At the same time, Korea's Hyundai pushed its exports to such an extent as to be accused in 1988 by the Canadian government of car dumping.

From this preliminary description of the auto industry in the three economies of Japan, South Korea, and Taiwan, we evince sharp differences in size, scope, and organization of the sector in each country. Japan's automakers are engaged in a mixture of competition and collaboration, what we would call competitive collusion among domestic manufacturers and with foreign partners. South Korean car manufacturers display no inclination to collaborate with each other; to the contrary, they compete fiercely for the same domestic and export markets, although they do so through different growth strategies. The Taiwanese carmakers do not have the high profile of either Japanese or Korean companies; rather, they concentrate on domestic production and have, until recently, avoided entering the international markets to achieve sector growth.

Ancillary Firms in East Asia's Auto Industries

Beyond the general differences among the automotive sectors of the three countries there are more substantive differences in the industrial organization which characterizes each sector internally. One way to demonstrate the sharp organizational differences of carmakers in the three economies is to look comparatively at the top automaker in each economy, as described in Table 3 below. The data demonstrate not only a great disparity in the sheer size of the three automakers, Toyota, Hyundai, and Yue Loong, but also in the organizational structure of each firm.

Table 3. Statistics on top three automakers in Japan, South Korea and Taiwan (1987 data)

	Japan	South Koreae	Taiwan
	Toyota Motor	Hyundai Motor	Yue Loong Motor
Vehicles Produced	3,970,404	606,816	80,725
% Passenger Cars	75	90	69
Sales (Millions US$)	41,455.0	3,437.4	814.8
Number of Employees	84,207	29,000	3,300
Vehicles/Employee	47	21	24.5
Sales/Employee (Thousands US$)	492	119	247

Sources: MVMA, *World Motor Vehicle Data*, 1989 edition, pp. 60-99.
Fortune's International 500, August 1, 1988.
Far Eastern Economic Review, June 21, 1990.

Data on vehicle production, sales, and number of employees for each firm show that compared to Hyundai and Yue Loong, Toyota produces twice the number of vehicles per employee, and displays four times the sales figure of Hyundai and twice the sales figure of Yue Loong. The large disparity in production and sales average figures is in part explained by greater automation and efficiency realized by Japanese carmakers, but beyond that factor, one must consider the degree to which each automaker relies on external subcontracting arrangements for the production of parts and components for auto assembly (for a history of affiliate firms of Nissan and Toyota, see Odaka et al. 1988).

In the Japanese industry, the extensive use of small and medium size subcontracting firms is well known. MITI estimates that half or more of small and medium sized firms with 300 or fewer workers are related through subcontracting agreements with larger firms. Manufacturing in the automobile sector follows this same pattern of an extensive division of labour among large auto assemblers, their subsidiaries and affiliates, and primary, secondary, and tertiary subcontracting firms. Adachi et al. (1983: 401) describe the Japanese organizational model as follows:

> A primary firm sits at the top of the hierarchical triangle whose base line is formed by a large number of ancillary firms, each of which maintains a close vertical relationship with the primary firm and at the same time keeps collaborative activities with fellow ancillary firms through their trade association. ... The primary firm, in turn, not only places indefinite standby procurement orders on the respective ancillary firms but also extends various forms of assistance to the latter in order to encourage their growth.

The subcontracting phenomenon is quite extensive throughout Japan's automobile industry. Shimokawa's 1985 study of the sector showed that major automakers have more than 30,000 subcontracting firms which are somehow incorporated in the production system. Relationships among assemblers, affiliates, and subcontractors are maintained through extensive webs of cross-holdings of stocks, dispatching of directors to affiliate firms' boards, extending financial loans for subcontractors' expansion of production, and providing them with technical assistance and know-how. The major advantage obtained by a system of extensive subcontracting is to achieve what Piore and Sabel (1984) call "flexible specialization" — the ability to enact rapid innovation and changes in products and production processes. The average time length for introducing new automobile models for major Japanese manufactures has been four years; and new models do not embody simply minor cosmetic changes of old models, but are totally new cars. In comparison, automobile models built by U.S. carmakers change after seven years or longer. The ability to update the introduction of new available technology into new automobiles is thus greatly enhanced in Japan, making its cars constantly among the best in terms of quality, reliability, performance, and cutting edge technology.

The organizational system of South Korea's auto industry is quite different from Japan's. The Korean government has been very active in promoting the domestic auto industry and has particularly encouraged the largest Korean *chaebol* groups' move into car manufacturing, but heavy state patronage has not been sufficient to turn Korea's auto industry into an overnight success. Although South Korea's major carmakers are, like their Japanese counterparts, members of major industrial groups, they do not enjoy the quantity or quality of close collaboration with subcontracting small and medium size firms observed in Japan. Ancillary firms in the auto industry had actually developed in South Korea before the emergence of major automakers, given the repair and replacement parts demand for military vehicles during and right after the Korean War. Also, it was the Korean government's policy to favour the development of the auto parts' industry through "horizontal subcontracting." According to government statistics, the domestic content of locally produced vehicles increased from 21% in 1966, to 38% in 1969, 70% in 1974, and 90% by 1980. The quality of domestically produced auto components, however, was historically below the quality required by international standards. A 1976 survey of the Korean Automobile Industry Association determined that only ten per cent of 1,200 items produced in South Korea in that sector met international quality standards. As Korean automakers sought to enter international markets, they became heavily dependent on foreign technology to improve the quality of their domestically manufactured products. While the official statistics on domestically produced components put the figure at 90%, it is widely believed that the actual localization rate is closer to 50% (*FEER* 18.1.1990). Major South Korean automakers are heavily dependent on Japanese manufacturers for major car components. Hyundai Motor Company relies on engines, gearbox, rear axle and suspension units from Japan's Mitsubishi Motor Company which owns 15% of Hyundai. Only in 1990 did Hyundai produce a project to develop its own engine, a step described by the Korean government as "a small revolution in the Korean motor industry" (*FEER* 18.1. 1990). The poorer quality of Korean auto manufacturing has plagued it in its export markets, especially in North America. Both Hyundai's smaller Excel and larger Sonata models received very poor marks concerning their manufacturing quality and reliability in the U.S.; similarly, GM's Pontiac LeMans, manufactured by Daewoo Motors, has scored very poorly in the U.S. market. One bright exception has been the good rating received by Ford's Festiva model, built by Kia Motors. The quality problems of Korea's automakers, together with the narrowing gap in the labour cost of Japanese and Korean auto workers, have made South Korea's success in the international auto industry problematic. The social organization of industry into competing *chaebol* fiefdoms prevents the financial and technological collaboration that strengthens Japan's automotive sector, and continues Korea's dynastic pattern of feuding families.

The organizational structure of business activities in Taiwan make it a very unlikely candidate for a strong automobile sector. Based on the family entrepreneurship of small businesses, and characterized by an arms-length relation with the Taiwanese government, the auto industry has shown little or no sign of ambition beyond its attempt to fill the modest demand of a small domestic market. Data for 1985 show that Taiwan's ten automakers combined sold a little over 150,000 automobiles that year — an average of 15,000 cars per firm. No Taiwanese carmaker is large enough to be able to embark on an export activity which requires car plants producing at least 200,000 vehicles a year. But in Taiwan, the production is instead fragmented among a large number of small automakers.

Henry Ford's visit to Taiwan in the late 1960s is significant of the policy pursued by the Taiwanese government regarding the car industry. Generalissimo Chiang Kai-shek offered Ford generous tax incentives and tariff benefits to set up a car plant in Taiwan. What Ford did not realize, however, was that the same privileged treatment was offered to any foreign carmakers who wanted to set up shop in Taiwan. "Chiang was not interested in the economics of the car industry; he just wanted to enhance national pride" (*FEER* 21.6.1990: 76). Today, Ford Lio Ho Motor is the largest automaker in Taiwan, having surpassed former industry leader Yue Loong Motor, but its production is still far below anything approaching export potential.

The events marking the decline of Yue Loong Motor are also telling of the inherent organizational problems of Taiwan's automobile firms. Yue Loong Motor was started as a family firm by T. L. Yen, a wealthy mainlander who had migrated to Taiwan and made Yue Loong the largest automaker in Taiwan; the family controls the firm with a 47% of stocks and runs the firm through personalistic family management. Jonathan Moore describes the events leading to the firm's decline:

> When the patriarch died in 1981, his widow, Vivien Wu, took over as chairwoman and began making decisions based on a personal whim and with little reference to executives lower down in the hierarchy.... The appointment of her U.S.-educated son, Kenneth, aged 25, as managing director and heir apparent led to the resignation of seven senior managers in 1988-89 (*FEER* 21.6.1990: 78).

Data from 1983 show that, in a typical Taiwanese fashion, Vivien Wu held multiple positions of management and stockholding in the ten firms making up the Yue Loong business group: she was director in seven firms, manager in two firms, and stockholder in four firms. Because of the familistic nature of private business enterprises in Taiwan, Vivien Wu and her son sought to maintain direct control of the family business through multiple management positions which allowed them to keep personal interaction reinforcing their authority position in each and every firm they owned. In response to the threatening growth of the distributing partner of Yue Loong Motor, Chinese Automobile Co., Wu looked for a second partner, a move that led to the abrupt end of the relationship with its former distributor and contributed to the crisis of Yue Loong Motor in 1988 and 1989. Because of the reduced size of their manufacturing firms, Taiwanese automakers have been focusing on the production of auto components for export as a more realistic goal in their firms' growth. Table 4 shows that Taiwan's export of auto components to the U.S. has had a more rapid growth in the early 1980s than either Japan or South Korea. Recent reports emphasize this trend in Taiwan's auto industry:

Some carmakers are trying to become integrated parts producers for their parent companies' regional affiliates. Renault wants to use San Fu's technology for components swaps with manufacturers. Yue Loong is investing in parts manufacturing to become a key supplier of cylinder blocks and other components to Nissan in Japan (*FEER* 21.6.1990: 77).

Table 4. U.S. imports of parts and accessories from Japan, South Korea and Taiwan, 1980 and 1984 (in 1,000 US$)

	Japan	South Korea	Taiwan
1980	2,828,725	120,313	110,084
1984	2,727,198	339,315	329,602
% change	-3.0	+64.5	+66.6

Source: Hoffman and Kaplinsky (1988: 302).

The metal products sector has traditionally been one of the strongest in Taiwan's export economy, and it is a more likely competitive niche for the small- and medium-size family firms seeking growth than the attempt to become competitive auto assemblers in the international market.

The State and the Auto Industry in East Asia

At the early stages of establishing an auto industry, the role of the government is crucial in providing directives and incentives for the development of capital intensive auto manufacturing capabilities in any economy. The different avenues taken by each state in the three economies we examined shows the effects of state institutions on economic outcomes.

Historically, the Japanese state had an interest in developing an auto industry since the turn of the century, but in practice it was only after World War II that such development took place. The Japanese government took the position that Japan had to develop its own auto industry instead of simply providing a cheaper labour force within an international division of labour. On the one hand, the state sought to upgrade the quality standards for auto parts in the late 1940s and early 1950s; on the other hand, the Ministry of International Trade and Industry launched the "Citizens' Car Project" in 1965, aiming at increasing the country's motorization by producing small passenger cars for wide domestic adoption. Through joint governmental agencies and business associations, the makers of auto parts were provided with financial assistance, technical expertise, and materiel procurement to strengthen the infrastructure of small- and medium-sized auto parts manufacturers. To develop a strong auto industry, it was paramount that ancillary firms be given the opportunity to acquire sophisticated technologies of production and to obtain the necessary capitalization required for firm expansion. The support was provided by the government in a joint effort with the large carmakers:

> The primary firms have extended financial, technological, and managerial assistance to their ancillary firms on the basis of the stable and exclusive relationships between them. On the other hand, the government ... has offered persistent and comprehensive support to both the primary and ancillary firms through various kinds of policy instruments. (Adachi et al. 1983: 391).

The success of the Japanese government's policy rested on its ability to promote simultaneously the development of strong primary firms and a strong basis of ancillary manufacturers of auto parts, covering both forward- and backward-linkages in the auto industry chain.

South Korea's government sought to emulate the Japanese in producing a national policy for a Korean auto industry, beginning with the first five-year development plan which included an "Automobile Industry Protection Law." As in the Japanese case, the government effort moved in two directions. On the one hand, with the 1969 "Automobile Industry Basic Promotion Plan", the Korean government sought to increase the localization of parts and components production by importing foreign technology and increasing the domestic content in auto manufacturing to 70% by 1974. On the other hand, with the 1974 "Long Term Automobile Promotion Plan", the government began to promote the development of an export-oriented auto industry. The plan was devised for a "Citizens' Car", similar to the Japanese plan, to meet about 80% of the domestic market demand, with a 95% domestic content. The three automakers designated as producers of the "Citizens' Cars" were Hyundai, Kia, and Saehan (later incorporated by

Daewoo Motor). The government goal was to achieve domestic production of 50,000 cars by 1975.

The major stumbling block in the development of a competitive auto industry in South Korea has been the lack of integrated effort between primary firms and ancillary firms in the sector, leading to a generally underdeveloped system of production. Kim and Lee (1983: 312-314) argue:

> The link between primary and ancillary firms is very weak in terms of equity share, technical assistance, financing, and supply of raw materials ... The reason seems to be that the ancillary firms in Korea have historically grown independently of primary firms catering to the repair and replacement market. Therefore, there were no close ties with primary firms from the beginning of ancillary firm development.

The inability of *chaebol* to nurture small subcontractors is directly traceable to the patrimonial logic that undergirds their organizational form: in a relentless attempt to bring all elements of production under the autarkic control of the patrimony, they vertically integrate, either by buying parts suppliers or producing their own components (Biggart 1990). Given the limited capabilities of the large *chaebol* firms themselves, both in terms of financial muscle and of technological capabilities, they were not only unwilling but unable to provide ancillary firms with the kind of tutelage which large Japanese automakers are able to provide their affiliates, subsidiaries, and subcontractors. As a consequence, the ancillary firms in South Korea are unable to support a strong, internationally competitive auto industry: "The Korean automobile industry, including the parts and components industry, will encounter greater difficulties in the future unless some measures are taken to resolve the problem of price and quality" (Kim and Lee 1983: 319).

In contrast to the strong leadership taken by both the Japanese and the South Korean governments, the Taiwan state maintained a hands-off approach in setting any kind of national policy for the auto industry. The Taiwanese government, to be sure, encouraged foreign automakers to set up shop in Taiwan and to engage in joint ventures with local manufacturers, but it never took it upon itself to stimulate the growth of the auto industry through massive infusion of capital in the auto industry or through the setting of national plans for a strong group of domestic automakers. In the absence of state leadership, the auto manufacturers remained relatively small, with an average production of 20,000 to 50,000 cars each in the mid-1980s, and with no ambition to turn their industry into an export sector, or even into a domestically self-sufficient supplier of automobiles. The niche which Taiwanese automakers could fill competitively in the international market was to export auto parts and components which required relatively low technological skills, and little or no help from governmentally orchestrated planning. The Taiwanese government understood that the auto industry would play a crucial role in economic development, as demonstrated by the government's attempt to promote a domestic heavy truck industry in Taiwan.

The motor vehicle industry was viewed as critical because of the backward linkages it creates. Taiwan officials knew that in the 1950s the automobile and truck sectors in Taiwan had spurred development in that country's steel, electronics, and precision machinery industries. The idea of building a heavy truck plant had the support of state-owned enterprises in related technological sectors, including China Steel and Taiwan Machinery Manufacturing Corporation (TMMC). It was hoped that such a plant would help expand and improve the automotive spare parts industry (Noble 1987: 687).

But the attempts on the Taiwanese government's part were too haphazard and sporadic to permit a sustained development of the auto industry as a whole. The heavy trucks joint venture between the state-owned TMMC and General Motors which had begun in early 1980 with the establishment of Hua Tung Heavy Trucks was abruptly terminated in 1982, when General Motors sold its 45% investment in the firm and withdrew from the project. The Taiwanese government ended up losing tens of millions of U.S. $ in the process. The development of a well-integrated auto industry was successful in Japan, and at least partially successful in South Korea. But Taiwan was partially unwilling, and partially unable to follow the same path for two major reasons. Noble (1987: 685) argues:

> First, the domestic market in Taiwan was simply too small to support the economies of scale required for efficient production in the truck industry ... Second, unlike textiles in which low-wage labor is crucial, or electronics in which Taiwan enjoyed not only low assembly costs but also a ready supply of basic components and well trained electrical engineers, the truck industry — highly capital intensive and requiring sophisticated mechanical engineering skills — is one in which Taiwan had neither a natural nor an acquired comparative advantage.

Accordingly, in the absence of strong governmental leadership, Taiwan's auto industry sought to maximize its comparative advantage in the international market by focusing its efforts on the production of auto parts and components for export to foreign auto manufacturers who have joint ventures in Taiwan.

Comparative Advantages of East Asian Auto Industries

The organizational characteristics in the auto industries in Japan, South Korea, and Taiwan, point to the distinctive place each one occupies in the larger global economy of that sector, and to their competitive advantages and disadvantages, both domestically and internationally. Japan's auto industry is characterized by a well-integrated effort among all major automakers, subsidiary, affiliate, and subcontracting firms, and the governmental agencies responsible for industrial planning at a national level. After massively importing foreign technology to catch up with western automobile firms, Japan eliminated its dependency on foreign firms and strengthened an infant domestic industry both at the level of primary firms and at the level of ancillary firms. Close collaboration throughout the production linkages made it possible to create a Japanese auto industry which is very competitive in international markets because of its ability to adopt and quickly implement cutting-edge technology in all steps of the production process, simultaneously assuring rapid innovation and quality products, far above most international competitors. In comparison, U.S. automakers, who rely more extensively on arms-length loose relations with parts subcontractors are much slower in marketing technological advances in the industry, bringing new models to the market, and achieving high levels of quality control in a short amount of time. General Motors' Saturn project demonstrated that wanting to introduce in the market a car which met the Japanese standards in terms of quality control ended up causing substantial delays in the production process. The ability of Japanese automakers to innovate rapidly while simultaneously maintaining a high standard of quality rests on an organizational structure which favours very close collaboration among major carmakers and the thousands ancillary firms they rely on for regular supply of constantly updated, defect-free parts and components. The clue to Japan's competitive advantage in the auto industry must therefore be sought in the interrelatedness of the firms which make up the sector, rather than in the singular strength of a particular group within that sector.

South Korea has tried to emulate Japan's success story in the auto industry by developing strong national plans, by favouring the emergence of a few strong primary firms, and by upgrading the quality of manufactured auto parts and components. The organization of the auto industry sector in South Korea, however, displays significantly lower levels of coordination among the economic actors involved. Resembling the organizational features of most other sectors of Korea's economy, the auto industry favoured the extreme competition of a few giant carmakers instead of a measured blend of competition and cooperation among a larger number of firms. In a parallel fashion, the ancillary firms in the auto industry developed independently of large firms with the result of a poorly integrated production process. The lack of leadership on the part of major Korean carmakers left ancillary firms unable to catch up in the acquisition of competitive technologies for the production of parts and components. Thus, Korean primary firms had to depend substantially on imported parts to achieve rapid growth in a short amount of time. The end result, however, is a precarious growth in the market share obtained by Korea's auto industry. Unless the problematic relation of primary firms to ancillary manufacturers is addressed systematically, it will be unlikely for the South Korean auto industry to achieve solid, competitive advantages in the international market.

Finally, in the case of Taiwan, the desire to build a strong domestic auto industry has been sporadic, if not altogether nonexistent, on the part of both major carmakers and of the Taiwanese government. Again, in a fashion which is typical of Taiwanese business patterns, the state preferred a hands-off policy regarding the growth of firms in the private sector; thus, it did not provide strong planning or guidance for an auto industry to emerge, and in the only instance when it tried it failed. For their own part, left to their own devices, the private entrepreneurs who were able to establish themselves in the auto industry had to rely heavily on foreign partners who had no interest in exporting cars but only in meeting the demands of the Taiwanese domestic market. Because of their inability to achieve a scale of production which would make them competitive in international markets, Taiwanese automakers realized that they should focus instead on the strong competitive advantage they held in the production of auto parts and components for export to foreign markets. This strategy capitalized on the flexible subcontracting arrangements that can be enacted among small and medium-size manufacturing firms in Taiwan, on the availability of a still relatively cheap labour force, and on production lines which require little technological upgrading and no research and development efforts. Taiwan's highly decentralized private economy has made it until now highly unlikely for a strong domestic auto industry to develop, and it is also unlikely for it to develop in the foreseeable future.

These three patterns of industrial development — Japan's collaborative competition among giant industrial groups, Korea's patrimonial rivalry among feuding family dynasties, and Taiwan's flexible family firms with low capitalization — can all be traced to pre-industrial patterns of political and economic organization (Hamilton and Biggart 1988). In each instance the automotive industry developed, or failed to develop substantially in the case of Taiwan, because institutional structures such as state-business relations or institutional logics of supplier-buyer relations, sustained particular orientations towards economic action.

The Electronics Industry in East Asia: Overview

If having a viable automobile manufacturing industry is the mark of an industrialized economy, having an electronics industry is often seen as the mark of an advanced industrial nation. The electronics industry is among the most technologically sophisticated of industrial sectors; it requires a degree of manufacturing expertise usually associated with only the most developed economies. It demands the ability to produce, or acquire, the latest basic and applied engineering research. Like few industries of the past or present, success in electronics is so interrelated with other areas of the economy that industrial nations feel pressed to develop a competitive electronics industry in order to protect their other economic sectors. As Duller put it, "Companies in market economy countries have no option but to adopt micro technology, create and upgrade products and processes, lest they be eliminated in short order" (1983: 28).

Although the U.S. grabbed the early lead in electronics production, most major industrialized nations are now involved in at least one of the three major electronics sub-sectors — electronic parts and components (such as semiconductors and microprocessors, as well as low technology parts such as capacitors, resistors, and transistors), industrial products (including defense, test equipment, and computers), and consumer products (such as cameras, audio and video equipment). These sub-sectors often integrate in products that become more technologically sophisticated, for example memory chips that include software information, or the marriage of cameras, test devices, and computers in medical imaging equipment.

The rapid development of technology and products, with constant permutation of the electronics industry subsectors, makes tracking the growth and pattern of electronics manufacturing more difficult. Indeed, even census figures in industrialized countries disagree on how to classify and enumerate electronics production: for example, is a largely mechanical dishwasher with digital controls an electronic product? Cross-national differences in data collection, and differences over time within a country, make comparison difficult.

Nonetheless, it is clear that although Japan, South Korea, and Taiwan are all major producers of electronics goods, and electronics are significant exports for each, they do not compete head-to-head in many subsectors. Japan is the technological leader in components, mainframe computers, consumer goods, and industrial products. *Keiretsu* firms have the financial and technological wherewithal to do the basic research and development to innovate and establish markets. South Korea's *chaebol* have targeted semiconductor component production, which requires a substantial capital outlay, and are becoming internationally significant producers of mass-produced chips. Korean *chaebol* are also significant producers of consumer products — not the cutting edge of products — but last generation audio and video products. Taiwan's myriad small- and medium-sized producers manufacture quality consumer-goods copies of Japanese and American products; a small, elite group of firms is establishing a reputation for high-Quality, technologically sophisticated software and personal computers.

Asian electronics production was almost exclusively of the low-technology variety until the early 1970s. Until then the U.S., where the transistor was developed at Bell Labs in 1947, held the undisputed world lead in electronics, both in sales and in technological sophistication. In 1974, however, Japan, known primarily as a low-cost assembler of last-generation products, introduced mainframe computers more advanced than the then-dominant IBM 370 models. In 1980 Nippon Telephone and Telegraph, Fujitsu, and NEC collaboratively developed the first 128K random access memory chip, (RAM) signaling that the technological lead in electronics would now be shared by the U.S. and Japan. Today Japan leads in consumer products such as calculators, videocassette recorders, and cameras, controls much of the office products industry for goods such as facsimile and copy machines, and dominates such industrial products as robotics and numerical control devices. Moreover, Japan is a major manufacturer of advanced components, not just for inclusion in its own products, but for export (Gregory 1985: 6-9).

In the fiscal year 1990 ending March 31, the largest 50 Japanese electronics firms sold U.S. $220.1 billion in goods, compared to U.S. $227.1 billion for the top 50 U.S. firms during calendar year 1989 (*Electronic Business Asia* [subsequently *EBA*] February. 1991: 38). The electronics industry, along with automobiles, dominates Japan's economy, especially the export sector. "Of the 15 Japanese companies that had the largest trade imbalances in 1989, eight were electronics companies. The rest were auto manufacturers" (*EBA* 1990: 54).

Japan is strong in all three electronics subsectors. In 1979 it became a net exporter of integrated circuits (ICs), and today shares the lead with the U.S. in developing ever more sophisticated advanced memory devices. While Japan and the U.S. are both capable of designing new generations of components, Japan took the lead in component production and production technology away from the U.S. in the 1980s. The U.S. component industry nearly collapsed during an industry recession in the 1980s, while networked Japanese firms were able to ride out the downturn with assistance from *keiretsu* affiliates.

Japanese companies challenge the best U.S. firms, including IBM, in the computer sub-sector, particularly in mainframes. Although the Japanese domestic PC industry is isolated by a different standard that is neither IBM — nor Apple-compatible (and dominated locally by NEC with more than

50% market share), Toshiba saw the future importance of laptops. By 1989, its IBM-compatible had 25% of the world laptop market. Japan is the undisputed world leader in consumer electronics. Companies such as Sony and Nintendo not only respond to consumer demand but shape it by producing innovative high technology products for mass markets. Japanese firms have miniaturized and digitized circuits in order to produce hand-held color TVs, video recorders, and electronic games. The Sony Walkman, Watchman, and Discman, and Nintendo's Gameboy revolutionized the category of personal entertainment. Even as a mature world leader in the electronics industry, Japan continues to post significant growth figures. The electronics industry in Japan grew 13% in 1988 and 1989, compared to 11% and 6% for the U.S. in those years (*EBA* February 1991: 39).

The Taiwanese electronics industry began in the 1960s much as the Japanese did a few years earlier: as a low-cost producer and assembler of components and low-technology consumer products such as transistor radios. Taiwanese firms were often subcontractors for American and Japanese companies. For example, Taiwanese companies made black and white TVs for General Electric, integrated circuits (ICs) for Texas Instruments, and terminals, printers, and computers for Digital Equipment Corporation. Subcontracting for technological superiors gave Taiwanese firms, particularly small- and medium-sized ones, the expertise for improving on foreign designs and selling them at even lower cost. Taiwan established a reputation in the 1980s for quality knock-offs, particularly in computer and consumer goods.

Although the electronics industry is dominated by myriad small producers, just as in automotive production, an elite corps of firms concentrated in Hsinchu Industrial Park, the "Silicon Valley of Taiwan", produce innovative products that compete successfully with Japanese and American producers in world markets, sometimes by utilizing original designs, often by reverse-engineering Japanese and American products. These firms, while numerically small, stimulate the industry in the country as a whole. Reverse engineering is growing more efficient and the lead time between redesigning the product and widespread local manufacturing is growing shorter.

Although electronics in 1988 was Taiwan's third largest export, and accounted for about 20% of the value of exports, electronics production represented only 4% of the country's total GDP. This small percentage suggests the diversity of economic output spread over myriad small producers.

The South Korean electronics industry, like Taiwan's, began with the assembly of transistor radios from imported parts and components in the late 1950s. In the 1960s Korean workers assembled components, mainly condensers and resisters, and in the 1970s assembled labour-intensive devices for black and white televisions. By the 1980s, however, Korean firms began producing more technologically sophisticated and capital-intensive products such as magnetic tape, color picture tubes, and mass-produced semiconductors for use in a wide range of consumer products. Until recently, South Korea has been known as a mass producer of labour-intensive consumer products and components.

During the 1970s and 1980s the average annual growth in the South Korean electronics industry was nearly 29%, in large part due to the coming on line of semiconductor manufacturing plants in the late 1980s. This compares to the still substantial growth rate of 16% for all Korean industries. In 1988 electronics overtook textiles as South Korea's biggest export, with U.S. $28.3 billion in total production, U.S. $16.6 in exports. The government estimates that by 1994 electronics production will be almost 25% of all manufacturing, and one third of exports by value (*EBA* April 1991: 10).

Korea is still noted for its substantial components production, representing more than 40% of electronics output, a figure likely to grow in the 1990s as major *chaebol* semiconductor plants become fully operative. Despite a significant components industry, South Korea was a large importer of semiconductors through the 1980s because it needed more technologically sophisticated components than it could produce domestically; most of its components imports, like its import of auto engines, come from Japan. Korea is also noted for its wide array of consumer products including TVs, microwave ovens, and stereos. These products typically compete with less expensive Japanese brands and OEM products made in Taiwan for American retailers under their brand names. The computer industry is small — in 1988 South Korea produced half as many personal computers as Taiwan, with just half the population of Korea — but entry into this market by Daewoo, Hyundai and the independent company Trigem (part-owned by Japan's Epsom) may expand this sub-sector's size in the 1990s, although entry into a crowded field is difficult. Computer manufacturers' strategy has been to produce cheaper clones of U.S. brands.

Structure of the Electronics Industry in East Asia

As in automobiles, large, networked firms dominate the Japanese electronics industry. Of the ten largest electronics firms in the world, six are Japanese; of the largest fifty, fifteen are Japanese. Again, like the automobile industry, these powerful corporations are networked into the Japanese economy, either as centrepieces of their own independent networks, or as members of *keiretsu*. For example, Matsushita, Japan's largest electronics firm and producer of National and Panasonic consumer products brands, is the core of its own independent group; it owns 65% of and controls Matsushita Electronics (Walter 1988: 42). It markets through an extraordinary 24,000-shop national retail network in Japan. Second largest producer, NEC, a communications, computer, and appliance manufacturer, is a member of Sumitomo group and negotiated an agreement with U.S. giant AT&T to develop gate-array chips, a technological advance. Toshiba, Japan's third largest electronics firm and world's largest producer of laptop computers, also produces heavy electrical equipment, instrumentation, and appliances. Toshiba, a member of Mitsui group, has almost 25% of the global 1 Mb (megabit) DRAM (dynamic random access memory) chip market. Fourth largest electronics firm, Hitachi, a highly diversified manufacturer, sits on the presidents councils of three *keiretsu* — Fuyo, Sanwa, and DKB — suggesting the interpenetration of firms. Hitachi unveiled its M-880 mainframe computer in June 1990, then the world's fastest. Number five Fujitsu, Japan's largest computer maker, is a DKB member and claims that its new M-1800 mainframe is the equal of Hitachi's top computer.

Table 5. Japan's top 50 electronics firms (in millions US$)

	Company	1990 Electronics sales	1990 Total sales	1989 Total sales
1	Matsushita Electric Industrial*	33,808	46,956	37,992
2	NBC Corp.	26,811	26,811	21,799
3	Nitachi, Ltd.	26,702	56,814	44,797
4	Toshiba Corp.	26,392	34,275	26,911
5	Fujitsu Limited	21,014	21,014	16,138
6	Sony Corp.	21,724	26,086	18,227
7	Mitsubishi Electric	12,498	22,318	18,838
8	Canon Inc.	12,270	12,521	8,550
9	LSharp Corp.	8,915	10,740	8,511
10	Sanyo Electric	8,871	10,665	8,643
11	Ricoh Co., Ltd.	5,471	6,496	5,288
12	Oki Electric Industry	4,782	4,782	3,987
13	Pioneer Electronic Corp.	4,296	4,296	3,239
14	TDK Corp.	3,814	3,814	3,024
15	Nintendo Co., Ltd.	3,629	3,629	1,843
16	Alps Electric Co., Ltd.	3,296	3,296	2,549
17	Ormon Corp.	3,261	3,261	2,634
18	Nippondenso Co., Ltd.	2,672	3,259	2,670
19	Kyoccia Corp.	2,700	3,333	42,665
20	Seiko Corp.	2,672	3,259	2,670
21	Citizen Watch Co., Ltd.	2,432	2,644	2,117
22	Casio Computer Co., Ltd.	2,391	2,391	1,929
23	Minolta Camera	2,110	2,740	2,198
24	Matsushita Electric Works	1,980	7,333	5,644
25	Murata Manufacturing	1,962	1,962	1,568

Table 5. Japan's top 50 electronics firms (in millions US$) (cont.)

	Company	1990 Electronics sales	1990 Total sales	1989 Total sales
26	Yokogawa electric Corp.	1,844	1,881	1,523
27	Nikon Corp.	1,696	2,174	1,800
28	Konica Corp.	1,565	3,913	3,222
29	Ryosan Co., Ltd.	1,563	1,563	1,317
30	Japan Radio Co.	1,518	1,518	1,212
31	Kenwood Corp.	1,481	1,481	435
32	Yamaha Corp.	1,413	3,623	3,157
33	Famac Ltd.	1,407	1,407	1,150
34	Tokyo Electron Limited	1,379	1,379	1,097
35	Olympus Optical Co., Ltd.	1,333	1,777	1,387
36	Clarion Co., Ltd.	1,305	1,374	1,007
37	Rohm Co., Ltd.	1,268	1,268	1,056
38	Shimadzu Corp.	1,216	1,415	1,137
39	Sanshin Electronics Co., Ltd.	1,215	1,215	932
40	Fujitsu General Ltd.	1,193	1,193	1,015
41	Mitsumi Electric Co., Ltd.	1,126	1,126	889
42	Sumitomo Bakelite Co., Ltd.	1,010	1,422	1,100
43	Kokusai Electric Co., Ltd.,	956	956	720
44	TEAC Corp.	906	906	699
45	Ryoyo Electro Corp.	904	904	766
46	Sanken Electric Co., Ltd.	878	878	685
47	Minebea Co., Ltd.	801	2,002	1,667
48	Asahi Optical Co., Ltd.	797	867	677
49	Nippon Chemi-Con	785	785	618
50	Anritsu Corp.	764	889	626

* Does not include contributions from MCA Inc.

Source: *Electronic Business Asia,* June 1991; FY ended March 1991.

The electronics industry in Japan is led by huge, inter-connected firms that dominate globally in important electronics subsectors. Forty-two of the top 50 Japanese electronics companies had sales of U.S. $ 1 billion or more for the fiscal year ending March 31, 1990 (*EBA* June 1991). Although Japan has a substantial domestic market for electronics goods, half of these firms' production was exported.

Although large exporting firms dominate, as in the automotive industry, small and medium-sized subcontractors that supply domestic producers are crucial to the industry. According to an *Electronic Business Asia* report:

> Most of Japan's huge electronics conglomerates have come to depend on elaborate networks of...subcontractors. The average conglomerate uses 183 subcontractors, while Hitachi Ltd., has more than 500. In turn, each of these subcontractors typically has some 60 sub-subcontractors of its own (September 1990: 84).

Suppliers, designers, and manufacturers are often within the same *keiretsu* or independent group network. This internal sourcing of key components and technologies distinguishes the Japanese industry from the Korean and Taiwanese industries, where there are fewer sources of domestic supply and a low level of integration between components manufacturers and electronic goods producers (although this may change somewhat in the 1990s for those Korean *chaebol* who are establishing semiconductor plants).

While individual Japanese electronics firms usually trace their affiliation to one (or occasionally more) groups, inter-group business relations are not uncommon in the industry. For example, Nippondenso, which began as an auto electrical supplier to Toyota, and is regarded as a member of Toyota Motor Corp. independent group, now supplies electronic systems to all domestic auto makers except Nissan; less than 60% of its output goes to Toyota. This "subcontractor" is now Japan's 19th largest electronics firm and does business with networks across the economy. No comparable firm could hope to do business with more than one *chaebol* in Korea, suggesting the qualitatively different relationship between suppliers and buyers in Japan. Taiwan's largest electronics firm, Tatung, made less than half of the U.S. $2.2 billion in revenues that Nippondenso posted in 1990, implying the quantitatively different scale of production in Taiwan.

Major Japanese firms cooperate in a range of projects, further linking them. Martin Fransman's study (1990) of inter-corporate electronics industry cooperation in Japan shows that major firms have often had ambivalent postures towards cooperative ventures with each other, fearing the loss of a competitive edge. In fact, however, the number and consequences of cooperative research, mostly stimulated by MITI, have been substantial including such major projects as VSLI (very large scale integration) circuit technology and HDTV (high-definition television).

South Korea's electronic industry is, like Japan's, dominated by large firms, although "large" is a relative term. Samsung Electronics, the biggest and most technologically advanced firm in Korea, posted U.S. $6.3 billion in revenues in 1990, compared to Japanese number one Matsushita's U.S. $27.3 billion in 1989-90. Ten Japanese electronics firms are larger than Samsung Electronics, eight of them twice as large or larger.

Korea's major electronics producers are overwhelmingly likely to be members of *chaebol* groups, although, as in Japan, there are notable independent firms. The top five South Korean electronics firms in 1991 were Samsung Electronics, Goldstar Co., Daewoo Electronics, Samsung Electron Devices, and Samsung Electro-Mechanics; the largest three firms contributed more than one-third of the country's total electronics production. Of the top 20 electronics firms listed on the stock exchange ranked by 1989 sales, eleven, including seven of the top 10, were affiliates of Samsung, Lucky-

Goldstar, and Daewoo *chaebol* (*EBA* December 1990: 49). If it had been publicly listed, privately held Hyundai Electronic Industries Co., maker of PCs and semiconductors, would have been fifth largest.

Table 6. Top 30 electronics firms in South Korea and Taiwan (1990, in millions US$)

	Company	Country	Electronics sales	Total sales
1	Samsung Electronics	Korea	6,371	6,371
2	Goldstar Co.	Korea	4,186	4,186
3	Daewoo Electronics	Korea	1,852	1,852
4	Tatung Co.	Taiwan	1,034	2,100
5	Samsung Electron Devices	Korea	1,003	1,003
6	Samsung Electro-Mechanics	Korea	596	596
7	Sampo Corp.	Taiwan	518	518
8	Acer Inc.	Taiwan	461	461
9	Orion Electric	Korea	406	406
10	Anam Industries	Korea	369	369
11	Teco electric & Machinery	Taiwan	367	367
12	Daewoo Telecom	Korea	298	298
13	Inkel	Korea	258	258
14	Goldstar Telecom	Korea	245	245
15	Goldstar Instrument & Electric	Korea	240	240
16	Taiwan Kolin	Taiwan	238	238
17	Maxon Electronics	Korea	236	236
18	Korea electronics	Korea	234	234
19	TriGem Computer	Korea	228	228
20	Goldstar Electric Machinery	Korea	204	204
21	Oriental Precision	Korea	168	168
22	Shihlin Electric & Engineering	Taiwan	155	207
23	United Microelectronics Corp.	Taiwan	148	148
24	Cal-Comp Electronics	Taiwan	148	148
25	Delta Electronic Industrial	Taiwan	134	134
26	Anam Electronics	Korea	130	130
27	Advanced Datum Information	Taiwan	111	148
28	Daewoo Electronic Components	Korea	106	106
29				
30	Goldstar Electric	Korea	105	105

Source: *Electronic Business Asia*, June 1991; FY ended March 1991.

Small- and medium-sized firms are numerically significant in South Korean electronics production — as much as 92% of the total number of electronics component firms; they produce low technology labour-intensive components and devices such as speakers. Unlike smaller Japanese subcontractors, though, these firms are not well integrated into *chaebol* production processes and do not provide the entrepreneurial innovations of independent Taiwanese subcontractors. Many are lower-cost producers of parts for foreign firms. Others "in the [South Korean] electronics sector, as many as 20% of the nation's parts suppliers rely on exclusive, almost feudal, supply contracts with the larger organizations for their existence"(*EBA* June 1990: 58).

According to Seo Sa-Hyeon, former Ministry of Trade and Industry (MTI) director, *chaebol* dominance of the industry keeps smaller firms from becoming engines of change and flexible responses to market shifts, as in Taiwan.

The *chaebol's* penchant for controlling every type of business also limits competition and opportunities for small and medium-sized companies. When refrigerator imports were liberalized [in 1988] Daewoo, Samsung, and Goldstar locked up the distribution and put them on sale for several times their landed price (*Business Week* 1990: 54).

Small and medium-sized Korean firms serve *chaebol* and foreign subcontractor needs and have little independent domestic role of significance, outside their patrimonial relationship, in shaping electronics sector directions.

Belatedly, the government has seen that the absence of a vibrant small-firm electronics presence means that the Korean industry has difficulty responding to market shifts, and further, has created economic monsters of the *chaebol*: politically unpopular and economically dangerous entities. For example, the electronics industry's boom period profits of the 1980s were spent by the *chaebol* on real estate speculation, not automation, and the industry is now suffering from high labour costs.

Those profits, had they been spread over more small- and medium-sized firms, would not have been able to corner the market in real estate, producing a politically destabilizing housing shortage, and more likely would have been diffused throughout the economy as a whole, perhaps to more productive purposes. Government has begun to conserve the production of some products, such as printed circuit boards, specifically to smaller firms. Ironically, it was government loans in the 1970s to those firms that could show the largest exports — *chaebol* firms — that spurred the dominance of large companies in South Korea.

Taiwan's electronics industry is segmented into numerous very small and a few medium-to-large companies. There are a thousand small companies producing consumer electronics, as well as a few substantial ones. Tatung, a producer of diverse appliances and other consumer goods, with U.S. $ 1 billion in 1990 sales, is by far the largest Taiwanese electronics firm. Tatung is expanding into Southeast Asia as domestic labour expenses climb, and is setting up plants in Europe. Its brand name is well known in Taiwan as a maker of appliances and consumer electronics, but like most Taiwanese firms, has little brand presence outside the country. Tatung is now selling SPARC workstation clones, having leased the rights from Sun Microsystems.

The next largest firms, Sampo Corp. and Acer Inc., with US$ 518 million and US$ 461 in 1990 sales respectively, are only half as large as Tatung. The fourth-largest firm, Taiwan Kolin, is only 25% as large. There are eleven electronics firms making U.S. $100 million or more a year in Taiwan, compared to 21 such firms in South Korea, with an economy half the size. While Taiwanese firms such as Tatung and Acer are large, although not in comparison to large Japanese and South Korean firms, they do not have nearly the economic dominance of leading firms in those other countries. Personal computer production, which is usually associated with good-sized assembly lines, is a case in point: the top *twenty* Taiwanese PC makers account for only 54% of the island's PC production (*FEER* 31.8.1989: 51).

Most of the smaller firms are engaged in low-technology production and assembly, but this is changing rapidly with the 50% upward valuation of the NT dollar in 1986-1990. Increasing labour costs and labour shortages are forcing Taiwanese producers to off-shore manufacturing to lower-cost sites, mostly in Southeast Asia. A small, but significant group of firms is producing medium technology custom components and industrial products for computers and workstations.

The Role of the State in Electronics

The role of the Japanese state in orchestrating Japan's post-war economic miracle is well-described (e.g. Johnson 1982; Vogel 1985 Prestowitz 1988). Although debate now rages as to precisely how influential the Ministry of International Trade and Industry (MITI), the Ministry of Finance (MoF), and government-controlled institutions such as the Bank of Japan in fact have been, it is clear that in comparison to the U.S. state, government activism has been an important economic factor, not least in the electronics industry.

The state, for example, has been crucial in targeting industries for development, including electronics. Targeted industries receive favourable loans, special depreciation rates, and tax incentives (Prestowitz 1988). Government has played an important role in organizing inter-firm research consortia in strategic electronics technologies such as high-speed computing, optical measurement and control, and future electronic devices (Fransman 1990). Although the state pays some research and organizing costs, it is not true that the state has a heavy-handed, directing role. As Vogel (1985: 64) put it:

MITI officials have power to grant licenses and patents and to determine which firms will participate in which projects, but the real power of MITI rests on the quality of its information, the care it takes in consulting with outsiders, the persuasiveness of its arguments, and the will to use its persuasiveness to favor those firms that cooperate.

The government's Agency of Industrial Science and Technology helps to establish industry standards, although not with uniform success. Matsushita's development of the VHS video standard eventually spelled the costly demise of Sony's Betamax; Sony is retaliating successfully with a Super-8 standard.

In electronics, as in other industries, an important government role has been to help sustain order in the domestic economy so that Japanese firms can aggressively pursue strategic global markets. This maintenance of "order" includes protection of the domestic market for major electronics firms. It is nearly impossible to buy European and U.S. brands of major electronic goods in Japan. The state works to maintain the profit level of domestic firms — Japanese tourists often find it less expensive to buy Japanese cameras and stereo equipment abroad than at home.

South Korea's government has been far more directive than Japan's. In the 1970s it targeted electronics as a crucial industry and gave substantial financial incentives to firms able to produce and export electronic goods. The incentives were based on gross export sales providing an incentive to *chaebol* firms to import parts for assembly in Korean factories, then shipping the finished goods abroad. Although electronics firms "grew", critical manufacturing processes were never developed domestically and imports, particularly from the Japanese, remained high in the 1980s causing a balance of payments problem.

In response to its earlier flawed efforts, the South Korean state began trying to organize research and development projects to help the electronics industry catch up technologically. As Electronic Business Asia reported:

Seoul is also encouraging Korean and other companies, particularly American concerns, to form strategic alliances, trading off market opportunities for Yankee know-how in hopes of sharpening the country's component making skills (April 1991: 9).

The government also removed the tariffs from advanced components to encourage more sources. Where the Korean state is acting aggressively to repair domestic distortions, some self-inflicted, the Japanese state is proactive in encouraging Japanese companies to develop new markets and technologies.

Although an aggressive actor in the economy, the size of the South Korean state limits what it can in fact do relative to competing nations. For example, the government is subsidizing electronics research and development, but where Korean electronics R&D was 4.3% of sales in 1989, more than double that of the entire manufacturing sector, it was substantially below other advanced industrial nations. "In the U.S. and Japan, for example, [electronics] R&D expenditure can range from an average 10 percent to 15 percent to heights of 30 percent in special cases" (*EBA* June 1990: 59). The South Korean government was expected to pay 35% of the U.S. $15 billion development expenditures targeted for 1990-94, half of which is for microelectronics.

The ability to maintain even that level of state funding is suspect, however. The government has encouraged *chaebol* firms to enter HDTV R&D consortia linking public research institutions and electronics manufacturers, including Samsung and Lucky-Goldstar (now LG Group). The project was divided into four sub-projects, but when the state has reneged on promised funding, *chaebol* participation waned.

One notable government success is a US$270 million public-private venture to catch up with the Japanese in the production of memory chips. Progress has been extraordinary and in keeping with Korea's strategic advantages. According to *Business Week*, "Concentrating on memory chips leverages Korea's strengths — low cost, high-volume manufacturing and large, vertically integrated companies" (1989: 69-70). Unfortunately the mass-market DRAMS this project produces, while used in many consumer products, are not among the most profitable components, and Korea has limited ability to get into more lucrative products such as microprocessors.

Because of the structure of the Taiwanese electronics industry, with its large number of very small producers, government impact is greatest on the few larger firms in the industry where it attempts to stimulate and coordinate projects, albeit selectively. Unlike state coordinated organization in Korea and Japan, the Taiwan government planning apparatus is as decentralized as the industry; there are at least six governmental and quasi-governmental bodies whose functions overlap that attempt to work with high-tech industry.

The government Computer and Communication Research Laboratory encourages R&D on targeted high technology projects. For example, in 1989 it organized a consortium to get Taiwan into the workstation market, but with mixed results. Only two of the six original members, Tatung and Datatech were still participating after two years. Acer, Copam Electronic Corp., and two smaller companies dropped out after Intel and Microsoft pressured them to stay away from Sun Microsystem's SPARC clone business, their competitor. While government can encourage and facilitate, it clearly cannot control.

Government has been successful in encouraging foreign firms to locate in Taiwan through the use of financial incentives. These firms often bring technology that stimulates domestic firms. Unlike either Japan or South Korea, the government has encouraged students to pursue engineering education, often abroad. Taiwan has one of the largest concentrations of well-trained, often American-trained, engineers in Asia.

Comparative Advantage in the Electronics Industry

The relative strengths and weaknesses of the electronics industries in Japan, South Korea, and Taiwan mirror very closely the strategic characteristics of their automotive industries. Japan's institutional character creates conditions under which group firms have access to large amounts of capital from affiliated banks, and *keiretsu* owners who are patient in waiting for returns on investment. Combined with a management system that encourages horizontal and vertical group coordination, Japanese electronic producers have ideal conditions for investing in large, cutting-edge projects whose returns promise to be substantial but only at a future moment. Mutually-supportive relations between large firms and subcontractors contribute to stability and innovation within the sector. Cooperative relations within networks and to some extent between networks, especially when coordinated by government, is ideal for the complex, multi-technology break-throughs that modern electronic systems demand. For example, HDTV, which had promised technological advances in television, is actually a coordinated system of many new processes and products. HDTV involves new studio cameras, audio standards, transmission equipment, not just television sets. A market setting that encourages the coordination of many innovators in producing such a complex system has a clear advantage. Observers almost all agree that the technology should it develop commercially, would most likely come first from Japan, not the U.S. Japan's ascendancy to the forefront in many, if not most, electronics markets demonstrates the strategic advantage a coordinated, competitive-cooperative system can produce. It is an advantage that leads to early market share and high profits at the beginning stages of product introduction, and eventually market dominance for high-end, high-quality goods.

Many have assumed that Korea would follow Japan's strategic lead and to some extent Korean electronics firms have tried. Although *chaebol*, like *keiretsu*, mass produce electronics goods, Korea is not able to produce cutting-edge technology. One might argue that it only a matter of time, that Korea is at an earlier developmental stage, but institutional characteristics of the Korean economy suggest that that country's trajectory is likely to be different from Japan's. The centralized, patrimonial *chaebol* have been very effective in concentrating capital for major industrial projects such as the mass production of semiconductors. Authoritarian, top-down relations, both at the level of the state and within *chaebol* groups, however, mitigate against the kind of innovation that puts a country at technological frontiers. Autocratic management styles, "feudal" relations with suppliers, and passionately antagonistic relations between *chaebol* do not augur well for market dominance in any significant electronic sub-sector except where mass production is key.

As South Korea has lost its low-cost advantage many of its firms are trying to develop higher quality and brand-name awareness. Samsung is probably farthest along in trying to move out from under its role as a subcontractor for firms such as General Electric and RCA; it now spends 1.5% of sales on advertising its own brand name (compared to 2% for Japanese brands). Most of its *chaebol* rivals, including Goldstar Co., however, continue to sell under the brands of mass merchandisers. Samsung's effort may be crucial because South Korean firms are "squeezed by countries like China at the low end, and Japan at the high end [and] could find itself trapped in the vanishing middle ground" (*FEER* January 1989: 52).

This process is already obvious in the personal computer market where South Korean industry is in a slump. Export sales dropped more than a third in 1990 compared to the year before. Korean firms could no longer compete on price because of a rising won and higher labour costs, and they offered no technological advantage. All six of Korea's PC makers had declines (*EBA* May 1991: 83). Hyundai, Daewoo, and Samsung are hoping that investment into dealer networks abroad will give them a distribution advantage in the 1990s.

Taiwan's strategic advantages are its skilled labour force, and small, flexible production networks. While there are few areas where Taiwan can hope to be a technological leader (although it has a reputation in some niche markets such as designer software), its institutional character allows it to rapidly piggy back on the advances made by the U.S. and Japan:

> One of the industry's strengths is its ability to adapt quickly to new technologies. The rapid move to laptop systems is one example. In 1988 when NEC launched the Ultralite, the world's first notebook PC, it sparked a stampede among Taiwan PC makers in 1989 and 1990 to replace desktops with laptops and notebook systems. According to a recent MIC report, about 200 computer makers were producing portable computer systems last year (*EBA* 1991: 80).

Taiwan is not without its problems, though. The appreciation of the NT dollar, rising wages, inflation, and the volatility of the stock market constrain development possibilities.

Taiwan has massive financial resources, though, and they are being used increasingly to allow the acquisition or merger with overseas companies. This is giving Taiwan new technological advantages and marketing channels. For example, Acer bought Altos Computer Systems, a U.S. firm, for access to both technology and distribution networks.

Conclusion

While Japan, South Korea, and Taiwan all have automotive and electronics industries, each has a different character and distinctive competitive advantage. While one might point to different economic factors as influential in shaping the structure of these industries — barriers to entry, or factor costs, for example — we would argue that even more fundamental is the institutional structure of each setting. Each nation has constructed an economy that adapts widely understood, even if not universally accepted, social patterns to economic ends.

Certainly, for example, South Korean patrimonialism has sparked political protest and labour unrest. It is limiting the way in which Korean industry can move forward. Nonetheless, patrimonialism is a familiar, institutionalized pattern of authority that has the force of long experience. While patrimonialism would be incomprehensible in most Western nations, and certainly unsuccessful as an organizing strategy in the industrialized West, it is a familiar way to organize social relations in Korean society. It was a model that subordinated individualism to the needs of industry and imposed the discipline of hierarchy on a war-torn nation. A centralized, patrimonial state was able to concentrate resources in a few, targeted industries. Importantly, it is an indigenous authority pattern, not one imposed by colonial experience. Although the limits of patrimonialism as an industrial organizing strategy are now becoming obvious, relying on institutionalized social patterns to spur economic development worked well in Korea, as it has in Japan and Taiwan.

This suggests that nations that search for the "best" or "most efficient" way to organize their economy, for example trying to emulate a hypothetical perfect market, are pursuing an illusory goal. Economies have social bases, and a successful economy cannot ignore the institutional playing field on which it rests. Nations that would hope to encourage development must look at the institutional structure, the social character of their nation, in order to formulate development plans. The path that worked for a neighbor nation, or that is ideally more efficient, will not necessarily make sense in another context. Attempting to eliminate market "imperfections", for example networks of social relations, may remove the very social means by which economic activity can be pursued, a point made recently at the firm level by scholars promoting a resource-based view of competitive advantage. We believe this insight works equally well at the level of industrial sectors and national economies.

Even if the Taiwanese attempted to emulate the Japanese approach to car manufacturing, research from a resource-based view of the firm affirms that enterprises cannot easily change strategies even when they want to, that there is an inertial character to strategic orientation. Unlike the economic view of strategy, "which views resources as immediately accessible on fungible factor markets, this view stresses the inherent immobility or stickiness of valuable factors of production and the time and cost required to accumulate those resources"(Collis 1991: 50). While it is not impossible for the Taiwanese to learn organizational routines and practices from the Japanese, it would require a wholesale makeover of their institutional character which would be both time-consuming and costly and hence likely not to their strategic advantage. To define strategic choice as a profit maximization problem, as neoclassical economics does, ignores the very real social, technological, and other investments in structure that are difficult and perhaps impossible to alter. Strategic choice, as Child described, involves both a consideration of external environmental and market factors, and of beliefs, structures, and institutionalized interests (1972).

It is clear that firm and national economic choices are limited by both "switching costs" and even the very impossibility of imagining alternative ways in which to relate in a socially-constructed taken-for-granted world, as institutional theory suggests, is well within the perspective of Weberian developmental sociology and evolutionary economics. Weber, while always leaving open alternative paths to development and the room for historical accidents, demonstrated clearly that the road to modern industrial capitalism was the product of a series of events that built upon the past and shaped future possibilities. Contemporary evolutionary economics, likewise argues that the economy is "path dependent" or shaped by the choices already made (Nelson 1994). If these perspectives are correct in claiming that strategic choices are constrained by deeply embedded cultural and technological frameworks inherited from the past, then it is quite clear that nations can only adopt easily economic routines that complement existing institutional structures. Comparative advantage, as the classical economists claimed, is a matter of building an economy on the resources with which one is endowed but that endowment, we would argue, is at least as much social as economic.

References

Adachi, F., K. Ono and K. Odaka (1983): "Ancillary firm development in the Japanese automobile industry" in Konosuke Odaka (ed.), *The Motor Vehicle Industry in Asia*. Singapore: Singapore University Press.

Balassa, B. (1981): "A stages approach to comparative advantage" in B. Balassa (ed.), *The newly industrializing countries in the world economy*, 149-164. New York: Pergamon.

Bain, J. (1956): *Barriers to new competition*. Cambridge, MA: Harvard University Press.

Bain, J. (1968): *Industrial organization*. New York: John Wiley and Sons.

Barney, J. (1991): "Firm resources and sustained comparative advantage." *Management Science* 17: 99-120.

Berger, P. (1984): "An East Asian development model." *The Economic News* 3079, September 17-23: 1, 6-8.

Bhaskar, K. (1980): *The future of the world motor industry*. London: Kogan Page.

Biggart, N.W. (1990): "Institutionalized patrimonialism in Korean business." *Comparative Social Research* 12: 113-133.

Biggart, N.W. and G.G. Hamilton (1989): "Explaining Asian business success: Theory no. 4." *University of Wales: Economic and Business Review* 5: 11-16.

Bloomfield, G. (1978): *The world automotive industry*. Newton Abbot: David and Charles.

Business Week (1989): "In Korea, all circuits are go." 9 July: 69-70.

Business Week (1990): "South Korea's new destination." 11 September: 50-54.

Castanias, R.P. and Helfat, C. (1991): "Managerial resources and rents." *Journal of Management* 17: 155-171.

Child, J. (1972): "Organizational structure, environment and performance: The role of strategic choice." *Sociology* 6: 1-22.

Collis, D.J. (1991): "A resource-based analysis of global competition: The case of the bearings industry." *Strategic Management Journal* 12: 49-68.

Connor, K. (1991): "A historical comparison of resource-based theory and five schools of thought within industrial organization economics." *Journal of Management* 17: 121-154.

Cosumano, M.A. (1985): *The Japanese automobile industry*. Cambridge, MA: Harvard University Press.

Dodwell Marketing Consultants (1986): Industrial groupings in Japan.

Duller, H.J. (1983): "Technique in Taiwan: the role of technology in Taiwan's past and present development." Monograph series, no. 4. Institute of the Three Principles of the People, *Academia Sinica*. Nankang, Taipei, Taiwan, November.

Electronics Business Asia (1990 and 1991): various issues.

Evans, P.B. (1979): *Dependent development: the alliance of multinationals, state and local capital in Brazil*. Princeton, NJ: Princeton University Press.

Far Eastern Economic Review (1989, 1990 and 1991): various issues.

Fortune (1988): "Fortune's International 500." 1 August.

Fransman, M. (1990): *The market and beyond: cooperation and competition in information technology development in the Japanese system*. Cambridge: Cambridge University Press.

Gereffi, G. (1994): "The international economy and economic development" in N. Smelser and R. Swedberg (eds.), *The handbook of economic sociology*, 206-233. Princeton and New York: Princeton University Press and Russell Sage Foundation.

Gerlach, M. (1992): *Alliance capitalism: the social organization of Japanese business*. Berkeley: University of California Press.

Gregory, G. (1985): *Japanese electronics technology: enterprise and innovation*. Chichester and New York: John Wiley.

Hamilton, G. and N.W. Biggart (1988): "Market, culture and authority." *American Journal of Sociology* 94: 552-595.

Hoffman, K., and R. Kaplinski (1988): *Driving force*. Boulder, CO: Westview Press.

Irwin, M.D. and J.D. Kasarda (1994): "Trade, transportation and spatial distribution" in N. Smelser and R. Swedberg (eds.), *Handbook of economic sociology*, 342-367. Princeton and New York: Princeton University Press and Russell Sage Foundation.

Johnson, C. (1982): *MITI and the Japanese miracle*. Stanford: Stanford University Press.

Kim, C.K. and C.H. Lee (1983): "Ancillary firm development in the Korean automobile industry" in Konosuke Odaka (ed.), *The motor vehicle industry in Asia*. Singapore: Singapore University Press.

Mason, E. (1939): "Price and production policies of large-scale enterprises." *American Economic Review* 29: 61-74.

Mill, J.S. (1871/1965): *Principles of political economy with some of their applications to social philosophy*. London: Routledge and Kegan Paul.

MVMA 1988 (1989): Motor vehicle facts and figures. World Motor Vehicle Data.

Nelson, R. (1994): "Evolutionary theorizing about economic change" in N. Smelser and R. Swedberg (eds.), *Handbook of economic sociology*, 108-136. Princeton and New York: Princeton University Press and Russell Sage Foundation.

Noble, G.W. (1987): "Contending forces in Taiwan's economic policymaking." *Asian Survey* 27: 683-704.

Odaka, K. (1983): *The motor vehicle industry in Asia*. Singapore: Singapore University Press.

Odaka, K., K. Ono and F. Adachi (1988): *The automobile industry in Japan*. Tokyo: Oxford University Press.

Orrù, M. (1991): "The institutional logic of small-firm economies in Italy and Taiwan." *Studies in Comparative International Development* 26: 3-28.

Orrù, M., N.W. Biggart and G.G. Hamilton (1991): "Organizational isomorphism in East Asia" in W.W. Powell and P. DiMaggio (eds.), *The new institutionalism in organizational analysis*, 361-389. Chicago: University of Chicago Press.

Piore, M. and C. Sabel (1984): *The second industrial divide*. New York: Basic Books.

Porter, M. (1985): *Competitive advantage*. New York: Free Press.

Powell, W.W. and P. DiMaggio (1991): *The new institutionalism in organizational analysis*. Chicago: University of Chicago Press.

Prestowitz, C.V. (1988): *Trading places: How we allowed Japan to take the lead*. New York: Basic Books.

Redding, G. (1990): *The spirit of Chinese capitalism*. Berlin: Walter de Gruyter.

Ricardo, D. (1817/1951): *On the principles of political economy and taxation*. Piero Sraffa (ed.). London: G. Bell and Sons, Ltd.

Saxenian, A. (1994): *Regional advantage: culture and competition in Silicon Valley and Route 128*. Cambridge, MA: Harvard University Press.

Shimokawa, K. (1985): "Japan's keiretsu system." *Japanese Economic Studies* 13: 3-31.

Smith, A. (1776/1843): *An inquiry into the nature and the causes of the wealth of nations*. Oxford: Clarendon Press.

Sorge, A. (1991): "Strategic fit and the societal effect in international cross-national comparisons of technology, organizations and human resources." *Organization Studies* 12: 161-90.

Vogel, E. (1985): *Comeback*. New York: Simon and Schuster.

Walter, I. (1988): *Microelectronics: an Industry in transition*. Boston: Unwin Hyman.

Ward's Automotive Yearbook (1988).

Japanese Industrial Groups and Cross-Shareholding: Is Agency Theory Really Relevant to the Communal Form?

Mark J. Scher

The organization of Japanese industrial groups has received much attention over the last several years as a critical factor in Japan's economic success. Some have gone so far as to advocate the "keiretsu" group form as a model for U.S. industry, implicitly presuming that this organizational structure is available to U.S. and European managers simply as a policy choice (Ferguson 1990; *Harvard Business Review* 1990; *Business Week* 1992; Burt and Doyle 1993). On the other hand, the lack of transparency of the interrelationships among firms, characteristic of Japanese groups, has become an issue in the ongoing trade negotiations between the U.S. and Japan, and it is thus no surprise that the U.S. side sees the existence of these group relationships as a major impediment to open markets.

Largely in reaction to rising external pressure, similar concern over the lack of transparency in business relations is also beginning to be voiced by Japanese in the academic and business worlds and in the press. Hitherto nonexistent issues of corporate governance and shareholder rights have newly thrust themselves into the consciousness of management through growing independent shareholder demands for changes in corporate dividend and voting policies. However, it can be argued that much of the criticized opaqueness of transactions, lack of accountability of management, and lack of access of foreign firms stems from entrenched cultural and legal antecedents within traditional Japanese society and is therefore intractable to short-term cure.

In fact, the unique qualities of industrial organization in Japan has been a favourite subject of study of both social scientists and economists. Organizational sociologists and cultural anthropologists have described Japan as a "community model" (Dore 1987); others have contrasted Japanese culture to Western culture as a "belonging model" versus a Western "contractual model" (Mito 1992); or as a model based on "obligational contractual relations" versus an "arm's-length contractual relations" model (Sako 1992); and by Whitley (1992), within the overall context of East Asian business systems, as a model built on high trust communal relations of village and family and an aloof state. Noting the special character of Japanese-style capitalism, some sociologists and economists have called it "Alliance Capitalism" (Gerlach 1992); "Network Capitalism" (Nakatani 1990); or even "Beyond Capitalism" (Sakakibara 1994), while others have attempted to create a J-model, by using game theory principles (Aoki 1984a). Other economists studying Japanese society have taken a different approach, placing the firm within the context of established Western economic conceptualizations like agency theory (Aoki 1984b; 1990; Sheard 1989; 1991).

The approach of agency theory (Berle and Means 1932; Jensen and Meckling 1976; Demsetz 1967; Alchian and Demsetz 1972) typically sees the firm as a nexus of linear contracts and is rooted in the concept of a bundle of freely marketable contractual rights historically embodied in the 17th-century Anglo-Dutch concept of the joint-stock company. The approach of transaction-cost analysis, which some economists have also applied to Japan, represents a continuum between two opposing idealized modes — the market mode versus the hierarchical mode (Coase 1937; Williamson 1975; 1985). Although claiming to be universalistic theories, both the transaction-cost and agency approaches (1) fail to account for some of the outstanding characteristics of the Japanese market, such as the quite notable lack of freedom, information, and transparency, *a priori* requirements for efficient marketplace theories to be relevant, and (2) ignore the social embeddedness of economic relations and transactions, the issues that are dealt with in the model advanced in this chapter.

This lack of fit between the terms of debate in management theory led by economists and the observations made of Japanese management practice by sociologists, among others, may well reflect a fundamental clash between the bias of Western-trained theorists who wish to see their models as universal and the observations of those who, as much as possible, look at the Japanese firm without those constraints. In this chapter I will examine the evidence used in developing what I call the Relational Access Paradigm.

Ouchi (1980) significantly expanded Williamson's (1975) dichotomy of the market form and the bureaucratic form into a trichotomy by adding a third category, the "clan form" to transaction cost theory's taxonomy of organizational forms. His usage of the term "clan" was derived from Durkheim's (1933) usage, denoting an organic association which resembles a kin network but which does not necessarily include blood relations. The members of the clan transact on an informal basis of shared information, personal trust, and equality.

In its internal governance Ouchi's clan form is based upon an understanding held in common by all parties to a particular transaction that, while imbalances in individual inducements and contributions may exist in the short term, in the long run balance will be restored and maintained. A generalized norm of reciprocity (Gouldner 1960) is part of the environment which will produce a state of "serial equity", as opposed to the "spot equity" characteristic of markets and, to some extent, of bureaucracies as well. It is also assumed that in certain transaction environments, where no explicit, prespecified measures of inducements and contributions exist, the parties to the clan form of transaction will trust in the generalized norm of reciprocity that underlies the relationship.

The willingness to permit short-term imbalances with the expectation of long-run balance or serial equity is an important feature of clan forms. In its internal manifestation it can be connected to lifetime employment together with personnel evaluation policies that emphasize qualitative rather than a purely quantitative evaluation. For example, managers who sacrifice their quantitative performance in the short term for the overall good of the company know that they will be appropriately recognized and compensated in the long run (Ouchi 1981; Barney and Ouchi 1984). In its external form, it is shown by the belief among transacting partners that short-term imbalances will be remembered and compensated.

Expanding the categories of the transactional forms described by Williamson, Ouchi and others, Boisot (1986), and later Boisot and Child (1988), added the "fief form." In a number of respects this form appears both to draw from Weber's (1921) "patrimonial bureaucracy" as well as to encompass the governance characteristics of household-style firms, both of which are discussed in a later section. Boisot and Child also restructured the hierarchy versus market dichotomy into a four-quadrant matrix of ideal types: bureaucracies, markets, fiefs, and clans. They differentiated these four forms on the basis of information asymmetries across two intersecting axes, a continuum of undiffused to diffused information and a second continuum of uncodified to codified information. Through its focus on information, this schema also was able to encompass and categorize: the nature of personal relationships intrafirm, impersonal or personal, hierarchical or competitive; goal-setting within the firm, superordinate or individualistic; coordination within the firm, horizontal or hierarchical; and whether necessity of shared values and beliefs are assumed.

High Context-Low Context/Power Relations: Towards a More Holistic Model

This chapter argues that, the addition of the above attributes to the description of the firm effectively transforms the transaction-cost perspective from a nonorganic into an organic concept in which the firm is viewed as an integral part of a broader context. Relationships and actions are no longer purely contractual and economic; rather, they have been broadened to include culturally-based governance structures. Furthermore, this more culturally inclusive model moves not only along an *x*-axis defined by the diffusion of information and bounded by the polarities of markets and hierarchies, but also along a new *y*-axis of codified to uncodified information of the Boisot-Child framework, which, I argue, is one of the key conditions differentiating the purely Western economic paradigm from communal models (see Table 1).

I further reinterpret and modify Boisot and Child's construction, which describes *intra*-firm transactions (they applied it to Chinese enterprises), to include *inter*-firm relationships and apply this matrix to firm-industrial group relationships. I argue that the nature of Japanese inter-firm relationships, specifically groups of enterprises that are only *informally* linked, has never fit the market-versus-hierarchy dichotomy which pointedly ignores the social embeddedness of economic relations and transactions (Granovetter 1985). Such analyses fail to account for relationships which are opaque to outsiders but which exert a commanding influence upon business groups, industries, and markets. When the information codification/diffusion model is extended to inter-firm analogs, two of the outstanding characteristics of Japanese inter-firm relations immediately stand out, namely, their common reliance on a superstructure of shared beliefs and their adherence to informal codes of behaviour.

This view is supported by the work of social scientists, such as Hofstede (1991) who placed Japanese society high on his Power Distance Index, indicating a propensity towards collectivist rather than individualistic actions. Hall (1977) classified Japan as a "high-context culture",[1] indicating a high degree of shared assumptions and outlook often taken for granted by members of the society, which is maintained by extensive networks, both formal and informal, for the diffusion of uncodified information. To incorporate Hofstede's and Hall's concepts, I further modify the matrix to include two key factors. In the model proposed here, Hall's concept of high-context, low-context culture is correlated to information diffusion and codification (high context/uncodified and low context/codified). The information diffusion axis is also modified, correlating it to Hofstede's concept of power distance relationships. This power relationship axis, when applied to inter-firm analogs, distinguishes the fief form (*keiretsu*) characterized by feudal/

asymmetrical power relations, from the clan form (*kigyo shudan*) characterized by collegial/non-competitive synergistic relations. Figure 1 illustrates the power relationships inherent in the two differing forms, as well as the relationship between the two forms, in contrast to the uni-dimensional schema usually used to represent the inter-firm relationships of the former *zaibatsu* groups.

Table 1. Information Codification and Diffusion, High-Low Context/Power Relations Matrix

	Undiffused Information Hierarchical Power Relations	Diffused Information Horizontal Power Relations
	Bureaucracies	*Markets*
Low Context Codified Information	• Information diffusion limited and under central control • Relationships impersonal and hierarchical • Submission to superordinate goals • Hierarchical coordination • No necessity to share values and beliefs • Explicit internal contracts, monitoring	• Information diffused, no control • Relationships impersonal and competitive • No superordinate goals — each one for himself • Horizontal coordination through self-regulation • No necessity to share values and beliefs • Explicit market contracts, monitoring
	Fiefs (Patrimonial Bureaucracy) *Keiretsu* — vertical Asymmetrical Power Relationships Subsidiary-like Affiliations	*Clans* (Kinship Network) *Kigyo Shudan* — horizontal Collegial Relationships Non-Competitive Synergistic Alliances
High Context Uncodified Information	• Information diffusion limited by lack of codification to face-to-face relationships • Relationships personal and hierarchical • Submission to superordinate goals • Hierarchical coordination • Necessity to share values and beliefs • Implict "internal" contracts, self-monitoring	• Information is diffused but still limited by lack of codification to face-to-face relationships • Relationships personal but nonhierarchical • Goals shared through process of negotiation • Horizontal coordination through negotiation • Necessity to share values and beliefs • Implicit relational contracts, non-monitoring

Adapted from Boisot & Child (1988) and the concepts of Durkheim (1933), Hall (1977), Hofstede (1991), Ouchi (1980), Weber (1921), Williamson (1975).

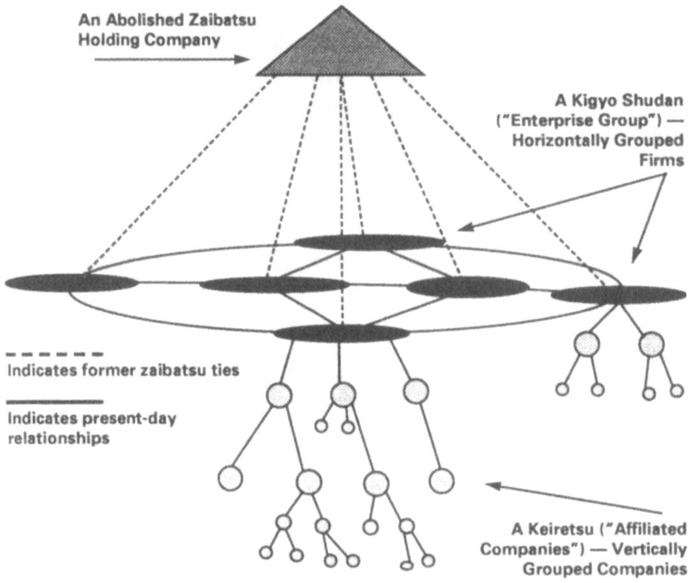

Figure 1. *Kigyo shudan-keiretsu* power relationships

At the top of Figure 1 is the *zaibatsu* holding company, the apex of a pyramidal control structure. These holding companies, abolished after World War II, were owned by the *zaibatsu* family. They held stock in the firms which today comprise the *kigyo shudan's* group member firms and their affiliated *keiretsu* firms' members. Today's *kigyo shudan* comprise a group of firms which are no longer owned by a holding company but instead are *horizontally* linked together and usually centered around the group's bank and/or trading company. For example, such former *zaibatsu* groups as Mitsui, Sumitomo, and Mitsubishi now consist of a number of related firms operating on essentially equal footing. A single member firm of such a *kigyo shudan* may in turn head a *keiretsu* of vertically affiliated companies. The old *zaibatsu* holding company system comprised both the *kigyo shudan* and the *keiretsu* structures.

A *kigyo shudan* typically includes a cross-section of major industrial firms which are sometimes incorrectly referred to as "financial keiretsu" or "inter-market keiretsu."[2] They have been frequently confused with *keiretsu*, their *vertically* affiliated subordinate companies, which usually reflect multi-tiered supplier and distributor relationships. The distinction between the *kigyo shudan* and *keiretsu* is important because the nature of the power relationship is not the same; in the former there is a collegial relationship among the member companies whereas in the latter there is a hierarchy between the company and its affiliated subordinates.

The *kigyo shudan* form is typified by joint projects, usually between two principal industrial members of the group which are forming a subsidiary to develop and manufacture a new product or service. Generally, the group trading company serves a supporting role in project planning, development, and marketing, while among the group's financial institutions the main bank supplies financial expertise and long term and short-term credits, and the group's trust bank may supply long-term project financing. Insurance companies, in addition to underwriting property and casualty insurance for the project, may also provide general financing, while other group companies provide logistical support in areas such as shipping and transport, or technical expertise. However, each company's primary concern is with its own bottom line, so that depending upon the particular group, only some 20% to 30% of *kigyo shudan* company contracts these days are with other group members, compared to some 80% among the prewar *zaibatsu*.

The *keiretsu* form is exemplified by such well-known Japanese subcontracting practices as "Just In Time" manufacturing (Fruin 1992), and black box design (Nishiguchi 1992). These practices, which shift inventory and product development costs to captive sets of subcontractors, are driven by a competitive dual-vendor pricing regime (Fruin 1992) which pits at least two suppliers for each and every component against each other. Suppliers are expected to absorb any increases in the cost of production. What may be long-term relationships within the *keiretsu* are dictated by short-term contracts that often require price reductions upon contract renewal (Sako 1992).

Some theorists have attempted to describe attributes of Japanese industrial groups to fit a market or bureaucracy profile. For example, agency economists have viewed the diffusion of information among Japanese firms in both the vertical hierarchy (*keiretsu*) and in the horizontal/collegial mode (*kigyo shudan*) as part of an agency relationship. The evidence tends to contradict such single-sided interpretation. Rather, in a high-context setting characterized by face-to-face relations, unlike either the bureaucracy or market forms, information diffusion tends to be personal, constant, wide-ranging, and generally unfocused.

The model proposed here brings together some of the outstanding shared attributes of the *keiretsu* (fief) and *kigyo shudan* (clan) forms, including informal communication among firms of the group, mainly through personal contact and membership in a culture of common values, while at the same time underscoring the key distinctions between the fief form's essentially vertical mode, characterized by hierarchical relations in which control often masquerades as negotiations, and the clan form's essentially horizontal mode, which operates through collegial negotiation between related parties. Most importantly, the model emphasizes an issue unaccounted for in other models: the significance of the defining relationship, which I address below.

The Relational Access Paradigm — The Third Dimension

The Japanese word for relationship, *"kankei"*, is composed of two parts: *"kan"* meaning a barrier-gate and *"kei"* signifying duty to the group familial system. (The familial system will be discussed in the next section.) These two elements capture and express the interplay of the basic concepts contained within the meaning of "relationship", namely, that access is determined by the nature of the relationship. "Access", first of all, as used in Japan, reflects a process not of opening doors but of controlling entry, determining who is allowed past the barrier-gate where passage through is determined by the specifics of the relationship. For example, in the exclusionary Japanese business practice known as *dango* (collusive rigged bidding) access is afforded relative to a fixed group of contractors — to the exclusion of those considered outsiders, such as domestic newcomers and foreign bidders.

In current Japanese business parlance, a relationship may be "wet" (intimate, supportive) or "dry" (purely transactional) or non-existent (*"kankei-nai"*) (no relationship and therefore no access at all). *Keiretsu torihiki,* group affiliated transactions, are mostly "dry", in contrast to transactions based, for example, on *giri*, in which obligational indebtedness makes the relationship very "wet." The nuanced and unstated though understood complexities of these relationships and the type of access each of them implies has led to the popularization by Japanese of the use of the English word "access", which skirts around the issues of implicit barriers and control. For example, for the past several years the official Japanese language texts of Japan-U.S. Trade Negotiations has employed the English "access" written in *katakana* (Japanese phonetic alphabet) without definition. Such lack of information and explicit definition is to be expected in an uncodified/high context society.

This concept of implicit access and relationship is key to an understanding of the nature of Japanese industrial group relations, which has often been misconstrued by false assumptions of what constitutes the degree of "access."[3] In the following discussion the essence of these relationships will be of some importance in understanding the consequences of access for group members, shareholders, investors, other stakeholders, and for the main bank relationship.

Normally the nature of transactions in the bureaucratic and the market forms are visible, with no opaque substructures to interfere with the efficient use of the market or the rational conduct of the bureaucracy. The fief and clan forms, that is, the *keiretsu* and the *kigyo shudan*, by contrast, are characterized by an opacity based on relationships and customs, the implicit rules governing access to information and commerce. Such opacity is, as was discussed, relative and wholly dependent on one's relationships — as an outsider trying to deal with the system or as an insider who is part of the system.

Relational access — as an *insider* or *outsider* — along the length of a defining third-dimension, an intersecting plane that ranges from "belonging" to "no relationship", transforms the model into a holistic paradigm of the Japanese firm and its inter- and intragroup relations. I call this plane the *uchi* (insider)-*soto* (outsider) continuum of graded relationships, reflecting spheres of relationships that exist within sets and subsets. For the model it is also the foundational dimension, the first distinction drawn before any other criteria are applied.

The *uchi-soto* continuum defines a third dimension which I call relational access (see Figure 2). As pointed out earlier, the linear market dichotomy was reconceptualized by the inclusion of context (codification of information) into a more complex four-quadrant matrix. This matrix is in essence a Cartesian plane based upon power relationships (information diffusion) as the x-axis, and high/low context (information codification) as its y-axis (see Table 1). The concept of relational access transforms the communal view of interfirm relationships beyond this four-quadrant Cartesian plane. The r-dimension of spatial relativity expands the paradigm to include one of the most primary priorities of the intra- and interfirm Japanese model, the necessity to place all relationships along an *uchi-soto* (insider-outsider) continuum of graded relationships.

The r-dimension of the *uchi-soto* continuum defines where one firm stands in relationship to another firm — from the centre of group membership to the outermost sphere of the spot transactional market (no relationship). In addition, in some contexts, a firm can be an insider because it is within a larger sphere while simultaneously an outsider, depending on its relative position within the concentric spheres of relationships surrounding any Japanese firm. Table 2 below describes the characteristics of the insider-outsider continuum.

According to this model, relationships follow a graded pattern based on a concentric, rather than a linear-contractual model; individuals are located in a work group, within the firm, situated in a industrial group, within a larger society (see Figure 3). For example, when applied to the *keiretsu* system (as illustrated in Figure 1), this graded system of relationships serves as an important distancing mechanism which excludes obligational relations of prime contractors from the affiliates of their sub-contractors. This has had enormous implications in terms of the hollowing-out of Japanese industry in recent years as primary contractors have expanded their outsourcing of parts production overseas, abandoning their supplier networks in Japan.

Table 2. Characteristics of the insider-outsider continuum

Insider *(Uchi)*	Outsider *(Soto)*
Access to other insiders	No relationship
Protection from outsiders	Competition
Obligations within sphere	No obligations

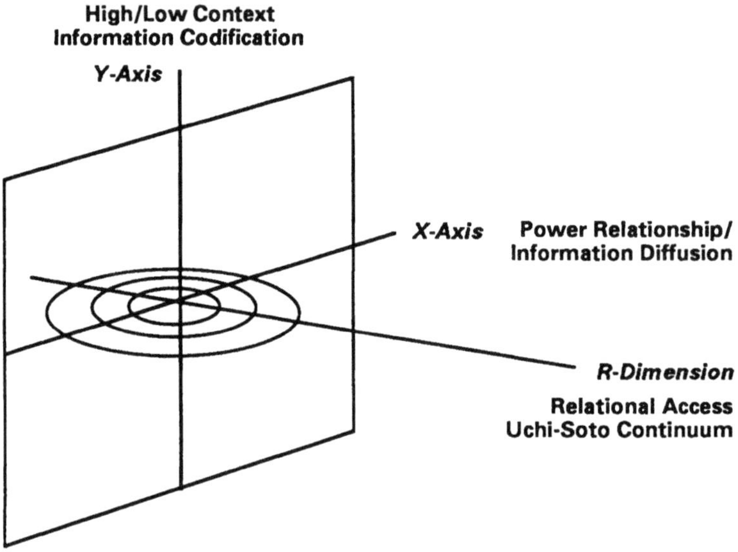

Figure 2. The relational access paradigm — The third dimension

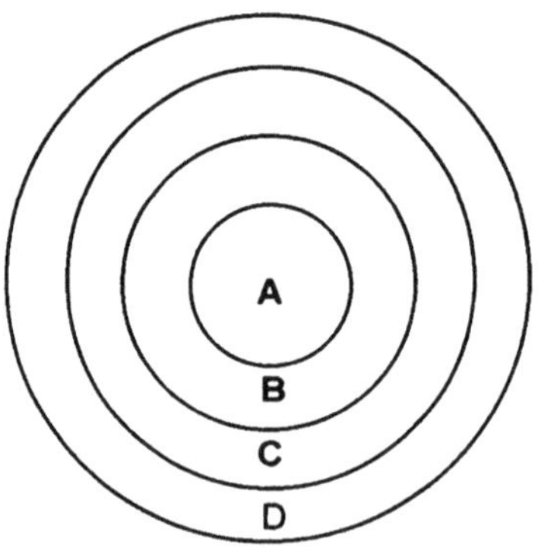

For example, in this illustration, firms A and B are insiders in relationship to firm C. Firm D is an outsider to firms A and B. Firm C may have some kinds of relationships with firm D because they border each other.

Figure 3. Insider-outsider relationships

The Japanese firm can thus be termed a "nexus of *implicit relational* contracts", indicative of its character as a high-context communal society. I argue that the theories of the firm promulgated by Western economists are caught in a mistaken and reductionist linearity. The boundaries of the concept of the firm and group companies should be extended beyond those drawn by *de jure* property rights theories to encompass a concept of the firm and group as participants in an arena of collective action in which viability as an institution is greatly dependent on the supportive milieu in which the firm and its group are situated.

Culture, Commerce and Communal Values

Although some Western scholars have credited Western influence for the successes of Japanese industrial management, the management styles so notable today are in fact rooted in the history of non-blood, fictive kinship-based economic units — the merchant "household-style" business unit. In Japanese society a very different construction of collective relations is contained in the concept of "household" and the distinctions between family and firm as compared to the West. This distinctive fictive concept of kinship relationships (Scher 1997) was firmly established by the mid-Tokugawa period of the eighteenth century and provided the basis for the distinctive Japanese long-term employment system, job advancement, and paternalism, characteristics of the management stability of modern Japanese industry. Similarly, today's enterprise group *(kigyo shudan)* and affiliated group (*keiretsu*) relationships may be seen as the direct descendants of the house-branch system of affiliated households, in which managers were allowed to open affiliated branches of the main household (Scher 1997).

Kinship is a phenomenon considered important in tribal societies but assumed by economists to be of little importance in an industrial society, who thus have tended to overlook critical aspects of the social embeddedness of economic relations and transactions (Granovetter 1985). This is particularly true of Japan where, for example, simulated kinship roles were not only of much importance in traditional occupations but continue in modern managerial practices as well (Bennett and Ishino 1963).

The inter-generational character of the family, exemplified in the paternalistic *oyabun-kobun* (parent status-child status) relationship, is yet another aspect of the *ie* (household) construct that underpins relationship patterns within Japanese businesses and Japanese society as a whole. In general, this relationship resembles the elements of Max Weber's description of patrimonial bureaucracy in his *Wirtschaft und Gesellschaft* (*Theory of Social and*

Economic Organization) (Weber 1921). However, *oyabun-kobun* goes well beyond Weber's mentor-student or master-apprentice relationship, by carrying with it an extensive web of interlocking obligations and duties called *on* and *giri* which pose a distinct contrast to the Western formulation of personal "rights and privileges." It is the reciprocity inherent in *oyabun-kobun* that binds the Japanese *kumi* (group) together, whether it be a team or guild, a company or even a corporation (Bennett and Ishino 1963).

Japanese relationships follow a graded pattern based on a concentric, rather than linear-contractual, model in which the household is located within the community within the larger country (*kuni*). In this Confucian-style system the household, whether based on blood or fictive relations such as the Japanese *ie,* (household) is situated within a *mura* (village), and in the case of the firm within its *kigyo shudan.* (See Figure 3 regarding the earlier discussion of insider-outsider relationships.) These sets of graded concentric relationships are grounded on the distinctions between the role of *uchi* (insiders) versus *soto* (outsiders), whom Japanese refer to as *kankeinai hito* — persons with whom one has no relationship and who therefore may be disregarded (see Figure 4).

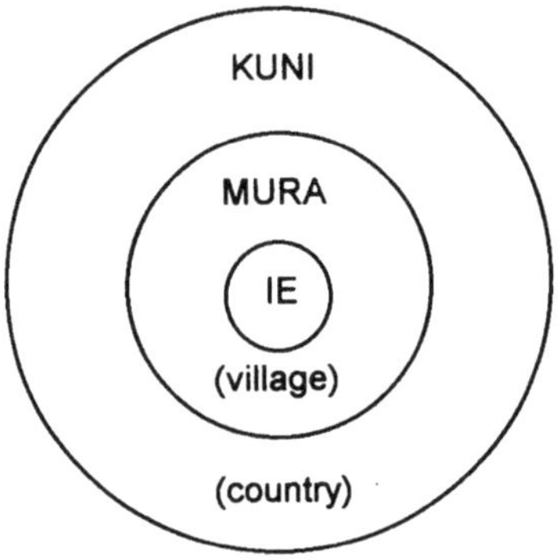

Figure 4. The Japanese Confucian-style system

The basic framework of the household system rests upon a tradition in which non-blood-related individuals function together as a simulated kinship group (Yoshino 1968). Even when the internal structure of a modern industrial enterprise grows beyond a small-sized business, traditional patterns of *on* and *giri* continue. Subsidiaries and sub-units assume the traditional obligations to their industrial workers (Bennett and Ishino 1963). Similarly, the traditional distinctions between insider and outsider are in play in the modern notion of the "lifetime employee", a modern-day embodiment of the traditional apprentice, an adoptive member of the *ie* (household). Today the most sought-after jobs for new university graduates are those not only with a prestigious company but also with a secure "family" culture. Only some 30% of Japanese employees are considered to have "lifetime" status; an employee may be classified as "temporary" or "part-time" even after working 20 years for the firm. The so-called temporary employee remains outside the network of reciprocities, without the expectation of a supportive *oyabun-kobun* relationship, "apprentice" status, a "share" in the *ie,* or job security.

The attributes of modern Japanese-style management, such as the lifetime employment system, promotion by seniority, and a paternalistic policy towards employees, have their historical basis in the annals of medieval seventeenth-century merchant households. These household codes governing the management of family businesses contained specific regulations on the theory and practice of long-term employment, seniority, and the good treatment of employees (Horie 1966, Mitsui Gomei-Kaisha 1933; Miyamoto 1984; Sakudo 1990).

The process of modernization in Japan may be viewed, in some very fundamental aspects, as the continuous development of native institutions rather than as the result of the abrupt introduction of Western ideas in the Meiji period of the late nineteenth century. Today, the values and beliefs associated with the *ie* (household) concept are alive not only in family-operated businesses but are reflected in the relationships and practices within firms and within industrial groups, whether horizontally or vertically structured. The traditional access given within one's extended *ie* are now given to those of one's group. The values placed on personal relationships implied in the informal channels of communication are indicative of the importance of a shared culture and value system.

Industrial Groups: Cross-Shareholding and Group Boundaries

I now turn to the governance of Japanese firms and industrial organizations, whose modern forms have been much studied and debated — both mechanistically and qualitatively. Studies taking a structural approach have focused on group boundaries (Gerlach 1992), others have studied bureaucratic influence (Schaede 1993; 1994), while still others have taken a contractual approach in their analysis (Gilson and Roe 1993). Hadley (1970), Aoki (1987) and Miyajima (1994) each provide a history of the transformation from prewar *zaibatsu* to postwar industrial groups. Some economists suggest that the group operates to distribute risk-sharing among the members (Nakatani 1984; Aoki 1984b). One issue which stands out as a key concern in the debate on governance structures is the implications of cross-shareholding, which I examine below.

It should be noted here that a number of Japanese studies have explored these same areas but have gone largely unnoticed in Western literature. These include research on the effect, if any, of cross-shareholding upon stock prices (Ikeo 1993; Kanesaki 1986; Kawakita 1992; 1993; Kobayashi 1991; 1992; Kumagai 1994; Kurasawa 1984; Ogishima 1993; Wakasugi 1982) and cross-shareholding from corporate governance perspectives (Ito 1993; Nomura Sogo Kenkyujo 1992; Okumura 1990). Two recent studies by Japanese research teams have analyzed management attitudes towards cross-shareholding based on corporate survey responses (Omura 1993; Fuji Sogo Kenkyujo 1993), focusing in particular on the firm's relationship with its main bank. Typically, none of the results of these Japanese studies have been included in discussions of Japanese industrial organization by the proponents of agency theory or, for that matter, by most other scholars outside of Japan.

Cross-shareholding

Kabushiki mochiai — mutual aid shareholding, is the Japanese term for what is antiseptically, but customarily, translated as "cross-shareholding", that is, bilateral shareholdings through which two companies hold stakes in one another. In 1987, cross-shareholdings represented 15.2% of the outstanding corporate stock issued in Japan by nonfinancial companies and some 22.7% when financial institutions are included (JFTC 1989). Cross-shareholdings, in turn, are a subset of what is known as *antei kabunushi* — quiescent stable shareholdings, held in trilateral, multilateral, or otherwise stable arrangements between companies, usually based on group and/or transactional relationships. Together, cross- and stable shareholdings comprise some 65% to 70% of all stock issued by publicly traded corporations in Japan. The remaining minority of shares are freely traded on the stock exchanges.

As I will show, however, cross-shareholding, when applied to Japan, describes more than a single-dimension ownership relationship and masks a culturally loaded connotation to those familiar with only its superficial meaning. The tacit mutual agreements that are often the real purpose of cross-shareholding are intended to avoid rather than confer shareholder rights. Designed to insulate management from any market threat of hostile takeover, the existence of the stable shareholding relationship is an essentially *anti*-corporate governance strategy.

For purposes of governance analysis, cross-shareholding may be divided into two categories: 1) cross-shareholding between members of an industrial group, or *kigyo shudan*, the core of stable shareholding arrangements, and 2) cross-shareholding that is indicative of business relationships between suppliers and customers. In the latter case, cross-shareholding arrangements are primarily a franchise to do business, a method of cementing of transactional relationships. In neither case, however, is the cross-shareholding intended to confer the ownership rights inherent in the Anglo-American model of corporate governance. It is also within this second category of transactional relationship that a bank's shares of cross-held stock with its major business client firms should be viewed. The same is true for insurance companies and trust banks which typically own shares in companies with which they do a significant amount of business, including selling insurance and pension fund products to the client firm and its employees. Such transaction-related shareholdings are to be considered separate from any holdings in the client firm's equity that these financial institutions may have in their investment portfolios.[4]

A third type of corporate shareholding exists which is unrelated to issues of corporate governance. It is a form of speculative financial investment within a firm's investment portfolio that was particularly popular during the "bubble period" of credit-induced asset price inflation of the late 1980s. Known then as *zaitech,* or financial engineering, such investments characterized a period when companies believed that financial investing would yield a greater return than their core businesses. It is only in this last category of shareholding that there has been any show of the selling of shares, primarily to cover losses on a firm's profit and loss statement.

Failure to Distinguish Between *Kigyo Shudan* and *Keiretsu*

Further complicating and often confusing the discussion has been the steady agglomeration of terminology, which has made defining the boundaries between reciprocal, inclusive relationships and competitive market relationships all the more difficult. This expansion of inaccurate vocabulary has led not only to the misuse of terms but in some cases to incorrect inferences. For example, Nakatani (1983), (as well as many other Japanese scholars), when writing in Japanese employ the correct usage "*kigyo shudan*", but incorrectly substitute "keiretsu" in the English version of their articles (Nakatani 1984). Gerlach (1992), as another example, imposes the use of the term "keiretsu" for a general description for all types of industrial groups. This acquiescence to misuse in nomenclature inevitably and predictably has popularized a mistake that is perpetuated by numerous scholars, journalists, and government officials, resulting in the blurring of clarity and critical understanding of important issues. The distinction between the *kigyo shudan* and *keiretsu* is important because the nature of the power relationships and relational access, as described earlier, are not the same.

Such misconstruing of *keiretsu* and *kigyo shudan,* by sheltering from scrutiny the formal and informal governance structures based on principles of relational access, leave issues such as lack of transparency and lack of information, inadequately examined. For example, in 1992 Japan's Economic Planning Agency (EPA) felt compelled to respond to U.S. criticism raised in the Strategic Structural Initiative (SSI) trade negotiations that cross-shareholding promoted unfair trading practices. Characterizing them as "merits", the EPA advanced three main economic justifications, among others, for cross-shareholding.

It argued that cross-shareholding provides a stable source of funding for businesses by ensuring partners who will be stable investors and buy new issues of stock whenever needed. Furthermore, according to the EPA, cross-shareholding strengthens the stability of corporate management by acting as a bulwark against the threat of hostile takeover. Such arrangements relieve management of the necessity of responding to excessive pressures from the capital markets, permitting it to develop operations according to a long-term perspective. Lastly, the EPA maintained, cross-shareholding stabilizes and strengthens business transactions between companies. The EPA White Paper of 1992 termed cross-shareholding a mutual "hostage" taking, which creates a captive relationship in the supply of goods or services and promotes long-term transactional relationships between cross-shareholding companies.

It is interesting to note that, while promoting these particular "merits", the Economic Planning Agency also conceded:

> Even though interlocking stockholding has the functions mentioned above, if it creates a relationship of 'conspiracy,' business may become inefficient. What is more important, in selecting the customers, if it is taken into account whether or not they have interlocking stockholding unrelated to their individual products or substance of service, or cartel relations come into existence between competitors, competition may be limited (Economic Planning Agency 1992: 181).

As we shall see, cross-shareholding arrangements spring from concepts of relational access in which such of its effects as anti-competitive practices and lack of management accountability are protected through reliance on principles of the *uchi-soto* continuum.

Kigyo Shudan Affiliation

Among the largest *kigyo shudan*, namely, those affiliated with the top six city banks, a distinction should be drawn between groups such as Mitsui, Mitsubishi, and Sumitomo, which are the direct descendants of the prewar *zaibatsu* of the same names, and groups which are affiliated with Dai-Ichi Kangyo, Sanwa, and Fuji Banks. Within the former, that is, the pre-war *zaibatsu* groups, the extent of cross-shareholding is far higher, 27.46% in 1989, with group members considering their trading company or the original core company within their group as the group's centre, although the group's bank also plays a significant role. Group identity and loyalties are thought to be far stronger among the more tradition-bound former *zaibatsu* groups than they are in the postwar bank-centered DKB, Sanwa, Fuji, *kigyo shudan*, where group identity and cross-shareholding is far weaker, 15.83% in cross-held shares in 1989 according to EPA calculations. Within all of the *kigyo shudan*, however, the group's bank and other financial institutions, together with the group's trading company, have the most global ties with all of the other group members by virtue of the basic nature of their transactional business.

Although the six largest *kigyo shudan* have been the most studied and analyzed, other significant groups exist, for example, around such banks as the Industrial Bank of Japan, the largest of the long-term credit banks, or client firms of the Tokai Bank, based in the Nagoya region. Indeed, there are many other groups of lesser size associated with smaller city banks with a strong regional base, or the regional banks themselves, and the second-tier regional (formerly *sogo* or mutual) banks, all of which have their "groups." It is the communal nature of Japanese society to coalesce in groups, and it is hard to imagine any entity in Japan no matter how small its size that does not consider itself to be a member of some group or another.

A common way of identifying firm membership in a particular *kigyo shudan* is by its membership in the group's *shacho-kai*, or Presidents Association.[5] Some scholars have translated *shacho-kai* as Presidents Club or Council. However, the Presidents Association is not a club in the usual social sense. Membership is solely *ex officio* and lasts only during the member's tenure as a president of a group company. Nor is it a council as has also been suggested. The word "council" implies a more deliberative function than actually transpires. Unsubstantiated assumptions as to the nature of the *shacho-kai*, apparently arising from the very existence of these organizations, has led some agency theorists to suggest that the *shacho-kai* plays a significant role in corporate governance (see for example Aoki 1987; Sheard 1989; 1991). The monthly meeting of the *shacho-kai* clearly does provide a venue for relationship building that is essential to conducting business. Indeed, the necessity of having a "relationship" is a *sina qua non* for conducting ongoing business in Japan. However, it would be considered indelicate, if not impertinent, for the *shacho-kai* to discuss its concerns about the business of a particular company, much less assume the collective right to exercise its influence on its management.

Not surprisingly, the prevalent view of scholars in Japan is that cross-shareholding is intrinsically *anti*-governance. There, critics have characterized the anti-governance effects of Japanese-style cross-shareholding as "demerits", particularly in terms of management accountability and anti-competitive practices. For example, with no effective oversight by shareholders of corporate operations and managerial performance, until recently Japanese managers have had little incentive to manage efficiently beyond their self-interested need to perpetuate the company. In the U.S., because shareholders, at least theoretically, oversee the effectiveness of corporate management, the possibility exists of shareholders exercising their rights to change management if operations become inefficient. Corporate management is thus incentivized to have an interest in the more effective operation of the company for the benefit of the shareholders (Ito 1993). However, because of the mutual agreements generally implied in a Japanese cross-shareholding relationship, Japanese corporate management is given a superabundance of discretion in making business decisions and in regulating itself. This lack of monitoring leads to inefficiencies that produce a low return on equity, since declaring shareholder dividends are neither a necessity nor even a priority concern to corporate managers (Nomura Sogo Kenkyujo 1992).

Critics in Japan also argue that the nature of cross-shareholding agreements can damage and even defraud shareholders. Viewed benignly, cross-shareholding merely represents an offsetting exchange of stock between companies, giving no advantage in funding because there is no injection of new outside capital. Only if equity financing is done at separate times and differing amounts of capital are raised will there be some limited merit for one side or the other. From the perspective of a third-party shareholder, however, these transactions can be seriously misleading. For example, normally when a company issues stock for ¥100 million in capital, the company then would end up owning assets worth ¥100 million. However, in a cross-shareholding arrangement, when one company issues stock to raise capital, there are no proceeds, just the receipt of new stock in exchange; the transaction is a purely paper one. The third party investor may thus be defrauded either because he does not receive capital or because he has decided to invest based upon the belief that there is actually that amount of capital in the company when, in fact, there is only paper (Okumura 1990).

The extent of cross-shareholding within the group's companies is often pointed to, particularly from abroad, as a measure of exclusionary, anti-competitive business practices in view of the fact that group companies tend to do business mainly with each other, thus discouraging foreign investment in Japan, as was pointed out at the Strategic Structural Initiative negotiations. Although not admitting that the practice is anti-competitive, the Japanese government nonetheless has agreed to monitor cross-shareholding transactions between companies within the same *keiretsu* group to prevent transactions that will encourage unfair competition. Thus, the government has promised to scrutinize whether a company, in choosing goods or services to purchase, is giving its cross-shareholding partners anti-competitive benefits (Economic Planning Agency 1992).

Cross-shareholding has also been criticized as having a negative effect on the stock market. It is argued that cross-shareholding will lead to fewer shares being traded on the exchange or in the secondary market. In other words, because the stocks of cross-held companies have a greater volatility in price, speculators can manipulate the market more easily. Such speculation in the Japanese stock market tends to discourage the trust of outside investors, and, in overall terms, would cause longer-term investors to leave the market.

Analysts taking the contrary view maintain, however, that under the efficient market hypothesis of the Miller-Modigliani theorem, stock price fundamentals are based upon the net value of the company, and cross-shareholding should not affect the company's value, and therefore the ultimate effect of cross-shareholding upon stock prices remains neutral (Ikeo 1993). Still other analysts believe it has positive effect on price/earnings ratios (Ogishima 1993), and some 82% of company executives surveyed held the belief that cross-shareholding has a beneficial effect in stabilizing their own company's stock price (Omura 1993).

In fact, despite the apparently wide-spread consensus that cross-shareholding has either nil or a positive effect on stock prices, evidence shows cross-shareholding to have the opposite effect. The assets of companies holding cross-held stock are more vulnerable to share price volatility to the extent the company holds such stocks. This is because their corporate earnings ultimately tend to rely upon the stock prices of cross-held shares. If stock prices go up, the company earns "hidden profits" from these stocks, but if these stocks' prices go down, they will have "unrealized losses." Japanese companies which showed a steady rise in their core business income between 1985 and 1991, suffered unrealized stock losses in cross-held shares when the stock market declined from 1989-1991. This resulted in an overall decline in their own company's stock price during those years, despite core business profits, to the extent that they held stock in cross-shareholding companies (Kawakita 1992). Thus, in this sense, their corporate earnings tend to depend upon cross-held stocks' prices.

Thus the very nature of cross-shareholding has multiple side effects — upon management, shareholders, competition, and even the price of stocks and corporate earnings. I would argue that this system of cross-shareholding is itself a product of a well-developed culture heavily reliant upon principles of relational access. The typically invisible barrier-gate operates not only against foreigners but against other outsiders, whether they be shareholders vis-à-vis management, or competitors, or non-group firms.

Conclusion

This chapter has presented an analysis of the Japanese firm and industrial group relations in which I have argued that core Japanese business practices are determined by sets of uncodified rules and obligations that are opaque to outsider scrutiny. The governing principle underlying these practices is described as "relational access", a continuum of relationship from insider to outsider by which inter- and intra-firm relations are determined.

Based upon this concept, I have presented a new model of Japanese firm and industrial group relations which I have termed the "Relational Access Paradigm." The paradigm proposes an *r*-dimension, an *uchi-soto* (insider-outsider) continuum which defines where one firms stands in relation to another. The paradigm intentionally extends the concept of the firm and group firms beyond the boundaries drawn by *de jure* property rights theories to encompass a concept of the firm and group as participants in an arena of collective action in which viability as an institution is greatly dependent on the supportive milieu in which the firm and its group are situated. In this sense, the Japanese firm and group can be viewed as a nexus of *implicit relational* contracts, indicative of a high-context, communal form of industrial organization, in contradistinction to the firm as a nexus of linear contracts in a freely negotiated market.

Central to the model of the Japanese firm presented here is a graded pattern of concentric relationships traceable from the *ie*-style merchant household of Tokugawa Japan to today's corporate relationships and the *kigyo shudan* and *keiretsu* industrial group forms. Within the concentric spheres, issues of ranking, relatedness, and identification as either *uchi* (insider) or *soto* (outsider) are as significant today as they were four hundred or more years ago. The formation of the production unit in Japan remains fundamentally coextensive with an elaborated meaning of kinship and household, and with the loyalties and allegiances which those inspire. Similarly the discussion of the *ie* (household) attempted not only to set forth some of the historical antecedents of modern Japanese managerial practices but, more fundamentally, to propose that a deeper, more culturally inclusive view of the nature of relationships among Japanese firms and industrial groups is critical to the current analysis of the Japanese firm.

I have argued that the agency approach to the Japanese industrial groups has been based upon a number of false assumptions, most frequently relating to corporate governance by the *shacho-kai* or Presidents Associations. As I see it, the failure of the proponents of agency theory to discern the nature of the *shacho-kai* arises from not drawing clear distinctions between the collegial relationships within the *kigyo shudan*, i.e. the clan form, and the hierarchical relationships of the *keiretsu*, i.e. the fief form.

The persistence of the current economic recession in Japan has led some observers to speculate that there will be a winding down of the cross-shareholding system as hard-pressed companies are forced to take capital gains from the sale of cross-held shares in order to dress up their bottom lines. However, statistical evidence to date indicates that among companies holding such shares, the required fiscal reports for the year ending 31 March 1993 reveal a slight *increase* in cross-shareholding patterns (Mabuchi 1993; Kumagai 1994). Indeed, it has been a very common practice for banks and other cross-shareholders, in an attempt to capture profits to dress up their annual statements, to sell and then immediately repurchase these shares at the current market price to realize the capital gains, leaving intact their ratio of cross-held shares. The fact that banks feel obliged to repurchase these shares is indicative that the purpose of this shareholding is strictly relational access, a necessary component for their maintaining close transactional ties to client firms, similar to the close vendor/supplier relations that non-financial companies also must maintain in with their cross-shareholding business partners. As one banker reported to the author, his bank's sale of any client shares requires the assessment of the relationship and approval of three departments before they may be sold.

In today's market far fewer gains can be captured by selling off shares. Indeed, it depends when those shares were initially purchased. For many banks, their so-called "hidden assets" are in fact unrealized losses, since those shares were initially purchased during the boom markets of the 1980s, or last repurchased for capital gains at a higher levels. If shares are sold for fundraising, then some care should also be taken to distinguish between the cross-held relational shares and those shares which were acquired by corporations as speculative investments during the *zaitech* era — the period of financial "engineering" of the late 1980s. Although the rationalization of speculative investments is to be expected, shares which were purchased as part of a cross-shareholding pattern based upon customer-supplier relationships are of a quite different character.

In sum, many of the supposed rationales of the mutual stockholding relationship, such as reduced share price volatility, are now in serious dispute. Other so-called benefits, such as the "smoothness" of shareholder meetings (the result of management steamrolling tactics), act primarily to protect management incumbency and are often explicitly anti-governance. The lack of correlation between capital ratios and mutual stock ownership eliminates any oversight for large companies. Responses by corporate executives to the questions of the Fuji Sogo Kenkyujo (1993) and Omura (1993) surveys indicate that corporate governance concerns have had little or no impact on cross-shareholding patterns and show no evidence of a devolution of mutual shareholding arrangements. Thus we can conclude only one significant purpose remains for maintaining stable business relationships, i.e. transactional relations between the cross-shareholding partner companies — as a franchise to do business with each other. This conclusion is in itself significant since these cross-held shares provides us here with what otherwise seldom exists, tangible evidence of these implicit relational contracts.

The concept of the ownership of the firm is poorly developed in the literatures of economics and management. In the case of Japan, economics-based theories which view the firm as essentially a commodity, i.e. a bundle of rights with marketable value linked to an expected profit stream, inevitably collide with management-based theories in which forces of collectivity overwhelm pecuniary factors. Whereas in the West the joint-stock company weakened the role of the household firm, recasting it in essentially commodity terms, through the *ie* system the Japanese firm was able to accomplish some of the same objectives as the joint-stock company while retaining the motivational aspects of a family business.

That Japanese business relationships still fall within this traditional pattern should not be perceived as an historical accident but rather as evidence that such a social system continues to be a necessary element in the success of Japanese capitalism. In the hierarchical *keiretsu* form the web of traditional relations can become a vast reservoir within which asymmetries of power are able to exploit ingrained societal relations. In the hypothesis of perfect markets these asymmetries are vitiated and such traditional reserves of relational obligations do not exist to be tapped in low-context, contractual societies. In a pure-market hypothesis in which everyone is a free agent and all of life is reduced to a series of spot transactions, all asymmetries and the opportunity for exploitation of these asymmetries theoretically is quickly lost to some free market equilibrium.

What has made Japanese capitalism so successful is that it has been able to tap into a traditional culture that supports the great exploitation of asymmetries, such as imperfect labour markets, to concentrate wealth. Although the opaque nature of *keiretsu* transactions has led some to presume that they are not dictated by power relationships between the parties and that such relations have no effect on price or exploitation, I conclude this view underestimates the fact that the essence of Japanese governance structures is not always predominantly synergistic, as the *kigyo shudan* form tends to be, but, as evidenced by the *keiretsu* form, is often rooted in the exploitation of asymmetries of information, labour, and a host of other variables in the sets and subsets of relationships that permeate Japanese society. Our holistic model, the Relational Access Paradigm, provides a framework to better understand the dimensions of power, information, and access that define Japanese governance structures.

Notes

1 "Culture", as used by anthropologists, is a term referring to a system for creating, sending, storing, and processing information developed by human beings. The terms *mores*, *tradition*, *custom*, and *habit* are subsumed under the umbrella of "culture" (Hall and Hall 1990).

2 Banks do have their own "keiretsu" relationships, but their vertical affiliations are with other financial institutions such as: regional banks, mutual banks, finance companies, casualty insurers, leasing companies and other financial services. Fifteen out of the top sixteen companies in which city, regional and long-term credit banks held shares were in fact other financial institutions (Zenkoku Shoken Torihikijo Kyogikai 1992).

3 Many Western scholars have come to mischaracterize Japanese long-term transactional relationships as dependent on "trust." This is not a concept or a word that is commonly used in Japan when describing *keiretsu torihiki* (group affiliated transactions). The right of "access" provided by a *keiretsu* relationship is seen as a franchise to do business that group membership affords, hence a "dry" relationship.

4 In the author's interviews with trust bank and insurance executives, they reported that they principally rely on fixed-income securities in their investment portfolios to meet their actuarial needs, and that the overwhelming percentage of client firm equities being held were for "relational" purposes.

5 The various *shacho-kai* groups meet monthly, and most are anonymously named by the day of the month they meet: Kinyo-kai — Friday Association (Mitsubishi); Nimoku-kai — Second Thursday Association (Mitsui); Sansui-kai — Wednesday Association (Sanwa); Sankin-kai — Third Friday Association (DKB); Fuyo Club (Fuji); and Hakusui-kai — White Water Society (Sumitomo).

References

Alchian, A.A. and H. Demsetz (1972): "Production, information costs, and economic organization." *American Economic Review* 62: 777-795.

Aoki M. (1984a): *The co-operative game theory of the firm*. Oxford: Oxford University Press.

Aoki M. (1984b): "Aspects of the Japanese firm" in M. Aoki (ed.), *The economic analysis of the Japanese firm*, 3-43. North-Holland: Elsevier.
Aoki M. (1987): "The Japanese firm in transition" in K. Yamamura and Y. Yasuba (eds.), *The political economy of Japan*, 263-288. Stanford, CA: Stanford University Press.
Aoki M. (1990): "Toward an economic model of the Japanese firm." *Journal of Economic Literature* 28: 1-27.
Barney, J.B. and W.G. Ouchi (1984): "Information cost and organization of transaction governance." Unpublished manuscript, Graduate School of Management, University of California Los Angeles.
Bennett, J.W. and I. Ishino (1963): *Paternalism in the Japanese economy: Anthropological studies of Oyabun-Kobun patterns*. Minneapolis: University of Minnesota Press.
Berle, A.A. and G.C. Means (1932): *The modern corporation and private property*. New York: Macmillan.
Boisot, M.H. (1986): "Markets and hierarchies in a cultural perspective." *Organization Studies* 7: 135-138.
Boisot, M.H. and J. Child (1988): "The iron law of fiefs: Bureaucratic failure and the problem of governance in the Chinese economic reforms." *Administrative Science Quarterly* 33: 507-527
Burt, D.N. and M.F. Doyle (1993): *The American Keiretsu: A strategic weapon for global competitiveness*. Homewood, IL: Irwin Publishing.
Business Week (1992): "American Keiretsu, Learning from Japan." 27 January: 52-60.
Coase, R. (1937): "The nature of the firm." *Econometrica* 4: 386-405.
Demsetz, H. (1967): "Toward a theory of property rights." *American Economic Association*, May: 347-359.
Dore, R. (1987): *Taking Japan seriously*. Stanford: Stanford University Press.
Durkheim, E. (1933): *The division of labor in society* (2nd edition. G. Simpson trans.). New York: Free Press.
Economic Planning Agency (1992): White paper: Economic survey of Japan, 1991-92. Tokyo.
Ferguson, C. (1990): "Computers and the coming of the U.S. Keiretsu." *Harvard Business Review* 68(4): 55-70.
Fruin, W.M. (1992): *The Japanese enterprise system*. New York: Oxford University Press.
Fuji, S.K. (1993): 'Main bank system oyobi kabushiki' ni tsuite no chosa (An investigation regarding the influence of shareholding on the main bank system). Research report, Tokyo.
Gerlach, M. (1992): *Alliance capitalism: The social organization of Japanese business*. Berkeley: University of California Press.
Gilson, R. and M. Roe (1993): "Understanding the Japanese Keiretsu: Overlaps between corporate governance and industrial organization." *The Yale Law Journal* 102: 871-906.
Gouldner, A.W. (1960): "The norm of reciprocity." *American Sociological Review* 25: 161-178.
Granovetter, M. (1985): "Economic action and social structure: The problem of embeddedness." *American Journal of Sociology* 91: 481-510.
Hadley, E.M. (1970): *Anti-trust in Japan*. Princeton NJ: Princeton University Press.
Hall, E.T. (1977): *Beyond culture*. Garden City, NY: Doubleday.
Hall, E.T. and M. Hall (1990): *Understanding cultural differences*. Yarmouth, ME: Intercultural Press.

Harvard Business Review (1990): "Can a Keiretsu work in America?" 68(5): 180-196.
Hofstede, G.H. (1991): *Cultures and organizations: Software of the mind.* Maidenhead: McGraw-Hill.
Horie Y. (1966): The role of the *Ie* in the economic modernization of Japan. *The Kyoto University Economic Review* 36(1): 1-16.
Ikeo K. (1993): "Kinyu no Micro-Keizaigaku — Kabushiki mochiai." (Microeconomics of cross-shareholding). Paper presented to Keizai Seminar, Nihon Hyoron-sha, March..
Ito K. (1993): "Kabushiki Mochiai: Sono Rasenkei 'Logic'" (Cross-shareholding: A spiral Logic) in T. Itami, T. Kagono and M. Ito (eds.), *Nihon no Kigyo System: Dai-ichi kann — Kigyo to Nani-ka,* (Japanese Enterprise System: Series 1 — What is an Enterprise?). Tokyo: Yushikaku Publishing.
Japan Fair Trade Commission (1989): *Kigyo shudan no jittai ni tsuite* (On the status of the enterprise groups). Tokyo.
Jensen, M.C. and W.H. Meckling (1976): "Theory of the firm: Managerial behavior, agency costs and ownership structure." *Journal of Financial Economics* 3: 305-360.
Kanesaki, Y. (1986): "Kabushiki mochiai ga aru baai-no kigyo kachi to CAPM" (Cross-shareholding's effect on the value of the enterprise and the Capital Asset Pricing Model). *Finansu Kenkyu* 5.
Kawakita H. (1992): "Kigyo zaimu wo mushibamu 104 choen no kabushiki mochiai" (¥104 trillion of cross-held shares eat away at company fiscal management). *Kinyu Zaisei Jijo,* 12.10.1992: 40-44.
Kawakita H. (1993): "Kabushiki antei hoyu no keisei to genjo" (The present situation of maintaining stable shareholdings), Shadanhojin Nippon Shoken Anaristu Kyokai. *Shoken Anaristu Janaru,* June.
Kobayashi T. (1991): "Kabushiki no jukyu to kabuka" parts 1-6 (The supply and demand of stocks and stock prices) Yasashii Keizaigaku. *Nihon Keizai Shimbun,* July: 12-18.
Kobayashi T. (1992): "Kabushiki mochiai to kabuka" (Cross-shareholdings and stock prices) in *Gendai Shoken Jiten* (Dictionary of Contemporary Securities). Nippon Shoken Keizai Kenkyujo-hen.
Kumagai, G. (1994): "Kabushiki shisan wa ROA jo, ALM jo asshuku sareru beki mono da" (ROA and ALM data require a cap on stock investments). *Kinyu Zaisei Jijo,* 12.9.1994: 32-36.
Kurasawa, S. (1984): "Kabushiki mochiai to kigyo kachi" (Cross-shareholding and the Value of an Enterprise) *Finansu Kenkyu* 2.
Mabuchi, H. (1993): *NRC Toshi Geppo.* November 1993, Tokyo: Nikko Research Centre Ltd.
Mito, T. (1992): "'Ie no ronri' to nippon shakai (2): keiyaku-gata to shozoku-gata — zangyo to tetsudai" ('Logic of *Ie*' and Japanese Society (part 2): Contract-model versus Belonging-model — Overtime work and helping-out). *Shosai no Mado* 3: 4-10.
Mitsui Gomei-Kaisha (Mitsui Unlimited Partnership) (1933): *The house of Mitsui. A record of three centuries: Past history and present enterprises.* Tokyo: Mitsui Gomei-Kaisha.
Miyajima H. (1994): "The Transformation of Zaibatsu to postwar corporate groups — From hierarchically integrated groups to horizontally integrated groups." *Journal of the Japanese and International Economies* 8: 293-328.
Miyamoto M. (1984): "The position and role of family business in the development of the Japanese company system" in A. Okochi and S. Yasuoka (eds.), *Family business in the era of industrial growth, its ownership and management,* 39-91. Tokyo: University of Tokyo Press.

Nakatani I. (1983): "Kigyo shudan no keizaiteki imi to ginko no yakuwari" (The economic significance of the enterprise groups and the role of banks). *Kin'yu Keizai* 202: 51-75.

Nakatani I. (1984): "The economic role of financial corporate grouping" in M. Aoki (ed.) *The economic analysis of the Japanese firm*, 227-258. North-Holland: Elsevier.

Nakatani I. (1990): "Opening up fortress Japan." *Japan Echo* 3: 8-11.

Nishiguchi T. (1992): *Strategic industrial sourcing*. London: Oxford University Press.

Nomura S.K. (1992): "Nihon kigyo no corporate governance" (Corporate Governance of Japanese Companies). *Zaikai Kansoku*, September.

Ogishima S. (1993): "Kabushiki mochiai ga kabuka keisei ni ateru eikyo" (The influence cross-shareholding gives to stock prices). Shadanhojin Nippon Shoken Anaristu Kyokai. *Shoken Anaristu Janaru*, June.

Okumura H. (1990): *Kigyo baishu — M&A no jidai* (Company buyouts in the M&A era). Tokyo: Iwanami Shoten.

Omura K. (1993): *Kabushiki mochiai no ishiki kozo* (How do Japanese companies consider cross-shareholding?). Report of International Finance Group, Keiei Academy, Tokyo.

Ouchi, W.G. (1980): "Markets, bureaucracies, and clans." *Administrative Science Quarterly* 25: 129-141.

Ouchi, W.G. (1981): *Theory Z: How American business can meet the Japanese challenge*. Reading MA: Addison-Wesley.

Sakakibara, E. (1994): *Beyond capitalism: The Japanese model of market economics*. Lanham MD: University Press of America/Economic Strategy Institute.

Sako, M. (1992): *Prices, quality and trust: Inter-firm relations in Britain and Japan*. Cambridge: Cambridge University Press.

Sakudo, Y. (1990): "The management practices of family business" in C. Nakane and S. Oishi (eds.) *Tokugawa Japan, The social and economic antecedents of modern Japan*, 147-166. Tokyo: University of Tokyo Press.

Schaede, U. (1993): "Understanding corporate governance in Japan: Do classical concepts apply?" CCC Working Paper No. 93-12, Center for Research in Management, University of California at Berkeley.

Schaede, U. (1994): "Corporate governance in Japan: Institutional investors, management monitoring and corporate stakeholders." *Industrial and Corporate Change* 2: 285-323.

Scher, M.J. (1997): *Japanese interfirm networks and their main banks* London: Macmillan.

Sheard, P. (1989): "The main bank system and corporate monitoring and control in Japan." *Journal of Economic Behavior* 11: 399-422.

Sheard, P. (1991): "The economics of interlocking shareholding." *Ricerche Economiche* 45: 421-448.

Wakasugi K. (1982): "Kabushiki mochiai no zaimuteki igi" (The financial significance of cross-shareholding) in *Nipponteki keiei zaimu no kaimei* (Views of Japanese Treasurers) by Nippon Keiei Zaimu Kenkyu Gakkai-hen. Chuo Keizai-sha.

Weber, M. (1921): (*Wirtschaft und Gesellschaft*) *The theory of social and economic organization*. Translated by A.M. Henderson and Talcott Parsons. Edited with an Introduction by T. Parsons. 1947 New York: Oxford University Press.

Whitley, R. (1992): *Business systems in East Asia: Firms markets and societies*. London: Sage Publications.

Williamson, O.E. (1975): *Markets and hierarchies: Analysis and antitrust implications*. New York: Free Press.

Williamson, O.E. (1985): *The economic institutions of capitalism: Firms, markets and relational Contracting*. New York: Free Press.
Yoshino M.Y. (1968): *Japan's managerial system, tradition and innovation*. Cambridge MA: MIT Press.
Zenkoku Shoken Torihikijo Kyogikai (1992): *Kabushiki Bunpu Jokyo Chosa* (Survey of the state of share distribution). Tokyo.

Between Democracy and Dictatorship: The Market Queen Institution of Ghanian Daily Markets*

Saija Katila

Introduction

West-African markets in general and Ghanian markets in particular are famous for their large size and female dominance. The majority of traders in Ghana are women, estimates varying between 70-85% (Clark 1994; Cutrufelli 1983), and being as high as 97% among fish traders (Essiem 1987). These large markets dominated by female traders appear to be exceptionally well organized thanks to a particular system of personalized ties between traders. The central component of this system is the "market queen" institution. A market queen is a democratically elected representative of traders trading a certain product or product group (Clark 1994; 1991; Omenukor 1989; Cutrufelli 1983). The smooth functioning of commodity markets in Ghana is assured by market queens who enjoy a considerable degree of economic power in society.

Trading, even on a small scale, has been an important source of income for many families in Ghana, but it has been of great importance to the women in West-Africa in general (Little 1973; Clark 1991). Purely female involvement in the market trade in Ghana began at the turn of the century. The introduction of jobs for men in cocoa farming and in the modern sector opened up the markets to women (Clark 1994; Sai 1971). Women's active involvement in the trading sector is also related to familial structures and the responsibilities assumed by women in Ghanian society, which limit their chances of getting, or accepting waged employment.

To meet the familial and economic demands society places upon market women, they combine their activities in such a way that child care and other domestic duties do not conflict with their trading activities and vice versa (see Grieco et al. 1996). The large number of infants present at the markets illustrates this well. This is not, of course, a Ghanian feature, but common to other, especially Third World, countries as well (Tripp and Swantz 1994; Epstein 1990; Omari 1989). Furthermore, women lack formal education —

over 50% of traders have never been to school (Clark 1994; Opoku-Boakye 1990; Essiem 1987). This is due, at least in part, to the high demand for female child labour in domestic, farming and trading activities (Grieco et al. 1996).

Given the low level of education of traders it is rather remarkable that they are so well organized, and have such economic power. Market women have been able to control the markets and the price of goods in Ghana for decades. At certain periods, this practice resulted in soaring prices and thus endangered both the national economy and political stability. Numerous attempts of governments to control prices have so far been unsuccessful (Omenukor 1989). In 1979 and 1982 government's frustration materialized in ideological attacks on market traders. They were accused of accumulating disproportionate wealth through predatory practices. The system of personalized ties between traders was seen as the main source of exploitation and abuse by traders. These arguments were used in political debates to justify the attempts to dismantle the informal power base of market traders (Clark 1994). In spite of serious allegations against the way commodity groups are organized, the role of this particular organizational form in securing the food supply in Ghana is essential. The majority of Ghanian food stuffs are both transported and sold by market women and trading in food staples has flourished with no formal sector competition (Clark 1994; Appiah-Asare 1992; Opoku-Boakye 1990; Essiem 1987; Ansah 1985; Vercruijsse 1983).

Through an ethnographic approach this chapter attempts to unravel the complexities and tensions inherent in the market queen institution. By giving a vivid description of the institution, this chapter invokes questions about the Western perceptions of organizing the labour process in general. It thus invites the reader to contest her/his Western distinctions of customer/competitor/colleague, legal/illegal, and privileged Western women/deprived African women. The study shows that in the Ghanian context these distinctions tend to acquire different meanings since the markets, with the mechanisms designed to institute and to regulate them, are deeply rooted in the traditional fabric of the Ghanian society.

After presenting the study design in the first section, the second section of this chapter discusses the cultural background against which the market queen institution is shaped. Following a brief description of Ghanian markets given in section three, the next section discusses the market queen institution and its economic and social significance. It is argued that this institution benefits individual traders by operating, among other things, as a mechanism to facilitate information flows, risk sharing and credit provision. It is shown that the institution serves a crucial social and economic function in assuring the smooth functioning of markets. Nevertheless, it also has some undesirable consequences in terms of economic efficiency and relations of social power. In the concluding section, the relative significance of these advantages and disadvantages are discussed in an overall appraisal of the specific form of Ghanian market organization.

Study Design

The study reported here was undertaken at Kaneshie Market Accra and in Koforidua. Kaneshie Market is a three-floored market complex and is the second most important market in Accra, the capital of Ghana. There are a total of 2,000 stalls and expansive space for those without stalls (Appiah-Asare 1992). In Koforidua (100 km from Accra, in the Eastern Region) traders from the Main and Anloa town markets, as well as some store keepers outside the walls of the Main market, were interviewed. The Main market is a walled area in the heart of the town which has concrete stalls and wooden sheds for traders. Anloa town market is an unwalled roadside market approximately 1,5 kilometers from the Main market where traders are scattered alongside the road. Mostly basic food stuffs and charcoal are sold there.

The field work was done during a five month period in Ghana in 1994 during which I spent a lot of time at the markets, especially at Kaneshie market. Being at the market place was useful not only to understand the organization of trade but also to gain the confidence of the interviewees. The latter were initially suspicious that I might have connections with the tax department. However, once these suspicions were dispelled, they were quite eager to speak to a white European woman. The initial questions were on how individual market traders organize and manage their work, the emphasis being on the technical aspects of trading (see Apt and Katila 1994; Katila 1996). Eventually, questions about the organization of the market were introduced.

The ethnographic evidence presented here is based on participant observation and in-depth interviews with 19 business owners and one market manager. Eighteen of the business owners were women between 24 to 56 years of age and one was a 27-year old man. They were all interviewed at least twice and some of them up to four times. It was important to carry out these interviews without disrupting the traders' business. Therefore, finding a suitable time for the interviews demanded my presence at the market during which I engaged in lengthy informal discussions with the traders. I sat down behind their counters observing the action and sometimes participating in it, for example by sorting and piling tomatoes, thus gaining valuable information on pricing and credit practices.

The interviews in Accra were conducted in English which is neither my nor the traders' native language. Nevertheless, it is widely spoken because of Ghana's history as a British colony. Furthermore, English is the school language in Ghana. I found my twelve interviewees in Accra by merely asking a trader whether or not she would be willing to participate in the study. Thus, the sample in Accra is biased towards traders who have at least the basic skills in the English language. The first round of interviews in Koforidua were conducted with the help of an interpreter who arranged the interviews for me. In the second round five out of the eight traders were willing to talk to me in English in private. I made notes during the interviews and later on typed them. Before the next interviewing session I asked all literate participants (17 in all) to read through the interviews and correct all mistakes and misunderstandings to improve the reliability of the interviews.

Market Queens and Queen Mothers

The origin of the market queen institution can be traced back to collective traditions of African societies in general and Ghanian society in particular. African societies give primacy to group membership over individual independence (Clark 1994; Mireku 1991; Malkamäki 1991; Lloyd 1967; Pellow 1978). Furthermore, every individual belongs to a group which, no matter how small, must have a leader (Debrunner 1961; Pellow 1978). Those chosen as such are senior members of the society reflecting the prestige and power given to age in African societies (Clark 1994; Nukunya 1992; Mireku 1991). But perhaps most importantly, the market queen institution is very similar to the traditional leadership system of Ghana — the queen mother institution.

The leader of all women in an Akan[1] chiefdom is called a queen mother — a title often used also of market queens. In fact, there are some easily discerned similarities between the role of a queen mother in the traditional political system and that of a market queen. One could suggest that some of the functions of the queen mother were transferred to the market context, along with some elements of social status and power connected with the office.

In the Akan political system a queen mother is a person next in order of importance to the chief or king. She has responsibility for the women in the chiefdom or town, but she has also a large say in selecting a new chief. All the decisions the chief makes must be discussed and agreed upon by the counselors, and queen mother, to whom the whole chiefdom has access through their family heads, lineage heads, village heads etc. (Clark 1994;

Nukunya 1992; Mireku 1991; Omenukor 1989). Also in other Southern Ghanian ethnic groups, the queen mother institution functions in parallel with the male chiefs. There are differences from group to group, but the basic roles can be identified. In Ewe[2] villages, the queen mother is elected and she has a council of elderly women as advisers and a linguist to speak for her. It is within the power of a queen mother to call all the women to work on communal tasks, such as repairs to the water and road system, and school buildings. The men are organized in a similar way, and both men and women are fined if they stay away from communal work without a valid reason. When a conflict arises between a husband and wife, an attempt at conciliation is made through representatives from the two families involved and a woman can ask the queen mother to represent her (Bukh 1979).

According to Clark (1994), although market queens are similar to queen mothers in some ways, they are different in others. One of the most significant differences is that market queens define their followers by occupation rather than by residence or citizenship, as in community leadership; or kinship, as in lineage leadership. However, the similarities seem to be more important than the differences. To summarize, both queen mothers and market queens are responsible for the women in the area, they both have elders (sub-queens) as advisers, they both can call women to work on communal tasks, and last but not least they both have an important role in dispute settlement. Furthermore market queens also have ceremonial duties like queen mothers. They are expected to attend funerals and community celebrations to keep up the public image of market traders.

The ceremonial representation by the market leaders is highly valued by group members. In Ghana funeral attendance is seen as a primary benefit of membership in any group, and it is seen to reflect its strength and cohesion. When a commodity group member dies, her market queen leads all the group members to attend her funeral, and the funeral of a market queen would be a market wide event (Clark 1994). In addition to ceremonial functions, the market queens also follow some other Akan traditions in order to gain and maintain their prestige. One of these traditions is speaking through a linguist. In Ghanian society a linguist is an official spokesman of the chief through whom all formal announcements from the chief are made. A chief does not speak directly to his subjects or to visitors (Nukunya 1992). As one of the market queens I interviewed told me:

> I am the queen and she is my linguist. So if you would be Ghanian you should go to her and she would introduce you to me. All the traders know this. They go first to her and then to me. I am an Ashanti but it would be this way no matter what ethnic group the queen comes from (Faustina, 45).[3]

It can be concluded that the collective traditions of Ghanian society and the adoption of the title queen and many of its procedural elements has made commodity groups internally strong and cohesive. Furthermore, the loyalty and discipline that give market queens their effective power derive from their presiding role in internal dispute settlement and from their highly valued ceremonial functions. This does not mean, however, that market leadership solely reflects the traditional forms. It shows, rather, that the contemporary challenges of organizing large markets are met with the aid of society-specific institutions that could only be understood with reference to their cultural context.

Crammed Buzzing Markets

The number of traders at a Ghanian market can vary from ten in a quiet village market to fifteen thousand at e.g. the giant Kumasi market. Most of the markets are places buzzing with life having smells, colours and noises of their own. Practically everything is sold at the larger markets: imports, exports and local products; to name a few, vegetables, grain, meat, smoked and fresh fish, cooking oil, charcoal, kitchen utensils, shoes, hand bags, jewelry, cloth, jeans, pottery, and refreshments. The markets are divided into commodity-specialized retail sections where a countless number of traders are selling exactly the same product in exactly the same form. All the items sold are neatly and often beautifully displayed. The largest markets also have various services such as tailoring, hair dressing and restaurants available. The scale of trading operations varies from large wholesale operations to small retail sales where the items sold may be placed on a single tray.

The main markets in Accra and Koforidua are full and no free stalls are available to be distributed to new traders. Thus the problem of getting access to market stalls on the crowded markets has made "bending of the rules" a common practice. Sharing, renting and inheriting a stall have become institutionalized practices upon which the formal market management has very little influence (Katila 1996; Clark 1994; Lardemelle 1992). In the most congested parts of markets traders sit side by side on small stools holding their goods on a tray in their laps.

In a situation where the population of traders is enormous and the trading space is limited, the option of hawking — headload carrying the goods around to reach passing customers — has become an attractive option for many. The practice of hawking at Kaneshie has resulted in the market area encroaching upon the bus station and the nearby pavements and overhead bridges. During rush hours catching a bus has become difficult, not to mention crossing the overhead bridges. In the months that I spent at the market there were some days when there were no illegal sellers on the pavements or bridges. They could be named "caning days" — then the city police force was ordered to drive away all illegal hawkers. When the police arrived the traders fled running from the site with their goods. Those who did not get away fast enough were hit with long bamboo canes, and all their produce was destroyed or confiscated. To a foreigner the practice looked pretty harsh, but it had very little effect on the illegal trading practices. In a couple of hours, at the latest by the next morning, all the hawkers were back on the site.

On busy days, the markets in Accra and in Koforidua look and feel chaotic, as if there were no rules, no order. But that is merely an illusion. The general rules of the market are set by the board of directors and they are, in theory, enforced by the market management. In practice, the market queens are the ones holding the reins. The everyday enforcement of the rules and regulations is in their hands. The management of the market has enough troubles of its own.

We have all the management problems that a market could have. The biggest problems are sanitation and congestion. We don't have information on the total number of sellers at Kaneshie market. If you count together the number of stalls and stores and multiply the figure by three you come quite close to the right figure. It is not under our control (Kaneshie Market Manager).

The Market Queen Institution

The formal organization of Ghanian markets co-exists with a powerful market queen institution. The institution operates as a mechanism to organize the labour process at the markets. In the market the term market queen is used to refer to a democratically elected representative of the traders of a certain product or product group. "Queen mother" or "elder" are also commonly used terms but for the sake of clarity the term market queen is used. The voluntary collegial commodity groups are based on egalitarian relations among and between groups of traders. They constitute the dominant structure of the marketplace system throughout Southern Ghana. The current commodity group structure was gradually formalized between the 1930s and 1950s (Clark 1994).

The number of market queens at the markets depends on the size of the market, the number of traders trading the same product, and the number of locations they are traded at. Some commodity groups have only one queen and some have one to three "sub-queens." In some cases the queens have separate roles as chairman, secretary and treasurer. Commodity group membership is limited to market traders. Store keepers right outside the boundaries of the markets do not participate in them. The groups are organized in varying degrees meeting usually once or twice a month depending on what the group has decided. Each market has also one democratically elected leading queen who is the leader of all the traders and market queens. Furthermore the market queens in Accra have their own formal association. Clark (1994) found that some commodity groups even have nationwide networks.

Market queens are often traders with substantial experience in the field. They are usually over forty years of age to be able to gain sufficient respect from inside and outside the group. Traders characterize queens as humble and simple women who can communicate well with their people. They must also have social skills as arbitrators. The queens are prominent members of their society both inside and outside the market. The importance of different queens varies according to the significance of their products in Ghanian society — most often according to the importance of the product in the Ghanian diet. Hence, yam, tomato and plantain queens are among the most important queens (see also Clark 1994).

Advantages of Group Membership

The market queen institution is a very powerful tool to promote traders' interests in large competitive markets. Commodity group membership carries significant advantages. The system of commodity groups organized around the market queen institution incorporates mechanisms of information dissemination, credit provision, risk sharing, and social security. It therefore presents a society specific alternative to formal institutions which fulfill these functions in Western market societies. Furthermore, market queens assume the responsibility of maintaining law and order by making sure that rules are obeyed, disputes do not get out of control, and the market place conforms to proper sanitary standards.

As in most economies, in Ghanian economy information is one of the key elements of market success. Traders need information about supply and demand, transportation, prices, credit and so on. Commodity group membership gives traders centralized access to this valuable market information (Clark 1991; 1994). Most of the information is orally transmitted, in other words, information spreads through the "grapevine." This is a necessity since over 50% of the traders are illiterate (Clark 1994; Opoku-Boakye 1990; Essiem 1987).

If there is a budget increase [referring to an increase in the fixed prices of grain] which rises the price of grain the market queen goes and tells her sellers to increase the prices (Joyce, 30).

Wholesalers and importers contact us market queens and we introduce them to reliable retailers at the market. If someone cannot pay off her debts to the wholesalers I advise her to the stall of this person, to able the wholesaler to confiscate as much of worth goods, as she owes her (Faustina, 45).

The last quote illustrates the importance of the status and information gained through group membership. Being known as a reliable commodity group member operates as a "social collateral" increasing one's chances of getting credit. Furthermore it helps individual traders to identify creditworthy colleagues thus limiting their risk when giving credit. Since banks play practically no role in financing market traders, informal sources of capital are crucial. Banks are unwilling to lend to female traders because they cannot offer acceptable collateral and also because the sums they require are often too small to be profitable (Appiah-Asare 1992; Opoku-Boakye 1990; Essiem 1987).

When traders are in need of working capital they turn to their colleagues, but in the case of start-up capital they most often rely on their family members (Katila 1996; Clark 1994; Pellow 1978). Fellow traders are better and more reliable sources of credit than other informal money lenders who often charge high interest rates. Informal money lenders in Zambia and Kenya have been found to charge 40-50% monthly interest which amounts to annual rates as high as 600% (Malkamäki 1991). Such excessive interest is rare in the Ghanian market context because traders who manipulate the credit terms beyond generally accepted limits face the risk of social and economic ostracism. Traders extend credit to each other in three forms: advances of goods, advances of capital and cash loans. Most traders pay promptly to be eligible for credit in the future. Traders also extend credit to consumers to have a competitive edge over other suppliers of the same good. Sales on credit can be a part of the bargaining process between the buyer and the seller and, moreover, it helps to gain consumer loyalty. The presence of loyal customers, in its turn, moderates the fluctuations of demand and thus reduces the traders' risk (Clark 1994).

All the traders are selling for the same price. My customers come back to me because they buy the goods from me on credit. I wouldn't give them credit until they have become regular customers and to make them become regular I dash them some extra grains (Joyce, 29).

Whenever there is a serious conflict between fellow traders concerning credit arrangements, or in any other issue for that matter, the market queen plays a presiding role in the dispute settlement. The rule of "no fighting" is clear in every trader's mind. There seems to be a good deal of hidden tension in the crowded and highly competitive Ghanian markets. When wandering around the markets heated arguments are commonly witnessed and sometimes in a matter of seconds the quarrels break out into violence between fellow traders. Traders themselves ranked internal dispute settlement as the most important duty of the market queens. Market queens operate as judges in dispute settlement although they have no enforceable legal jurisdiction. Market women prefer their mediation to formal legal channels which they often find completely useless. Market queens depend on peer pressure and the disputants' mutual interest in maintaining an orderly market (see also Clark 1994).

The market queen's duty is to see that there is sanity and peace. Market women like to quarrel, so the market queen settles the arguments. There should be no quarrels at the market. When you are found quarreling you will be fined or suspended for 6-12 months but when you are found consulting or calling oracles you will be suspended for a year (Elisabeth, 45).

All official letters concerning market activities for examples new regulations are sent to the leading market queen. She delivers the information to traders by sending a messenger boy who gongs and yells as he goes 'market queen says'. If the message is upsetting traders complain to the market queen who negotiates about the issue with the authorities (Faustina, 45).

In addition to internal dispute settlement between market traders, market queens also settle traders' disputes with non-traders such as farmers, drivers and porters. They also operate as important mediators between the market management and the trading community at large. Their informal jurisdiction extends as far as to negotiation with state authorities such as government officials and military personnel (Clark 1994).

In addition to disputes one of the main problems at the markets is sanitation. General cleaning is organized by the market management, but now and then the market needs "spring cleaning." Every trader should participate in these cleaning operations, but the authority of the management is not enough to mobilize approximately 3,000 individual traders in Kaneshie market. Market queens are left in charge of the practical mobilization of traders in cleaning operations. Furthermore, they have important roles as educators and "health inspectors." They advise traders in matters regarding sanitation and supervise that the general rules and regulations concerning the sale of food stuffs are followed.

You have to obey the order of your elders. If the leading market queen tells us to clean, and close your shop for the time, we have to do it (Charlot, 48).

My duty is to make sure that the bread sellers keep their spots in order by sweeping them every day and keeping their bread covered. I go around the market with my sub-queens to check the spots are clean and all the bread is covered. If someone does not take care of the hygiene around her spot I go and remind the particular seller. If that does not help I report the case to the leading market queen. If a seller refuses to sweep the leading queen can tell her to keep off the market (Felicia, 43).

The market queen institution also has a role to play in the realm of social welfare in times of crises affecting a trader's family economy. The formalization of commodity groups involves the introduction of membership lists and dues. From the dues, donations are made to needy members of the commodity groups. Donations are most frequently given in the case of death of a close relative, but they are also made in the case of birth or theft. Funeral donations is a typical Ghanian convention. Funerals in Ghana present a heavy financial burden on the individual(s) in charge — they are celebrated like big weddings in Europe. The donations are of vital importance to the economic and social survival of traders, and can thus be regarded as a rudimentary form of social security.

It can be concluded that the market queen institution is essential to the smooth functioning of Ghanian daily markets — its benefits stretch beyond the commercial advantages of individual traders. The lack of formal mechanisms of market regulation in Ghana has called for indigenous organizational forms such as the market queen institution. The latter has been the women's own way to organize the labour process which they have intentionally kept outside traditional labour unions (Clark 1994). The institution has substituted many of the formal mechanisms of intervention found in Western countries such as trade unions, banks, state jurisdiction and legislation, and execution of government regulations. The institution is, therefore, highly valuable for the Ghanian society at large. While serving a number of useful functions in the society, the market queen institution also has, however, some disadvantages.

Coercion and Control: Market Queens' Order

The institution has the potential to create certain problems in terms of economic efficiency and inequality of socioeconomic power. More specifically, it blocks free entry, intervenes in the price mechanism in a way to cause divergences from competitive market equilibrium, and introduces relations of subordination which might acquire an arbitrary and undemocratic character. Moreover, the system can be abused by certain market queens who might use their power for purposes of personal economic gain.

Clark (1994) characterized traders' commodity groups as voluntary self-help associations. She found that over 60% of traders did not participate in commodity groups in the Kumasi market in late 1970s. The extra costs of group membership made the threshold too high for the poorest traders. However, this study suggests that for the markets under study the voluntary nature of the groups is questionable. At the present, membership seems to be more or less obligatory. Out of the 19 traders I interviewed only one did not belong to a commodity group. All the others wanted to belong, or they felt that they had no choice in the matter, so severe were the social and illegal financial sanctions imposed if traders refused to join. Market queens have very little formal control over the allocation of market locations and they have no legal right to block the access of a trader to a particular market. However, they can hamper the business operations of traders not conforming to agreed group rules and can thus make trading at the location difficult. The first rule concerns the payment of dues.

A new seller can come and join the group meeting. We meet once a month to discuss about our sales. You are not allowed to sell if you don't come to the meeting and pay the monthly dues. What can you do about the system, if you don't pay you cannot sell (Joyce, 29).

I pay 200 cedis dues per month. The money collected is used as donations in case of funerals. You cannot say that you don't pay. It is a regulation that you have to pay. They will call you and talk to you if you don't pay. If you don't pay they take some of your plantain until you pay (Beatrice, 38).

The tight control of membership has benefits in terms of extending credit and information, and maintaining order. However, it creates some potential for domination and possibilities for personal economic gain by the market queens willing to take advantage of their fellow traders. Clark (1994) found that market queens take only token dues which hardly compensate for the amount of work and time they spend in dispute settlement or meetings. This seems to be the usual situation. However, some queens do manipulate members' loyalty in the pursuit of their own economic interest by collecting, for example, extra dues over and above the commonly agreed dues and funeral donations.

I would not like to be a market queen. I don't like that thing. When plantains are plenty they come and collect one plantain from each seller every Wednesday and Saturday. Now we don't have any plantain to give so they collect 50 cedis every Wednesday and Saturday. There is no record of the money collected. We don't know where it goes. This is Ghana. A lot of bad things. Life is hard in Ghana (Beatrice, 38).

One generally known practice, and widely disapproved of by traveling traders and the general public, is toll collection. It is used as a mechanism of personal accumulation by some corrupt market queens. However, its main aim is to regulate the inflow of goods at the markets. The practice benefits resident traders at the expense of traveling traders who are not group members. According to Clark (1994), toll collection was not common at Kumasi Central Market. However, this study indicates that these days it is quite a common practice in Accra, as well as elsewhere. Even the Kaneshie market manager reported farmers complaining about it (see also Lardemelle 1992).

Market queens collect tolls from farmers and traveling traders who come to sell their produce at the markets. A traveling trader cannot come to a new market to sell produce without consulting the appropriate market queen. If a trader and the queen can come to an agreement on the toll, and on the price the goods can be sold for, the trader is allowed to sell her produce at the market. If not, she is forced to take her produce elsewhere. Often traders have to accept the tolls because they are dealing with perishable foodstuffs which rot quickly in the hot, humid climate.

I get the mangos from the bush. I go to the bush by car and buy the boxes, and then I drive them to Coastal areas (Takoradi, Tema, Accra, Cape Coast). When I reach the market in a particular town I'll contact the queen of mangos. She comes and stands beside me and fixes the price. I negotiate the price with her. If the price is not good enough for me, I take my goods elsewhere. She can try to make you sell at too low prices, so that you make loss. When we come into an agreement on the price, I give the market queen 200 per each box you sell at that market. This money goes to the queen, it is her commission. When the price is settled I go and sell the mangos to my customers. When they come to me once they'll come again (Agnes, 43).

According to Clark (1994), market queens have limited role in regulating daily commerce in Kumasi market since they have very little influence on the total supply there. Hence, she concludes that the commodity groups in Kumasi do not operate as cartels as suggested by anecdotal reports from Accra. The present study implies, however, that in 1994 some commodity groups both in Accra and Koforidua did form cartels, through which they effectively regulated the demand and supply, as well as prices of goods at the markets. Market queens tend to control especially the supply and demand of highly seasonal products like tomatoes and mangoes. They assigned volume quotas and delivery days to each traveling trader participating in the commodity groups, and simultaneously tried to block the entry of other traveling traders. Anything other than the strict adherence to rules was socially and financially sanctioned.

We are divided into groups. One group off loads in one of the market days, and the other one in the next market day. When we arrive to the market with the goods the market queen collects 2,000 cedis from every group. We share the cost so everybody has to pay 300-400 cedis. The queen also collects two tomatoes from every box and sells them herself. 30 petty sellers buy from me. There are 65-70 middlewomen at the market who are getting their tomatoes from the bush. We are divided into about seven groups. Three to four groups go into the bush at a time. You can be suspended from the market if you go to the bush with your own car and collect tomatoes on a day that it is not your turn. They can suspend you or collect four boxes of tomatoes from you and sell them, if you have broken the law. When this happens you can go to the council and make a complaint. The queens will never allow you to sell. They drive you away from the market. Then you go to the regional office and they give you the permission to sell and you can come back and sell. The queens cannot do anything more about it, but they will insult you and try to talk you out of it. Sellers are afraid of the queens and the sanctions, so they obey the rules (Agnes, 43).

The costs of these arrangements should of course be weighed against their benefits. It is clear that resident traders have a lot to gain from cartel like control exercised on supply which effectively eliminates price and income fluctuations. Thanks to such controls, the sellers of seasonal products enjoy a considerable degree of price/income stability even during glut periods. On the other hand, apart from the non-group suppliers, consumers and farmers are the losers. As a result, the relationship between traders and the parties that are harmed by supply controls can be quite tense. High prices throughout the year make the customers angry while farmers are furious when their produce is left to rot in the fields because market queens would not allow sales above the commonly set quotas. This, obviously, is not the way competitive markets would function and the outcome in terms of quantities and prices is far from being economically efficient. There is, in fact, ample indication that the prices are negotiated and not market determined. Fixed prices, a common characteristic of many Third World markets (Epstein 1990; Cassidy 1974), tend to dominate Ghanian markets.

Buyers will not give you a good price if tomatoes are coming to the market in abundance. The market queen will not allow you to buy more than the agreed quantity. You cannot sell for lower price than others. We get together and make 'one mouth' in other words an agreement on how we are going to sell. You have to follow the agreement. You will not be suspended for breaking this rule but they will abuse you (Agnes, 43).

When asking for prices in Koforidua or Kaneshie markets it rapidly becomes clear that the price is uniform in many commodities at the markets, and in some it is uniform even throughout the town. Clark (1991; 1994) in her study of Kumasi Central Market suggests that high levels of price information in one location results in high levels of price uniformity. In contrast this study suggests that the uniform price is a negotiated one and is maintained not only by high levels of information, but by social and financial sanctions as well. The rule of uniform price is perceived by the traders more or less like a law which cannot be broken.

Price uniformity is especially common in foodstuffs which usually are not refined or differentiated in any way. Traders of perishable items do, however, have different prices and customers for premium, ordinary, and inferior quality grades. Foodstuffs are sorted and sold usually in small neat heaps or bundles, each of which is offered at a unit price. The seemingly identical displays of the retail line provide vital supply information. As pointed out by Clark (1994) the price uniformity is illusionary in the sense that traders get around it. Instead of changing the price they change the quantity by "dashing" the customer, i.e. by changing the quantity sold after the deal is done. She furthermore found some variation in bargaining practices depending on the product and quantity sold. For example, wholesale transactions most often involve price bargaining because of fixed wholesale units. However, this study implies that even though traders get around price uniformity in sales, there is a strong effort to maintain price uniformity at the markets as indicated by the statements of the interviewees quoted above, as well as the following one:

> The market queen sends scouts to check the prices. They go around and ask different sellers for their prices and report the wrong prices to the market queen. Then the market queen comes personally to meet those individuals to tell them to sell at the right price. Those who do not obey the rules of the market are suspended for two or three months. I have not had any arguments with other sellers. Competing sellers may start arguing with the ones who do not sell at the right price. The market queen sees that everything is in order. She makes sure that no one is selling for too high prices. Kaneshie and Makola Market queens do negotiate about prices. Profit margin is fixed in all markets in Accra (Joyce, 24).

The study reveals that the more differentiated the products are, the less power the market queens have over the price. This is the case, for example, with underwear and shoes. Nowadays, there is plenty of variety in such products and their prices may already vary substantially at the wholesale level. Thus the queens cannot exercise the same control over the retail prices of these goods.

Where the market queens can effectively control quantities and supplies, they can cause significant divergencies from economic efficiency. Moreover, their dictatorial behaviour manifested in the imposition of extra dues and unfair tolls, or in the limitation of quotas and delivery days can constitute a burden on traders and create an obstacle for more entrepreneurial merchants wishing to develop their businesses. Nevertheless, one must bear in mind that these practices are carried out with the common consent of the majority of traders. Although they have no legal basis, these commercial conventions are followed as if they were formal laws. Group loyalty remains strong even where the market queen abuses her authority in her own self-interest and at the expense of her fellow traders. The fear of social and economic ostracism, as well as the characteristics of traditional culture from which the authority of market queens is in part derived, seem to play an important role in maintaining group discipline.

Conclusions

This chapter investigated the role of the market queen institution in female dominated Ghanian markets. Through an ethnographic approach, I have tried to assess the cultural factors from which the institution derives its legitimacy and to evaluate its positive and negative aspects.

The sources of the organization of Ghanian markets dominated by the market queen institution are seen to originate from the collective traditions of African societies as well as from the political system of traditional Ghana where the queen mother institution has a central role. The market queen institution follows those traditional patterns from which it derives its prestige and effective power. As such, it has strong symbolic and functional value in Ghanian markets.

The market queen institution serves to maintain law and order in the market process and it incorporates mechanisms of information dissemination, credit provision and social security. It thus appears as a substitute for a number of formal mechanisms of intervention that one encounters in Western countries.

However, it also operates like a cartel and like all cartels presents an impediment to the efficient functioning of the market mechanism. It has considerable disadvantages for certain third parties such as consumers, farmers and traders that are outside the commodity group. Moreover, it leaves ample room for abuse by some market queens who use the power conferred by their position for personal material gain at the expense of the majority of traders.

These disadvantages should, nevertheless, be evaluated by keeping in mind the contributions of this particular organizational form to the social power and economic survival of a large number of female traders. Trading has offered an important opportunity for women to subsist, especially in the urban areas (see Grieco et al. 1996). Because of the ease of entry into the informal sector in general (Swaminatham 1991) and to the trading sector in particular (Clark 1994; Epstein 1990; Lamptey 1987), masses of women have participated in the activity. In 1984 over 50% of the female working population in the Greater Accra region were traders, the total number being over 45,000 (Statistical Service 1987). Since then the number of traders has continually increased due to decreasing employment opportunities in the formal sector (Ninsin 1991). The possibilities of traders to accumulate excessive wealth in the highly competitive markets is thus limited. Most of the traders are trading at subsistence level to feed their families in a country where the formal welfare system is often unable to support them. Approximately 56% of female traders in urban centres are heads of their households, in other words, widows, divorcees, abandoned wives or single parents often having a number of dependents (Ardaytio-Schandorf 1994; see also Grieco et al. 1996).

Under these circumstances, maintaining at least a minimal standard of living for traders is not an easy task which could perhaps be achieved only by controlling supply and fixing the prices at higher than competitive levels to help the group members to avoid business failure. Commodity groups organized around the market group institution also incorporate social support mechanisms that assure the survival of their members in exceptionally difficult periods of their life. Moreover, it is thanks to the existence of commodity groups that Ghanian markets have fairly egalitarian networks that exclude the domination of poorer traders by a few wealthy ones. It is undeniable that these positive contributions have a cost to be paid in terms of the loss of economic efficiency. Still, from the point of view of the people involved, the benefits of the system seem to outnumber its disadvantages.

Notes

* I would like to thank Andrew Sturdy and the editors of this book for their helpful comments on earlier drafts of this chapter. I would further like to extend my thanks to Margaret Grieco for giving me the opportunity to work in Ghana, and last but not least, I am truly grateful to the traders for their patience, co-operation and friendship.

1 The Akans are the largest ethnic group in Ghana, and the majority live in Eastern, Central, Western, Ashanti and Brong-Ahafo regions.

2 Ewes are an ethnic group dominating the Volta region near the Togolese border.

3 The quotations are based on my interview notes. When taking notes special emphasis was placed in writing down the answers in as a verbatim form as possible. Therefore the quotations are provided with no corrections in the English language of my informants. Possible clarifications of the quotations are placed in brackets.

References

Ansah, G.K. (1985): "Increasing food production: The role of market women." Unpublished bachelors dissertation, University of Ghana, Legon.

Appiah-Asare, H. (1992): "The flow of food stuffs into urban markets: A case study of kaneshie market in Accra." Unpublished bachelors dissertation University of Ghana, Legon.

Apt, N. and S. Katila (1994): "Gender and inter-generational support: Comparative issues for South Africa." *Southern African Journal of Gerontology* 3(2): 23-29.

Ardaytio-Schandorf, E. (1994): "Household headship and women's earnings in Ghana" in E. Ardayfio-Schandorf (ed.), *Family and development in Ghana*, 30-47. Ghana University Press, Accra.

Bukh, J. (1979): "The village women in Ghana." *Publications from the Centre for Development Research, Copenhagen. No 1*. Uppsala: Scandinavian Institute of African Studies.

Cassidy, R. Jnr. (1974): *Exchange by private treaty*. Austin, University of Texas.

Clark, C. (1991): "Colleagues and customers in unstable market conditions: Kumasi, Ghana." *Ethnology: An International Journal of Cultural and Social Anthropology* 30: 31-48.

Clark, C. (1994): *Onions are my husband. Survival and accumulation by West African market women*. Chicago: The University of Chicago Press.

Cutrufelli, M.R. (1983): *Women of Africa*. Bath, UK: Pitman Press.

Debrunner, H. (1961): *Witchcraft in Ghana*. Accra, Ghana: Presbyterian Depot.

Epstein S.T. (1990): "Female petty-entrepreneurs and their multiple roles" in S. Vyakarnam (ed.), *When the harvest is in. Developing rural entrepreneurship*, 254-265. London: Intermediate Technology Publications.

Essiem, H. (1987): "Fish distribution at Tema fishing harbour." Unpublished bachelors dissertation, University of Ghana, Legon.

Grieco, M., N. Apt, and J. Turner (1996): *At Christmas and on rainy days. Transport, travel and the female traders of Accra*. Aldershot, England: Avebury.

Katila, S. (1996): "From mother to daughter: Social networks and entry into the occupation of trading." *Piccolo Impresa/ Small Business* 1:117-130.

Lamptey, G. (1987): "The Changing Variation in Employment of Ghanian Women in Accra (Ghana)." Unpublished bachelors dissertation, University of Ghana, Legon.

Lardemelle de, L. (1992): "Report on two case studies on improved market-places in Accra, Ghana." Unpublished report, Food and Agricultural Organization of the United Nations.

Little, K. (1973): *African women in towns. An aspect of Africa's social revolution*. London: Cambridge University Press.

Lloyd, P.C. (1967): *Africa in Social Change*. Middlesex, England: Penguin Books.

Malkamäki, M. (1991): "Banking the poor. Informal and semi-formal financial systems serving the micro enterprises." *University of Helsinki Institute of Development Studies Report B* 22: 1-132.

Mireku, E. (1991): *Which way Ghana. Restoring hope and confidence in the Ghanian*. Accra, Ghana: Asuo Peabo.

Ninsin, K. (1991): *The informal sector in Ghana's political economy*. Accra, Ghana: Freedom Publications.

Nukunya, G.K. (1992): *Tradition and change in Ghana. An introduction to sociology*. Accra, Ghana: Ghana Universities Press.

Omari, C.K. (1989): "Rural women, informal sector and household economy in Tanzania. Working Papers 79: 3-83.

Omenukor, V. (1989): "A study of the evolution of the politics of African women in the traditional and modern period: The case of ashanti (matrilinear) and ibo (patrilinear) societies." Unpublished dissertation, University of Hamburg.

Opoku-Boakye, J. (1990): "The role of traders on the distribution of local food stuffs in Accra: the case of 31st December Makola Market." Unpublished bachelors dissertation, University of Ghana, Legon.

Pellow, D. (1978): "Work and autonomy: Women in Accra." *American Ethnologist* 5(5): 760-784.
Sai, H. (1971): "The market women in the economy of Ghana." Unpublished M.S. Thesis, Cornell University.
Statistical Service (1987): *1984 Population census of Ghana. Demographic and economic characteristics*. Accra, Ghana: Statistical Service.
Swaminathan, M. (1991): "Understanding the 'Informal Sector': A survey." *Wider Working Paper WP* 95: 1-39.
Tripp, A.M. and M.L.Swantz (1994): "Limits of self-interest: Alternative logics of economic decision-making among small-scale women entrepreneurs in Uganda and Tanzania." Unpublished manuscript.
Vercruijsse, E. (1983): "Fishmongers, big dealers and fishermen: Co-operation and conflict between the sexes in Ghanian canoe fishing" in C. Oppong (ed.), *Female and Male in West Africa,* 180-191. UK: George Allen and Unwin.

Putting Nationalism back into National Business Systems: The Ideological and Institutional Context of Global Competition

Ray Loveridge

Introduction

Whatever view of the history of industrialization is taken, it seems clear that, over time, the economic health of the community has come more and more to be attributed to the effects of good governance and less and less to acts of God. In many instances the connection was made most obvious through the seeming unfairness of central taxation; as the Massachusetts rebels chanted in 1773 "No taxation without representation!". In more recent times the citizens of Boston, Mass. have come to believe, as have the citizens of Kuala Lumpur, that good governance is associated with a broader concept of economic well being. Whether their continuing increase in personal living standards is achieved through setting the right conditions for market growth or through direct government intervention as investor or customer, a plurality of citizens in liberal democracies tend to vote in national elections according to their various assessments of the current administrations' ability as an economic manager (Olson 1982).

In a similar fashion the emergence of the modern nation state has been attended by an increasing resort to comparisons of economic development as measured by indices such as *per capita* income, productivity etc. While invidious comparison was previously normal between the royal courts of each region of Europe, by the mid-18th century the exiled Voltaire was extolling the economic significance of the status held by English merchants to his Parisian compatriots. Thanks to their freedom and emancipation they were able to prosper so well that they could lend money to the Government to finance the English navy, sending it to all corners of the globe, in protection of their trade (Voltaire 1733/1964). (His published comments earned him further exile from his native France!)

By the late 19th century it had become normal for British and other European political economic commentators to make comparisons with US and German economic development and to relate these to the characteristics of their own national institutions. Perhaps the most comprehensive of these comparisons appears in the evidence and report of the British Royal Commission on Causes of the Great Depression (1884). The significance of key areas of institutionalized practice drawn then have been rediscovered by several subsequent generations of scholarly commentators (for example Shonfield 1965; Lane 1989). However over that period the role of the UK as an international exemplar, a position held by virtue of its economic precedence in global trade, has clearly given place to the USA. Indeed, over the last century the "American way-of-life" and of doing business has come to be seen by many observers as the archetype of modernism upon which other nations have been converging (Kerr et al. 1960; Rostow 1960; Servan-Schreiber 1965). With the apparent demise of the so-called Communist bloc this interpretation has been revived as the "end of ideology" and "end of history" theses (Fukuyama 1992).

However an alternative view that emphasizes the *persistence of differences* in social systems based on the institutionalized norms and the role of *strategic choice* across varying modes of capitalism has also remained alive. The comparison of national institutional frameworks has recently become a dominant theme in scholarly commentary on national economic development (Peet 1991) Following the evident economic success of Japan over the latter part of this century business strategies and structures adopted by Western corporations have also come to be assessed by reference to this new national archetype (Best 1990). This has led to many notable attempts to isolate elements of the institutional structure of the recently emerging economies of South East Asia (the so-called Newly Industrialized Countries or NICs) and to construct alternative idealized archetypes of modernist business systems at both macro and micro levels of society (Clark and Mueller 1996).

In this chapter two sets of constructs are particularly addressed. The first has become known as the National Innovation Systems (NIS) approach and includes the work of scholars such as Nelson (1992), Lundvall (1992), and Kogut (1992). The other is the National Business Systems approach. This can be defined loosely to include many current and past writers that have emphasized the institutional shaping of markets and of inter-organizational business relationships within national or cultural boundaries. In this chapter the work of Whitley (1992) is taken to represent a synthesis of the most recent scholarship in the field and one that provides an example of the trend towards the adoption of a socio-economic analytical frame of "new institutionalism."

The chapter attempts a critique of the structural-functionalism implicit, and, sometimes, explicit, within both approaches. It suggests that the underlying explanatory concept of "uncertainty reduction" that has been extrapolated from an essentially functionally based analysis of organization behaviour, becomes increasingly inadequate in explanation of the pre-requisites and dynamics of nation-formation. Instead institutional evolution is seen as an *ongoing* process, subject to prevailing demands of the evolving needs of the actors, rather than as the end point of an apparently linear trajectory. In both approaches the complementarity and cohesion present (or not) across elements of the system are often seen to be bound by a characteristic "trustfulness" between actors, a term applied across a variety of relationships that appear, empirically, not only as extremely various but often, potentially, dysfunctional. It will, instead, be suggested that the architecture of the nation states emerges from a series of arenas for collectivized interest in which the architectural boundaries are themselves disputed and therefore in flux. At periods of disjuncture and discontinuity in socio-economic relationships, opportunities present themselves for a re-alignment of interests which can provide new strategic orientations for emergent coalitions which can, in turn, lead to radical new directions in systemic trajectories.

The Systems Analysis of National Institutions

The systems approach to societal analysis is, of course, one of the oldest, and in modern times has been expressed in the explicitly biological metaphors used by Spencer (1882) and Parsons (1966) among others. In a more focused and descriptive manner it underlies the chapter headings for most texts on industrial economics (Allen 1933) and the more dynamic analyses of developmental economists (Marx 1887/1967; Rostow 1960). In many ways the recent emergence of two different, but related, approaches to the analysis of what are described as either National Business Systems (NBSs) or National Innovation Systems (NISs) reflect the same concerns as those of the drafters of the 1884 British Report on Causes of the Great Depression mentioned earlier. All tend to stress the importance of financial institutions that provide sustained levels of relatively cheap credit and of educational institutions that provide the labour force with vocational preparation for design and implementation of new technologies.

The NBS concept is implicit in a great many cross national studies of the last quarter century or more, most notably that of Shonfield (1965) and Best (1990). In his recent seminal contributions Whitley has attempted to define the NBS in more abstract and generalizable terms, viz.:

(...) business systems are distinctive configurations of hierarchy-market relations which become institutionalized as relatively successful ways of organizing economic activities in different institutional environments. Certain kinds of activities are co-ordinated through particular sorts of authority structures and interconnected in different ways through various quasi-contractual arrangements in each business system. Thus, what resources are organized by differently structured hierarchies and markets varies between these systems as do preferred ways of developing business and making choices. They develop and change in relation to dominant social institutions, especially those important during the process of industrialization. The coherence and stability of these institutions, together with their dissimilarity between nation states, determine the extent to which business systems are distinctive, integrated and nationally differentiated (Whitley 1992: 13).

All of Whitley's empirical evidence is drawn from secondary sources and, as such, he attempts to interpret the work of many notable North American anthropologists and development economists such as Amsden (1989), and Hamilton and Biggart (1988). Two key groups of characteristics are used to define systemic differences, *background* social institutions and *proximate* institutions. Of the first Whitley suggests: "These reflect more general and underlying principles of trust, co-operation and subordination which have become institutionalized in different societies and which are usually derived from: (1) the pre-industrial political system and its legitimation principles; (2) traditional elite attitudes towards privately controlled concentrations of wealth and; (3) the organization and control of agricultural activities" (Whitley 1991: 21). Shared social response to these exercises in power break down into six dimensions: (1) Degree and basis of trust between non-kin; (2) Commitment and loyalty to collectivities beyond the family; (3) Importance of individual identities, rights and commitment; (4) Depersonalization and formalization of authority relations; (5) Differentiation of authority roles; (6) Reciprocity, distance and scope of authority relations.

Of the "proximate" institutions those which institutionalize property rights, those which give access to financial resources and to different kinds of labour power are seen as "clearly important." They are listed as:

(1) Business dependence on strong cohesive state; (2) State commitment to industrial development and risk sharing; (3) Capital market or credit based financial system; (4) Unitary or dual education and training system; (5) Strength of skill based trades unions; (6) Significance of publicly certified skills and professional expertise.

While it is difficult to single out any one of the 105 combinations of these factor dimensions that Whitley suggests can be derived from his matrix, it is clear that, in common with other contemporary writers on NBS, he places some significance on the presence and purposes of a variety of intermediate bodies — inter-firm associations, occupational associations, large federal companies (e.g. Korean *chaebols*) and cross-national family businesses (specifically Chinese) — standing between business units and the national government. It is equally clear that within successful NBSs the functioning of these intermediate institutions is largely directed at the absorption of the uncertainty and risk of disequilibrium seen to be pervasive to the business context in which the firm is embedded (Whitley 1994).

Of the two systemic approaches the NIS is defined most narrowly and yet, more variously. Its proponents are students of science and technology policy, most of whom have been strongly committed advocates of greater State intervention in this field for many years. In a recent introduction to a collection of readings on different national systems the institutional economist Nelson suggested that "the concept is a set of institutions whose interactions determine the innovation performance... of national firms" (1992: 4). Elements of this system seem to include the provision of a national infrastructure for business activities that will provide both research poles and conduits along which information can flow in a targeted manner. Lundvall (1992) stresses the importance of strategic uses of technological information and suggests, like Porter (1990), that nations are characterized by their peculiar capabilities within particular sectors in which they have developed a regional comparative advantage. These included the development of inter-firm networks which facilitate both incremental innovation and its rapid diffusion within particular regions. NIS writers again lay stress on the role of venture capital and availability of long term finance or credit, as well as on higher education in the provision of human capital.

How Open are "Open Systems"?

Clearly the use of systemic analysis enables the isolation of significant elements that contribute to societal activity and the identification of hypothesized interdependencies between these elements. In this sense it appears useful in directing business research to the effects of the wider social system in which the firm is embedded and of which it is part (Marshall 1919; Granovetter 1985). At its most basic Whitley's classifications bring together data from a range of single nation case studies in a manner that allows comparison. Analytically speaking it appears more rigorous than the broadly descriptive taxonomies of NIS scholars. What he describes as "background elements" of the business system accord closely with what Parsons (1966) described as the pattern maintenance and socialization functions designed to sustain normative order within the wider social system. His proximal elements appear very close to the adaptive or economic sub-system in Parson's model of society. One interpretation of Whitley's NBS might, then, be that of demonstrating the importance of the pattern-maintenance elements in society in shaping its adaptive functioning in a manner that produces "trustful" relations (or not) in business. This purpose might be compared with that of the many prescriptive managerial works over the last decade or so that have urged such a relationship upon a Western business audience.

This is an interpretation of his work that one anticipates would be rejected by Whitley since it is clear from his introductory assumptions that the actor's beliefs, preference and expectations are to be given determinant value in an apparently reflexive process of activity. However there is a danger that in making the effectiveness of the firms' performance the focus of a systemic analysis of the national society as a whole there is a danger of teleological and even tautological analysis (Giddens 1979). Whilst providing detailed evidence of a history of military and socio-economic coercion over the histories of the South East Asian populations on which he chooses to focus his most detailed analysis, Whitley offers no amplification on how these events or forces interact with the actors' social responses, seen to have become institutionalized in the structures he delineates. We are left with no basis upon which to predict what factors might interrupt the stable reflexivity apparent in the expectations of actors in a way that might lead to a different interpretation of "background" structures of reciprocity and *apparent* trust.

Institutions and the Process of Institutionalization

Over the 1980s a revival of what is described by some sociologists and economists as the "New Institutionalism" (NI) has brought a renewed emphasis in organizational analysis upon to the longevity of institutionalized patterns or structures, of behaviour within "societies." In his introduction to his recent seminal text on NI, Scott (1995: ix) reveals that "(W)ith the benefit of hindsight, I now can see clearly that from my earliest days I have been an institutionalist." Perhaps it is not too cynical to suggest that before the wave of phenomenological criticism of structural sociology in the 1970s (see e.g. Burrell and Morgan 1979) the analysis of the social institutions provided its intellectual core. Even so the empirical study of institutions before that period never lost its focus on individual *commitment* to the rules within an organized "society." In his own work Scott (1995) provides a three part typology of the basis for personal compliance to control by social institutions. These cover, personal expedience in the face of coercive force; moral obligation in response to internalized norms; and habitual "taken for granted" actions responding to mimetic comparison and "isomorphism." It is, of course, upon the latter type of "taken-for-granted" nature of institutional authority that much of the recent sociological NI approach to the analysis of institutions appears to rest, although not generally well explored. (see e.g. Powell and DiMaggio 1991).

In his earlier analysis of the duality of organizational control and compliance Etzioni (1961/1975) placed emphasis on utilitarian (remunerative) power and a calculative or instrumental response in modern societies. In many approaches to the development of "modern" societies, including most comprehensively, that of Parsons (1966), a distinction is made between the affective bonding of institutions in so-called traditional or pre-industrial societies (Gemeinschaft in Tönnies terms) and the contractually neutral nature of relationships under legal-rational (Gesellschaft) regimes. NI economists tend to approach the analysis of institutional functioning on the basis of the latter assumption, that is that rational profit taking actors adopt and retain institutional frameworks that reduce their costs or risks within an opportunistic market place. This is, for example, a fundamental precept of the transaction cost school primarily represented in the work of Williamson (1975; 1985). As against this perspective North (1990) and, earlier, Commons (1924) come closer to a sociological stance in seeing the workings of markets as inextricably linked with the concept of personal or collective "property", or monopoly over the services of a resource, without which exchange between autonomous parties would not be possible. These are seen as deriving from institutionalized rules, while "organizations" are often brought into existence by associational actors with the intention of changing those rules. Perhaps the importance of the latter authors for the present analysis is to be seen in their acceptance of the importance of "interest", both personal and collective, in determining choices between "social and cultural repertoires."

Like Giddens (1979), Wilkinson (1996) argues for an area of autonomy for social agents in the enactment of events. What he describes as "culturist" explanations of the configuration of national business systems tend to focus on various elements of articulated belief systems such as Confucianism or those of organized religion. These are translated by culturist writers into a range of specific contemporary practices in a manner and extent that is often contradictory and of "post hoc rationalization: of gross assumptions about causal links: of the danger of racism: and of an absence of historical understanding" (Wilkinson 1996: 424). "The institutionalist account", suggests Wilkinson (1996: 434), "then, replaces an economic determinism with a socio-cultural determinism: economic actors are 'passively embedded in' rather than 'engaged with', a social environment (Whittington 1992)." In opposition to this privileging of cultural embeddedness in shaping organizational structures and processes, Wilkinson proposes that modern business elites are continuously prevailed upon to legitimate and to justify their strategic choices: they are naturally most likely to do so in terms that support extant relations of domination.

Like "culture" and "institution" the term "ideology" is capable of both specific and universalistic meaning and is usually defined in a manner that allows considerable overlap across the contingent phenomena being described. At their most extreme cultural theorists see all languages as expressing a social order that is hegemonic and all encompassing (for example Bourdieu 1978), and therefore the ultimate source of institutionalized belief systems. But in the societal explanations offered by NBS theorists the term "institutional" is also used in the common place manner as a term of reference for organizing collectively functional activities such as creating financial credit, protecting and socializing children, maintaining the labour force etc. Even here one might see a historical difference between the time honoured practices of social acceptable modes of biological reproduction and the manner in which later developing governments consciously imitate the actions of a 17th century English court in the creation of a national bank (differences obscured by the use of terms such as "isomorphism" perhaps?).

Evidently consciousness or a heightened awareness of strategic options can become apparent to social actors at particular junctures and can lead them to social or to collective actions. Sociological explanations of this phenomenon usually contain references to the volatility of shared aspiration or to the significance of comparisons with normative reference groups (Smelser 1959; Urry 1973). The process of systematizing and articulating individually held ideologies in paradigmatic ideals is however one that is in "normal" times seen to be performed by discrete groups such as intellectuals, and political and business elites and the organized religions. Such ideals are most likely to gain a more generalized currency when what appears as "exogenously" provoked change in socio economic reward structures leads to an apparent need for wider explanation. As both NBS theorists and their critics acknowledge this eventuality normally leads a prevailing elite to enlist various elements of traditional or existent beliefs and requisite language forms.

Hence, for example, terms such as "world standard", "organizational reengineering", and "down-sizing" evoke the language of technical efficiency and convey the impression of a controlled response to the combined effects of information technology and Asian new entrants to markets formerly dominated by Western capital. The generalized usage of such managerial language to explain widespread structural change in society at large (including the response of satirists) might be seen as illustrating either the hegemonic nature of the state in the manner suggested by Althusser (1984) or as disguising an inability to coordinate action across its diverse agencies. Certainly the response of French truck-drivers to their government's actions in November 1996, suggests that this very interdependency can leverage the exercise of countervailing power within some business systems.

Appropriative Learning as the Institutionalization of Property Rights

By and large NIS theorists describe themselves as Schumpeterians. This appears to imply that business systems are driven by the interaction of two forces — one is that leading to the routinization of corporate innovation, the other to its disruption and to discontinuities in technological trajectories. For Schumpeter (1934; 1939; 1950) competition, or oligopolistic contest, in 20th century capitalism was based on technological innovation rather than price. In earlier times entrepreneurialism was the source of innovation but increasingly innovations stem from path-dependent incremental improvements stemming from the routinized capabilities of large corporations (Nelson and Winter 1982). In many ways those institutional economists who emphasize the routinization of design-innovation come closest to the habituation assumptions of NI sociologists. Sectoral boundaries stem from the emergence of known populations of firms following a socially accepted script or recipe for "best practice" in the production of a particular good or service (Clark and Staunton 1989). Other followers of Schumpeter emphasize the effects of long term cycles caused by shifts in the nature of generic technologies, i.e. those affecting most sectors such as power sources, steam to electricity/gasoline or most recently micro electronics (Freeman et al. 1982). In his recent work the latter author has offered the micro electronic revolution as his explanation for the business success of the "Four Tiger" economies (Freeman 1995). More usually Schumpeterians tend to take the role of MITI in Japan as their prescriptive model for the orchestration of the sectoral life cycle (Johnson 1982).

The present author (Loveridge 1972; 1983b; 1987; 1990) has suggested that historically, shifts in generic technologies have led to long periods of organizational learning. Over this time existing and newly realised collective interests emerge to compete for appropriation of the new resource. The shaping of sectoral relationships and the acquisition of external reputation for unique competencies emerges from an initial period of "architectural" turbulence and, often, internal strife within existing and nascent forms of organization. A major focus of the conflict concerns the basis upon which new knowledge is codified and interpreted. Often this knowledge is tacit and artisanal, deriving from operational adaptations of existing technologies. This was certainly true of the early applications of water and steam energies but was equally true of the first successful applications of gasoline power to the "horseless carriage" and to flight. In the year, 1903, that the US Mid-West bicycle repairers, Orville and Wilbur Wright, made the first formally recorded "heavier-than-air" flight, the Royal Aeronautical Society in London published a paper proving its impossibility according to existing physical theory! (RAS Archives: Author) Even the creation of the early semiconductor depended crucially on tacit operational skills in the "baking" process: success rates of 10-15% were normal in the production of early transistors in the 1960s and early 1970s (Braun and Macdonald 1978).

However the development of the new technologies takes place within a growing bureaucratic differentiation between the performance of design tasks and those of operational implementation. A third and critical role is that of acquiring and maintaining a corporate credibility and creditworthiness with financial institutions — or along appropriate corporate networks — to financially sustain the initial exploration of the inventions. Uncertainty as to the expected returns to investment in the new technology and the growing social distance between financial controllers and design professionals enhances the importance of reputable corporate agents and financial analysts. (See Chandler 1990 and Lazonick 1991 for differing perspectives with remarkably similar interpretations of these functionally differentiated networks.)

Recognition of new occupational identities by such corporate agencies has always been problematic since, besides prestige, these identities provide the basis for collective claims for quasi-rents or added-value. In the analysis of occupations the distinction is sometimes made between the comparative analysis of structures (e.g. professions) and of processes (e.g. attempted strategies of profession*alization*). In the first the emphasis is placed on providing taxonomies of institutionalized ways of *resolving* or *absorbing* the uncertainty of clientele: in the second upon describing attempted strategies for closing and monopolizing opportunities in an ongoing struggle for scarce resources (prestige, authority and market position) which may be obtained through political recognition and legitimation. (Murphy 1988).

While the institutionalization of occupational monopoly over particular bodies of skills and knowledge is a common feature of societal structuration in pre-industrial as in modern society, in the latter phase it may be seen to be in a constant tension with managerial activity in the coordination and control of the value-adding process and in the creation and implementation of new technology.

In the process of bureaucratic routinization and standardization of tasks it is often assumed that the expropriation of knowledge moves from the operational performance of tasks to abstract design through the application of Scientific Management (Braverman 1974). In practice, as Pettigrew (1980) has demonstrated, the introduction of new technology, such as novel computerized systems, is equally as likely to trigger appropriative conflict between existing design specialisms in jurisdictional disputes (see also Child and Loveridge 1990). Indeed across most Anglo-Saxon accounts of innovation the assumption of resistance to innovation and of the need for "product champions" and "sponsors" rests on a tournament metaphor (e.g. Maidique 1980).

Much the same distinction between structural and processual analysis can be seen in different approaches to corporate strategy and to the development of cross-firm associations within industries. The analysis of the emergence of the electronics sector in Europe carried out by Cawson et al. (1990) provides a rare example of the dynamic analysis of ongoing corporate attempts appropriate and to close sectors to new entrants. Like collective attempts at occupational closure, corporate action is evidently directed at appropriating unique capabilities which will enable the corporate group to establish reputational power along stable networks of exchange (Teece 1981). Collectively shared ideologies are used to justify attempts to institutionalize newly achieved "rights" through accepted procedures which will ensure their acceptance and legitimation by significant others (both peers and national or supra-national governments). In the business management literature these convert into Porter's (1990) famous taxonomy of the "5-forces", in the population ecology literature they are subsumed within the processes of isomorphism (Freeman and Barley 1990).

The *process* by which an industrial or sectoral set emerges and leads to associational linkages at all three levels of interaction (corporate creditworthiness, professional design know-how and operational predictability) has not been well explored in a comparative and systematic way. The public role of the State as sponsor and coordinator, particularly in the corporatist prototypes provided by Germany and Japan, have been systemically described (Johnson 1982; Schmitter and Streek 1985; Best 1990). The role of government in both sponsoring and phasing-out industrial clusters of national firms has been most clearly analyzed in the case of Japan by Okimoto (1989) and more widely in NICs by Evans (1995). As mentioned above Freeman (1995) ascribes the rapid economic growth of the four East Asian Tiger countries (South Korea, Taiwan, Singapore and Hong Kong) to their focus on the export of microelectronic products. Originally reliant on FDI in assembly, the movement into domestically designed products was in some cases orchestrated by the national government, but was in all cases supported by government investment in the higher education of technologists with knowledge appropriate to the new industries. The existence of a *shared* view of long term strategy ensured that these graduates found employment in corporate career structures.

The Ethnic Myth?

Occupations have been seen by most modern social theorists as providing the cement of social order, not simply at the sectoral level but within wider society. Durkheim (1893/1964), no less than Marx (1887/1967), was acutely aware of the part played by the employment relationship in creating commitment to a wider sense of community. It is still possible to see many European writers on NBSs as focusing on the labour process in their analysis of such national systems (e.g. Maurice and Sellier 1979; Sorge and Warner 1986; Lane 1989). But as James (1996) has recently remarked, this concern for the internal cohesion of "societies" in classical social theory can be compared with the almost total neglect of *nationhood* and the claims for recognition of appropriative sovereignty over territories and their populations that it entails. Marx and Engels (1859/1976) described the nation-state as a purely temporary phenomenon believing that a uniform experience of positioning within the labour process would bring about a cross national awareness of class affiliations. After nearly a century of industrialized warfare between modern nation states the possibility of a more primordial basis for social identity is still largely unacknowledged in the organizational literature. Over the past 20 years or so, and with increasing urgency, this neglect has been remedied in other areas of social science. But in the NBS/NSI frameworks the assumption of national hegemony is provided with little empirical or theoretical justification other than the evidence of contemporary workings of functionally inter-dependent organizations. Historical accounts of their emergence sometimes even imply a national consensus or, at least, voluntary concurrence with prevailing arrangements on the part of a majority of national residents. Arrival at this concurrence might, even from the brief historical descriptions that most business writers provide, appear to be rather less than voluntaristic, sometimes involving civil war between factions led by rival elites or directed at colonial or dominant ethnic oppressors.

The achievement of a national identity providing, as it evidently often does, an overarching cognitive frame within which other citizen affiliations can be placed, is usually accompanied by the kind of shared process of emulative comparison described in the introduction to this chapter. It is often accompanied by a heightened collective awareness caused by the potential threat of military invasion or external economic dominance. This was evidently the case in those countries strung along the East-West divide over the period of the Cold War. It can also be found in the early histories of relations between ASEAN members and, before that, in Europe, particularly in French/German relations over the first half of the 20th century and in the subsequent ambiguity of feeling towards German re-armament over the latter half.

In the process of achieving what Du Preez (1980) has called a collectively shared "identity set", the emergence of an ideology which articulates aspirations of what *ought* to exist, may be more significant in shaping action than an *existing* institutional frame (Keesing 1974). In much of the recent analysis of national development ethnicity has come to be seen as the most pervasive and prevalent source of a nationalistic ideology (Gellner 1994; Smith 1986). Ethnic identity uses primary socialization within the family unit as its main referent. Social closure rests on shared beliefs related to racial or family origins and is usually contained in coded rituals, foods, clothes etc. and, most importantly, language. In order for such beliefs to be translated into nationalistic ideologies a "value-added" process of the kind outlined by Smelser (1959) may be seen to occur. This involves the shift of self identity with a local or proximal group through increasingly higher levels of abstraction in definition. Translation into feelings of patriotism must, necessarily, include identification with historically occupied territory. Claims to collective sovereignty are normally articulated in a nationalistic way that can be understood both internally and by rivals for that territory. Ultimately these must result in functionally effective modes of governance or statehood. Recognition of this functional imperative is not, however, always apparent or necessary (Merton 1957). Usually groups are more immediately motivated by opportunistic appropriation, comparative emulation and/or relative deprivation in seeking external recognition of the closure of their collective identity and sovereignty (Urry 1973).

James (1996) describes this process as the creation of "abstract community" and sees it as one that may, eventually, lead to a higher and even more distal identity with a global community. Most political theorists distinguish between claims to sovereignty put forward by absolute monarchs on the basis of a theocracy whether, in medieval Europe or some contemporary nations (Weber 1924/1947). The emergence of the "modern" state is usually identified with the slow and often conflictful establishment of what Marshall (1964) described as the basic rights of citizenship — legal (judicial), political (emancipatory), and social (welfare) for the emergent middle and later, working classes. England is generally seen to have been the first nation to have commenced this progress towards what we may call a *civic* society through "bottom-up" claims for rights achieved in everyday custom and practice from Tudor times onwards. France articulated and proselytized the concept of civic society in a formal logic that was imposed through "top-down" intellectual and military action. European immigrants created a model of a pluralistic civic society in the resource abundant insularity of North America (see Greenfeld 1992)

As already indicated in the introduction most developmental theorists see claims to nation-hood as ultimately related to collective economic aspirations and more particularly to the experience of industrialization. Gellner (1983) speaks of ethnicity as a myth created by elites to mobilize support for their material ambitions. The institutional frame that is created in the name of such normative beliefs is one designed to ensure the continued economic domination of the nation-building elite. Kerr et al. (1960: 8) began their famous post-World War II project on "Industrialization and Industrial Man" by asking the question, "Who begins the march to industrialization?". The five part typology of contemporary elites they produced in response to this question included a detailed description of the mobilizing devices, belief systems and institutional procedures adopted by each. Although focused on industrial relations (how to motivate an agrarian population to move into urban factories) their analysis appears in some respects more comparatively dynamic than much of current business literature. Their conclusion that all systems would converge on that of the "middle class", North American, elite continues to be more quoted than the systemic distinctions they draw between the different start-points for industrializing strategies, those of either dynastic oligarchies or colonial administrators or revolutionary intellectuals or nationalistically inspired movements or of an aspiring middle class elite.

For heuristic purposes these differing start-points might be placed along the value-adding historical process of creating a national identity. Pre-industrial dynastic and anti-colonial movements might be seen as drawing more readily from an ethnic or religious source of legitimacy than those in which civic rights were already widely achieved, especially among a middle class population. This is not to discount the role of religion. Weber (1905), of course, emphasized the nature of the Protestant Ethic in justifying and legitimating Western individualism. (His comparison with the stultifying role of Confucianism and Taoism in China (Weber 1919) provides an interesting contrast with contemporary interpretation of the effect of these belief systems in NBS/NIS theory). Habermas (1975) saw Christianity as providing a "strategic-utilitarian morality" in legitimating the rise of the Western bourgeoisie, Marx and Engels (1848/1962) more famously as the "opiate of the masses." Certainly throughout the period of so-called Western Enlightenment religious metaphors appears to have been far more used in everyday life than reference to legal-rational authority. Surprisingly little is said in NBS theory of the current role of formal religion, particularly the Church of Unification in South Korea, or the varying interpretations of Islam across NICs. Morishima (1982) suggests that Confucianism was the *consciously* pursued doctrine of the pre-industrial Tokgama regime in Japan. Masahiro and Ng (1996) also suggest that the Confucian ethos has been *systematically* fostered in Taiwan and South Korea in order to consolidate labour-management relations and legitimate the state's steering role in the labour arena.

Civic and Romantic Ideologies

Nevertheless the "first new nation", as the USA has been described, drew from a well articulated notion of *civic* society in which ethnicity was, formally at least, discounted against citizenship rights within contract and property by an aspirant middle class elite. In Britain too, a civic society was well developed before the emergence of industrialization and its institutional framework ensured the rapid emergence of a middle class. (Perkin [1969/1985] has suggested the existence of two competing ideals in Britain of traditional toryism and individualistic liberalism at the beginning of the 19th century.) Both countries now serve to provide archetypal models of "individualistic" capitalism in the business literature (Lodge and Vogel 1987). Their functionally related institutions are seen to shape short-term, opportunistic modes of market based behaviours. In both countries associations of citizens tend to take the form of interest groups while state agencies often originate as responses to grievances aired in an *ad hoc, post facto* way and resolved, especially in Britain, through resort to common law precedents. Olson (1982) has gone so far as to suggest that the transaction costs of administering the Anglo-Saxon civic state are such as to inhibit national economic growth after a critical level of pressure group activity has been reached.

The contrasting archetype is, of course, that provided by Germany and Japan in which what is variously described as collaborative, or comparative, or alliance capitalism is seen to exist. These are societies in which, as both Marx (1887/1967) and Weber (1924/1947) remarked, the middle class was relatively poorly developed over the period in the late 19th century in which national sovereignty was claimed, in Germany's case by a pre-industrial, dynastic Prussian elite led by Bismarck. Perhaps more importantly was the manner in which this claim was articulated through what is now labelled as the "romantic" movement of the early 19th century. At first an anti-modernist reaction to industrialization, it became converted into the patriotism of Disraeli's "One Nation" Conservatism in Britain, and in Germany to the ardent pan-German nationalism of Fichte and the mercantilist economics of List (1844/1910). For over a century up to 1945 the romantic Germanic ideology was used to justify and legitimate personal and collective acts of supreme technological and artistic creation and of the most primordially brutal ethnic aggression.

Heuristically it is possible to see the two types of industrializing ideologies, civic and romantic, as representing polarities that have, historically, helped to shape different institutional forms. Since the European Enlightenment civic liberalism has provided an all pervasive ideal for the teaching of classical political economy. But in the absence of a politically influential or aware middle class, able to *assert* their rights to citizenship, most later developing countries have tended to be led by dynastic or nationalistic elites that have mobilized populations with a romantic or ethnically based ideal. In his famous analysis of differing national routes to modernization Moore (1966) offers the communist ideology as a third alternative to those described above and the one most likely to prove attractive to *peasant* societies. It is, of course, the case that strong communist movements existed in most NICs in the 1950s and 60s and engaged US, British, French, Dutch, Australasian and United Nations military forces in South East Asia on and off from the mid-century onwards.

The Role of Middle Class — Service Class

As mentioned above, what is now seen as the prototype of cooperative capitalism was labelled by both Marx and Weber as the "German problem." Giddens (1972) interprets Weber's position as being one of public support for the Junkers (and Kaiser Wilhelm). In the absence of a politically strong middle class that could direct and constrain the state bureaucracy that he (Weber) thought necessary for German economic development a charismatic leader seemed a preferable alternative! More recently Morishima (1982) and many other authors have made similar analyses of modern Japanese history. Whitley's (1992) own description of the separate histories of NBSs in South East Asia supports the view that anti-colonial nationalists as well as dynastic elites have utilized strongly ethnically based ideologies to recruit, maintain and to constrain a state bureaucracy. Like Bismarck, leaders often appeal to workers in a populist way in order to check what might be seen as divisive factional movements, particularly among students. In a comparison of government structures and strategies across Burma, Singapore, Indonesia, Thailand and Malaysia, Brown (1994) demonstrates how successful elites from a dominant culture, such as that of Singapore, have skillfully orchestrated the conflicting aspirations of minority ethnic groups towards their goals of economic development.

Working in a Weberian tradition Evans (1995) sees the transition from traditionally based organizational authority to a legal rational one as critical to the economic success of new nations. Like most previous developmental theorists he locates the bridge from one state to the other in the emergence of a middle class and, more specifically, in the creditation of an effective bureaucratic framework. He compares the interaction of national governments with private corporations in Taiwan, South Korea, Brazil, India and Zaire. The latter two ex-colonial countries had, of course, adopted the formal parliamentary and judicial structures of their Western sponsor. Both, too, had like many externally sponsored states, to accept national boundaries that cut across ethnic groupings and incorporated multiple ethnic cultures and languages. The combination of a constitutionally enshrined right to represent collective grievances and of the simultaneous creation of such grievances might appear to contain elements of structural instability from the beginning of the long "march to industrialization" undertaken by India and Zaire. It is, perhaps, therefore not surprising that neither had achieved the economic success of the first two comparators — Taiwan and South Korea.

In all five countries transactions between private firms and state bureaucracies were characterized by clientism and "rent-taking" (bribery). For Evans the distinguishing feature was, however, that in Taiwan and South Korea these practices took place within a well established elite of young, well educated senior civil servants and corporate executives not unlike that of the French administrative class. Personal gain was constrained, both by the higher ultimate objective of national success and by a professional acceptance of the technical demands to be met in achieving that success. Hence goals set by government (or the president) tended to be organized around task-related project teams which, while socially cohesive, were both technically competent and embedded in external financial and professional networks that crossed the boundaries of private and public bodies.

By contrast this was rarely achieved in Brazil, even less so in India and not at all in Zaire. In these countries desire for personal gain usually over rode consideration for technical pre-conditions for collective success and, in the face of the resulting strategic uncertainty, acted to confirm actors in their initially opportunistic behaviour. It might seem from Evans' case histories that this uncertainty became multiplied at the operational level of organizations. Unable to depend on predictable directions from above, those responsible for the delivery of goods and services worked on a similar basis of clientism and rent-taking — all the more justified by their meager and unpredictable wages.

What Evans' empirical research confirms is the importance of a professionally oriented middle class to successful economic development. That is to say, that as Perkin (1989) has recently suggested, the replacement of the feudal ideal of hierarchical *mutuality* of service can be that of a modern professional ideal of *expert* service to a national community based on an accredited competence. The bridge between the ascriptive values of pre-industrial ethnicity and that of meritocratic achievement has, of course, to be linked to that of a shared feeling of *national* achievement through an outwardly oriented view of a global contest. Dore (1976) emphasized the "ornamental" value of formal qualification in his analysis of the tide of "credentialism" that swept across the new nations following WW2. But Japan became a normative reference or archetype in the post war development of qualification as entry into a corporately organized career in which altruistic as well as mendacious motives could be satisfied. In this way the individualistic instrumentalism (or Zweckrationalitat) is legitimized through identification with the goals of the national community and transcendental hierarchy of the state (Wertrationalitat). This is not to say that alternative sources of communal identity do not exist: the success of the Reverend Moon's Church of Unification among the South Korean middle class offers a parallel with the success of Methodism under the charismatic leadership of John Wesley in the early years of British industrialization.

Reticulism and Appropriative Learning

Essentially Evans' explanation of the "embedded autonomy" of the state bureaucracy in relation to corporate management is not so much one of *institutional constraint* as of *shared ideology*. This might be likened to the Western liberal notion of "enlightened self-interest" but for the much greater patriotic fervour and concern for what is sometimes described as the "techno-professionalism" of ASEAN management.

Though employing very different modes of formal organization these, like firms in other later developing countries, including the prototypical German corporations, continue to maintain large centralized corporate staffs – unlike their Anglo-Saxon counterparts who have "down-sized" in an attempt to become "virtual corporations" (Kase 1996). Paradoxically this has probably reduced the capability of the latter to "network" on the basis of anything other than a short-term contract for services provided. In the appropriation of new knowledge this can be the least effective way of absorbing an understanding of new practices into the institutionalized behaviours of existing staff. The use made of permanent corporate staff representatives at international conferences, professional and academic meetings, trade fairs and, perhaps nowadays most importantly, sectorally related meetings called by national and supra-regional governmental bodies is a characteristic of large corporations in later developing countries who seem to follow the German pattern of attaching great importance to strong representation at such events and, indeed, in sponsoring them on a regular basis (Hughes and Christie 1995; Loveridge 1996). In Germany itself the ongoing association between corporate and professional bodies make this a more routine activity (Schmitter and Streek 1985). In ASEAN countries the more obvious intention is to gain access to professional knowledge networks in Western countries, although the contribution from corporately or university based researchers in these nations is growing in some "leading edge" sectors (Aoki and Dore 1995; Jeong 1995).

This type of networking, or reticulism, is not new. In the author's research it appears that many innovations in the design of aerospace and automobile components earlier in the century derived from chance meetings at trade fairs (Loveridge 1993). However at the birth of these sectors "the firm" was little more than the inventor-entrepreneur. In the creation or transformation of new sectors at the end of the 20th century internal reticulism, or the movement of information along networks *within* large firms involves overcoming boundaries both *vertically* between corporate and operational activities and *horizontally* across departmental specialisms (Kanter 1990). Failure to attain such a free diffusion of knowledge and commitment to its use in a creatively shared manner has led to two apparently contradictory responses from Anglo-Saxon executives. The first is that of adopting a strategy of outsourcing, described above, the other is that of the attempted "cultural engineering" of trustful involvement of "core" employees through "high commitment" operational management after the manner of Japanese corporations. While such a strategy can be seen as a rational attempt to segment the internal labour market on the basis of an assessment of transaction costs (Williamson 1975; Loveridge 1983a) its lack of moral coherence within the institutionalized values of Western NBSs has brought its long-term viability into question (Legge 1995).

The Role of the State

Perhaps the most important level of reticulism from the NBS perspective might be considered to be that occurring along the corporate networks or in marxian terms — the circuit of capital. Of these the formal interaction between state agencies and corporate planners in coordinative planning mechanisms such as the Japanese Ministry of International Trade and Industry (MITI) have attracted most attention. The role of large industrial banks in these countries and, prototypically, in Germany, has also been regarded as being one of both protecting "national champions" and advancing their long term expansionist goals (Royal Commission 1884; Shonfield 1965; Best 1990). Jepperson and Meyer (1991) have expressed the institutionalization of relations between state and constituent interests in the four part typology illustrated below.

In a historical explanation of forces leading to the degree of collective institutionalization of public functions within civil society their analysis of the processes of legitimation lead Jepperson and Meyer to differentiate between a collective identity with the state along the horizontal axis and the degree of decentralization of authority to firms and to interest associations along the vertical axis. France provides their exemplar of a statist society with high decentralization but held together by a strong belief in the overriding rationality of the state. The Anglo-Saxon countries are decentralized but lack such a commitment to a statist rationale. South American states are "segmentalized" in much the way that Evans describes Brazil and Zaire while Germany, Austria, Switzerland and to a lesser extent Nordic Scandinavia are portrayed as strongly corporatists in the manner in which "(I)ndividuals gain standing not as actors with autonomous interests, but as functionaries — as members of groups with legitimate functional needs and responsibilities" (Evans 1995: 217).

		Degree of Collective Institutionalisation of Public Functions and Functional Relations	
		Low	High
Degree of Authorization of Social Sub-units as Public Actors	High	Liberal Individualistic	Statist
	Low	Segmental	Corporatist

Source: Adapted from Jepperson and Meyer (1991).

Figure 1. Four main types of modern rationalized polity

Like much of the NI analysis this typology is an attractive one in exposing and simplifying key institutional characteristics that require a deeper processual analysis and explanation in order to understand, not simply its historical trajectory, but also its likely resilience to change. It tends to ignore the significance of internal contradiction within national systems, not least the tension that exists between the universally articulated principles of a liberal civic ideology as manifested in the belief that the State should hold the ring, or at best act as a countervailing power in retaining a balance of interests in a pluralistic contest, and the more positive view of the State as a sponsor of private interest in the form of "national champions" in global competition (Best 1990). Within all nation states the social networks that bring together representatives of government departments with those of private corporate interests and which, crucially, involve the mediation of financial institutions, is critical to the economic well-being of the country. What has, earlier in this chapter, been described as a "national elite" evidently comprises such a network. The relative openness or closure of such an elite is one criterion of democracy within civil society (Giddens 1973/1983).

In the study of these relationships in Western countries most academic research has taken the pressure-group or "bottom-up" model as its basis (e.g. Streeck 1992). A separate strand of research has attempted to trace networks or filières on the basis of interlocking directorates and cross-holdings of stock or credit between corporate bodies (Stokman et al. 1985). In practice it is difficult to assess the manifold strands of meaning within such formal and informal transactions or their importance to the long term survival of institutions. What seems certain is that what is often described as "trustful collaboration" in recent NBS analysis, would in a different national setting be regarded as "corrupt" and, often, illegal conjoining of private and public interest.

There is an evident degree of scepticism displayed towards the continuous demands from Anglo-Saxon governments for a "level playing field" in international trade (e.g. Tyson 1993). This scepticism was best expressed by the founder of romantic economics Friedrich List (1844/1910) warning all Europe against "the crafty and spiteful commercial policy of England" which wished to deny to others the use of instruments of state power and protectionism that had been responsible for establishing Britain's own commercial hegemony (quoted by Shonfield 1965: 80). It remains true that a strong attachment to a civic (liberal) ideology as the basis for legitimate governance demands a formal distancing of the regulator role of government from involvement with the sponsoring and promoting of private interest. In the past appeals to the "national interest" have been treated somewhat sceptically by pressure groups in civic states and by the electorate in general; it is most usually invoked for matters concerning "the defence of the realm" or in exceptional peace-time conditions of crisis such as Roosevelt's somewhat belated, New Deal programme (much of which was revoked by the US Senate within two years).

The manner in which national governments and their corporate elites, handle this tension is a major characteristic of the working of the NBS and, of course, their political democracy. In nations such as France typified by Jepperson and Meyer (1991) as "statist" disputes over "national interest" tend to be resolved in periodic, open and sometimes violent, confrontations at national level. In corporatist states responsibility as well as authority is shared within a densely interlocked hierarchy of public agencies and private associations with statutory powers (including financing) such as chambers of commerce. In both modes the assumption that private interest *can* be made compatible with a prevailing definition of public concerns appears axiomatic. It is an assumption that is periodically challenged by the formally radical ideologies of opposition movements but, on the whole, the view of the state taken by all parties is a much more holistic monolithic concept than that which exists in the liberal civil ideologies that shaped Anglo-Saxon nation states (Moore 1966, 1984 edn.).

Towards a Romantic Convergence?

Over the last quarter of the 20th century the emergence of the entrepreneurial state (Loveridge 1996) among South East Asian countries has brought about a considerable redefinition of the role of government among civic societies as well. What was formerly conceived of as the "national interest" was normally seen as being confined to the provision of an infrastructure essential to the welfare of the community where economies of scale resulted in large external benefits for consumers of an "essential service." Thus the provision of postal and telecommunications services, of electricity and carbon fuel gas were often publicly owned or subsidized and heavily regulated by government agencies. By contrast the production of mass consumer durable goods, and most particularly automobiles, tended to be treated as sources of revenue and as means to controlling national economic stability through indirect monetary and fiscal means.

An interesting case in point is that provided by a comparison of the 20th century development of the aircraft industry and the automobile industry within Western states. Both developed from the invention of the internal combustion engine but the former was identified from the beginning as a potential threat to national sovereignty and was therefore sponsored by liberal governments equally as much as more authoritarian regimes. Sector boundaries in aerospace have followed the limits set by national government sponsorship to the almost total exclusion of manufacturers who did not receive recognition in the exclusive bidding rings through which both the military and civil designs for air frames were considered (Edgerton 1991). The effects of such national exclusivity are still to be seen in the current problems of the European industry in producing regional corporate champions to compete with the rationalized US aerospace sector.

By contrast automobile manufacturers in both Britain and the USA have been much more exposed to both foreign competition and to domestic regulation in pursuit of consumer advantage in a free market. Over the first half of the century car manufacturers in these countries were the dominant exporters to foreign markets. But in Germany and Italy the achievements of fascist regimes in the 1930s are rarely emphasized for evident reasons. In the former country major road building equalled that of the USA and the production of automobiles increased by 40% per annum compound over the period 1933-1939, with GM subsidiary, Adam Opel, producing four times as many cars as Mercedes Benz (Bardou et al. 1982). The fact that first Japan and then South Korea, closely followed by Malaysia, should, in the latter part of the 20th century, choose to "leap-frog" the development of their domestic markets in durables to export and, more latterly, to invest directly, in the relatively open US market can be seen as part of a mimetic process in the adoption of appropriative strategies by nation states.

However these nationalistic strategies have sponsored the emergence of the multi-national corporation (MNC) as a major actor in what is now described as the process of globalization (Mueller and Loveridge 1995). Paradoxically the very embeddedness of such organizations in the institutional context of the nation-state has provided the state itself with what appears to be a major threat to its sovereignty. Another paradox can be seen in the manner in which Anglo-American governments provided a lead to other nations in adopting a traditionally market-based approach to institutional change through the, so called, privatization of those infrastructral services formerly considered to be in the domain of the state. The provision of such essential services thus pass into the ownership and ultimate control of MNCs located outside of the boundaries of the state. In some sectors such as telecommunications the nature of technologically advance makes it difficult, in any case, to monitor or police the service provision at national frontiers (Loveridge and Mueller 1996).

In this situation some observers such as Reich (1991) see the role of the nation-state as becoming one in which governments compete in the provision of human resources, or in creating an educated labour force, for the MNC. In addition, however, the state is seen as providing an external civic framework from which labour, as citizens and as consumers, claim rights within the governance structures of competing MNCs. A further paradox is, perhaps, to be found in the greater awareness of the need for such constitutional rights among the later developing nations than in the ideologies of earlier civic societies such as Britain. The intense localism of segmentation discovered within the British middle class appears to make it ill-equipped to provide the kind of romantic leadership that once inspired Voltaire!

Conclusions

It has not been the intention of this chapter to discount the importance of nationally discrete institutional structures in shaping economic development: they evidently constrain choices available to elites, no less than the populations of developing nations, and mould elite responses to perceived challenges to the operational viability of their governance and legitimacy. However, this process is not necessarily a self-confirming one: change does not only follow a linear trajectory as NI theory appears to stress. Achieving a balance between satisfactory business results with rising and, often conflicting, aspirations of national populations appears a problematic to be solved in each epoch rather than extrapolated from past states of apparent social order. Contradictions present at every level of complex social systems enter into ongoing transactions (Giddens 1979) but are particularly apparent in the appropriative contests that characterize modern capitalistic relationships. On one hand such contests often rest on gaining, so-called, competitive advantage, or proprietorial rights particularly over unique technological capabilities. On the other hand the closure of such opportunities often seems to involve cooperation among those wishing to generate or acquire such capabilities. These joint ventures may be defensive or appropriative and provide the basis for occupational closure, as well as the birth of corporations or firms, industrial and sectoral associations and, of course, the nation state itself.

NI approaches to comparative taxonomies tend not to extend to a systemic analysis of the process by which boundaries are erected and how they are legitimated in ideologies. These latter can provide the moral lubricant of future changes in institutional boundaries and perceptions of contingent pressures for change. In this chapter it has been proposed that nationalistic ideologies are a critical complement to economic development and have been more efficacious in newly industrializing countries than in the earliest modern states. A number of factors contribute to this efficacy in some NICs rather than others. It is suggested that nationalism is most efficacious when rooted in ethnicity, and hence in family ties. External referents are used both to accentuate boundaries and to provide archetypes. German industrialization provided an important reference for later developing countries in that a pre-industrial traditional elite were able to legitimate the creation of a deferential and patriotic techno-professional class whose self interest was firmly embedded in the modernization of the nation's economy. The Japanese experience was more closely modelled on that of Germany than on the US exemplar or that of other European states. It was, itself, obviously to become a more proximally specific referent for neighbouring ASEAN collaborators.

The contrasting model of civic society has been seen as being at the heart of liberal democracies such as the USA and UK. In these older industrializing countries a nascent middle class elite already enjoyed a range of citizenship rights in the early stages of modernism and acceded these to workers in a negotiated political process. in which market based interests played an important part. Thus, in the establishment of what constitutes a "national interest" ,state action is often judged to be against what might equally be claimed as individual interest within a competitive, contractually based market. This tension in opposing elements in civic belief systems is rarely reflected in the institutional analysis of contemporary business institutions, rather patterns of behaviour (e.g. short versus long termism) are taken to have structural significance and often lead on to prescriptive "good" (Germany, Japanese romanticism) and "bad" (Anglo-Saxon liberalism) judgements on the effect of current institutions. In practice it can be demonstrated that "the national interest" can be interpreted differently across different sectors and the national governments of the latter countries have adopted different stances towards two technologically related industries, automobiles and aerospace, for socio-political reasons. However, it seems equally clear that in the working out of similar national ideological stances to similar industries the institutionalized structures of US and UK governments did contribute to their relative business success over most of the 20th century

By the closing years of the century the pressures of competition created by new entrants from developing countries governed according to romantic principles is having an effect on relations between industry and government in civic societies. That is to say that the national interest is being defined in a way that aligns government with private capital in an attempt to attract sponsorship from foreign and home based MNCs. But equally it appears from the evidence that the patriotic self-discipline of members of the service classes in Japan and South Korea could be giving place to a more individualistic ideology — i.e. consumerism. Should this be the case it seems conceivable that organizational citizenship within the MNC might, indeed, one day become as effectively and emotionally a source of moral power as the nation-state. However the present importance of nationalism as the basis of commitment to the institutions of the state and of personal identity with communally shared objectives seems very great indeed. It therefore seems inadequate to analyse the institutions of NBSs without taking this overarching frame of beliefs into account. At the end of what well might have been the bloodiest century in human history and one in which much of the violence can be said to have stemmed from an ethnically based nationalism it seems insufficient merely to echo Vladimir's observation near the end of Samuel Beckett's *Waiting for Godot*. "The air is full of our cries. But habit is a great deadener."

References

Allen, G.M. (1933): *British industries and their organisation*. London: Green and Co.

Althusser, L. (1984): *Essays in ideology*. London: Verso.

Amsden, A. (1989): *Asia's new giant*. New York: Oxford University Press.

Aoki, M. and R. Dore (eds.) (1995): *The Japanese firm*. Oxford: Clarendon Press.

Bardou, J.P., J.J. Chanaron, P. Fridenson and J.M. Laux (1982): *The automobile revolution* (trans. J.M. Laux). Chapel Hill: University of North Carolina Press.

Best, H.M. (1990): *The New Competition*. Oxford: Polity.

Bourdieu, P. (1978): "Pouvoir et langage." *Communications* 28: 21-27.

Braun, E. and S. Macdonald (1978): *Revolution in miniature: The history and impact of semi conductor electronics*. Cambridge: Cambridge University Press.

Braverman, H. (1974): *Labor and monopoly capitalism* New York: Monthly Review Press.

Brown, D. (1994): *The state and ethnic politics in South East Asia*. London: Routledge.

Burrell, G. and G. Morgan (1979): *Sociological paradigms and organisational analysis*. London: Heinemann.

Cawson, A., K. Morgan, D. Webber, P. Holmes and A. Stevens (1990): *Hostile brothers: Competition and closure in the European electronics industry*. Oxford: Oxford University Press.

Chandler, A. (1990): *Scope and scale*. Cambridge, MA: Belkap Press.

Child, J. and R. Loveridge (1990): *Information technology in European services*. Oxford: Blackwell.

Clark, P. and F. Mueller (1996): "Organisations and nations: From universalism to institutionalism?" *British Journal of Management* 7: 125-139.

Clark, P. and N. Staunton (1989): *Innovation in technology and organisation*. London: Routledge.

Commons, J.R. (1924): *The legal foundations of capitalism*. New York: Macmillan.

Dore, R. (1976): *The diploma desease*. London: George Allen and Unwin.

Du Preez, P. (1980): *The politics of identity — Ideology and the human image*. Oxford: Blackwell.

Durkheim, E. (1893/1964): *The division of labour in society*. New York: Free Press.

Edgerton, D. (1991): *England and the aeroplane*. London: Macmillan.

Etzioni, A. (1961/1975): *A comparative analysis of complex organizations*. New York: Free Press.

Evans, P. (1995): *Embedded autonomy*. Princetown, NJ: Princetown University Press.

Freeman, C. (1995): *Unemployment and the diffusion of information technology: The two edged nature of technical change*. Brunel University: ESRC Programme on Information and Communication Technology.

Freeman, C., J. Clark and L. Soete (1982): *Unemployment and technical innovation — A study of long waves and economic development*. London: Pinter.

Freeman, J. and S.R. Barley (1990): "The strategic analysis of inter-organizational relations in biotechnology" in R. Loveridge and M. Pitt (eds.), *The Strategic Management of Technological Innovation*, 127-156. Chichester: Wiley.

Fukuyama, F. (1992): *The end of history and the last man*. New York: Free Press.

Gellner, E. (1983): *Nations and nationalism*. Oxford: Blackwell.

Gellner, E. (1994): *Encounters with nationalism*. Oxford: Blackwell.

Giddens, A. (1972): *Politics and sociology in the thought of Max Weber*. London: Macmillan.

Giddens, A. (1973/1983): *The class structure of the advanced societies*. London: Hutchinson.
Giddens, A. (1979): *Central problems in social theory*. London: Macmillan.
Granovetter, M. (1985): "Economic action and social structure." *American Journal of Sociology* 91: 481-510.
Greenfeld, L. (1992): *Nationalism*. Cambridge, MA: Harvard University Press.
Habermas J. (1975): *Legitimation crisis* (trans. T. McCarthy). Boston: Beacon Press.
Hamilton, G. and N.W. Biggart (1988): "Market culture and authority." *American Journal of Sociology* 94 (supplement): 552-594.
Hughes, K. and I. Christie (1995): *UK and European science policy — The role of cooperative research networks*. London: Policy Studies Institute.
James, P. (1996): *Nation formation*. London: Sage.
Jeong, J. (1995): "The failure of recent state vocational training policies in Korea from a comparative perspective." *British Journal of Industrial Relations* 33(2): 237-252.
Jepperson, R.L. and J.W. Meyer (1991): "The public order and the construction of formal organizations" in W.W. Powell and P.J. Di Maggio (eds.), *The new institutionalism in organizational analysis*, 204-231. Chicago: The University of Chicago Press.
Johnson, C. (1982): *MITI and the Japanese miracle: The growth of industrial policy 1925-1975*. Stanford: Stanford University Press.
Kanter, R.M. (1990): *When giants learn to dance*. London: Unwin.
Kase, K (1996): "The corporate centre in Japanese management." Unpublished DBA Thesis, University of Manchester, Manchester Business School.
Keesing, R.M. (1974): "Theories of culture." *Annual Review of Anthropology* 3: 73-97.
Kerr, C., J.T. Dunlop, F. Harbison and C.A. Myers (1960): *Industrialism and industrial man*. Cambridge, MA: Harvard University Press.
Kogut, B. (1992): "National organizing principles of work and the erstwhile dominance of the American multinational corporation." *Industrial and Corporate Change* 1(2): 285-326.
Lane, C. (1989): *Management and labour in Europe*. Aldershot: Edward Elgar .
Lazonick, W. (1991): *Business organization and the myth of the market economy*. Cambridge: Cambridge University Press.
Legge, K. (1995): *Human resource management — Rhetorics and realities*. London: Macmillan.
List, F. (1844/1910): *The national system of political economy*. London: Macmillan.
Lodge, G.C. and E.F. Vogel (1987): *Ideology and national competitiveness — An analysis of nine countries*. Boston, MA: Harvard Business School Press.
Loveridge, R. (1972): "Occupational change and the development of interest groups among white collar workers in the UK: A long term model." *British Journal of Industrial Relations* 10(1): 340-365.
Loveridge, R. (1983a): "Contingency control and risk" in J. Edwards, C. Leek, R. Loveridge, R. Lumley, J. Morgan and M. Silver (eds.), *Manpower strategy and techniques in an organizational context*, 113-154. Chichester: Wiley.
Loveridge, R. (1983b): "Sources of diversity in internal labour markets." *Sociology* 17(1): 44-46.
Loveridge, R. (1987): "Social accommodations and technological transformations: The case of gender" in G. Lee and R. Loveridge (eds.), *The manufacture of disadvantage*, 176-197. Milton Keynes: Open University Press.
Loveridge, R. (1990): "Incremental innovation and appropriative learning styles in direct services" in R. Loveridge and M. Pitt (eds.), *The strategic management of technological innovation*, 339-368. Chichester: John Wiley.

Loveridge, R. (1993): "The production and diffusion of managerial and organisational knowledge." Paper presented to the 11th European Group on Organizational Studies Colloquium, Paris, July.
Loveridge, R. (1996): "Global networks and national assets: Living and learning with the multi-national corporation." Paper presented to the Cross-Cultural Technology Transfer Seminar, University of Brunei, Darassalam.
Loveridge, R. and F. Mueller (1996): "Putting the corporate agent back into national business systems." Paper presented to the EMOT Workshop on Economic Performance Outcomes in Europe: The Role of National Institutions and Forms of Economic Organisation, Berlin.
Lundvall, B.A. (1992): *National systems of innovation*. London: Pinter.
Maidique, M.A. (1980): "Entrepreneurs, champions and technological innovation." *Sloan Management Review* Winter: 59-76.
Marshall, A. (1890/1919): *Principles of economics*. London: Macmillan.
Marshall, T.H. (1964): *Class, citizenship and social development*. New York: Doubleday.
Marx, K. and F. Engels (1848/1962): "The manifesto of the Communist Party." *The Essential Left*, 7-48. London: Unwin.
Marx, K. and F. Engels (1859/1976): *The German ideology*. New York: International Publishers.
Marx, K. (1887/1967). *Capital*. New York: International Publishers.
Masahiro, M. and S.K. Ng (1996): "The role of the state and labour's response to industrial development: An Asian 'drama' of three new industrial economics" in I. Nish, S.G. Redding and S.K. Ng (eds.), *Work and society: labour and human resources in East Asia*, 215-232. Hong Kong: Hong Kong University Press.
Maurice, M. and F. Sellier (1979): "A societal analysis of industrial relations." *British Journal of Industrial Relations* 17 (3): 322-336.
Merton, R.K. (1957): *Social theory and social structure*. Glencoe, Ill: Free Press.
Moore, B. (1966/1984): *Social origins of dictatorship and democracy*. Harmondsworth: Penguin.
Morishima, M. (1982): *Why has Japan succeeded?* Cambridge: Cambridge University Press.
Mueller, F. and R. Loveridge (1995): "The 'second industrial divide'? The role of the large firm in the Baden-Wurtenburg model." *Industrial and Corporate Change* 4(3): 167-199.
Murphy, R. (1988): *Social closure: The theory of monopolisation and exclusion*. Chicago: University of Chicago Press.
Nelson, R.R. (1992): *National innovations systems — A comparative analysis*. Oxford: Oxford University Press.
Nelson, R. and S. Winter (1982): *An evolutionary theory of economic change*. Cambridge, MA: Harvard University Press.
North, D.C. (1990): *Institutions, institutional change and economic performance*. Cambridge: Cambridge University Press.
Okimoto, D.I. (1989): *Between MITI and market*. Stanford: Stanford University Press.
Olson, M. (1982): *The rise and decline of nations*. New Haven: Yale University Press.
Parsons, T.A. (1966): *Societies: Evolutionary and comparative perspectives*. Englewood Cliffs, NJ: Prentice Hall.
Peet, R. (1991): *Global capitalism: Theories of societal development*. London: Routledge.
Perkin, H. (1969/1985): *Origins of modern English society*. London: Arc.
Perkin, H. (1989): *The rise of the professional society*. London: Macmillan .

Pettigrew, A. (1980): *The Politics of organizational decision making*. London: Tavistock.
Porter, M.E. (1990): *The competitive advantage of nations*. New York: Free Press.
Powell, W.W. and P.J. Di Maggio (eds.) (1991): *The new institutionalism in organizational analysis*. Chicago: The University of Chicago Press.
Reich, R.B. (1991): *The work of nations — Preparing ourselves for 21st century capitalism*. New York: Alfred Knopf.
Rostow, W.W. (1960): *The stages of economic growth*. Cambridge: Cambridge University Press.
Royal Commission on Causes of the Great Depression (1884), London, HMSO.
Schmitter, P.C. and W. Streek (1985): "Preface" to A. Cawson, *Organized Interests and the State*, 1-12. London: Sage.
Schumpeter, J.A. (1934): *The theory of economic development*. Cambridge, MA: Harvard University Press.
Schumpeter, J.A. (1939): *Business cycles: A theoretical, historical and structural analysis*. New York: McGraw Hill.
Schumpeter, J.A. (1950): *Capitalism, socialism and democracy* (2nd ed.). New York: Harper and Bros.
Scott, W.R. (1995): *Institutions and organizations*. London: Sage.
Servan-Scheiber, J.J. (1965): *The American challenge*. Harmondsworth: Penguin.
Shonfield, A. (1965): *Modern capitalism*. Oxford: Oxford University Press.
Smelser, N. (1959): *Social change in the industrial revolution*. Chicago: University of Chicago Press.
Smith, A. (1986): *The ethnic origins of nations*. Oxford: Blackwell.
Sorge, A. and M. Warner (1986): *Comparative factory organization*. Aldershot: Gower.
Spencer, H. (1882): *The principles of sociology*. New York, Appleton.
Streeck, W. (1992): *Social institutions and economic performance*. London: Sage.
Stokman, F.N., R. Ziegler and J. Scott (1985): *Networks of corporate power*. Oxford: Blackwell.
Teece, D.J. (1981): "The market for know-how and the efficient international transfer of technology." *The Annals of the American Academy of Political and Social Science* 458, November: 81-96.
Tyson, L.D. (1993): *Who's bashing whom?* Washington DC: Institute for International Economics.
Urry, J. (1973): *Reference groups and the theory of revolutions*. London: Routledge and Keegan Paul.
Voltaire (1733/1964): "10. lettre sur le commerce." *Lettres philosophiques*, 66-67, Paris: Flammarian.
Weber, M. (1905/1970). *The Protestant ethic and the spirit of capitalism*. London: George Allen and Unwin.
Weber, M. (1919/1947): "Konfuzianismus und Taoismus" in *Gesammelte Aufsätze zur Religionssoziologie*, 112-134. Tübingen: Universität Tübingen.
Weber, M. (1924/1947): *The theory of social and economic organization*. New York: Oxford University Press.
Whitley, R. (1991): "The social construction of business systems in East Asia." *Organization Studies* 12(1): 1-28.
Whitley, R. (1992): *Business systems in East Asia — Firms, markets and societies*. London: Sage.
Whitley, R. (1994): "Dominant forms of economic organization in market economies." *Organization Studies* 15(2): 153-182.
Whittington, R. (1992): "Putting Giddens into action: Social systems and managerial agency." *Journal of Management Studies* 29: 693-712.

Wilkinson, B. (1996): "Culture, institutions and business in East Asia." *Organization Studies* 17(3): 421-447.
Williamson, O.E. (1975): *Markets and hierarchies: Analysis and anti-trust implications*. New York: Free Press.
Williamson, O.E. (1985): *The economic institutions of capitalism: Firms, markets, relational contracting*. New York: Free Press.

Notes on Contributors

Nicole Woolsey Biggart is Professor of Management and Sociology at the University of California at Davis. She is interested in theoretical issues in economic sociology and has studied the relationship between society and economy in Asian business, the direct selling industry, and popular culture. She is author of *Charismatic Capitalism: Direct Selling Organizations in America* (University of Chicago Press, 1989) and *The Economic Organization of East Asian Capitalism* with Gary G. Hamilton and Marco Orrù (Sage, 1996). She is on the Executive Council of the Society for the Advancement of Socio-Economics, and the editorial boards of *Organization Studies, California Management Review*, and *Organization*.

Mailing Address: Graduate School of Management, University of California, Davis, CA 95616, U.S.A.

Ayşe Buğra is Professor of Economics at Boğaziçi University, Istanbul. Her research interests are in methodology related problems of economics and development studies, state-business relations, and the political economy of human needs and consumption patterns. Her publications include *On Economists and Human Behaviour* (in Turkish, 1989; 2nd ed., 1994) and *State and Business in Modern Turkey: A Comparative Study* (State University of New York Press, 1994). She has published in such journals as *Current Anthropology*, *Technological Change and Forecasting*, *Review of Radical Political Economics*, *Interventions Economiques*, *MAUSS*, and has contributed to several edited volumes. She has translated *The Great Transformation* by Karl Polanyi into Turkish.

Mailing Address: Department of Economics, Boğaziçi University, P.K. 2, Bebek, 80815 Istanbul, Turkey.

Laszlo Czaban was lecturer at the Technical University of Budapest from 1986 to 1990; researcher at the Research Institute for Economic and Social Studies from 1990 to 1991; and economist for the EU Delegation in Budapest, 1992-1993. He was Research Fellow at the Manchester Business

School in 1993. His publications in the late 1980s and early 1990s were mainly on international financial systems and on Hungary's external indebtedness.

Mailing Address: Manchester Business School, The University of Manchester, Booth Street West, Manchester M15 6PB, U.K.

Christina Garsten has a Ph.D. in Social Anthropology from Stockholm University and is currently Assistant Professor at SCORE (Stockholm Centre for Organizational Research) at Stockholm University and Stockholm School of Business. Her work has been focused on organizational culture and globalization processes in organizations. She has also studied the social effects of unemployment in Sweden. More recently, she has been engaged in research on the increasing reliance upon temporary workforce in organizations, entailing a comparative study of California, Sweden and Belgium. The aim is to study relations between temp agencies, temporary personnel and client organizations, with particular emphasis on effects on professional identity and integrity.

Mailing Address: SCORE (Stockholm Centre for Organizational Research), Stockholm University, 106 91 Stockholm, Sweden.

John Hassard is Professor of Organizational Behaviour at Keele University. Previously he taught at the London Business School and Cardiff University. His publications include *Time, Work and Organization* (1989), *The Theory and Philosophy of Organizations* (1990, edited volume), *Sociology and Organization Theory: Positivism, Paradigms and Postmodernity* (1993), and *Postmodernism and Organizations* (1994, edited volume). He is currently engaged on an ESRC-funded study of enterprise reform in the Chinese steel industry.

Mailing Address: School of Management, Keele University, Keele, Staffordshire ST5 5BG, United Kingdom.

Jeffrey Henderson is a Senior Lecturer in Economic Sociology and Organizational Analysis in the Manchester Business School, University of Manchester. Formerly Reader in Sociology at the University of Hong Kong, he has held visiting professorships at universities in the U.S.A. and Australia. His publications include *The Globalisation of High Technology Production* (Routledge, 1989) and *States and Development in the Asian Pacific Rim* (Sage, 1992). He is the co-editor of the journal *Competition and Change: The Journal of Global Business and Political Economy*.

Mailing Address: Manchester Business School, The University of Manchester, Booth Street West, Manchester M15 6PB, U.K.

Willem Hulsink is now Assistant Professor at the Rotterdam School of Management. Before taking up this position he was a research fellow at the Science Policy Research Unit of the University of Sussex (Brighton, UK), and previously an assistant professor in policy and organization studies at Tilburg University, The Netherlands. He has published on the diffusion of new media, European telecommunication policies, organizational innovation, privatization and regulatory reform, and consumer protection. His current research interests include: trans-European (information) networks and European integration, regulation of utility sectors, national systems of innovation, and competition/industrial policy.

Mailing Address: Rotterdam School of Management, Erasmus University Rotterdam, P.O. Box 1738, 3000 DR Rotterdam, The Netherlands.

Saija Katila is a Research Fellow at The Basic Research Institute of the Helsinki School of Economics and Business Administration. Her research interests include understanding the less rational, more intuitive and emotional aspects of organizational life in general and in small businesses in particular. Her most recent research activities have focused on an ethnographic study of new farm-based businesses in Finland. Other interests include gender and environmental management.

Mailing Address: Helsinki School of Economics, Runeberginkatu 22, 00100 Helsinki, Finland.

Gyorgy Lengyel is Head of the Department of Sociology at the Budapest University of Economic Sciences. He is the author of numerous papers in Hungarian and English publications, as well as the editor of *Hungarian Economy and Society during World War II* (Atlantic Research Publications, 1993).

Mailing Address: Budapest University of Economic Sciences, 1093 Budapest, Fovam Ter 8, Hungary.

Raymond Loveridge is currently Professor in the Strategic Management Group at Aston Business School, Aston University, Birmingham, a Visiting Fellow at Science Policy Research Unit, University of Sussex, and a Visiting Professor in Strategic Management, Ecole Superieure des Sciences Economiques et Commmerciales, Paris, France. He has consulted with various public and private service organizations. His recent publications include *Information Technology in European Services* (Blackwell, 1990); *The Strategic Management of Technological Innovation* (Wiley, 1990); *Continuity and Crisis in the National Health Service* (Open University, 1992); "Technology and Organizations", in M. Warner (ed.), *Encyclopaedia of Business Management*; "Language, Cognition and Information Technology", in R. Ceseria and P. Shockley-Zalabak (eds.) *Organization Means Communication* (SIPI, 1995), and "The Role of the Large Firm in the Baden-Wuerttemberg Model", *Industrial and Corporate Change*, 4 (3). His research interests include development of global alliances between transnational corporations, defining and developing corporate/regional core capacity, and managing primary care networks in health care delivery.

Mailing Address: Aston Business School, Birmingham, B4 7ET, United Kingdom.

Marco Orrù is late of the University of South Florida where he was Professor of Sociology before his death in 1995. Marco Orrù received his Ph.D. at the University of California, Davis. His dissertation became the best-selling theory book *Anomie* which traced this important sociological concept from ancient usage to classical sociological thought. In recent years Marco Orrù wrote widely on topics in comparative economics and development, much of which is collected, along with previously unpublished research, in *The Economic Organization of East Asia* (Sage, 1996).

Mark J. Scher is Senior Research Fellow at the Institute of Financial Affairs (Japan), New York office. The former editor and publisher of *Japan Financial Market Report* received his Ph.D. from the University of Manchester and the Manchester School of Management (UMIST). The chapter in this volume draws upon his book *Japanese Interfirm Networks and their Main Banks,* which was the result of in-depth research interviews within the banking community in Japan over the last four-years.

Mailing Address: Japan Market Research, 609 Columbus Avenue, New York, NY 10024, U.S.A.

Jackie Sheehan took her first degree in Chinese Studies at Cambridge University and went on to do a Ph.D. in Chinese History at the School of Oriental and African Studies, London University. Her doctoral dissertation, on conflict between workers and the party-state in China since 1949, is to be published by Routledge. She lectures in International History at Keele University, and is one of a group of researchers there now working on an ESRC-funded project on enterprise reform in the Chinese steel industry.

Mailing Address: History Department, Keele University, Keele, Staffordshire ST5 5BG, United Kingdom.

Arndt Sorge has worked on the organization and management of industrial enterprises, vocational education and training, personnel policy and industrial relations. In particular, he has taken part in international comparisons and has studied the development and utilization of new technology. Since 1972, he has had university or research positions in Germany, England, France and the Netherlands. He is presently the Editor-in-chief of *Organization Studies*, and he was the sub-editor for the Organization Behaviour articles in the *International Encyclopaedia of Business and Management* (Routledge 1996). From 1992-97, he was Professor of Industrial and Organizational Sociology at Humboldt University, Berlin, and is now a research professor and the Director of WORC, the Work and Organization Research Centre, at Tilburg University in The Netherlands.

Mailing Address: Tilburg University, WORC, PO Box 90153, 5000 LE Tilburg, The Netherlands.

Yohanan Stryjan, is Associate Professor (Docent) in sociology (Uppsala) and currently project director at the Stockholm School of Business, and Visiting Professor/PHARE fellow at the Faculty of Economics and Management, CZU, Prague. He is the author of *Impossible Organizations* (Greenwood Press, 1989) and numerous articles. He is a member of the scientific board of CIRIEC and the ICA research committee executive. He is currently conducting a research project on the transformation of the Swedish welfare service sector and engaged in several international projects on social economy.

Mailing Address: Stockholm University, School of Business, 106 91 Stockholm, Sweden.

Behlül Üsdiken is Professor in the Department of Management, Boğaziçi University, Istanbul. His current research interests are in comparative organization theory, evolution of management and organization studies in Turkey, and top management teams and managerial succession. He has published in *Organization Studies*, *Strategic Management Journal*, *British Journal of Management*, *Scandinavian Journal of Management* and *International Studies of Management and Organization*. He has served on the editorial board of *Organization Studies* since 1987 and is currently a co-editor of the journal.

Mailing Address: Department of Management, Boğaziçi University, P.K. 2, Bebek, 80815 Istanbul, Turkey.

Richard Whitley is Professor of Organizational Sociology at the Manchester Business School, University of Manchester and is Co-Director of the European Science Foundation's Programme on "European Management and Organizations in Transition." Recent publications include *Industrial Transformation in Europe* (Sage, 1995), edited with E. Dittrich and G. Schmidt and *The Changing European Firm* (Routledge, 1996), edited with P.H. Kristensen.

Mailing Address: Manchester Business School, The University of Manchester, Booth Street West, Manchester M15 6PB, U.K.